Of Men a...

'Susan Shillinglaw and Jackson J. Benson understand better than
anyone the motivating force in all of his best work . . . Steinbeck
seldom wrote with more conviction or with more honesty than in
his non-fiction. Nowhere, for instance, has he written with more
fervour than when reporting on the migrant labour force of
inter-war California . . . [a] heartfelt testament to his life and work'
Robert Edric, *Spectator*

'A good, worried man . . . his journalism has lasted so well – it is
intensely personal' Allan Massie, *Daily Telegraph*

'What a rare talent he was. He had a capacity for describing injustice
without emoting, for bringing home to the readers just how
unacceptable the state of affairs was and for showing no mite of
equivocation when faced with the strong ganging up on the weak'
Eamonn Sweeney, *Sunday Tribune*

'Here is the democratic American voice in all its glory: friendly,
courageous, compassionate, keen to go everywhere, see
everything, and capture it all in pacy, spirited prose'
Boyd Tonkin, *Independent*

'There is the spiritedness, the blend of conversation and descriptive,
the centred-self and, above all, the feel of writing that's shaped
and honed and worried into words that will weather the judgment
of passing decades. It has coherence and integrity – born from
within . . . As a warning beacon Steinbeck was matchless'
Tom Adair, *Scotsman*

'Steinbeck's journalism feels effortless, written with conversational
ease, and there are many witty passages in this collection'
Michael Greenberg, *The Times Literary Supplement*

John Steinbeck was born in Salinas, California, in 1902 and grew up in a fertile agricultural valley near the Pacific coast: both valley and coast would serve as settings for some of his best fiction. Throughout his life he wrote regularly, both journalism and fiction, and left behind him a large body of work. Some titles have been accorded the status of American classics, particularly *The Grapes of Wrath* and *Of Mice and Men*. Steinbeck died in 1968, having won the Nobel Prize for Literature in 1962.

Susan Shillinglaw is a Professor of English and Director of the Center for Steinbeck Studies at San Jose State University. She has edited several books on Steinbeck, published essays and introductions on his work, and is Editor of *Steinbeck Studies*.

Jackson J. Benson has published twelve books on modern American literature, among them, *John Steinbeck, Writer: A Biography*, which won the PEN West Award for non-fiction, and *Wallace Stegner: His Life and Work*, which won the Evans Biography Award. He was twice a Fellow of the National Endowment for the Humanities.

OF MEN AND THEIR MAKING

The Selected Nonfiction of John Steinbeck

EDITED BY

Susan Shillinglaw and Jackson J. Benson

PENGUIN BOOKS

PENGUIN BOOKS

Published by the Penguin Group
Penguin Books Ltd, 80 Strand, London WC2R 0RL, England
Penguin Putnam Inc., 375 Hudson Street, New York, New York 10014, USA
Penguin Books Australia Ltd, 250 Camberwell Road, Camberwell, Victoria 3124, Australia
Penguin Books Canada Ltd, 10 Alcorn Avenue, Toronto, Ontario, Canada M4V 3B2
Penguin Books India (P) Ltd, 11, Community Centre, Panchsheel Park, New Delhi – 110 017, India
Penguin Books (NZ) Ltd, Cnr Rosedale and Airborne Roads, Albany, Auckland, New Zealand
Penguin Books (South Africa) (Pty) Ltd, 24 Sturdee Avenue, Rosebank 2196, South Africa

Penguin Books Ltd, Registered Offices: 80 Strand, London WC2R 0RL, England

www.penguin.com

This edition first published in the USA by Viking Penguin, a member of Penguin Putnam Inc.,
as *America and Americans and Selected Nonfiction* 2002
First published in Great Britain by Allen Lane The Penguin Press under the present title 2002
Published in Penguin Books 2003

5

The acknowledgements on page 430 constitute an extension of this copyright page

The moral right of the editors has been asserted

Printed in England by Clays Ltd, St Ives plc

ISBN 978-0-14-118723-5

www.greenpenguin.co.uk

CONTENTS

INTRODUCTION

MOST AMERICANS know John Steinbeck's name, and many know his novels: *The Grapes of Wrath, Of Mice and Men, Cannery Row,* and *East of Eden.* His books, both fiction and nonfiction, still sell millions of copies every year, and one or another is part of the curriculum in schools throughout the United States. Few writers become beloved, their writing read with affectionate response long after their death. And few writers as popular as Steinbeck have written books that have for so long withstood critical and cultural crosscurrents. Like some other authors, such as Mark Twain, Robert Frost, and Willa Cather, John Steinbeck became beloved because he was so essentially American, a writer for and about the people.

But while his novels are familiar to many, his nonfiction is hardly known. From 1936 to 1966, Steinbeck wrote scores of short nonfiction pieces published in a variety of magazines and newspapers here and abroad. Most were read widely at the time and then gradually forgotten. By and large, however, these pieces are curiously modern and relevant. Steinbeck was a writer fully engaged in social currents, politics, and history. He takes on issues vital to the twentieth century—the environment, poverty and homelessness, America's moral decline, major wars, racism, ethnicity. Other essays recount his life, his travels, his ideas, his projects. The range is impressive, the style unadorned and engaging, and the voice remarkably varied—reportorial, witty, impressionistic, impassioned.

This volume, published in celebration of Steinbeck's centennial, brings together for the first time representative articles, essays, and columns from his role as journalist and commentator. Also reprinted here for the first time since its original publication in 1966 is his last book, a series of commentaries on American life, *America and Americans*. Included also is the final, heretofore unpublished, chapter of *Travels with Charley* (1962). Some of these articles and essays are provocative, some moving, some thoughtful, and others amusing.

"What can I say about journalism?" he wrote in 1956. "It has the greatest virtue and the greatest evil. It is the first thing the dictator controls. It is the mother of literature and the perpetrator of crap. In many cases it is the only history we have and yet it is the tool of the worst men. But over a long period of time and perhaps because it is the product of so many men, it is perhaps the purest thing we have" (*SLL* 526).* In many ways, this selection of Steinbeck's nonfiction is the "purest" record of a writer immersed in his times. What reviewer Lewis Gannett said of *Sea of Cortez* may be extended to Steinbeck's corpus of literary journalism—there is here "more of the whole man, John Steinbeck, than in any of his novels."

Like Mark Twain before him, Steinbeck was a great democrat, skeptical of power and privilege, seeking to encourage the best that is in us and doing so sometimes in sorrow, sometimes in frustration or even anger, but sometimes, too, with tongue in cheek and a sly smile. In his roles as novelist or journalist, he always did his best—he cared deeply about his work, but like Twain, he seldom took himself too seriously. When he volunteered to cover the national political conventions in 1956, he wrote to the editors of the syndicated newspapers who would publish his columns: "Walter Lippmann, the Alsops and David Lawrence have nothing to fear from me. I have no sources—dependable or otherwise. If I should make a prediction, it will probably be assembled out of information from the wife of the alternate delegate from San Jose, California, plus whispers from the bell-hop who has just delivered a bucket of ice to 'usually dependable sources' " (*SLL* 526).

Steinbeck had a knack for choosing topics, as well as taking an approach, that would be of interest to ordinary people, usually putting himself in their place. But above all he had the ability through it all to entertain and inform. Indeed, these articles form a series of snapshots of a

---

*Source notes in the editors' introductions refer to works listed in "Works Cited"; unpublished letters, primarily the Harry Guggenheim/John Steinbeck letters, are cited by date.

man who, through his compassion, concern, and sense of fun, has endeared himself to the American public, both in his life and since his death. It's in the spirit of that great range that the book is organized—by topics that suggest the power of his thinking, the scope of his enthusiasms, and the varied approaches he took to the craft of literary nonfiction.

John Steinbeck was lucky enough to live at a time when the concept of journalism as a profession was a fairly flexible notion. Newspapers sent novelists to cover stories, and Steinbeck, his reputation firmly grounded in the American psyche after *The Grapes of Wrath,* was fortunate to have his pick of material. Publications were usually happy to have his work, not only because of his name, but because he developed a reputation for applying his skills to even the most casual of pieces. From the time he published his first article in 1936 to his last in 1966, he took the writing of these little articles seriously, fretting over each one of them. "You know as well as I do that I have never turned out a really easy piece of copy in my life," he wrote his agent Elizabeth Otis during a frustrating moment on assignment in 1952. "These articles are going to be just exactly as hard as anything I have ever done" (*SLL* 451).

Journalism was seldom effortless in large part because Steinbeck was always the novelist, shaping, arranging, creating characters and scenes and conversations, occasionally drifting into the fanciful or mining the fantastic. His work in both nonfiction and literary journalism always teases the border between fiction and nonfiction, between the fanciful and factual. If his "migrant material" of the 1930s swings toward the documentary and reportorial, his work of the 1950s and 1960s freely mixes moods, narrative approaches, and fictional techniques. Some of this may have been temperament—he was, in fact, fired from a reporting job in 1925 on the *New York American* because his news stories drifted from the facts—but some he may have picked up from muckraking journalist Lincoln Steffens, who lived near Steinbeck in the 1930s. Steffens was undoubtedly Steinbeck's political mentor; it was he who, in 1935, urged the writer to interview strike organizers hiding out on the Monterey Peninsula. Abandoning his initial notion to write a biography of an organizer, Steinbeck published *In Dubious Battle* (1936), the first of three labor novels. But Steffens, whose *New York Commercial Advertiser* had run a "new

kind of journalism" that was, as his biographer observes, "personal, literary, immediate," may also have schooled Steinbeck in his concept of "descriptive narrative" (Kaplan 82). A good news story should contain "only
life." Steffens taught not only New York reporters at the turn of the century
but also scores of Stanford journalism students making pilgrimages to his
Carmel home in the 1930s—and John Steinbeck by 1935. When Steinbeck
wrote his first feature series in 1936, "The Harvest Gypsies," he knew
how to "see" things as they are, in line with Steffens's advice to reporters.

From 1936 on, Steinbeck published his articles in more than three
dozen different newspapers and magazines. Many pieces were reprinted,
and many were syndicated and ran in a number of newspapers throughout the country. Four series—or parts thereof—were collected and published separately: *Their Blood Is Strong* in 1938 (originally "The Harvest
Gypsies," which ran in the *San Francisco News* in 1936), *Once There Was
a War* in 1958 (originally war dispatches that ran in the *New York Herald
Tribune* in 1943), *A Russian Journal* in 1948 (parts of which ran in the *Herald Tribune* in January 1948), and *Un Américain à New-York et à Paris* in
1956 (seventeen of the pieces written for *Le Figaro Littéraire* in 1954).
America and Americans was written as a book, Steinbeck's last, and then
published as a series in Long Island's *Newsday.* Other newspaper series
have never been collected. His *Le Figaro* articles were collected only in a
French edition, although a few of the pieces were published separately in
American and English magazines. Two lively series for the Louisville
Courier-Journal are scarcely known: one was Steinbeck's coverage of the
1956 political conventions, and the other a series on his European travels
a year later. And the 1966 and 1967 series called "Letters to Alicia," his
last and most controversial newspaper work, written for *Newsday,* is difficult to locate. Selections from all these series, with the exception of *A
Russian Journal,* are included here.

He often wrote longer pieces for magazines. During the time that he
wrote for them, from the late 1940s to the early 1960s, magazines were an
important source of family entertainment. General-interest magazines,
like *Collier's,* published articles, short stories, and serialized novels, often
with accompanying photographs or illustrations, as well as cartoons and
editorials. After the war, such popular magazines gradually decreased the
amount of fiction they published and eagerly sought essays. *Holiday*, a

glossy pictorial magazine that published descriptions of possible vacation sites and travel narratives, ran several of Steinbeck's essays, among them two of his most personal and incisive, "Always Something to Do in Salinas" and "Conversation at Sag Harbor." With their circulations in the millions, *Collier's* and *Holiday* and *The Saturday Evening Post* aimed at the ordinary American, providing Steinbeck a perfect platform for the expression of his ideas. While he was not in the strictest sense an intellectual, he was a man of ideas who responded thoughtfully, often passionately, to the problems he saw around him.

Steinbeck had the advantage not only of fame but also of competent agents in the United States and abroad who were willing to undertake the extra labor of finding placement for his literary journalism. Although many of his assignments were arranged by them, he set up a surprising number through friends: Mark Ethridge, staunch liberal and editor of the Louisville *Courier-Journal;* Alicia Patterson and Harry Guggenheim, owners of Long Island's *Newsday;* Lewis Gannett, book editor of the *New York Herald Tribune;* and Norman Cousins, editor of *The Saturday Review.* Steinbeck and Cousins, for example, were both liberals and shared a firm support for the United Nations. In the mid-1950s, Cousins wanted Steinbeck to write a weekly column: "It would have been an important triumph for *SR* to have been able to publish him in every issue," Cousins asserted (Benson 775), but it was an honor that the author declined, reluctant to take on journalism full time. His eventual role as "Editor-at-Large" allowed him to contribute when he could, an agreement that he struck with newspapers and magazines whenever he could from the 1950s on. Although he was capable of turning out copy regularly, as he did when he first went to London as a correspondent during World War II, normally he hated to meet weekly deadlines and preferred to sign agreements for occasional articles, writing about whatever struck him as significant. He became a contributor to *Newsday* in 1965 because Harry Guggenheim told him to "write when the spirit moves you and send the copy on. . . . If you don't feel like writing don't write" (3 Sept. 1965).

This collection of Steinbeck's nonfiction and literary journalism is organized not chronologically but thematically, to highlight the diversity of Steinbeck's concerns. Each topic is briefly introduced. Throughout, however, a few trenchant points about Steinbeck's nonfiction need to be kept in mind: the urgency of his desire to witness and judge for himself; his lifelong fascination as to what reporting with objectivity meant; his determined focus on the commonplace, the ordinary, the neglected detail; and, finally, his idealism, the urge to set things right somehow.

Steinbeck's career in journalism began in 1936, when he wrote a series of seven exposés about migrant labor for the liberal *San Francisco News*. In 1943, eager to contribute to the war effort, he went overseas for a few months as a war correspondent for the *New York Herald Tribune*, and after the war he did a series on Russia for the *Tribune*, published in 1948. These three series, all collected as books, reveal the essence of Steinbeck's journalistic impulse—his need to observe firsthand people, locales, and events and to represent them as honestly as possible in all their dimensions. His best work emerges from his perspective as eyewitness, as the one who strives to see fully and place in perspective. That is true of every assignment he accepted, whether travel articles, war journalism, or his breezy series on the 1956 conventions. To snag the latter assignment, he wrote to Mark Ethridge, publisher of the Louisville *Courier-Journal*, and, as Ethridge recalled, "confessed an ambition to cover the conventions." "I have never been to a National Convention," he announced in a letter to the Syndicated Newspaper Editors. "That is my main reason for wanting to go" (*SLL* 525).

The same impulse sent him frequently overseas. Although Steinbeck is known through his fiction as a Western writer who evoked a strong sense of place, it is equally true that he was compelled to travel abroad. After frequent trips to Mexico and the war reporting of the 1940s, he went on in the 1950s and 1960s to take several trips to France, Italy, England, and Ireland and to report on the state of Israel and on the war in Vietnam during his final assignments, supporting months-long journeys by writing for popular magazines such as *Collier's, Holiday,* and *Esquire*. He agreed to write travel series for the *Courier-Journal* and *Newsday*. While in Europe, he wrote for *Punch* in England and *Le Figaro* in France, the latter an assignment that began with a typical measure of enthusiasm:

Here in France I get interviewed all the time. I spend hours with journalists helping them to make some kind of a story and then

when it comes out it is garbled and slanted and lousy. I wondered
why I did not write my own interviews and charge for those hours of
time and have it come out my way. . . . [It might be] called something like an American in Paris—observations, essay, questions, but
unmistakably American. (*SLL* 480)

His willingness to write for *Le Figaro,* however, was strained by the
fact that his work would have to be translated into French. With his usual
fretting over every piece of writing, the addition of the translation process
caused him considerable anxiety. He wanted each piece, no matter how
small, to be good. His secretary, Marlene Gray, tried several translators,
including several that were suggested by *Le Figaro,* but she felt in each
case that the results were inadequate. She finally found another writer,
rather than a professional translator, to do it, someone who could reproduce the spirit rather than just the letter of what was written. She had realized that it was the way he saw things and the way he wrote about
what he saw that was "Steinbeck." Indeed, the "Steinbeck" tone and "unmistakably American" approach could be the stamp on all his writing,
whether about growing up in a California small town or about French
fishing habits in Paris—it was American in spirit.

Through much of Steinbeck's writing, but particularly in *Cannery
Row* and *Sea of Cortez*, seeing fully was set out as his primary task, while
finding connections among discrete ways of seeing was a major motif. At
the heart of both books is the all-important matter of perspective. One
can see with one's heart as well as with the head. At the beginning of *Sea
of Cortez*, for example, he writes:

We wanted to see everything our eyes would accommodate, to
think what we could, and, out of our seeing and thinking, to build
some kind of structure in modeled imitation of the observed reality.
We knew that what we would see and record and construct would
be warped, as all knowledge patterns are warped, first, by the collective pressure and stream of our time and race, second by the
thrust of our individual personalities. But knowing this, we might
not fall into too many holes—we might maintain some balance between our warp and the separate thing, the external reality. The one-
ness of these two might take its contribution from both. (2)

Steinbeck acknowledges—here and elsewhere—that anything he wrote was far from "objective," for it was necessarily colored, "warped," by his perceptions and his times. It was "a" Russian Journal, not "the" definitive viewpoint on the Soviet Union; it was what Paris looked like to the average American, a "tourist's" report; it was Steinbeck watching a bomber crew prepare for combat. Long before Charles Kuralt, Steinbeck more or less invented *On the Road*. He differed from the usual journalist in his lack of detachment—he simply could not keep his feelings out of his reporting, but that, whether in his fiction or nonfiction, is what endears him to us.

Some twenty-five years after he published *Sea of Cortez,* during his first visit to Israel and on his penultimate trip abroad, he is still mulling over the problem of how and what an observer sees in "Letters to Alicia," a long passage but worth quoting in full:

It occurs to me to wonder and to ask how much I see or am capable of seeing. It goes without saying that our observation is conditioned by our background and experience, but do we ever observe anything objectively, do we ever see anything whole and as it is? I have always fancied myself as a fairly objective looker, but I'm beginning to wonder whether I do not miss whole categories of things. Let me give you an example of what I mean, Alicia. Some years ago the U.S. Information Service paid the expenses of a famous and fine Italian photographer to go to America and to take pictures of our country. It was thought that pictures by an Italian would be valuable to Italians because they would be of things of interest to Italy. I was living in Florence at the time and I saw the portfolio as soon as the pictures were printed. The man had traveled everywhere in America, and do you know what his pictures were? Italy, in every American city he had unconsciously sought and found Italy. The portraits—Italians; the countryside—Tuscany and the Po Valley and the Abruzzi. His eye looked for what was familiar to him and found it. . . . This man did not see the America which is not like Italy, and there is very much that isn't. And I wonder what I have missed in the wonderful trip to the south that I have just completed. Did I see only America? I confess I caught myself at it. Traveling over those breathtaking mountains and looking down at the shimmering deserts . . . I found myself saying or agreeing—yes, that's like the Texas panhandle—

that could be Nevada, and that might be Death Valley. . . . [B]y identifying them with something I knew, was I not cutting myself off completely from the things I did not know, not seeing, not even recognizing, because I did not have the easy bridge of recognition . . . the shadings, the nuance, how many of those I must not have seen. (*Newsday,* 2 Apr. 1966)

Steinbeck's journalism is the record of a man who wanted to get it right, who wanted to see clearly and accurately, without superciliousness—and without ever claiming that his was the definitive, or even a fully accurate, view. He always tried for the human perspective, as much as possible without prejudice, reporting from the street level rather than from the platform or penthouse. The "greatest human excitement," Steinbeck wrote in his foreword to Ed Ricketts's handbook *Between Pacific Tides,* is "that of observation to speculation to hypothesis. This is a creative process, probably the highest and most satisfactory we know" (vi).

Furthermore, he reveled in the odd angle, the small incident, the ordinary person, topics not often considered by most journalists to be "stories." Once again trying to explain his penchant for journalism, he stated in a 1965 open letter to writer Max Lerner why he "succumbed to the fatal itch and joined the gaggle of columnists":

Maybe it's like this, Max—you know how, when you are working on a long and ordered piece, all sorts of bright and lovely ideas and images intrude. They have no place in what you are writing, and so if you are young, you write them in a notebook for future use. And you never use them because they are sparkling and alive like colored pebbles on a wave-washed shore. It's impossible not to fill your pockets with them. But when you get home, they are dry and colorless. I'd like to pin down a few while they are still wet. (*Newsday,* 4 Dec. 1965)

Finally, there is an urgency about many of his social pieces—particularly, of course, *America and Americans,* his last work of nonfiction. He didn't preach, but he cared. Behind reporting things as he saw them, focusing on the small but telling experiences in life, he was also a moralist and idealist. All his life he was essentially an idealist; that is, he searched to find the essence of things, the meanings or patterns behind what he observed. That's what he was doing as his life came to an end—interpreting America.

Perhaps it was his experience in California's Central Valley during the 1930s, working out of his old bread truck so as to not draw attention to himself, mingling with the migrants, that set the pattern for a lifetime of reporting. He looked away from himself, observing the commonplace and the common people in order to see the whole picture as a democratic vista as accurately as he could. This is precisely Casy's stated mission in *The Grapes of Wrath* as he joins up with the Joads for the trip to California. Steinbeck lived that mission throughout his career—to see the whole as clearly as possible and to see it with his heart as well as with his head.

I.

PLACES OF THE HEART

EXTRAORDINARILY SENSITIVE to his environment, John Steinbeck "brings together the human heart and the land," to borrow a phrase from environmentalist and writer Barry Lopez (Lopez 71). Like Lopez, Steinbeck urges his readers to consider two primal landscapes: external landscapes—our relations to the land, to oaks, to the whir of night frogs—and interior landscapes, often shaped by the places where we reside. Some of Steinbeck's best nonfiction considers the writer's internal landscapes, places he lived and loved: Salinas, California, where he was born in 1902 and lived until age eighteen; San Francisco, where he resided briefly during the 1920s; the Monterey Peninsula, where he wrote his early fiction from 1930 to 1936; and the East Coast—New York City and Sag Harbor—where he spent the last eighteen years of his life.

His reflections on these places are sometimes meditative and serious, as in "A Primer on the '30s" and in that marvelous piece "Conversation at Sag Harbor." But more often his view is colored with humor, a humor that is sometimes impish, sometimes touched with irony. Always we sense the connection of the writer to the places he lived. To a certain extent these pieces form a kind of autobiography, and considering how badly he was treated by some people in both Salinas and Monterey (where the landlord of an office building wouldn't rent him space after he returned to live on the peninsula in 1944) and how terrible was his struggle during his first experience in New York, they are remarkably free of bitterness.

The Salinas valley, twenty miles inland, and the Monterey Peninsula, where his parents had a beach cottage, have become "Steinbeck Country" because so much of his fiction is located there or nearby. Few writers have put such an indelible imprint on a region. Tourists often visit the area to see it not for what it is but for what Steinbeck made of it. But as is clear from "Always Something to Do in Salinas," the author had mixed emotions about his hometown. Although it was a fine place for a boy to roam the countryside on his pony, the community's conservatism chafed. As he got older, the town's puritanical respectability and antilabor biases grated increasingly—although he could in retrospect treat the rigidity of the Salinas burghers with some levity. In opposition to Salinas, he set up Monterey as more relaxed and diverse, a place more tolerant of both bohemians and ne'er-do-wells. The whole peninsula, he wrote in the mid-1940s, "has a soul which is lacking in the east" (*SLL* 28). In particular, he loved Monterey's Cannery Row, a street of fish canneries, warehouses, bordellos, groceries, and fishermen's shacks—a place throbbing with life. Surprisingly, when asked in 1957 to write about redevelopment of the abandoned canneries and warehouses—the sardine industry had collapsed in 1948—he did not endorse nostalgia. He recommended that "young and fearless and creative architects" be hired "to design something new in the world, but something that will add to the exciting beauty" of the Pacific coastline. Steinbeck would later mourn changes in his native turf, but he was realistic about the need for evolutionary growth (*Monterey Peninsula Herald,* 8 Mar. 1957).

His time in San Francisco was relatively short. As his memoir recalls, "The City," as most northern Californians referred to it, was the place where, when he was young, his mother took him for culture—the opera, museums, the theater. His nostalgic memories of his bohemian life in the city as an adult are based on the nearly two years he spent there in the late 1920s, when he relocated to be near his future wife, Carol, who worked as a secretary for the Schilling spice company. His nights on the town with her were idyllic, but he fails to mention his long hours of muscling bales of hemp in a bayfront warehouse. He would never fully embrace urban life. Yet his appreciation of the other great city where he lived for a number of years, New York, suggests that he could adapt and become attached to nearly any environment: "When you really live in New York," he writes to his college roommate, Carlton Sheffield, "it is more rural than country. Your district is a village and you go to Times Square as once you went to San Francisco" (*SLL* 456). Settled there, first in the early 1940s, permanently from 1950 on, he sometimes embraced it wholeheartedly. "New York is everything," he wrote for a radio broadcast in 1955. "It is tireless, and its air is charged with energy. I can work longer and harder without weariness in New York than any place else" (*The Saturday Review,* 26 Nov. 1955).

But city life, no matter how enthusiastic his boosterism, was not fully satisfying to a man who needed space, contact with the land, access to the sea. In particular he missed the ocean, the smell of it, the seabirds, and the people who ran boats out to fish. "We have an urban civilization," remarked Arthur Miller, "and John was not an urban man. He liked to think he was sometimes. . . . He was trying to find a community in the United States that would feed him, toward which he could react in a feeling way, rather than merely as an observer or a commentator. And I don't know if there is such a place left in the world" (Benson 701–2). With his third wife, Elaine, Steinbeck found in the old whaling village of Sag Harbor on Long Island a place reminiscent of Monterey, a place he could respond to "in a feeling way." In 1954 they bought a small cottage located on a point overlooking a cove of the bay. They weatherized it so that it could be used in the winter, and it became more than a summer home. They made friends, and Steinbeck could wear his old clothes and his sailor's cap, and could walk to town for morning coffee. He bought a boat—several boats in time—and would fish, or pretend to fish, with his two boys, agent Shirley Fisher, and guests to the cottage. In Sag Harbor, Steinbeck could shed his fame, talk to the locals, read, spend endless hours inventing small innovations, sail on the bay, and, of course, write in the tiny octagonal study that he had built for himself on the point, "Joyous Garde." "Out here," he wrote his editor at Viking, Pascal Covici, "I get the old sense of peace and wholeness" (Benson 784).

Steinbeck's essays on the places he cared about serve as a kind of memoir, testimony to one of the most endearing qualities of Steinbeck's prose, his attachment to place.

Always Something to Do in Salinas

ARLY MEMORIES of Salinas are so confused in my mind that I
don't know, actually, what I remember and what I was told I remembered. I am fairly clear on the earthquake of 1906. My father
took me down Main Street and I remember brick buildings, spilled outward. Our own wooden house was not injured, but the chimney had
completely turned around without falling. And my sharpest memory is
that a phonograph we had obtained by subscribing to the *San Francisco
Call* for two years—our first talking machine—leaped from a shelf and
destroyed itself. There were two thousand five hundred people in Salinas
then, but boosters confidently predicted that it would someday be a metropolis of five thousand.

Tradition was strong in Salinas and my town never forgot nor forgave
an injury. For example, in the Fourth of July hosecart race in 1900, run
against Watsonville, the Salinas team ran out its hose smartly and with a
substantial lead, then found to its horror that the threads of the coupling
had been filed smooth. They could not couple up and get water and so
lost the race. Watsonville had obviously cheated. For a decade after, a
man could get a fight in a bar at any time simply by bringing up the subject. I thought of Watsonvillians as foreigners and cheats. I wouldn't have
thought of trusting them.

The old Camino Real, the royal road that threaded California together, moved up the valley and did not come near Salinas for a very
good reason. The place that was to become Salinas was a series of tule-
grown swamps, which toward the end of the summer dried and left a
white deposit of alkali. It was this appearance of salt that gave the place
its name. The stagecoaches on the royal road stopped at Natividad, a

pleasant little town on the higher ground of the Gabilan foothills, free of fog and swamp and mosquitoes, protected from the fierce daily winds which funneled up the valley center. Natividad had a small college, perhaps the first in California.

There is no understanding the impulses of humans. Someone built a blacksmith shop in the swamp and houses clustered around it: Main Street went in, and little bridges were built over the dark and noisome swamps. On this least likely site, Salinas grew while Natividad died. The adobe college lost roof and windows. The royal road became a country lane. By the time I came along much of the swamp had been filled in, but there was plenty left so that the night roared with frogs. I was pretty big before I learned that silence was not made up of a wall of frog song.

Salinas was never a pretty town. It took a darkness from the swamps. The high gray fog hung over it and the ceaseless wind blew up the valley, cold and with a kind of desolate monotony. The mountains on both sides of the valley were beautiful, but Salinas was not and we knew it. Perhaps that is why a kind of violent assertiveness, an energy like the compensation for sin grew up in the town. The town motto, given it by a reporter ahead of his time, was: "Salinas is." I don't know what that means, but there is no doubt of its compelling tone.

As the swamps were drained and the black odorous mud exposed, it became known that this land was rich beyond belief. And Salinas became rich, the richest community per capita, we were told, in the entire world. I suppose this was true. Certainly we Salinians never questioned it even when we were broke. It was a town of wooden frame houses, the trading center of the valley, the social center of the whole world as we knew it.

The social structure was a strange and progressive one. First there were the Cattle People, the First Families of the Salinas Valley, gentry by right of being horsemen and dealing in gentry's goods, land and cattle. Theirs was an unassailable position, a little like that of English royalty. Then Claus Spreckels came from Holland and built a Sugar Factory (in capitals) and the flatlands of the valley around Salinas were planted to sugar beets and the Sugar People prospered. They were upstarts, of course, but they were solvent. The Cattle People sneered at them, but learned as every aristocracy does that not blood but money is the final authority. Sugar People might never have got any place socially if lettuce had not become the green gold of the Valley. Now we had a new set of upstarts: Lettuce People. Sugar People joined Cattle People in looking down their noses. These Lettuce People had Carrot People to look down on and these in turn felt odd about associating with Cauliflower People. And all the time the town stretched out—the streets extended into the country. Farmland became subdivisions. Salinas became five thousand and then ten thousand. Enthusiasts thought that twenty thousand was not too high a mark to shoot at. We had a brick high school and a National Guard armory for dances. And we had the rodeo in the summer to attract tourists.

This celebration had started as a kind of local competition. One's uncles and even athletic aunts entered the roping contests. The ranchmen from the valley in the foothills rode in on saddles decorated with silver, and their sons demonstrated their skill with unbroken horses. Then gradually the professionals moved in and it became "show business." A working cowman hadn't time to attain the circus perfection of the professionals and soon even the wild horses and the Brahma bulls were imported, and cowboy clowns, who moved from show to show, took the places of the sons of Lynches and Abernathys and Bardins.

I remember Salinas best when it had a population of between four and five thousand. Then you could walk down Main Street and speak to everyone you met. Tom Meek the policeman, and Sheriff Nesbit, Jim Bardin, Mr. Pioda, manager of the Sugar Factory, and any one of a multitude of Hugheses. The generations of Portuguese and Swiss and Scandinavians became American so that the names of Tavernetti and Sveresky and Anoitzbehere and Nissen no longer sounded foreign to our ears.

I wonder whether all towns have the blackness—the feeling of violence just below the surface. Of course it was the only town I knew. Are they all full of dark whispers? There were whispers of murders covered up and only hinted at, of raids on the county funds. When the old courthouse burned down it was hinted that the records would have been dangerous to certain officeholders. It was a blackness that seemed to rise out of the swamps, a kind of whispered brooding that never came into the

open—a subsurface violence that bubbled silently like the decaying veg-
etation under the black water of the Tule Swamps. I do not think Salinas
was a gay place in those days. Monterey was gay but not Salinas. Maybe it
was the wind beating every day on the nerve ends. Perhaps it was the
months of high, sad, gray fog.

People wanted wealth and got it and sat on it and it seemed to me
that when they had it, and had bought the best automobile and had
taken the hated but necessary trip to Europe, they were disappointed and
sad that it was over. There was nothing left but to make more money.
Theater came to Monterey and even opera. Writers and painters and
poets rioted in Carmel, but none of these things came to Salinas. For
pure culture we had Chautauqua in the summer—William Jennings
Bryan, Billy Sunday, The World of Art, with slides in a big tent with
wooden benches. Everyone bought tickets for the whole course, but Billy
Sunday in boxing gloves fighting the devil in the squared ring was easily
the most popular.

Mr. Rowling, the violin teacher, tried for years to breathe life into a
small orchestra but the town preferred to hear Joe Conner sing Irish
songs. Now and then of course we were shaken loose. Once Tetrazzini
came to Del Monte, eighteen miles away. We in grammar school
learned the Italian words to "Santa Lucia," written phonetically on the
blackboard, and we journeyed to Del Monte, each one of us clutching a
wilted bouquet of violets. We sang for her and threw our violets at her
and went sadly home. She was a corseted, fat woman and she cried. I
don't remember that she sang. Perhaps our singing threw her and maybe
she was laughing, not crying.

One section of Salinas was called Kidville—a district where the less
prosperous lived and procreated violently. Kidville kids were kind of
"across the tracks."

Andy was a Kidville kid, one of the nicest boys I ever knew. A quiet,
lonely boy who went about by himself and yet loved to be with others.
No matter how early you got to the West End School yard, Andy would
be there, squatting against the wooden fence, waiting. Andy was a boy
who walked about early in the morning. In any kind of excitement you
would see Andy on the sidelines, silent but present. If men talking privately said, "Get that kid out of here," that kid would be Andy. All of us

were in love with the fourth-grade teacher, it turned out Andy most of all, but as usual Andy was quiet and inward.

We had excitements in Salinas besides revivals and circuses, and now and then a murder. And we must have had despair, too, as when a lonely man who lived in a tiny house on Castroville Street put both barrels of a shotgun in his mouth and pulled the triggers with his toes. That morning Andy was not first in the schoolyard, but when he arrived he had the most exciting article any Salinas kid had ever possessed. He had it in one of those little striped bags candy came in. He put it on the teacher's desk as a present. That's how much he loved her.

I remember how she opened the bag and shook out on her desk a human ear, but I don't remember what happened thereafter. I have a memory block perhaps produced by a violence. The teacher seemed to have an aversion for Andy after that and it broke his heart. He had given her the only ear he or any other kid was ever likely to possess.

We had many of what are now called characters in Salinas. Looking back it seems to me now it was solid characters, but at the time I thought everyone lived that way.

There was Hungry Anderson, who was known to be a tight man with a dollar. He and his wife lived about a mile out of town. He got his name on an occasion when he had some carpenters working on the roof of his house. At noon it took them about six or seven minutes to get down off the roof, and by the time they did, Hungry had eaten their lunches. He explained that when they were late, he had thought they didn't want to eat. He was called Hungry Anderson from that day on, and people began to say he was a miser. To prove that he wasn't he bought a shiny Chalmers automobile, but his instincts were too strong for him. He kept the car in a shed in town and came in with his horse and buggy, motored about town, put up the car and trotted back to his farm.

We had a man who wore long hair and looked very distinguished. We had heard that it was because the tips of his ears were clipped, a common punishment for stealing sheep.

And we had misers, lots of misers. Heaven knows what they were, but we needed misers, perhaps with visions of counting gold pieces and hiding treasures. In those days many transactions were carried out in gold. Paper was highly suspected simply because it was unusual. One of our rich men used to sweat with nervousness when he had to pay a bill in gold. Paper saved him considerable painful emotion because it didn't really seem like money to him.

We had, however, one whooping dolager of a miser who gave us a great deal of pleasure. Of course now I know he was nuts, but then it was a different thing. He and his wife and his daughter lived in a dark little house in an apple orchard right in town. He was reputed to be a miser. My father had a feed store at that time and this man used to buy five pounds of middlings, which is somewhere between flour and bran. Every week he bought middlings and apparently that is all he bought. That is what the family ate, middlings and apples.

First the daughter died and a year later the wife died. The doctor who signed the certificates was said to have said, four times removed, that they had died of starvation. And now our miser was living all alone in his dark house in his dark orchard.

Naturally he was a pushover for us kids. We used to creep up close to his window at night and peek in at him sitting beside a kerosene lamp writing in a big ledger. Every once in a while he would stand up and make a speech to no one at all. We could hear his voice and see his gestures but could not make out his words. Then we discovered a delightful thing. If he sat still too long we could stir him up by knocking gently and in a ghostly manner on the wall. He would leap to his feet and deliver great speeches, waving his arms and shaking his fist while his face contorted with emotion and saliva dripped from his mouth. If we worked him over for quite a while, we could sometimes get him rolling on the floor. There was always something to do in Salinas.

Then one day he was gone and we were very sad because we thought he had gone away. But he hadn't. He was inside there and in about ten days somebody found him and the coroner had to take him away in a rubber blanket and spray the house with creosote.

Well, gold fever ran through us. We dug holes at the roots of every apple tree in his orchard. We got a window open and searched the house, holding handkerchiefs over our noses. The big ledger was there and we could make out sentences like "Go good god goodly like liver line god do devil darn dawn." It didn't make any sense except to a psychiatrist and they hadn't been invented. Anyway we tried to find secret hiding places, rapped on the walls and even took up some floor boards. Finally we had to give it up. Then a distant relative looked in a place we had neglected, under the sink in the elbow of the U-trap. He found a flour bag containing eight thousand dollars in gold. I still get the shudders when I think we might have found it. It would have changed our whole lives and our parents' lives.

Salinas had a nice balance of lodges—Elks for the gay men, Woodmen of the World, Knights of Pythias and, later, Knights of Columbus. We were a Masonic family, my father a Mason and my mother an Eastern Star. My father was a medium Mason, not as high a degree as some and higher than many. There must have been some ceremonies that were semipublic because I can remember clearly Louis Schneider, the local butcher, red-faced and short and fat and with a handlebar mustache. I can see him now sitting on a throne, I think it must have been of the order of the Royal Arch. He wore a royal robe with an artificial ermine collar and on his head was a golden crown studded with gems about the size of half chicken eggs. Louis' blue serge trouser cuffs and box-toed shoes were the only unregal things about him.

Salinas had a destiny beyond other towns. The rich black land was one thing, but the high gray fog and coolish to cold weather which gave it a lousy climate created the greatest lettuce in the world, several crops a year and at a time when no other lettuce in the United States matured. The town named itself The Salad Bowl of the World and the refrigerator cars moved in a steady stream out of the railroad yards toward Chicago and New York. Long packing sheds lined the tracks and the local iceman who had used to bring a fifty-pound block on his shoulder for ice cream made a vast fortune.

The need for labor became great. We brought in Filipinos to cut and chop the lettuce and there were interesting results. No Filipino women were allowed in and the dark, quick little men constantly got into trouble with what were called "white women." The Filipinos lived and worked in clots of five or six. If you had a fight with one, you had six on you. They bought automobiles cooperatively by clots and got women the same way. The wages of five or six mounted up and they could afford to buy themselves a pretty fair communal woman. For some reason this outraged the tender morals of certain of our citizens who didn't seem to be morally sensitive in other directions. There used to be some pretty fine gang fights in the poolrooms of Market Street of a Saturday night.

In addition to the Filipinos for chopping the lettuce, the cutting and packing sheds required labor. Women and men to prepare the lettuce for the crates, and icers and nailers. These were migrant people who went from one place to another as the crops came in. There were a great many of them and they worked, some by the hour and some by piecework.

Eventually, as was inevitable, these people decided that they wanted to have a union. It was happening all over and they didn't want to be left out. The owners yelled that communists were behind it all, and maybe they were. Nobody ever proved anything one way or another, but the union got formed. I guess wages were pretty low and profits pretty high. So, now [that] they had a union, the shed people made demands for higher wages and when they were refused, went on strikes.

Now what happened would not be believable if it were not verified by the Salinas papers of the time. A man suddenly appeared, went to the owners and the sheriff and announced himself as an expert in handling strikes. He must have been a commanding figure. The sheriff turned the situation over to him.

The General took a suite in the Geoffrey House, installed direct telephone lines to various stations, even had one group of telephones that were not connected to anything. He set armed guards over his suite and he put Salinas in a state of siege. He organized Vigilantes. Service-station operators, owners of small stores, clerks, bank tellers got out sporting rifles, shotguns, all the hundreds of weapons owned by small-town Americans who in the West at least, I guess, are the most heavily armed people in the world. I remember counting up and found that I had twelve firearms of various calibers and I was not one of the best equipped. In addition to the riflemen, squads drilled in the streets with baseball bats. Everyone was having a good time. Stores were closed and to move about town was to be challenged every block or so by viciously weaponed people one had gone to school with.

Down at the lettuce sheds, the pickets began to get apprehensive.

The General sat in his guarded suite at the Geoffrey House issuing orders and devising tactics. He may have believed that Salinas was in danger of being annihilated. I have no way of knowing. Suddenly he issued the information that the Longshoremen of San Francisco, a hundred miles away, the most powerful and best disciplined union in the State, were marching on Salinas, singing "The Internationale." A shudder of excited horror ran through Salinas. Orders were issued from Headquarters. The townsmen marched to the outskirts determined to sell their lives dearly. The sheriff seems to have become a kind of runner for the General.

Then a particularly vigilant citizen made a frightening discovery and became a hero. He found that on one road leading into Salinas, red flags had been set up at intervals. It was no more than the General had anticipated. This was undoubtedly the route along which the Longshoremen were going to march. The General wired the governor to stand by to issue orders to the National Guard, but being a foxy tactician himself, he had all of the red flags publicly burned in Main Street.

All might have gone well if at about this time the Highway Commission had not complained that someone was stealing the survey markers for widening a highway, if a San Francisco newspaper had not investigated and found that the Longshoremen were working the docks as usual and if the Salinas housewives had not got on their high horse about not being able to buy groceries. The citizens reluctantly put away their guns, the owners granted a small pay raise and the General left town. I have always wondered what happened to him. He had qualities of genius. It was a long time before Salinians cared to discuss the episode. And now it is comfortably forgotten. Salinas was a very interesting town.

It is a kind of metropolis now and there must be nearly fourteen thousand people living where once a blacksmith shop stood in the swamp. The whole face of the valley has changed. But the high, thin, gray fog still hangs overhead and every afternoon the harsh relentless wind blows up the valley from King City. And the town justifies the slogan given it when it was very young . . . Salinas is!

The Golden Handcuff

HAVE YOU EVER NOTICED how attempts to write about San Francisco invariably turn into autobiography? And could it be that she is such a personal even subjective city that, once you know her, you can never again sort out which is San Francisco and which is you? One advantage of this confusion of identities is that she never gets dull. There are as many San Franciscos as she has lovers and she has many. I am one and I have known her on several levels.

Being born in Salinas, I do not recall as a child ever using the name San Francisco. She was The City, and I guess by that we meant all cities, which isn't a bad evaluation for a kid.

My first knowledge of The City was derived from my Uncle Joe Hamilton, who came from King City and ascended the Acropolis to work on the old *San Francisco Wasp*. At least that's what he said. He also said he had sat in the chairs once occupied by Mark Twain and Bret Harte. I was a little kid then and I learned The City from Uncle Joe on his infrequent visits.

I figure that Julius Caesar was stabbed near the arched entrance of the old Ferry Building, that Market Street led under the Arch of Titus, past the Forum which was of course the Palace Hotel, and went thence up the Capitoline or Nob Hill. It was obvious that Joan of Arc was burned in Union Square with her eyes fixed on the Fairmont, that Moses went up Twin Peaks to receive the Tables of the Law. You may understand that through my uncle's star-dusted eyes, I knew The City quite well before I ever went there.

My second level did not diminish the first although it was different. My mother was a lady with a high church attitude toward culture. She always knew what she liked and, to a surprising degree, what she liked turned out to be art. As a medium-sized kid I was taken to The City to be blooded with culture.

Music in Salinas was George Rowling on piano and his nice sister working away on a sweet and sour violin and never getting it sawed through, plus Joe Conner singing "When Irish Eyes Are Smiling" and "The Rosary." You must admit it was pretty heady to fall without preparation into Caruso, Melba, Tetrazzini, Scotti and the rest of that fantastic band of Archangels. And then a little later I saw, heard and felt Eleonora Duse and even though she played *Ghosts* in Italian, it didn't matter. Even at that age it seemed to me that she brought something to the theater that was lacking in our seasonal Chautauqua or the Salinas High School's version of Mrs. Bumpstead-Leigh. There was no conflict of interests. Salinas was Salinas but The City was magic.

My third San Francisco came to me when I was going to Stanford. I was very broke and couldn't indulge in as much sweet-scented sin as I wished, but what I did manage to chisel in on was in San Francisco. Who needed Paris or the silken sewers of Rome when there were Bush Street apartments and the Pleasure Domes of Van Ness Avenue? Much later I found Pigalle and the glitter-works of the Right Bank kind of saltless by comparison.

Finally, when I was what we used to call educated I moved up to San Francisco for my tour of duty as an intellectual bohemian. I don't remember all the places I lived in but they were many and they all had one thing in common, they were small and they were cheap. I remember a dark little attic on Powell Street. It was in the best tradition with unsheathed rafters and pigeons walking in and out of a small dormer window. Then there was a kind of cave in North Beach completely carpeted wall to wall with garlic. The rest, in my memory, were small pads whose only charm lay in cheapness.

We of that period might, or should have been called the Unfortunate Generation because we didn't have a Generation nor the sense to invent one. The Lost Generation, which preceded us, had become solvent and was no longer lost. The Beat Generation was far in the future. But we did have one thing they had. We were just as broke as they were, and we hated it just as much, and we gloried in it insofar as we were able. An acquaintance with money was fair game. We tried to trade our dubious talents for love and understanding and amazingly enough sometimes we succeeded. We pounded away at our deathless prose and even worse poetry, but if we had ever tried to read any of it aloud in a bar we would have been given the quickest A and C on record. Bars were for drinking, fighting, arguing and assignation, not poetry.

But in other ways we didn't let the side down. We lived on sardines and buns and doughnuts and coffee in the best tradition. Now and then we got sick and didn't know that what we had was a touch of scurvy. . . . Meanwhile I walked the streets absorbing life, yearned passionately toward the sidewalk flower stands, made friends with some dubious characters and was rejected by others. I even took jobs without shame, for I was ever a maverick. I did common labor at which I was very good, tried door-to-door selling at which I was lousy, worked in department stores during holidays, never enough though to lose my standing as free spirit and enlightened bum.

And what a place for it. My God! How beautiful it was and I knew then how beautiful. Saturday night with five silver dollars laughing and clapping their hands in your pocket. North Beach awakening with lights in a misty evening. Perhaps a girl with you, but if not then, surely later. Dinner at the Cafe Auvergne! I don't remember its real name but I remember the long tables clad in white oilcloth, the heaped baskets of sour bread, the pots de chambre of beautiful soup du jour, then fish and meat, fruit, cheese, coffee, 40 cents. With wine, and that means lots of wine, 50 cents.

And after dinner to the shining streets again with more wine to carry in your hand, superior wine not rot gut, a half gallon 38 cents. And then a night of Bacchic holiness, love perhaps behind a bush, and a streetcar ride to the Beach and lying breathless and dry-mouthed in the shelter of a rock while the fog-dancing dawn came up over you. How innocent we were and how clever, for we put up and took down our cynicisms like shutters.

And then, hungover and happy, back to the secret room with narrow bed, straight chair, typewriter and naked electric bulb with two sheets of copy paper pinned around it to shield the eyes. In such places we learned our trade, or tried to. We had to. Jobs were hard to get. Magazines didn't want our stories. Publishers were leery of first novels and rightly so. I wish they had been leerier of some of mine. No one ever offered me a job in advertising or motion pictures. I wonder whether I would have refused. I'll never know, but I suspect that I would have jumped at it—temporarily, of course, as they all do. It is true that we learned our trade because there were no better offers but we learned it in the magic heaped on the hills of San Francisco. And you know what it is? It's a golden handcuff with the key thrown away.

Ask anyone about San Francisco and the odds are that he'll tell you about himself and his eyes will be warm and inward—remembering.

A Primer on the '30s

S URE I remember the Nineteen Thirties, the terrible, troubled, triumphant, surging Thirties. I can't think of any decade in history when so much happened in so many directions. Violent changes took place. Our country was modeled, our lives remolded, our Government rebuilt, forced to functions, duties and responsibilities it never had before and can never relinquish. The most rabid, hysterical Roosevelt-hater would not dare to suggest removing the reforms, the safeguards and the new concept that the Government is responsible for all its citizens.

Looking back, the decade seems to have been as carefully designed as a play. It had beginning, middle and end, even a prologue — 1929 gave contrast and tragic stature to the ensuing ten years.

I remember '29 very well. We had it made (I didn't but most people did). I remember the drugged and happy faces of people who built paper fortunes on stocks they couldn't possibly have paid for. "I made ten grand in ten minutes today. Let's see — that's eighty thousand for the week."

In our little town bank presidents and track workers rushed to pay phones to call brokers. Everyone was a broker, more or less. At lunch hour, store clerks and stenographers munched sandwiches while they watched the stock boards and calculated their pyramiding fortunes. Their eyes had the look you see around the roulette table.

I saw it sharply because I was on the outside, writing books no one would buy. I didn't have even the margin to start my fortune. I saw the wild spending, the champagne and caviar through windows, smelled the heady perfumes on fur-draped ladies when they came warm and shining out of the theaters.

Then the bottom dropped out, and I could see that clearly too because I had been practicing for the Depression a long time. I wasn't involved with loss.

I remember how the Big Boys, the men in the know, were interviewed and re-interviewed. Some of them bought space to reassure the crumbling millionaires: "It's just a natural setback." "Don't be afraid—buy—keep buying." Meanwhile the Big Boys sold and the market fell on its face.

Then came panic, and panic changed to dull shock. When the market fell, the factories, mines, and steelworks closed and then no one could buy anything, not even food. People walked about looking as if they'd been slugged. The papers told of ruined men jumping from buildings. When they landed on the pavement, they were really ruined. The uncle of one of my friends was a very rich millionaire. From seven millions he dropped to two millions in a few weeks, but two millions cash. He complained that he didn't know how he was going to eat, cut himself down to one egg for breakfast. His cheeks grew gaunt and his eyes feverish. Finally he shot himself. He figured he would starve to death on two millions. That's how values were.

Then people remembered their little bank balances, the only certainties in a treacherous world. They rushed to draw the money out. There were fights and riots and lines of policemen. Some banks failed; rumors began to fly. Then frightened and angry people stormed the banks until the doors clanged shut.

I felt sorry for Mr. Hoover in the White House. He drew on his encyclopedic arsenal of obsolescence. His gift for ineptness with words amounted to genius. His suggestion that the unemployed sell apples became the "Let them eat cake" of the Thirties. His campaign slogans—"Prosperity is just around the corner; a chicken in every pot"—sounded satiric to the shuffling recruits on the bread lines. Visiting the Virgin Islands, recently purchased from Denmark, he called them the garbage dump of the Caribbean. The Islanders still remember that.

Brigades of Bonus Marchers converged on Washington. Congress had voted the bonus money, but for later. Some of these men might have been hustlers and perhaps there were a few Communists among them, but most were ex-soldiers who had served the nation, frightened men with hungry families. The ragged hordes blocked traffic, clung like swarming bees to the steps of the Capitol. They needed their money now. They built a shack town on the edge of Washington. Many had brought their wives and children. Contemporary reports mention the orderliness and discipline of these soldiers of misfortune.

What happened in the seats of power? It looked then and it still looks as though the Government got scared. The White House, roped off and surrounded by troops, was taken to indicate that the President was afraid of his own people. The rumor spread that Mr. Hoover had stocked his Santa Cruz Mountain estate with food for three years. It doesn't matter whether or not it was true. People believed it. And there must have been fear in the Administration because only the frightened fall back on force. The Army got called out to disperse the hungry and tattered ex-Army.

Four companies of infantry, four troops of cavalry, a machine-gun squadron and two tanks drove the petitioners from the streets of Washington, moved under a cloud of tear gas on the scrap-and-kindling shanty town and burned that pitiful citadel of misery. It is interesting that the commandant was General Douglas MacArthur. Of course he was under orders. They cleared the ragamuffins out.

I speak of this phase at length because it was symptomatic of many of the positions of leadership. Business leaders panicked, banks panicked. Workers demanded that factories stay open when their products were unsalable. People on all levels began hoarding nonperishable food as though for an invasion. Voices shrill with terror continued to tell the people that what was happening couldn't happen. The unfortunate Mr. Hoover was quoted as having said Prohibition was a noble experiment. He didn't say that; he said noble in intent.

The noble intention had created inner governments by gangster, little states which fought wars, committed murders, bought officials, issued patronage and sold liquor. Not only was this new aristocracy supported by any citizen who had the high price for a bottle of bad liquor, but successful gangsters were better-known, even more respected, than any other Americans save movie stars. Their lives, loves, felonies and funerals were fully reported and hungrily read. Important citizens courted their acquaintance and favor. They seemed the only people in the land who weren't confused nor afraid.

Then Mr. Hoover, running for reelection with a weary momentum, came up with another beauty. He said grass would grow in the streets if Roosevelt were elected. He should have looked. Grass was already growing in the streets. Farmers dumped milk, burned crops to keep prices from collapsing. Armed neighbors guarded homes against mortgage-foreclosing sheriffs. Grass was growing not only in the streets but between the rusting tracks of factory railroad sidings.

There wasn't much doubt of the election's outcome. In Dizzy Dean's immortal words, Franklin D. Roosevelt slud home.

I guess Mr. Roosevelt was called more names and accused of more crimes than any man in history, but no one ever thought or said he was afraid. Furthermore, he spread his fearlessness about among the whole people. Much later, when business picked up and business leaders howled with rage against Government control and Mr. Roosevelt, they seemed to forget that they had laid their heads in his lap and wept, begged him to take over, to tell them what to do and how to do it, that they had marched and shouted and fought for the Blue Eagle, that symbol of Government control—but they had.

There are whole libraries of books about the Thirties—millions of feet of films, still and moving. It is a completely recorded and documented period. But to those of us who lived through the period and perhaps were formed by it, the Thirties are a library of personal memories. My own recollections will not be exactly like others, but perhaps they will set you thinking and raise up your memories.

The Depression was no financial shock to me. I didn't have any money to lose, but in common with millions I did dislike hunger and cold. I had two assets. My father owned a tiny three-room cottage in Pacific Grove in California, and he let me live in it without rent. That was the first safety. Pacific Grove is on the sea. That was the second. People in inland cities or in the closed and shuttered industrial cemeteries had greater problems than I. Given the sea a man must be very stupid to starve. That great reservoir of food is always available. I took a large part of my protein food from the ocean. Firewood to keep warm floated on the beach daily, needing only handsaw and ax. A small garden of black soil came with the cottage. In northern California you can raise vegetables of some kind all year long. I never peeled a potato without planting the skins. Kale, lettuce, chard, turnips, carrots and onions rotated in the little garden. In the tide pools of the bay, mussels were available and crabs and abalones and that shiny kelp called sea lettuce. With a line and pole, blue cod, rock cod, perch, sea trout, sculpin could be caught.

I must drop the "I" for "we" now, for there was a fairly large group of us poor kids, all living alike. We pooled our troubles, our money when we had some, our inventiveness, and our pleasures. I remember it as a warm and friendly time. Only illness frightened us. You have to have money to be sick—or did then. And dentistry also was out of the question, with the result that my teeth went badly to pieces. Without dough you couldn't have a tooth filled.

It seems odd now to say that we rarely had a job. There just weren't any jobs. One girl of our group had a job in the Woman's Exchange. She wasn't paid, but the cakes that had passed their salable prime she got to take home and of course she shared so that we were rarely without dry but delicious cakes. Being without a job, I went on writing—books, essays, short stories. Regularly they went out and just as regularly came back. Even if they had been good, they would have come back because publishers were hardest hit of all. When people are broke, the first things they give up are books. I couldn't even afford postage on the manuscripts. My agents, McIntosh and Otis, paid it, although they couldn't sell my work. Needless to say, they are still my agents, and most of the work written at that time has since been published.

Given the sea and the gardens, we did pretty well with a minimum of theft. We didn't have to steal much. Farmers and orchardists in the nearby countryside couldn't sell their crops. They gave us all the fruit and truck we could carry home. We used to go on walking trips carrying our gunny sacks. If we had a dollar, we could buy a live sheep, for two dollars a pig, but we had to slaughter them and carry them home on our backs, or camp beside them and eat them there. We even did that.

Keeping clean was a problem because soap cost money. For a time we washed our laundry with a soap made of pork fat, wood ashes and salt. It worked, but it took a lot of sunning to get the smell out of the sheets.

For entertainment we had the public library, endless talk, long walks, any number of games. We played music, sang and made love. Enormous invention went into our pleasures. Anything at all was an excuse for a party: all holidays, birthdays called for celebration. When we felt the need to celebrate and the calendar was blank, we simply proclaimed a Jacks-Are-Wild Day.

Now and then there came a bit of pure magic. One of us would get a small job, or a relative might go insane and enclose money in a letter— two dollars, and once or twice, God help me, five. Then word would fly through the neighborhood. Desperate need would be taken care of first, but after that we felt desperate need for a party. Since our clothing was increasingly ratty, it was usually a costume party. The girls wanted to look pretty, and they didn't have the clothes for it. A costume party made all manner of drapes and curtains and tablecloths available.

Hamburger was three pounds for a quarter. One third of that weight was water. I don't know how the chain stores got so much water in the meat. Of course it cooked out, but only a fool would throw the juice away. Browned flour added to it and we had delicious gravy, particularly with fresh-gathered mushrooms or the big black ones we had gathered and dried. The girls shampooed their hair with soap root, an onion-shaped plant that grew wild; it works too. We rarely had whisky or gin. That would have ruined the budget. There was local wine—and pretty good too; at least it didn't kill us. It was twenty cents a gallon—take your own jug. Sometimes we made it ourselves with grapes the vineyardists let us pick. And there you had a party. Often we made them quite formal, a kind of travesty on the kind of party we thought the rich gave. A wind-up phonograph furnished the music and the records were so worn down that it could be called Lo-Fi, but it was loud.

I remember one great meat loaf carried in shoulder high like a medieval boar's head at a feast. It was garnished with strips of crisp bacon cut from an advertisement in *The Saturday Evening Post*. One day in a pile of rubbish behind Holman's store I found a papier-mâché roast turkey, the kind they put in window displays around Thanksgiving. I took it home and repaired it and gave it a new coat of paint. We used it often, served on a platter surrounded with dandelions. Under the hollow turkey was a pile of hamburgers.

It wasn't all fun and parties. When my Airedale got sick, the veterinary said she could be cured and it would cost twenty-five dollars. We just couldn't raise it, and Tillie took about two weeks to die. If people sitting up with her and holding her head could have saved her, she would have got well. Things like that made us feel angry and helpless. But mostly we made the best of what we had because despondency, not prosperity, was just around the corner. We were more afraid of that than anything. That's why we played so hard.

It's not easy to go on writing constantly with little hope that anything will come of it. But I do remember it as a time of warmth and mutual caring. If one of us got hurt or ill or in trouble, the others rallied with what they had. Everyone shared bad fortune as well as good.

Relief came along and was welcomed. We got some food—blocks of cheese and canned Government beef. I remember the beef well. It tasted like boiled laundry and had about as much food value. Private enterprise processed it from Government-bought cattle. They processed the hell out of it and at that time a rich beef essence went on sale. We ate the boiled laundry from which it probably came.

When WPA came, we were delighted because it offered work. There were even writers' projects. I couldn't get on one, but a lot of very fine people did. I was given the project of taking a census of all the dogs on the Monterey Peninsula, their breeds, weight and characters. I did it very thoroughly and, since I knew my reports were not likely to get to the hands of the mighty, I wrote some pretty searching character studies of poodles and beagles and hounds. If such records were kept, somewhere in Washington there will be a complete dog record of the Monterey Peninsula in the early Thirties.

All over the country the WPA was working. They built many of the airports we still use, hundreds of schools, post offices, stadia, together with great and permanent matters like the stately Lake Shore Drive in Chicago.

By that time some business was beginning to recover and it was the fixation of businessmen that the WPA did nothing but lean on shovels. I had an uncle who was particularly irritated at shovel-leaning. When he pooh-poohed my contention that shovel-leaning was necessary, I bet him five dollars, which I didn't have, that he couldn't shovel sand for fifteen timed minutes without stopping. He said a man should give a good day's work and grabbed a shovel. At the end of three minutes his face was red, at six he was staggering and before eight minutes were up his wife stopped him to save him from apoplexy. And he never mentioned shovel-leaning again. I've always been amused at the contention that brain work is harder than manual labor. I never knew a man to leave a desk for a muck-stick if he could avoid it.

Meanwhile, wonderful things were going on in the country: young men were reforesting the stripped hills, painters were frescoing the walls of public buildings. Guides to the States were being compiled by writers' projects, still the best source books on America up to the time they were printed.

A fabulous character named Hallie Flanagan was creating a National Theatre. And playwrights and actors were working like mad for relief wages. Some of our best people grew to stature during that time. We might still have a National Theatre if some high-minded Senators had not killed the whole thing on the ground that *Getting Gertie's Garter* was an immoral play.

In Pacific Grove we heard that business was improving, but that hadn't much emphasis for us. One of the indices of improvement was that the men who had begged the Administration to take over and tell them what to do were now howling against Government control and calling Mr. Roosevelt highly colored names. This proved that they were on their feet again and was perfectly natural. You only tolerate help when you need it.

The factories were slowly coming to life again and the farmers were as optimistic as farmers can be, which isn't much. And then the weather gods reared back and let us have it. The rains simply went away. A weather map of 1934 is a dismal history—dry, poor, drought, arid—West, Middle West, Southwest—the great meat, cereal and vegetable area of the nation, shriveled and desiccated and cracked. Cows were racks of bones and pigs were shot to stop their hunger squeals. The corn came up and collapsed.

Prohibition had been repealed by then and crudely painted signs went up everywhere: "You gave us beer. Now give us water!" On the great plains, the root carpet of buffalo grass had been long plowed away and the earth lay bare and helpless under the sun. When the strong winds blew, the topsoil rose into the sky in gritty clouds, put out the sun and then drifted back against houses and fences like dark snow. Photographs taken then show our richest areas looking like moonscapes, desolate and frightening. Cattle died or were shot, and people fled to save themselves, abandoning everything they could not carry. They ran to the fringes of moisture—California, Oregon and Washington, where the cold of winter would not be an added problem. America was like a boxer, driven to the floor by left-hand jabs for a seven count, who struggles to his feet to catch a right-hand haymaker on the point of his chin.

In the early days of the migration, some groups got trapped by other kinds of weather. For example, about three thousand, encamped in King's County, California, were caught in a flood. They were huddled and starving on high ground surrounded by water and mud-logged fields.

I had a friend, George West of the San Francisco *News*, who asked me to go over there and write a news story—the first private-enterprise job I could remember. What I found horrified me. We had been simply poor, but these people were literally starving and by that I mean they were dying of it. Marooned in the mud, they were wet and hungry and miserable. In addition they were fine, brave people. They took me over completely, heart and soul. I wrote six or seven articles and then did what I could to try to get food to them. The local people were scared. They did what they could, but it was natural that fear and perhaps pity made them dislike the dirty, helpless horde of locusts.

The newspaper paid me some money and about that time I had a little windfall so I went to live with these migrant people, traveled back to their home base to see why they were leaving it. It wasn't philanthropy. I liked these people. They had qualities of humor and courage and inventiveness and energy that appealed to me. I thought that if we had a national character and a national genius, these people, who were beginning to be called Okies, were it. With all the odds against them, their goodness and strength survived. And it still does.

In Pacific Grove a part of our social life was politics; we argued and contended and discussed communism, socialism, labor organization, recovery. Conversation was a large part of our pleasure and it was no bad thing. With the beginning of recovery and the rebirth of private business, strikes began to break out. I went to see them to find out what it was about, felt them, tasted them, lived them, studied them and did quite a bit of writing about them. Fantastically, a few people began to buy and read my work even when they denounced it. I remember one book that got trounced by the Communists as being capitalist and by the capitalists as being Communist. Feelings as always were more potent than thought.

And feelings in the Thirties ran high. People were not afraid to express them as they have become recently. If you believed a thing, you shouted it. We lived or at least talked excitement.

We discussed what was happening in Europe. Hitler was rising on the despair of defeated ex-soldiers, Mussolini riding up on Italian poverty and confusion.

And in America maybe we were weary too. We had been up and down too many times in a short period. We have always had a tendency in confusion to call for a boss. A baseball scandal, a movie difficulty with morals, and we yell for one man to take over. Oddly enough we always call him a Czar, but, fortunately, so far we have never let him get very big.

But in the Thirties when Hitler was successful, when Mussolini made the trains run on time, a spate of would-be Czars began to arise. Gerald L. K. Smith, Father Coughlin, Huey Long, Townsend—each one with plans to use unrest and confusion and hatred as the material for personal power.

The Klan became powerful, in numbers at least. In Pacific Grove, KKK was painted in huge letters on the streets and several times a small red card was slipped under my door which read, "We are watching you," signed "KKK."

The Communists were active, forming united fronts with everyone. We had great shouting arguments about that. They were pretty clever. If you favored justice, or the abolition of poverty, or equality or even mother love, you were automatically in a united front with the Communists. There were also Lovestoneites and Trotskyists. I never could get them straight in my mind except that the Stalinists were in power in Russia and the others were out. Anyway, they didn't like each other. The Stalinists went about with little smiles of secret knowledge and gave the impression that they had sources of information not available to ordinary people. It was only later that I realized this was not so. We were all united in a dislike for dictators (Stalin was not a dictator if you were properly educated in dialectics).

When the stunning news of the Hitler-Stalin pact was printed, I came on one of my Communist friends in the street. He began shouting before I got near him: "Don't ask me. I don't know, God damn it. They didn't tell us." As it turned out, the Kremlin didn't tell the American Communists anything. Someone told me later they didn't trust them.

Except for the field organizers of strikes, who were pretty tough monkeys and devoted, most of the so-called Communists I met were middle-class, middle-aged people playing a game of dreams. I remember a woman in easy circumstances saying to another even more affluent: "After the revolution even we will have more, won't we, dear?" Then there was another lover of proletarians who used to raise hell with Sunday picnickers on her property.

I guess the trouble was that we didn't have any self-admitted proletarians. Everyone was a temporarily embarrassed capitalist. Maybe the Communists so closely questioned by investigation committees were a danger to America, but the ones I knew—at least they claimed to be Communists—couldn't have disrupted a Sunday-school picnic. Besides they were too busy fighting among themselves.

During the early years of the Thirties, my literary experience was unfortunate, but not unique. Every time a publisher accepted one of my books, he went bankrupt. One book was accepted by one publisher, printed by a second and issued under a third. But it didn't sell anyway. I began to feel like the Typhoid Mary of the literary world. But as the Thirties progressed, a little solvency began to creep in on me. I remember when a story of mine called *The Red Pony* was bought by the now defunct *North American Review*. They paid ninety dollars for it. I didn't believe there was that much money in the world. The pure sparkling affluence of it went to my head for weeks. I couldn't bear to cash the check, but I did.

By 1936 the country must have been on the upgrade. When a writer does well, the rest of the country is doing fine. A book of mine which had been trudging wearily from publisher to publisher was finally bought and brought out by Pat Covici. It sold well enough so that it was bought for motion pictures for three thousand dollars. I had no conception of this kind of dough. It was like thinking in terms of light-years. You can't.

The subsequent history of that book is a kind of index of the change that was going on. The studio spent a quarter of a million dollars having my book rewritten before they abandoned it. Then they fired the man who had bought it in the first place. He bought it back for three thousand and later sold it for ninety thousand dollars. It shows how values change. But I still think of that original three thousand dollars as about as much money as there is in the world. I gave a lot of it away because it seemed like too much to be in private hands. I guess I wasn't cut out for a capitalist. I even remained a Democrat.

During the Depression years and the slow recovery, the world of gadgets called science had passed us by in Pacific Grove. One of our friends owned a Model T Ford, high ceiling, cut-glass vases, a fairly dangerous vehicle since its brake band was gone and the reverse band had been moved over to the high-low-forward drum. It could be used for emergencies if we could come by a quart of gasoline.

I had at one time come by a radio, tickler and crystal affair with headphones. But sitting tapping my foot to music or laughing at jokes no one else could hear caused my wife to threaten divorce. Now in my growing affluence I bought a magnificent secondhand radio for fifteen dollars. Architecturally it was a replica of the Cathedral of Notre Dame, lacking only gargoyles. The set itself was good and still is. Now we had access to the great world of music and particularly to news. We gathered close to the speaker because a nearby X-ray machine had a way of coming on at the most vital times. On this set we heard Mr. Roosevelt's fireside chats, listened to the doom tones of Gabriel Heatter and the precise, clipped reporting of H. V. Kaltenborn. But also we heard the recorded voice of Hitler, a hoarse screaming and the thundering *Heils* of his millions. Also we listened with horror to the mincing sneers of Father Coughlin. One night we got Madison Square Garden, a Nazi meeting echoing with shrill hatred and the drilled litany of the brown-shirted audience. Then a dissenter's voice broke through and we could hear the crunch of fists on flesh as he was beaten to the floor and flung from the stage. America First came through our speaker and it sounded to us very like the Nazi approach. Lindbergh was proposed to ride the White Horse, which must have saddened him. We had also heard the trial of the man who had stolen and murdered his baby.

Prosperity had returned, leaving behind the warm and friendly associations of the dark days. Fierce strikes and retaliations raged in Detroit, race riots in Chicago: tear gas and night sticks and jeering picket lines and overturned automobiles. The ferocity showed how frightened both sides were, for men are invariably cruel when they are scared.

The Spanish War split America's emotions. The people we knew favored the Republic. We could not see how justice could be on the side armed and supplied by Hitler and Mussolini. We watched with dismay while our Government cut off supplies to the Loyalists and forced them to turn to the Russians for help. It was a crazy time that came to us through that great episcopal radio.

Shirley Temple, then a little girl, was denounced by the Dies Committee for sending money for medical aid to Loyalist Spain. And I had one hilarious experience because I also had contributed toward an ambulance. Everyone knows at least one telephone joker. Ours was a woman who loved to call the zoo and ask for Mr. Bear. One day I answered the phone (oh! yes, we had a telephone by now). I thought it was our joker because the voice said: "This is the Monterey *Herald*. You were denounced before the Dies Committee today. Would you care to comment?"

And I, still thinking it was the joker, replied: "What's good enough for Shirley Temple is good enough for me."

But it was true. I had been denounced for giving money for medical aid to Spain. My reply got printed all over and apparently the committee didn't think it as funny as many others did. They wouldn't even answer my wire asking to be heard. But from then on I was a Communist as far as the Dies Committee was concerned. It was at this time that everyone was a Communist or a Fascist depending on where you stood.

My books were beginning to sell better than I had ever hoped or expected and while this was pleasing it also frightened me. I knew it couldn't last and I was afraid my standard of living would go up and leave me stranded when the next collapse came. We were much more accustomed to collapse than to prosperity. Also I had an archaic angry-gods feeling that made me give a great lot of my earnings away. I was a pushover for anyone or any organization asking for money. I guess it was a kind of propitiation. It didn't make sense that a book, a humble, hat-in-hand, rejected book, was now eagerly bought—even begged for. I didn't trust it. But I did begin to get around more.

I met Mr. Roosevelt and for some reason made him laugh. To the end of his life, when occasionally he felt sad and burdened, he used to ask me to come in. We would talk for half an hour and I remember how he would rock back in his chair behind his littered desk and I can still hear his roars of laughter.

One night at John Gunther's apartment in New York I met Wendell Willkie, who was running for the Presidency. I liked him very much, although I was opposed to him politically. He seemed a warm and open man. Very late at night after a number of whiskies I brought up something that had always interested me. I asked him why he wanted to be President. It seemed the loneliest and most punishing job in the world. He rolled his highball glass slowly between his palms and stared into it. And finally he said: "You know—I haven't the slightest idea."

I liked him even more then. He didn't give me any bull.

The strange parade of the Thirties was drawing toward its close and time seemed to speed up. Imperceptibly the American nation and its people had changed, and undergone a real revolution, and we were only partly aware of it while it was happening.

Now war was coming. You didn't have to be an expert to know that. It was patent in every news report, in the clanging steps of goose-stepping Nazis. It had been in the cards since the first German put on his brown-shirted uniform. The practice wars—Ethiopia, Spain, the Ruhr, the Czech border—we had watched with paralyzed attention. At any early moment it could have been stopped—or could it? America knew it was coming even while we didn't believe it. We watched the approach of war as a bird helplessly watches an approaching rattlesnake. And when it came, we were surprised as we always are.

But the strange designlike quality of the Thirties continued to the end. It was as though history had put up markers, dramatic milestones at either end of the decade. It started with the collapse not only of financial structure, but of a whole way of thought and action. It ended with perhaps the last Great War.

A few weeks ago I called on a friend in a great office building in midtown New York. On our way out to lunch he said, "I want to show you something."

And he led me into a broker's office. One whole wall was a stock ex-change trading board. Two young men moved back and forth swiftly fill-ing in changes, rises, falls, buying, selling. Behind an oaken rail was a tight-packed, standing audience, clerks, stenographers, small business-men. Most of them munched sandwiches as they spent their lunch hour watching the trading. Now and then they made notations on envelopes. And their eyes had the rapt, glazed look one sees around a roulette table.

Making of a New Yorker

NEW YORK IS the only city I have ever lived in. I have lived in the country, in the small town, and in New York. It is true I have had apartments in San Francisco, Mexico City, Los Angeles, Paris, and sometimes have stayed for months, but that is a very different thing. As far as homes go, there is only a small California town and New York. This is a matter of feeling.

The transition from small town to New York is a slow and rough process. I am writing it not because I think my experience was unique; quite the contrary. I suspect that the millions of New Yorkers who were not born here have had much the same experience—at least parallel experiences. Perhaps my account may remind them of all the painful, wonderful times in their own lives.

When I came the first time to New York in 1925 I had never been to a city in my life. (From Stanford University I had made undergraduate trips to San Francisco and thought naturally that I knew all about it, particularly as related to sin in my income bracket. I was twenty-three years old and my bracket was low.) I arrived on a boat, tourist, one hundred dollars. It was November. Besides my one hundred dollars, I had when I sailed out of San Francisco another hundred dollars to see me started in New York. If I had been a little richer, or a little more experienced, I wouldn't have taken the pretty girl around Havana in a carriage, nor been charmed and worldly about the broad rum drinks like tubs of soaking fruit. I don't know what I thought I was going to do with that very pretty girl once I got to New York—marry her, I guess, and take her into my penthouse on Park Avenue, where my guest list had no names but those of the famous, the beautiful and the dissolute. Anyway, it didn't pan out, and in the process my hundred dollars for New York was reduced to three.

From a porthole, then, I saw the city, and it horrified me. There was something monstrous about it—the tall buildings looming to the sky and the lights shining through the falling snow. I crept ashore—frightened and cold and with a touch of panic in my stomach. This Dick Whittington didn't even have a cat.

I wasn't really bad off. I had a sister in New York and she had a good job. She had a husband and he had a good job. Now, in California, when a relative visited, there was always a good bed—maybe under the eaves, but it was yours for as long as you wanted to stay. My sister had one of the really nice apartments. It consisted of one large room, a tiny bathroom and a screened alcove where the lightest of cooking could be done and wasn't. There wasn't any question of staying with her. One double studio couch that acted as a sitting place in the daytime was the total sleeping space. My brother-in-law loaned me thirty dollars and put me up at a hotel for the first night. The next day he got me a job as a laborer on a big construction job and I found a room three flights up in Fort Greene Place in Brooklyn. That is about as alone as you can get. The job was on Madison Square Garden, which was being finished in a hurry. There was time and a half and there was double time. I was big and strong. My job was wheeling cement—one of a long line—one barrow behind another, hour after hour. I wasn't that big and strong. It nearly killed me and it probably saved my life. I was too tired to see what went on around me.

Most of the men in the line were Negroes—stringy men who didn't look big and strong at all, but they dollied those 150-pound barrows along as though they were fluff. They talked as they went and they sang as they went. They never seemed to get tired. It was ten, fifteen, and sometimes eighteen hours a day. There were no Sundays. That was double time, golden time, two dollars an hour. If anybody slipped out of the line, there were fifty men waiting to take his place.

My knowledge of the city was blurred—aching, lights and the roar of the subway, climbing three flights to a room with dirty green walls, falling into bed half-washed, beef stew, coffee and sinkers in a coffeepot, a sidewalk that pitched a little as I walked, then the line of barrows again. It's all mixed up like a fever dream. There would be big salamanders of glowing coke to warm our hands and I would warm mine just for the rest, long after I couldn't feel my hands at all. I do remember a man falling from a scaffold up near the ceiling about ninety feet and landing about four feet from me. He was red when he hit and then the blood in his face drew away like a curtain and he was blue and white under the working lights.

I don't even remember how long the job went on. It seems interminable and was maybe a month or six weeks. Anyway, the Garden got finished for the six-day bicycle races and Tex Rickard congratulated us all, without respect to race or color. I still get a shiver from the place sometimes.

About that time, my rich and successful uncle came to town from Chicago. He was an advertising man with connections everywhere. He was fabulous. He stayed in a suite at the Commodore, ordered drinks or coffee and sandwiches sent up any time he wanted, sent telegrams even if they weren't important. This last still strikes me as Lucullan. My uncle got me a job on a newspaper—the *New York American* down on William Street. I didn't know the first thing about being a reporter. I think now that the twenty-five dollars a week that they paid me was a total loss. They gave me stories to cover in Queens and Brooklyn and I would get lost and spend hours trying to find my way back. I couldn't learn to steal a picture from a desk when a family refused to be photographed and I invariably got emotionally involved and tried to kill the whole story to save the subject.

But for my uncle, I think they would have fired me the first week. Instead, they gave me Federal courts in the old Park Row Post Office. Why, I will never know. It was a specialist's job. Some of the men there had been on that beat for many years and I knew nothing about courts and didn't learn easily. I wonder if I could ever be as kind to a young punk as those men in the reporters' room at the Park Row Post Office were to me. They pretended that I knew what I was doing, and they did their best to teach me in a roundabout way. I learned to play bridge and where to look for suits and scandals. They informed me which judges were pushovers for publicity and several times they covered for me when I didn't show up. You can't repay that kind of thing. I never got to know them. Didn't know where they lived, what they did, or how they lived when they left the room.

I had a reason for that, and it was a girl again. I had known her slightly in California and she was most beautiful. I don't think this was only my memory. For she got a job in the Greenwich Village Follies just walking around—and she got it with no trouble whatever. It was lucky because that's about all she could do. She got a hundred dollars a week. I fell hopelessly in love with her.

Now New York changed for me. My girl lived on Gramercy Park and naturally I moved there. The old Parkwood Hotel had some tiny rooms— six walk-up flights above the street—for seven dollars a week. I had nothing to do with New York. It was a stage set in which this golden romance was taking place. The girl was very kind. Since she made four times as much money as I did, she paid for many little dinners. Every night I waited for her outside the stage door.

I can't imagine why she went to the trouble of trying to reform me. We would sit in Italian restaurants—she paid—and drink red wine. I wanted to write fiction—novels. She approved of that in theory, but said I should go into advertising—first, that is. I refused. I was being the poor artist, shielding his integrity. I wonder now what would have happened if anyone had offered me a job in advertising. I was spared that choice.

During all this time, I never once knew or saw one New Yorker as a person. They were all minor characters in this intense personal drama. Then everything happened at once. And I am glad it happened in the sequence it did. The girl had more sense than I thought. She married a banker from the Middle West and moved there. And she didn't argue. She simply left a note, and two days later I was fired from the *American*.

And now at last the city moved in on me and scared me to death. I looked for jobs—but good jobs, pleasant jobs. I didn't get them. I wrote short stories and tried to sell them. I applied for work on other papers, which was ridiculous on the face of it. And the city crept in—cold and heartless, I thought. I began to fall behind in my room rent. I always had that one ace in the hole. I could go back to laboring. I had a friend who occasionally loaned me a little money. And, finally, I was shocked enough to go for a job as a laborer. But by that time short feeding had taken hold. I could hardly lift a pick. I had trouble climbing the six flights back to my room. My friend loaned me a dollar and I bought two loaves of rye bread and a bag of dried herrings and never left my room for a week. I was afraid to go out on the street—actually afraid of traffic—the noise. Afraid of the landlord and afraid of people. Afraid even of acquaintances.

Then a man who had been in college with me got me a job as a workaway on a ship to San Francisco. And he didn't have to urge me, either. The city had beaten the pants off me. Whatever it required to get ahead, I didn't have. I didn't leave the city in disgust—I left it with the respect plain unadulterated fear gives. And I went back to my little town, worked in the woods, wrote novels and stories and plays, and it was eleven years before I came back.

My second assault on New York was different but just as ridiculous as the first. I had had a kind of a success with a novel after many tries. The royalties that poured in seemed to me princely. There must be some background to this. Three of my preceding novels did not make their advance and the advance was four hundred dollars. The largest amount I had ever got for a short story was ninety dollars. That was for *The Red Pony* and the payment was large only because the story was very long. When royalties for *Tortilla Flat* went over a thousand dollars, and when Paramount bought the book for $3,000—$2,700 net—I should have been filled with joy but instead I was frightened. During the preceding years I had learned to live comfortably, and contentedly, on an absolute minimum of money—thirty-five to fifty dollars a month. When gigantic sums like $2,700 came over the horizon I was afraid I could not go back to the old simplicity.

Whereas on my first try New York was a dark hulking frustration, the second time it became the Temptation and I a whistle-stop St. Anthony. I had become a fifth-rate celebrity. People in a narrow field went out of their way to be nice to me, invited me places, and poured soft and ancient beverages for me. And I, afraid I would lose my taste for twenty-nine-cent wine and red beans and hamburger, resisted like a mule.

As with most St. Anthonys, if I had not been drawn toward luxury and sin, and to me they were the same thing, there would have been no temptation. I reacted without originality: today I see people coming to success doing the same things I did, so I guess I didn't invent it. I pretended, and believed my pretense, that I hated the city and all its miles and traps. I longed for the quiet and contemplation of the West Coast. I preferred twenty-nine-cent wine and red beans. And again I didn't even see New York. It had scared me again but this time in another way. So I shut my eyes and drew virtue over my head. I insulted everyone who tried to be kind to me and I fled the Whore of Babylon with relief and virtuous satisfaction, for I had convinced myself that the city was a great snare set in the path of my artistic simplicity and integrity.

Back to the West I plunged, built a new house, bought a Chevrolet and imperceptibly moved from twenty-nine-cent wine to fifty-nine-cent wine. Royalties continued to come in. Now I made a number of business trips to New York and I was so completely in my role of country boy that I didn't look at it because I must have been enjoying my triumph over the snares and pitfalls. I had a successful play but never saw it. I believed I wasn't interested but it is probable that I was afraid to see it. I even built up a pleasant fiction that I hated the theater. And the various trips to New York were very like the visits of the Salvation Army to a brothel—necessary and fascinating but distasteful.

The very first time I came to the city and settled was engineered by a girl. Looking back from the cool position of middle age I can see that most of my heroic decisions somehow stemmed from a girl. Some basic healthiness in me had never permitted me to add girls to my catalogue of sins. And I who distrusted luxuries was a pushover for those most expensive luxuries of all—women.

I got an apartment on East Fifty-first Street between First and Second Avenues but even then I kept contact with my prejudices. My new home consisted of the first and second floors of a three-story house and the living room looked out on a small soot field called a garden.

Two triumphant Brooklyn trees called ailanthus not only survived but thumbed their noses at the soft coal dust and nitric acid which passed for air in New York.

It is so strange to look back. I was going to live in New York but I was going to avoid it. I planted a lawn in the garden, bought huge pots and planted tomatoes, pollinating the blossoms with a water-color brush. But

I can see now that a conspiracy was going on, of which I was not even aware. I walked miles through the streets for the exercise, and began to know the butcher and the newsdealer and the liquor man, not as props or as enemies but as people.

I have talked to many people about this and it seems to be a kind of mystical experience. The preparation is unconscious, the realization happens in a flaming second. I remember when and where it happened to me.

It was on Third Avenue. The trains were grinding over my head. The snow was nearly waist-high in the gutters and uncollected garbage was scattered in the dirty mess. The wind was cold, and frozen pieces of paper went scraping along the pavement. I stopped to look in a drugstore window where a latex cooch dancer was undulated by a concealed motor—and something burst in my head, a kind of light and a kind of feeling blended into an emotion which if it had spoken would have said, "My God! I belong here. Isn't this wonderful?"

Everything fell into place. I saw every face I passed. I noticed every doorway and the stairways to apartments. I looked across the street at the windows, lace curtains and potted geraniums through sooty glass. It was beautiful—but most important, I was part of it. I was no longer a stranger. I had become a New Yorker.

Now there may be people who move easily into New York without travail, but most I have talked to about it have had some kind of trial by torture before acceptance. And the acceptance is a double thing. It seems to me that the city finally accepts you just as you finally accept the city. Born New Yorkers will not know anything about this and I don't know whether they are lucky or unlucky.

A young man in a small town, a frog in a small puddle, if he kicks his feet is able to make waves, get mud in his neighbor's eyes—make some impression. He is known. His family is known. People watch him with some interest, whether kindly or maliciously. He comes to New York and no matter what he does, no one is impressed. He challenges the city to fight and it licks him without being aware of him. This is a dreadful blow to a small-town ego. He hates the organism that ignores him. He hates the people who look through him.

And then one day he falls into place, accepts the city and does not fight it anymore. It is too huge to notice him and suddenly the fact that it doesn't notice him becomes the most delightful thing in the world. His self-consciousness evaporates. If he is dressed superbly well—there are half a million people dressed equally well. If he is in rags—there are a million ragged people. If he is tall, it is a city of tall people. If he is short the streets are full of dwarfs; if ugly, ten perfect horrors pass him in one block; if beautiful, the competition is overwhelming. If he is talented, talent is a dime a dozen. If he tries to make an impression by wearing a toga—there's a man down the street in a leopard skin. Whatever he does or says or wears or thinks he is not unique. Once accepted this gives him perfect freedom to be himself, but unaccepted it horrifies him.

I don't think New York City is like other cities. It does not have character like Los Angeles or New Orleans. It is all characters—in fact, it is everything. It can destroy a man, but if his eyes are open it cannot bore him.

New York is an ugly city, a dirty city. Its climate is a scandal, its politics are used to frighten children, its traffic is madness, its competition is murderous. But there is one thing about it—once you have lived in New York and it has become your home, no place else is good enough. All of everything is concentrated here, population, theater, art, writing, publishing, importing, business, murder, mugging, luxury, poverty. It is all of everything. It goes all right. It is tireless and its air is charged with energy. I can work longer and harder without weariness in New York than anyplace else.

It is the fate of every outlander who comes to live in New York to have visitors from the place of his origin. They come in with a list of shows and places they want to see. For a week you take them about—restaurants, theaters, nightclubs. You start drinking cocktails at four o'clock. You get no sleep; your work goes to pieces. You fight with your wife and are mean to the children. And when your guests leave they invariably say, "We don't see how you can stand the pace." It takes you two weeks to recover from their visit.

I live in a small house on the East Side in the Seventies. It has a pretty little south garden. My neighborhood is my village. I know all of the storekeepers and some of the neighbors. Sometimes I don't go out of my village for weeks at a time. It has every quality of a village except nosiness. No one interferes in our business—no one by any chance visits us without first telephoning, certainly a most civilized practice. When we close the front door, the city and the world are shut out and we are more private than any country man below the Arctic Circle has ever been. We have many friends—good friends in the city. Sometimes we don't see them for six or eight months and this in no way interferes with our friendship. Anyplace else this would be resented as neglect. We accept invitations or refuse them without explanation or recrimination.

When we give a party, we ask whom we wish and a friend not invited is not mortally injured. Sometimes we go to bed at eight in the evening and sometimes we don't go to bed at all. When friends we love call and ask if they may call, we can say no without hurting their feelings. We eat in restaurants and go to the theater exactly when we wish. The explanation "I'm working" is accepted at its face value. There seems to be very little venomous gossip but surely there is discussion. No one knows nor cares when we go out or come in. I am a mild celebrity but there are a hundred thousand more important. In New York celebrityness is no burden. This is a matter of horror to some Hollywood visitors.

Everyone at one time or another tries to explain to himself why he likes New York better than anyplace else. A man who worked for me liked it because if he couldn't sleep he could go to an all-night movie. That's as good a reason as any.

Every once in a while we go away for several months and we always come back with a "Thank God I'm home" feeling. The only explanation I can think of to describe my feeling about the city is that if you have lived in New York no place else is good enough. New York is the world with every vice and blemish and beauty and there's privacy thrown in. What more could you ask?

My War with the Ospreys

M Y WAR with the ospreys, like most wars, was largely accidental and had a tendency to spread in unforeseen directions. It is not over yet. The coming of winter caused an uneasy truce. I had to go into New York while the ospreys migrated to wherever they go in the winter. Spring may open new hostilities, although I can find it in my heart to wish for peace and even friendship. I hope the ospreys, wherever they may be, will read this.

I shall go back to the beginning and set down my side of the affair, trying to be as fair as I possibly can, placing Truth above either propaganda or self-justification. I am confident that until near the end of the association my motives were kind to the point of being sloppy.

Two years and a half ago I bought a little place near Sag Harbor, which is quite near to the tip of Long Island. The outer end of Long Island is like the open jaws of an alligator and, deep in the mouth, about where the soft palate would be, is Sag Harbor, a wonderful village inhabited by people who have been here for a long time. It is a fishing town, a local town which has resisted the inroads of tourists by building no motor courts and putting up no hotels.

Sag Harbor was once one of the two great whaling ports of the world and was, according to local accounts, not at all second to Nantucket Island. At that time no fewer than one hundred and fifty whaling bottoms roved the great seas and brought back their riches in oil. Sag Harbor and Nantucket lighted the lamps of the world until kerosene was developed and the whaling industry languished.

With the wealth brought back by the whalers, beautiful houses were built in the village during the early 1800s, houses of neo-Greek architecture with fluted columns, Greek key decorations, with fanlights and

Adam doors and mantels. Some of these magnificent old houses have widow's walks, those high balconies on which the women kept watch for the return of their men from their year-long voyages. Some of these old houses are being rediscovered and restored. Many of the streets of Sag Harbor are named after old whaling men. My own place is near Jesse Halsey Lane and he is still locally known as Old Cap'n Jesse. I have a picture of his rough and whiskered face.

The place I bought is not one of the great old houses but a beautiful little point of land on the inland waters, a place called Bluff Point, with its own little bay—incidentally a bay which is considered hurricane-proof. Ordinarily only two boats are moored there, mine and one other, but during hurricane warnings as many as thirty craft come in for anchorage until the all-clear is broadcast.

My point, just under two acres, is shaded by great oak trees of four varieties and there are many bushes and pines to edge it on the water side. I myself have planted a thousand Japanese black pines, furnished by the State of New York to edge my point, to hold the soil with their roots and eventually to curve beautifully inward, urged by the wind which blows every day of the year—sometimes a zephyr and sometimes a fierce and strident gale.

Greensward grows on my place. On the highest point I have a small, snug cottage and in front of it a pier going out to nine feet at low water so that a fairly large boat can dock. My own boat, the *Lillymaid*, with Astolat as her port of registry, is named for my wife. She, the boat, is a utility craft twenty feet long, a clinker-built Jersey sea skiff. Her eight-foot beam makes her highly dependable and seaworthy. Many of these specifications could also describe my wife. She is not clinker-built, however. The *Lillymaid* has a Navy top to put up when the weather gets too rough and she has a hundred-horsepower engine so that we can run for it if a storm approaches. She is a lovely, efficient and seaworthy craft and all we need for the fishing and coastal exploring which is our pleasure.

Our house, while very small, is double-walled and winterized so that we can drive out during cold weather when the not-so-quiet desperation of New York gets us down.

My young sons, ten and twelve, but eight and ten when the osprey war began, adore the place and spend most of their summers here, exploring about in their skiffs or quarreling happily on the pier or on the lawn under the oak trees. My wife, who I believe was realistically skeptical when I bought the place, has become its staunchest defender.

Our association with the village people of Sag Harbor is, I think, pleasant to all of us. I come originally from a small town on the West Coast, a fishing town where my people have lived for a long time. And I find that what applies in my home country is equally acceptable in Sag Harbor. If you pay your bills, trade locally as much as possible, mind your own business and are reasonably pleasant, pretty soon they forget that you are an outlander. I feel that I belong in Sag Harbor and I truly believe that the people of the village have accepted us as citizens. I do not sense the resentment from them which is reserved for tourists and summer people.

But I must get back to the ospreys, because with them I have not only failed to make friends but have, on the contrary, been insulted, have thrown down the gauntlet and had it accepted.

On the West Coast, in California's Monterey County where I was born, I learned from childhood the grasses and flowers, the insects and the fishes, the animals from gopher and ground squirrel to bobcat and coyote, deer and mountain lion, and of course the birds, the common ones at least. These are things a child absorbs as he is growing up.

When I first came to Long Island I knew none of these things. Trees, grasses, animals and birds were all strange to me; they had to be learned. And sometimes the natives could not help me much because they knew the things so well and deeply that they could not bring them to the surface.

Thus with books and by asking questions I have begun to learn the names of trees and bushes, of berries and flowers. With a telescope, a birthday present from my wife, I have watched muskrats and a pair of otters swimming in our bay. I have tried to identify the migrating ducks and geese when they sit down in our bay to rest from their journey.

The mallards mate and nest in the reeds along our waterline and bring their ducklings for the bread we throw to them from the pier. I have watched my boys sitting quietly on the lawn with the wild ducks crawling over their legs to get pieces of doughnut from their fingers.

The baby rabbits skitter through my vegetable garden and, since I like the rabbits better than my scrawny vegetables, I permit them not only to live but to pursue happiness on my land.

Our house has a glassed-in sun porch and outside its windows I have built a feeding station for birds. Sitting inside I do my best to identify the different visitors with the help of an Audubon, and I have not always, I confess, been successful. There is one common blackish bird which looks to be of the grackle persuasion but his bill is the wrong color and I don't know what he is.

In the upper branches of a half-dead oak tree on the very tip of our point, there was, when I took possession, a tattered lump of trash which looked like an unmade bed in a motor court. In my first early spring a native named Ray Bassenden, our contractor and builder, told me, "That's an osprey's nest. They come back every year. I remember that nest since I was a little boy."

"They build a messy nest," I said.

"Messy, yes," he said professionally, "but I doubt if I could design something the winds wouldn't blow out. It isn't pretty but it's darned good architecture from a staying point of view."

Toward the end of May, to my delight, the ospreys came back from wherever they had been, and from the beginning they fascinated me. They are about the best fishermen in the world and I am about the worst. I watched them by the hour. They would coast along hanging on the breeze perhaps fifty feet above the water, then suddenly their wings raised like the fins of a bomb and they arrowed down and nearly always came up with a fish. Then they would turn the fish in their talons so that its head was into the wind and fly to some high dead branch to eat their catch. I became a habitual osprey watcher.

In time, two of my ospreys were nudged by love and began to install new equipment in the great nest on my point. They brought unusual material—pieces of wood, rake handles, strips of cloth, reeds, swatches of seaweed. One of them, so help me, brought a piece of two-by-four pine three feet long to put into the structure. They weren't very careful builders. The ground under the tree was strewn with the excess stuff that fell out.

I mounted my telescope permanently on the sunporch and even

trimmed some branches from intervening trees, and from then on, those love-driven ospreys didn't have a moment of privacy.

Then June came and school was out and my boys trooped happily out to Sag Harbor. I warned them not to go too near the point for fear of offending the nest builders, and they promised they would not.

And then one morning the ospreys were gone and the nest abandoned. When it became apparent that they weren't coming back I walked out to the point and saw, sticking halfway out of the nest, the shaft and feathers of an arrow.

Now Catbird, my youngest son, is the archer of the family. I ran him down and gave him what for in spite of his plaintive protests that he had not shot at the nest.

For a week I waited for the birds to come back, but they did not. They were across the bay. I could see them through the telescope building an uneasy nest on top of a transformer on a telephone pole where they were definitely not wanted.

I got a ladder and climbed up to the nest on our point and when I came down I apologized to Catbird for my unjust suspicions. For in the nest I had found not only the arrow, but my bamboo garden rake, three T-shirts belonging to my boys and a Plaza Hotel bath towel. Apparently nothing was too unusual for the ospreys to steal for their nest building. But our birds were definitely gone and showed no intention of returning. I went back to my Audubon and it told me the following:

"Osprey (fish hawk) *Pandion haliaëtus*, length 23 inches, wingspread about 6½ feet, weight 3½ pounds.

"Identification—in flight the wings appear long and the outer half has a characteristic backward sweep.

"Habits—(age 21 years) Provided they are not molested, ospreys will nest wherever there is a reasonably extensive body of clear water and some sort of elevated nest sites exist. The birds have little fear of man and are excellent watchdogs, cheeping loudly at intruders and driving off crows and other birds of prey. For this reason platforms on tall poles are often erected to encourage them to nest about homes and farmyards. Their food consists entirely of fish. These they spot from heights of thirty to one hundred feet, then, after hovering for a moment, they half close their wings and plunge into the water. The fish is seized in their talons, the toes of which are used in pairs, two to a side. This and the rough surface of the foot gives them a firm grip on the most slippery prey. After a catch, they rise quickly . . . and arrange the fish head first."

There followed a list of the kinds of fish they eat and their range and habits. Those were our boys, all right.

I must admit I had been pleased and a little proud to have my own osprey nest, apart from being able to watch them fish. I had planned to observe the nestlings when they arrived. The empty nest on the point was a matter of sorrow and perplexity to me. The summer was a little darkened by the empty nest, and later the winter winds ripped at its half-completed messiness.

It was in February of 1956 that the answer came to me. If people put up platforms on poles, why could I not build a nest so attractive as to be irresistible to any passing osprey with procreation on his mind? Why could I not win back my own birds from the uncomfortable nest which the power company had meanwhile torn off the transformer? I had been to Denmark and had seen what the country people there did for storks. And the storks loved them for it and had their young on the roof tops and year by year brought luck to their benefactors.

In the late winter I went to work. Climbing the oak tree on the point, I cleaned away the old debris of the nest. Then I mounted and firmly wired in place horizontally a large wagon wheel. I cut dry pampas grass stalks and bound them in long faggots. Then with the freezing blasts of winter tearing at my clothes, I reascended the tree and wove the reeds into the spokes of the wheel until I had a nest which, if I had any oviparous impulses, I should have found irresistible.

My wife, dressed in warm clothing, stood dutifully on the ground under the trees and hooked bundles of reeds on the line I threw down to her. She has a highly developed satiric sense which on other occasions I have found charming. She shouted up against the howling wind: "If anybody sees you, a middle-aged man, up a tree in midwinter, building a nest, I will have trouble explaining it to a sanity commission."

Misplaced humor can, under some circumstances, almost amount to bad taste. Silently and doggedly I completed what I believe was the handsomest nest in the Western Hemisphere. Then I went back to my sunporch to await eventualities.

I did have some difficulty explaining the project to my boys. To my oldest son Thom's question "Why do you build nests for birds?" I could only jocularly reply, "Well, I can build a better nest than they can, but I can't lay eggs, so you see we have to get together."

The winter was long and cold and there was hardly any spring at all. Summer came without warning about June 1. I had trouble with the novel I was writing since I had to rush constantly to the telescope to see whether the ospreys, my prospective tenants, had returned.

Then school was out and my boys moved to Sag Harbor and I put them on watch.

One morning Catbird charged into my study, which is a corner of the garage.

"Ospreys!" he shouted. "Come running—ospreys!"

"Sh!" I shouted back. "Keep your voice down. You'll disturb them."

I rushed for my telescope, bowling Catbird over in my rush and tripping over Thom's feet.

There were the ospreys all right. But they weren't settling into my beautiful nest. They were dismantling it, tearing it to pieces, lifting out the carefully bound reed pads and carrying them across the bay and propping them clumsily on top of the same transformer.

Of course my feelings were hurt. Why should I deny it? And on top of all my work. But on the heels of injury came anger. Those lousy, slipshod, larcenous birds, those ingrates, those—those ospreys. My eyes strayed to the shotgun that hangs over my fireplace, but before I could reach for it a Machiavellian thought came to me.

I wanted to hurt the ospreys, yes. I wanted revenge on them, but with number-four shot? No. I ached to hurt them as they had hurt me in their feelings—psychologically.

I am an adept at psychological warfare. I know well how to sink the knife into sensibilities. I was coldly quiet, even deadly in my approach and manner, so that my boys walked about under a cloud and Thom asked, "What's the matter, Father, did you lose some money playing poker?"

"You stay out of the garage," I said quietly.

I had made my plan. I declared the garage off limits to everyone. My novel came to a dead stop. Daily I worked in the garage using pieces of chicken wire and a great deal of plaster of Paris.

Then I paid a call on my neighbor, Jack Ramsey, a very good painter, and asked him to come to my workshop and to bring his palette and brushes. At the end of two days we emerged with our product—a life-size perfect replica of a nesting whooping crane. It is my belief that there are only thirty-seven of these rare and wonderful birds in the world. Well, this was the thirty-eighth.

Chuckling evilly I hoisted the plaster bird up in the tree and wired her firmly in the nest where her blinding white body, black tail and brilliant red mask stood out magnificently against the sky. I had even made her bill a little overlarge to take care of foreshortening.

Finally I went back to the sun porch and turned my telescope on the ospreys, who pretended to go about their nest building on the transformer as though nothing had happened. But I knew what must be going on over there, although they kept up their façade of listlessness, and I must say they were building an even messier nest than usual.

Mrs. Osprey was saying, "Lord almighty, George! Look who has moved into the apartment *you* didn't want. Why did I listen to you?"

To which he was replying, "I didn't want—what do you mean *I* didn't want? It was you who said the neighborhood wasn't good enough. Don't you put words in my mouth, Mildred."

"Everybody knows you have no taste or background," she was replying. "Your Uncle Harry built his nest over a slaughterhouse."

And I laughed to myself. These are the wounds that never heal. This is psychological warfare as it should be fought.

Two days later, Thom came running into my study in the garage.

"The nest," he cried. "Look at the nest."

I bolted for the door. The ospreys in jealous rage were dive-bombing my whooping crane, but all they could accomplish was the breaking of their talons on the hand surface of the plaster. Finally they gave up and flew away, followed by my shouts of derision.

I did hear my oldest boy say to his brother, "Father has been working too hard. He has gone nuts."

Catbird replied, "His id has been ruptured. Sometimes one broods too much on a subject and throws the whole psychic pattern into an uproar."

That isn't quite where it rests.

It is true that the ospreys have not attacked anymore, but we have had other visitors, human visitors.

One morning I looked out the window to see a rather stout lady in khaki trousers and a turtle-neck sweater creeping across my lawn on her hands and knees. Field glasses dangled from her neck and she held a camera in front of her. When I went out to question her, she angrily waved me away.

"Go back," she whispered hoarsely. "Do you want her to fly away?"

"But you don't understand—" I began.

"*Will* you keep your voice down," she said hoarsely. "Do you know what that is? The club will never believe me. If I don't get a picture of her I'll kill you."

Yes, we have had bird watchers—lots of them. You see, our whooping crane can be sighted from a long way off. After a time they discovered the nature of the thing, but they would not listen to my explanation of the ruse. In fact, they became angry; not at the ospreys, where the blame rests—but at me.

As I write, it is autumn of 1956 and from the coldness and the growing winds, an early winter and a cold one is indicated. I have taken my whooping crane down and restored the nest to its old beauty. When the spring comes again—we shall see what we shall see. No one can say that I am unforgiving. The nest is ready and waiting. Let us see whether the ospreys are big enough to let bygones be bygones.

My wife says that if she has to go through another year like this she will—no, I won't tell you what she says. Sometimes her sense of humor seems a little strained.

Conversation at Sag Harbor

The north wind doth blow,
And we shall have snow,
And what will the robin do then—
                    Pore thang!

He sit in the barn,
To keep himself warn,
And put his head under his wang—
                    Pore thang!

I DO NOT SUBSCRIBE to Togetherness, which seems to me to foster active dislike between American parents and their children. A father being a pal to his son not only is nonsense but can be dangerous. Father and son are natural enemies and each is happier and more secure in keeping it that way.

My friend Jack Ratcliff has reduced the problem to two sentences. "If you can catch them, hit them," he says. "If you can't catch them, bribe them."

My two sons understand and admire the principle of Apartness, and this being so, we sometimes take an exclusively masculine trip during their spring vacation in March, the coldest, meanest and most treacherous part of the winter.

My boys were thirteen and fifteen years old. They had all the faults and some of the virtues of their ages. They are inmates of separate boarding schools, and although well equipped in delinquency, neither of them has so far made the pokey, but they have been close.

Last year we decided to go to Sag Harbor, near the end of Long Island. Ours is no attempt to be pals but rather for each side to spy out and neutralize the changing weapons of the other. I have a warm and cozy little fishing cottage there, set on a point of land that extends into a protected bay. Going alone permits us to eat, talk and act in ways that would not be possible under the civilizing influence of femininity—in other words to be slobs.

It was very cold, the longest cold spell of any recorded March. The hundred-mile highway from New York was high-walled on either side with snow tossed up by the plows, but snow doesn't bother us much. My vintage station wagon wears snow tires from November until May. We were a traveling nightmare—the car radio yowled and the boys tapped their feet, patted rhythm with their hands, squirmed and occasionally threw a secret punch at each other. I'll be glad when they are old enough to drive and I can sit back and criticize. "Watch out! You're going too fast! For God's sake don't pass on the right!"—that kind of thing.

At exactly halfway we stopped at a big silver diner. They loaded the jukebox and each boy had three hamburgers and a bottle of Coke. For dessert one had chocolate ice cream with chocolate sauce, and the other vanilla ice cream with chocolate sauce. Their main problem seems to be getting from one meal to the next without starving to death. While I paid the bill, they bought candy bars to tide them over until dinnertime.

Back in the car they were a little sluggish and conversational, too sluggish to squirm. In honor of the occasion we took new names. This does for us what a new hairdo or a flowered hat does for a woman. My oldest son became The Tingler, and the younger The Fly, a character from another horror picture. I kept my old calypso name, Insidestraight, which was awarded me in Trinidad.

We passed a few guarded remarks—weather, how we felt, how good it was to be together—not really fighting, just feinting and getting the range but enough for me to relearn the always amazing fact that in the short time since I had seen them at Christmas they were changed, grown, enlarged.

The Fly has become arrogant—an arbiter of manners, clothes and ideas, and his standard is strict. He described many persons, ideas and things as corny, square or sentimental.

I threw a sneak punch. "The only people I know who are afraid of being corny or sentimental are adolescents and second-raters. Homer wasn't afraid of it. Neither was Shakespeare. And can you think of a cornier character than Albert Einstein?" I don't think I got over.

"It's a sign of insecurity," said The Tingler. And lest you think this profound, I must explain that just as The Fly uses "corny" and "square," The Tingler substitutes "insecure" for the same qualities. The boys were a little edgy. They knew the infighting was to come.

It was evening when we got to Discove Point and the sun was bleeding into the clouds over the hills to the south of Great Peconic Bay. The Point was deep-drifted. We had to shovel out a road to get the car in the garage. Our own bay was frozen over with only tide channels of open water. The huge oak trees on the Point were black against the whiteness of the snow and the steel blue of the ice. Our little shingled cottage with its good oil furnace was lovely and warm and immaculate. At least it was clean when we arrived. We lighted the water heater and loaded the refrigerator with the exotic and indigestible foods we had brought from town.

Then it was night and the beauty thing was the full moon, white and serene and lonely. The ridged ice of the bay was piled in high wreckage along the shores where the tides had thrust it. The plumed stalks of the pampas grass whispered wonderfully in the night wind. On the frozen surface of the bay the seagulls in congress assembled stood like hunchbacked old men, beaks into the wind to keep their feathers down. In the open water of the tide race the wild ducks gabbled, shovelers in transit now, competing with the mallards which never leave us. A blue heron lives on our shore, a friend and neighbor named Poor Harry. He stood on one leg, his head scrunched down, his long sword of a beak hidden in his breast feathers. Because he stands upright, he turns his back to the wind to keep his feathers down, a pitiful, doleful-looking bird. In the sterling silver of the moon-white night, the ice cricked and rustled on the falling tide. And O, the limbs of the oaks were as black against the sky as those Sung paintings in ink made from fir smoke and the glue from wild asses' hides. Jack pines were yellowy from the cold, and the naked grape vines hung like ragged spiderwebs on the white walls of the garage. Far away, almost like Aurora Borealis, the winking town lights of Sag Harbor put up a dome of glow.

Most of the houses in sight were closed up for the winter. We walked about on the Point, our feet crunching through the crusted snow, and it was a joy to see the lights of the cottage, and to smell the pine smoke of the new-built fire.

The Fly is a hot trumpet boy. He roared up the phonograph, and with head thrown back and glazed eyes, he sat in and belted out riffs with some of the best sidemen in the business.

Tingler unpacked his drawing board. We are designing a catamaran entirely new in principle and method which will undoubtedly make our fortune, and we can use it—a fortune, I mean.

Best not to describe our dinner. Strong and competent women have been known to flag and fail at our menus. We finished, however, with our *spécialité de la maison*, known as *pousse* capudding, a handsome dessert made by pouring every known kind of do-it-yourself pudding in layers, black, white, pink, yellow, green.

The Fly was a good hour away from his trumpet. He cooked the dinner and he cannot play while eating. Pudding gums up the valves. He took his ease while The Tingler and I cleaned the kitchen—not the dishes, the whole bloody kitchen. The Fly had prepared his Sag Harbor *mignon*, which puts up a mushroom cloud of real mushrooms and has a fallout of hamburger particles.

The Tingler is in what has been called his God and Girl Period. Sometimes he can't tell them apart. I remember it myself, a kind of half-strangling sensation and sudden urges to laugh or weep and an outer layer of utter cynicism for show.

I asked, "How's the girl situation?"

"Just the same," he said. "You've either got too many or none at all. I don't know which is worse. Makes you insecure."

"And it won't get any better," I reassured him.

"I wish I didn't love them so much," he said, " 'cause I hate 'em."

"Well, at least you didn't invent them. Look, I know I didn't get all the grease off those plates, but you might do me the honor of wiping it off. How's your religion? Still aiming to be a Catholic?"

"I'm an atheist," he said.

"That's a hard religion to live up to. Better leave yourself an escape hatch for walking under ladders and wishing on the new moon."

"I don't believe in *anything*," he said fiercely.

"Hallelujah! What's her name?"

"Helen."

"A brute, eh?"

"A bitch," said The Tingler.

"Shall we join The Fly? At least he believes in C-sharp minor."

"He's just a kid," said The Tingler.

He was watching a newborn fly, his namesake, crawling heavily up the new-warmed windowpane. "Say," he asked, "how much does it cost an hour to fly a jet 707?"

"I don't know. Pretty much, I guess. Why?"

"Oh, nothing."

Then I heard the sound too—the droning cry of a flight of jets from an airfield not far away. We went outside to look for them and they flew across the white face of the moon. Then they crashed the barrier with a sound that always makes me think the furnace has exploded. In our shirt-sleeves the cold air bit deep and raised goose bumps on our arms, so that we went inside again.

The Fly asked, "Why are they pouring the heat on those poor disk jockeys?"

"Payola," I said.

"Plugola," The Tingler said.

"What's wrong with it?" The Fly demanded. "He plays records and maybe somebody gives him a buck. Is it against the law?"

I put on my fatherly-logic-and-reason tone. How they must hate it. "I don't know whether it's against the law or not, but it is said to be immoral."

Tingler explained to his brother, whom he considers a little kid and probably always will. "You see, people buy what they hear. It's not what's good but what gets played. The DJ's play the ones they get paid to play. They say some of the jocks own part of the recording companies. They spin their own cookies."

You can see how valuable these outings are in the matter of language.

The Fly fixed us with a glittering self-righteous eye. (I might mention here that neither of my kids has ever made or brought home an honest or a dishonest dime.) "Those Eisenhower kids got a vacation in Puerto Rico," said The Fly. "They went in an Air Force jet 707."

"Jealous?" I asked.

"Sure I am. What did it cost the taxpayer?"

"What do you care?" I said. "You don't pay any taxes."

Then an uneasy silence fell on that pleasant room. I could feel the boys brace themselves against the usual lecture, or at least prepare not to listen. I'd been thinking about it for a good time, and I let the silence ride.

"Well, I guess we might as well get to it," I said at last.

The boys exchanged a glance that said, "Oh, brother, here it comes."

"I have prepared a few remarks," I began.

The Fly looked as though he had bitten down on a No. 5 shot in a piece of wild goose. Tingler put on the earnest and Oriental look that means he is courteously not listening.

"At intervals, it becomes my duty, through the accident of being your father, to give you what for."

"Yes, sir," they said in unison, the rotters.

"I have in hand the reports of your teachers and masters, who urge me to influence you. You, Tingler, have done a little better in school but not nearly well enough. You, Fly, are a scholastic disgrace. Not only have you done little or no work, you have engaged in a contest of wills with a master and caused pain and anxiety. Are these facts correct?"

"Yes, sir"—synchronized.

"Have you excuses?"

"Yes, sir. We mean, no, sir."

"Have I not given you good and fatherly advice in letters and in speech?"

"Yes, sir."

"Do you believe what I've told you?"

"Yes, sir."

"And you continue your lives of sin and gold bricking."

"It creeps up on you," said The Fly.

"I'm at my wits' end," I said. "And I mean that literally. I've told you all I know and it isn't much but you've had it."

I paused for answer, but the sons of guns know when to keep still. The room was silent and then from far off—a gunshot.

"Somebody shooting ducks with a flashlight," Tingler observed.

"All right—all right. Don't change the subject or the mood. After much thought I am prepared to do something painful, something drastic."

Both boys looked at the floor. They were trying to look pitiful, humble and respectful waiting for the blow to fall. I have a feeling they weren't very scared. "Yes, sir."

"I am going to give you your freedom."

"Sir?"

"I'm getting off your back."

"How do you mean?"

"I mean no more lectures, no more come-uppances. You are crowding manhood and you'll have to take some of the pain. You are free."

"How do you mean free?"

"I'll tell you. If you get a good grade, it's your grade. If you fail, it's your failure. That's what freedom means and it's awful." I think for the moment I had caught their attention.

"What's awful about it?" The Fly asked.

"I'll tell you, but you'll have to find it out yourselves. Freedom is the worst slavery of all. No boss to cheat, no teacher to fool. No excuses that work. And nobody to bitch to."

"Do you mean it? About—getting off—our backs?"

"I mean it, all right. It's a lonely feeling, isn't it?"

I could feel their dishonest little minds scurrying about looking for a trick, and I answered their thoughts.

"It's not a trick," I said. "Of course if you get in trouble beyond your control, I'll stand by. But I want no more details. That part of your lives is over."

Tingler said, "I'll bet the masters won't go for that."

"No, of course they won't. Neither will the cop, neither will the judge if you come before him. But that's your business. Being a man is a good thing, maybe the best, but a man has to do his own time, take his own rap, be his own man."

"Yes," said Fly, "but how about all those people on the couch, or the drunks?"

"They're sick or they're children but they aren't men. I think the lecture is over; I think it's over for good. I've taught you everything I know. From now on we can only discuss."

I could hear them let out their breaths like a slow leak in a tire. "Let's put on coats and go for a walk," I said. "The moon is beautiful."

The outside was crisp and crusted as a pie. We heard the ice crackling around the piles of our small pier as the tide changed level. Just above the high-water mark in the thick pampas grass a colony of muskrats live, nice secret little creatures, so silent and quick that we had not been able to see one up close. Someone had told us that muskrats love parsnips. We set one of those Havahart wire traps baited with parsnips by the burrows in the pampas grass. The trap doesn't hurt an animal. We planned to look at a customer for a little while and then turn him loose. We also have a pair of otters on our shore, but they are much harder to catch.

The Fly took his trumpet to the end of the pier. He keeps the mouthpiece warm in his breast pocket. He blew taps to break the hearts of neighbors two miles away, and then to prove his virtuosity he did it again, three times in different keys. If he would give the attention to his school work that he lavishes on his trumpet, he would be in Princeton's Institute for Advanced Study right now.

Hopelessly, whitely beautiful as was the night and sweet and bitter the wind and attractive the conversation of the mallards, we got blue with cold and our ears felt like wounds. We rushed back to the warm house and played the whole album of the Benny Goodman concert at Carnegie Hall. The only difference was that we played it much louder than the original could possibly have been. I drank a beer and the kids made a horrid mixture of chocolate that poured like fudge. Then we went to bed, half praying for a snowstorm. The Point is wonderful when the good snow blows over it riding the wind like a horse.

(Note 1—Must winter-spray my fruit trees tomorrow if possible.)

(Note 2—Take lawn mower to town to be repaired against the time when we will have a lawn.)

(Note 3—Stay off their backs.)

We slept sweetly and long.

The morning was sharp and clean as a blade. Even the tide channels were crusted over with ice. Tingler cooked a fine breakfast. He will make a late-sleeping woman very happy some day. He's a good cook because he loves to eat. The Fly doesn't give a damn. He'd eat his socks if not reminded.

Coffee time is a good time and one to prolong, sitting in the little glassed-in porch with the sun pouring in, just staring at the distant hills furry with leafless trees. I swear they seemed to be changing toward green already. I always think so even when I know it isn't true. The crested bluejays worked away at the seed-and-suet cake in a basket on the tree outside the window. A herd of brownish birds fed like sheep on the bare place that will be a lawn later in the year. Wonder what they find to eat? Wonder what kind of birds they are? I look them up every year and then forget.

One thing I could truly say and know it isn't wishfulness. The lilac buds were indeed swelling and getting a glossy milky look. If you squeeze them they run sticky juice. It's good to have one true and provable thing on a morning in the sun, a golden quiet time, no loud music for the moment.

With our first rising we had gone out to look at the trap. No muskrat. The parsnips were untasted and a little withered.

A beastly clamor broke out near the kitchen steps. An old lady mallard nests regularly in our reed bed. She has a game leg she uses for show. Now she came limping to the house for bread crusts, complaining bitterly about how attractive she is to drakes and what a burden it is to her.

"Here comes Gimpy," said The Fly. "Don't you know people like her? And there's that big old bull-bitch of a rabbit at the carnations again. I thought you trapped her and took her halfway to East Hampton."

"I did," I replied. "She came back."

The theory that kids wake up bright as buttons is nonsense. Mine wake up as though they were coming out of ether.

"Do you remember my lecture last night?" I asked.

"Sure do."

"Well, I meant it. But just as a matter of discussion, Fly, what was your difficulty with the master that caused so much fuss?"

"Well, he—" and then he grinned. "I don't remember how it started. But I'd do something and then he'd do something until we were so far out we couldn't get together anymore. We just didn't like each other."

"I understand that very well. I'm not suggesting it but simply stating a fact. If you were to say that last sentence to him, you might make a good and lasting friend."

"I couldn't," he said. "I don't think I could."

"Bothered you, didn't it?"

"Sure." The Fly has moments of devastating honesty. "It got so I blamed him for things I didn't do."

"I know how it is. I remember—you may not believe it but I really do remember. One of you turn on the radio for the news."

The report was a detailed account of Eisenhower's tremendous success in Europe and India—millions of people, millions of children waving flags.

"He sure is popular," I said.

Fly said cynically, "You give me a half holiday and a flag and I'll wave at King Kong. Who's going to walk away from a parade?"

"What a monster I have spawned," I said. "Tingler, sometimes in the morning you are a kindly and a loving child. Exude some honey, will you?"

"I've got a friend at school that his father is on Madison Avenue."

"I wish you had a friend who speaks good English."

"You ought to hear him," Tingler said enthusiastically. "That boy can speak pure Madison Avenue. Can't understand a word of it."

"I've read some of it in John Crosby's column. What shall we do today? We could put the catamaran in the water and see whether our invention works."

"We'll freeze our twinks, but I'm game. We can wear that Navy storm stuff you got war-surplus."

Launching the new-type catamaran which will make our fortune was not easy. We edged it out on the ice and then inched it along toward the tide channel and every moment we expected to plunge through into the icy water. The old, refrozen holes of the eel fishermen were all about it. They cut holes in the ice and probe the bottom with many-tined spears until they jam into a big eel. Out in the channel a few small outboard boats were anchored, for the spring flounder were beginning to pay attention. The men crouched in the boats were bundled up like feather beds, hooded and helmeted so that nothing but their noses and eyes could be seen. This early in the season the flounder are sleepy and sluggish with cold. The fishermen drag a piece of iron or an old bedspring back and forth along the bottom a few times to stir the lazy things awake. Then before they settle back to rest, they will sometimes take a bait. It is just one of the fishing theories and it works.

As we neared the open water, the ice became more mushy and treacherous so that we put most of our weight on the pontoons of the catamaran and pushed it along with one foot like boys pushing a scooter. I broke through once and half filled a boot with water. Finally we were afloat in the wind-rippled open with a strong tide running. We set our motor where we thought it should be and started it and the craft jumped like a horse and nearly reared over backward. Fortunately we stalled the motor in time and changed its position, giving it a very generous safety factor.

I freely admit that most of our inventions are dogs, but not this one. A couple of adjustments and we went skittering along like a blinking bobsled. I don't know what speed we made. We got so cold bouncing into the wind that we couldn't feel our fingers at all even with gloves on. Even my worldly sons were impressed. They admire anything that goes very fast or very high or very deep, and I must say I do, too, but we began to realize we were slowly freezing to death and we had to turn about and run in. Kids are all alike.

Once we made the ice, they would have run for shelter, leaving me to bring back the boat, if I had not used the kitchen-chair-and-whip method on them.

"Poor little pitiful blue-fingered waifs," I said. "I could put you out on the streets selling matches and I would make my fortune."

"While you sit in front of the fire and count the money?"

"Sure, why not?"

Tingler said, "Quote 'there must be easier ways of making a living' unquote. I want to go inside the house and look out at it. I'm cold."

We built an enormous fire in the fireplace and hung our icicled garments over the screen to drip dismally on the hearth. It's an odd fact that you really get to shivering when you hit warm air. Fly figured that if his lip wasn't ruined for all time, with the shakes he had, he could blow a vibrato you could throw a dog through.

It was my night to cook. I served corned-beef hash, *ancien chameau*,

the parsnips the muskrats had sneered at and cherries carnivale. The
boys weren't enthusiastic but they ate it. They would have eaten each
other. I dug out some old jam-session records and wiped the dust from
them—Eddie Condon, Peewee Russell, Wild Bill Davison, Bobby Hack-
ett—and it was pretty nice sitting there with the smell of roasting clothes
in the air, and two charming children doing a lousy job on the dishes,
while the ghosts of the old Chicago hyperharmonic boys ripped the walls
out and broke water tumblers. After that the silence sounded like a rushing wind. The sunset was green-gold, almost the way it is in the tropics.

"What's that you're drawing?" Tingler asked.

"I am inventing a self-filling bird feeder made with an overturned
flower pot suspended over a dish. You see, the pot is suspended by this
knot in the rope and it releases the seeds into the dish as they are needed.
They will hang in the trees and be painted in lovely colors like bells.
Pretty, aren't they? It will probably make our fortune."

The Fly said, "We make our fortune every day and we're still broke."

"Bad luck. Say, when I was in school a thousand years ago, we used
to have bull sessions—I guess that's a corny term now."

"Sure is."

"Do they still go on?"

"Sure, couple of bottles of bootleg Coke."

"Well, what are the subjects of discussion outside of girls?"

"You name it and we discuss it."

"Any big dramatic subjects?"

Automatically they clammed up, as they ought to. Never trust an
adult. That's the first rule. And then I could almost hear them remember
they were free, and it was a kind of a shocking thought.

Tingler said, "Biggest we had started with Dick Clark."

"Did you?" Fly asked. "So did we."

"Are disk jockeys that important to our civilization? Don't answer
that! I remember when Rudy Vallee was."

"It only started with Dick Clark."

"But it went on—"

"You going to tell or am I?"

"You mean the same discussion went on in two schools two hundred
miles apart?"

"Sure—Fly and I talked about it."

"Look, fair children, unless you can tell in unison, I suggest that you take turns."

"Yes, sir, fair father," said Tingler. "You see, in chapel and assembly we get all this honesty-is-the-best-policy jazz."

"And all the time the payola goes on right to the top."

They were breaking in on each other.

"Some of the kids say what good is it? You stay honest—you stay broke. Now—do you think that's important?"

"I sure do. How do the boys know all this?"

"They read the papers. *New York Times* is required reading."

"Doesn't anybody stand up for honesty?"

"Well, it's kind of hard to argue when you read who's been taking it. If it was only mugs and cops, but it's not."

"Give us an argument, fair father. We need one."

"You've got to live with yourself."

Fly said. "That's crazy. I've got to live with everybody."

"There have always been crooks."

"In high office? I'd love to have an argument to take back."

"You mean even in school the ranks of virtue are thinned?"

"No—but you can see when chapel and assembly don't tell the same story as the papers, it's pretty confusing."

"I agree. It's never been easy. There are millions of honest citizens."

"Yes, and where does it get them?"

"Is that your stand?"

"I'm just telling you the arguments. It's confusing."

"Why not warm up your trumpet?"

"That's a good idea," said The Fly. "You can't fake good jazz."

"Maybe we should take a turn around Dog Island. Is the moon up?"

Tingler cupped his hands against the window and looked out. "It's overcast," he said. "The wind's up too."

"Tell me this—do you ever discuss the juvenile-delinquency problem?"

Fly asked, "Do you mean gangs and rumbles or one kid going sour?"

"I'd be interested to know what's said."

"Well, the kids got to believe in something. They don't believe in cops and government so they make their own. May not be good but it's all they've got."

"And how about the lone kid?"

"I know what I think," said The Tingler. "I think they're confused. When you get confused, you get scared and then you get mad."

"You're telling me," I said. "And what's your cure, professor?"

"Stick to something they can believe in without being dopes."

"I think you've got something."

"I'm going to make some chocolate," said The Tingler. "You want some, fair father?"

"No, but if you'd open me a can of beer, I'd thank you kindly."

And then there came a sharp ticking on the windows.

"Snow," they shouted. "Maybe we won't have to go to town tomorrow. Maybe we'll be snowed in."

We snapped on the outside floodlights. Ghosts and winding sheets of small hard flakes came wind-driven over the Point, frozen snow that did not stick to the trees but blew along the ground like white dust. On the edge of the reed bed we saw Poor Harry, the heron, standing on one leg. He was all scrunched down, his beak buried in his breast feathers and his back to the snowy wind.

"I wonder what muskrats do like?" said The Fly.

II.

ENGAGED ARTIST

JOHN STEINBECK stood witness to some of the most significant upheavals of the twentieth century—the Depression of the 1930s, World War II, the McCarthy hearings, the Cold War, Vietnam. A man of compassion and intelligence, he developed into a writer who was constantly engaged with the manners, morals, and controversies of the world around him. He had the journalist's urge to participate, to see for himself. And he had the moralist's urge to comment, evaluate, and find solutions. As a Stanford University friend, Toby Street, noted in an interview, "John was actually a missionary. He was essentially a journalist, you know, that is, I think he could see things going on. . . . I mean journalist in the power of observation. I think some of his so-called tendencies toward you might say the 'left wing' were motivated by this strong missionary urge to set things right." His passionate resistance to tyranny and his equally heartfelt empathy for the marginalized and lonely, the disillusioned seekers and restless idealists, were wellsprings of his fiction as well as his nonfiction. He was ever the champion of the common person, so often caught in crosscurrents of politics and social unrest.

Both outrage and compassion are evident in his earliest journalism, represented here by three articles Steinbeck wrote before beginning the final draft of *The Grapes of Wrath* in May 1938. His first important essay appeared in the liberal national weekly *The Nation* only six months after the same magazine ran Mary McCarthy's searing indictment of *In Dubious Battle* as an "academic, wooden, inert" novel (11 Mar. 1936). With sweeping strokes, Steinbeck's "Dubious Battle in California" sets the record straight and, in addition, sets the writer's course for the next two years—the piece surveys the history of California's migrant problem. In the late summer of 1936, Steinbeck witnessed the migrants' suffering firsthand when he traveled to Arvin, near Bakersfield, to talk and tour camps with Tom Collins, manager of the Arvin government camp. Out of this trip came the far grittier and more detailed exposé of the migrant situation "The Harvest Gypsies," a series of seven articles published in October 1936 in the *San Francisco News,* a Scripps-Howard paper committed to a workingman readership. Reprinted as *Their Blood Is Strong* in 1938, the series was introduced by novelist and journalist John Barry: "Steinbeck is a unique figure. He has come forward at a time when revolutionary changes are going on in the world. He will be a factor in those changes" (*WD* 147). Indeed, that was Steinbeck's mission. His third piece of migrant nonfiction, "Starvation Under the Orange Trees," is his most incendiary, one that *Life* magazine, having commissioned a photo-text with photographer Horace Bristol, refused. Published in the small *Monterey Trader* in April 1938, the essay adumbrates the most explosive section in *The Grapes of Wrath,* Chapter 25: "Carloads of oranges dumped on the ground. The people came for miles to take the fruit, but this could not be. How would they buy oranges at twenty cents a dozen if they could drive out and pick them up? And men with hoses squirt kerosene on the oranges. . . . A million people hungry, needing the fruit—and kerosene sprayed over the golden mountains." These three forays into nonfiction chart Steinbeck's approach in *The Grapes of Wrath* itself: general overview, muckraking indictment, editorial wrath. Majestically symbolic, epic in scope, *The Grapes of Wrath* is at the same time insistently journalistic in its fidelity to the way people spoke, the land they crossed, the conditions they endured. This novel's roots—like those of much of what Steinbeck wrote—are in reportorial prose.

While Steinbeck sympathized with the migrants and, to some extent, with unionization, he opposed communism—although he was often labeled a Communist after publication of *The Grapes of Wrath.* His stance is clearly outlined in "I Am a Revolutionary," first published in *Le Figaro*'s magazine in 1954. Throughout his career, Steinbeck tried to maintain his position as a liberal, supportive of workers and organizing, but antagonistic to communism. That middle position was often misunderstood. Responding to a question sent to several writers in 1938, "Are you for or are you against the legal government and the people of Republican Spain," Steinbeck concludes his remarks: "I am treasonable enough not to believe in the liberty of a man or a group to exploit, torment, or slaughter other men or groups." He supported the rebels against the tyranny of Franco; the Joads against the tyranny of the Associated Farmers; the people of Russia against the tyranny of Stalin; and the South Vietnamese against what he saw as the tyranny of the Chinese-inspired North Vietnamese attacks. Several articles here—as well as comments punctuating *A Russian Journal* and "Letters to Alicia"—give testimony to his dislike of the ways in which communism dampened individual creativity, stifled initiative, fostered lies to achieve ends. In "Duel Without Pistols," he recounts an episode that occurred during a visit to Rome in 1952 when he was greeted by a critical "Open Letter to John Steinbeck" published in the Italian Communist paper *L'Unità*. He responded in print to Ezio Taddei's attack as he would respond in 1966 to Yevgeny Yevtushenko's poem chastizing Steinbeck for supporting the war in Vietnam, a poem first published in the Moscow newspaper *Literaturnaya Gazeta* and translated for the *New York Times* as "Letter to John Steinbeck" (see "An Open Letter to Poet Yevtushenko" in Part VII). In both cases, Steinbeck publicly outlined his anti-Communist stance and defended self, America, and the democratic process; he also invited Yevtushenko to accompany him on a proposed tour of both North and South Vietnam, a trip that never materialized. As was so often the case, Steinbeck channeled anger and outrage into words, most often a carefully crafted position. Other pieces here set forth his objections to McCarthy's tactics on the House Un-American Activities Committee; racial inequality; and, in a more relaxed tone, his responses to the Presidential inauguration—a final chapter omitted from *Travels with Charley*. He was a staunch advocate of democracy and fair play, and when they were threatened, he wrote passionately in their defense.

From 1955 to 1966, Steinbeck published extensively in *The Saturday Review*, where he was an "Editor-at-Large," submitting pieces on a wide range of topics. His name on the banner was a coup for a magazine whose aim was broad treatment of ideas and the arts. Norman Cousins, who took over the editorship of the popular literary magazine in 1940, said of Steinbeck, "I found him genuinely shy, extremely reluctant to get into public debate but deeply concerned and even agitated over public issues" (Cousins 195). Steinbeck's friend and fellow writer John Hersey concurred: "John was highly opinionated, but his opinions were thoughtful and clear. He apparently liked to write in the short, essayistic form, and the results were often quite fine. There was a large and admiring readership for these opinion pieces" (Parini 383), like "Atque Vale," reprinted here. An article like "Some Thoughts on Juvenile Delinquency" (not included here) is highly representative of much of Steinbeck's social commentary: he muses on a problem, gives it historical context (his passion for history is evident throughout his nonfiction), and links it to a well-thought-out moral or philosophical position. In this piece, Steinbeck concludes that "man is a double thing—a group animal and at the same time an individual. And it occurs to me that he cannot successfully be the second until he has fulfilled the first"(22). This remark goes a long way toward clearing up critical controversy concerning Steinbeck's supposed shift in perspective from his 1930s interest in group behavior to his subsequent focus on individual moral responsibility—as in *East of Eden*. The two strands are not, for Steinbeck, to be severed. Mutual and individual responsibilities are inseparable, he asserts, and "units," like individuals, engage in actions that must be read contextually.

By the late 1950s, the author felt keenly that America had gone morally flabby, a position sketched in an often reprinted piece first published in *Newsday*, "Adlai Stevenson and John Steinbeck Discuss the Past and the Present." (Steinbeck's part of this piece is reprinted here as "Dear Adlai.") Much of his work of the late 1950s and 1960s, both in fiction and nonfiction, is a jeremiad, exhorting Americans to consider their excesses and mend their collective ways. He objected to racism, certainly, to the disappearing sense of community and the destruction of the environment, certainly, but particularly to our growing materialism and loss of bedrock values: honor, courage, duty, love of country, and compassion for one's fellow man. Steinbeck's love of the Arthurian legends and what he thought were the enduring values of that time colored his response to America, and later to the Vietnam War. In America, as he wrote Stevenson, he recognized the "creeping, all pervading, nerve-gas of immorality which starts in the nursery and does not stop before it reaches the highest offices both corporate and governmental." Such comments sparked a "national controversy" and generated a symposium published in *The New Republic* titled "Have We Gone Soft?" (15 Feb. 1960), with comments by Harvard historian Arthur M. Schlesinger, Sr.; theologian Reinhold Niebuhr; Harry Golden, author of *Only in America;* and the Rev. Thurston N. Davis, editor of *America* magazine. "Mr. Steinbeck's fears are valid," writes Golden, "because his whole concern as an original thinker has been with the *tomorrow.* At this point in our history we have stopped living for the tomorrow" (15). Niebuhr concurred: "[O]ur moral and political complacency exposes us to the dangers which all soft nations of history have encountered" (15). Steinbeck had given voice to the anxiety that percolated beneath the bland surface of the 1950s.

This section includes one example of Steinbeck's political coverage. Whether he is writing for an English or an American audience, his tone changes from reflective to gently ironic. Most articles were written for the *Courier-Journal* in 1956, when, Steinbeck reports, "It occurred to me that a politically untrained reporter might be healthy" (12 Aug. 1956) and he offered to cover the national political conventions for the paper. His offer was accepted immediately by publisher Mark Ethridge, a friend of the Steinbecks since the couples had met a couple of years earlier on a return trip from Europe. "I can promise your readers," Steinbeck announced at the beginning of his series, "that I will be just as wrong as any of my competitors, only I hope to be more interesting than some" (12 Aug. 1956). He was. His twelve front-page columns, also syndicated in forty papers around the country, are filled with vintage Steinbeck, "a Peeping Tom and an eavesdropper at heart" (18 Aug. 1956). He delights in worm's-eye views, grubbing for the political insights of his cab driver, "the man at Gate 2-A" (14 Aug. 1956), and "the nice woman who has been serving me hot dogs and Cokes all week" whose arms have been burned repeatedly by lifting the hot dog steamer (19 Aug. 1956). By the end of the Democratic convention, exhausted by speechifying and "standing behind the mighty," Steinbeck writes, "Maybe it's perverse in me, but I find in myself a kind of hunger for a dishonest, cowardly, inhumane, and nongreat American" (18 Aug. 1956). It is this vein in Steinbeck that long endeared him to readers: the dry humor, the affinity for the "nongreat," and the ability to fix attention on what would seem, to a less practiced eye, a perfectly ordinary detail—and make that detail tell a whole story: "The Republicans have much better and bigger badges than the Democrats: In Chicago, I had a little old plastic card to pin to my lapel. Here in San Francisco they have given me a glorious bronze medal on a white ribbon, a combination of sharpshooter's medal and the Order of the Golden Fleece. I may wear this permanently and pass it on to my children."

After watching the "gutterfighting of the Democrats" and the "calm, the smooth and ordered mediocrity" of the Republicans, Steinbeck concludes his election coverage with his own political stance: "I find to my consternation that I am basically, intrinsically and irresistibly a Democrat" (25 Aug. 1956).

Dubious Battle in
California

IN SIXTY YEARS a complete revolution has taken place in California agriculture. Once its principal products were hay and cattle. Today fruits and vegetables are its most profitable crops. With the change in the nature of farming there has come a parallel change in the nature and amount of the labor necessary to carry it on. Truck gardens, while they give a heavy yield per acre, require much more labor and equipment than the raising of hay and livestock. At the same time these crops are seasonal, which means that they are largely handled by migratory workers. Along with the intensification of farming made necessary by truck gardening has come another important development. The number of large-scale farms, involving the investment of thousands of dollars, has increased; so has the number of very small farms of from five to ten acres. But the middle farm, of from 100 to 300 acres is in process of elimination.

There are in California, therefore, two distinct classes of farmers widely separated in standard of living, desires, needs, and sympathies: the very small farmer who more often than not takes the side of the workers in disputes and the speculative farmer, like A. J. Chandler, publisher of the Los Angeles *Times*, or like Herbert Hoover and William Randolph Hearst, absentee owners who possess huge sections of land. Allied with these large individual growers have been the big incorporated farms, owned by their stockholders and farmed by instructed managers, and a large number of bank farms, acquired by foreclosure and operated by superintendents whose labor policy is dictated by the bank. For example, the Bank of America is very nearly the largest farm owner and operator in the state of California.

These two classes have little or no common ground; while the small farmer is likely to belong to the Grange, the speculative farmer belongs to some such organization as the Associated Farmers of California, which is closely tied to the state Chamber of Commerce. This group has as its major activity resistance to any attempt of farm labor to organize. Its avowed purpose has been the distribution of news reports and leaflets tending to show that every attempt to organize agricultural workers was the work of red agitators and that every organization was Communist-inspired.

The completion of the transcontinental railroads left in the country many thousands of Chinese and some Hindus who had been imported for the work. At about the same time the increase of fruit crops, with their heavy seasonal need for pickers, created a demand for this mass of cheap labor. These people, however, did not long remain on the land. They migrated to the cities, rented small plots of land there, and, worst of all, organized in the so-called "tongs," which were able to direct their efforts as a group. Soon the whites were inflamed to race hatred, riots broke out against the Chinese, and repressive activities were undertaken all over the state, until these people, who had been a tractable and cheap source of labor, were driven from the fields.

To take the place of the Chinese, the Japanese were encouraged to come into California; and they, even more than the Chinese, showed an ability not only to obtain land for their subsistence but to organize. The "Yellow Peril" agitation was the result. Then, soon after the turn of the century Mexicans were imported in great numbers. For a while they were industrious workers, until the process of importing twice as many as were needed in order to depress wages made their earnings drop below any conceivable living standard. In such conditions they did what the others had done; they began to organize. The large growers immediately opened fire on them. The newspapers were full of the radicalism of the Mexican unions. Riots became common in the Imperial Valley and in the grape country in and adjacent to Kern County. Another wave of importations was arranged, from the Philippine Islands, and the cycle was repeated—wage depression due to abundant labor, organization, and the inevitable race hatred and riots.

This brings us almost to the present. The drought in the Middle West has very recently made available an enormous amount of cheap labor. Workers have been coming to California in nondescript cars from Oklahoma, Nebraska, Texas, and other states, parts of which have been rendered uninhabitable by drought. Poverty-stricken after the destruction of their farms, their last reserves used up in making the trip, they have arrived so beaten and destitute that they have been willing at first to work under any conditions and for any wages offered. This migration started on a considerable scale about two years ago and is increasing all the time.

For a time it looked as though the present cycle would be identical with the earlier ones, but there are several factors in this influx which differentiate it from the others. In the first place, the migrants are undeniably American and not deportable. In the second place, they were not lured to California by a promise of good wages, but are refugees as surely as though they had fled from destruction by an invader. In the third place, they are not drawn from a peon class, but have either owned small farms or been farm hands in the early American sense, in which the "hand" is a member of the employing family. They have one fixed idea, and that is to acquire land and settle on it. Probably the most important difference is that they are not easily intimidated. They are courageous, intelligent, and resourceful. Having gone through the horrors of the drought and with immense effort having escaped from it, they cannot be herded, attacked, starved, or frightened as all the others were.

Let us see what the emigrants from the Dust Bowl find when they arrive in California. The ranks of permanent and settled labor are filled. In most cases all resources have been spent in making the trip from the Dust Bowl. Unlike the Chinese and the Filipinos, the men rarely come alone. They bring wives and children, now and then a few chickens and their pitiful household goods, though in most cases these have been sold to buy gasoline for the trip. It is quite usual for a man, his wife, and from three to eight children to arrive in California with no possessions but the rattletrap car they travel in and the ragged clothes on their bodies. They often lack bedding and cooking utensils.

During the spring, summer, and part of the fall the man may find some kind of agricultural work. The top pay for a successful year will not be over $400, and if he has any trouble or is not agile, strong, and quick it may well be only $150. It will be seen that rent is out of the question. Clothes cannot be bought. Every available cent must go for food and a reserve to move the car from harvest to harvest. The migrant will stop in one of two federal camps, in a state camp, in houses put up by the large or small farmers, or in the notorious squatters' camps. In the state and federal camps he will find sanitary arrangements and a place to pitch his tent. The camps maintained by the large farmers are of two classes—houses which are rented to the workers at what are called nominal prices, $4 to $8 a month, and camp grounds which are little if any better than the squatters' camps. Since rent is such a problem, let us see how the houses are fitted. Ordinarily there is one room, no running water; one toilet and one bathroom are provided for two or three hundred persons. Indeed, one large farmer was accused in a Growers' Association meeting of being "kind of communistic" because he advocated separate toilets for men and women. Some of the large ranches maintain what are called model workers' houses. One such ranch, run by a very prominent man, has neat single-room houses built of whitewashed adobe. They are said to have cost $500 apiece. They are rented for $5 a month. This ranch pays twenty cents an hour as opposed to the thirty cents paid at other ranches and endorsed by the Grange in the community. Since this rugged individual is saving 33⅓ percent of his labor cost and still charging $5 a month rent for his houses, it will be readily seen that he is getting a very fair return on his money besides being generally praised as a philanthropist. The reputation of this ranch, however, is that the migrants stay only long enough to get money to buy gasoline with, and then move on.

The small farmers are not able to maintain camps of any comfort or with any sanitary facilities except one or two holes dug for toilets. The final resource is the squatters' camp, usually located on the bank of some watercourse. The people pack into them. They use the watercourse for drinking, bathing, washing their clothes, and to receive their refuse, with the result that epidemics start easily and are difficult to check. Stanislaus County, for example, has a nice culture of hookworm in the mud by its squatters' camp. The people in these camps, because of long-continued privation, are in no shape to fight illness. It is often said that no one starves in the United States, yet in Santa Clara County last year five babies were certified by the local coroner to have died of "malnutrition," the modern word for starvation, and the less shocking word, although in its connotation it is perhaps more horrible, since it indicates that the suffering has been long drawn out.

In these squatters' camps the migrant will find squalor beyond anything he has yet had to experience and intimidation almost unchecked. At one camp it is the custom of deputy sheriffs, who are also employees of a great ranch nearby, to drive by the camp for hours at a time, staring into the tents as though trying to memorize faces. The communities in which these camps exist want migratory workers to come for the month required to pick the harvest, and to move on when it is over. If they do not move on, they are urged to with guns.

These are some of the conditions California offers the refugees from the Dust Bowl. But the refugees are even less content with the starvation wages and the rural slums than were the Chinese, the Filipinos, and the Mexicans. Having their families with them, they are not so mobile as the earlier immigrants were. If starvation sets in, the whole family starves, instead of just one man. Therefore they have been quick to see that they must organize for their own safety.

Attempts to organize have been met with a savagery from the large growers beyond anything yet attempted. In Kern County a short time ago a group met to organize under the AF of L. They made out their form and petition for a charter and put it in the mail for Washington. That night a representative of Associated Farmers wired Washington for information concerning a charter granted to these workers. The Washington office naturally replied that it had no knowledge of such a charter. In the Bakersfield papers the next day appeared a story that the AF of L denied the affiliation; consequently the proposed union must be of Communist origin.

But the use of the term "communism" as a bugbear has nearly lost its sting. An official of a speculative-farmer group, when asked what he meant by a Communist, replied: "Why, he's the guy that wants twenty-five cents an hour when we're paying twenty." This realistic and cynical definition has finally been understood by the workers, so that the term is no longer the frightening thing it was. And when a county judge said, "California agriculture demands that we create and maintain a peonage," the future of unorganized agricultural labor was made clear to every man in the field.

The usual repressive measures have been used against these migrants: shooting by deputy sheriffs in "self-defense," jailing without charge, refusal of trial by jury, torture and beating by night riders. But even in the short time that these American migrants have been out here there has been a change. It is understood that they are being attacked not because they want higher wages, not because they are Communists, but simply because they want to organize. And to the men, since this defines the thing not to be allowed, it also defines the thing that is completely necessary to the safety of the workers.

This season has seen the beginning of a new form of intimidation not used before. It is the whispering campaign which proved so successful among business rivals. As in business, it is particularly deadly here because its source cannot be traced and because it is easily spread. One of the items of this campaign is the rumor that in the event of labor troubles the deputy sheriffs inducted to break up picket lines will be armed not with tear gas but with poison gas. The second is aimed at the women and marks a new low in tactics. It is to the effect that in the event of labor troubles the water supply used by strikers will be infected with typhoid germs. The fact that these bits of information are current over a good part of the state indicates that they have been widely planted.

The effect has been far from that desired. There is now in California anger instead of fear. The stupidity of the large grower has changed terror into defensive fury. The Granges, working close to the soil and to the men, and knowing the temper of the men of this new race, have tried to put through wages that will allow a living, however small. But the large growers, who have been shown to be the only group making a considerable profit from agriculture, are devoting their money to tear gas and rifle ammunition. The men will organize and the large growers will meet organization with force. It is easy to prophesy this. In Kern County the Grange has voted $1 a hundred pounds for cotton pickers for the first picking. The Associated Farmers have not yielded from seventy-five cents. There is tension in the valley, and fear for the future.

It is fervently to be hoped that the great group of migrant workers so necessary to the harvesting of California's crops may be given the right to live decently, that they may not be so badgered, tormented, and hurt that in the end they become avengers of the hundreds of thousands who have been tortured and starved before them.

The Harvest Gypsies:
Squatters' Camps

THE SQUATTERS' CAMPS are located all over California. Let us see what a typical one is like. It is located on the banks of a river, near an irrigation ditch or on a side road where a spring of water is available. From a distance it looks like a city dump, and well it may, for the city dumps are the sources for the material of which it is built. You can see a litter of dirty rags and scrap iron, of houses built of weeds, of flattened cans or of paper. It is only on close approach that it can be seen that these are homes.

Here is a house built by a family who have tried to maintain a neatness. The house is about ten feet by ten feet, and it is built completely of corrugated paper. The roof is peaked, the walls are tacked to a wooden frame. The dirt floor is swept clean, and along the irrigation ditch or in the muddy river the wife of the family scrubs clothes without soap and tries to rinse out the mud in muddy water. The spirit of this family is not quite broken, for the children, three of them, still have clothes, and the family possesses three old quilts and a soggy, lumpy mattress. But the money so needed for food cannot be used for soap nor for clothes.

With the first rain the carefully built house will slop down into a brown, pulpy mush; in a few months the clothes will fray off the children's bodies, while the lack of nourishing food will subject the whole family to pneumonia when the first cold comes.

Five years ago this family had fifty acres of land and a thousand dollars in the bank. The wife belonged to a sewing circle and the man was a member of the Grange. They raised chickens, pigs, pigeons and vegetables and fruit for their own use; and their land produced the tall corn of the Middle West. Now they have nothing.

If the husband hits every harvest without delay and works the maximum time, he may make $400 this year. But if anything happens, if his old car breaks down, if he is late and misses a harvest or two, he will have to feed his whole family on as little as $150.

But there is still pride in this family. Wherever they stop they try to put the children in school. It may be that the children will be in a school for as much as a month before they are moved to another locality.

There is more filth here. The tent is full of flies clinging to the apple box that is the dinner table, buzzing about the foul clothes of the children, particularly the baby, who has not been bathed nor cleaned for several days.

This family has been on the road longer than the builder of the paper house. There is no toilet here, but there is a clump of willows nearby where human feces lie exposed to the flies—the same flies that are in the tent.

Two weeks ago there was another child, a four-year-old boy. For a few weeks they had noticed that he was kind of lackadaisical, that his eyes had been feverish.

They had given him the best place in the bed, between father and mother. But one night he went into convulsions and died, and the next morning the coroner's wagon took him away. It was one step down.

They knew pretty well that it was a diet of fresh fruit, beans and little else that caused his death. He had had no milk for months. With this death there came a change of mind in this family. The father and mother now feel that paralyzed dullness with which the mind protects itself against too much sorrow and too much pain.

Here, in the faces of the husband and his wife, you begin to see an expression you will notice on every face; not worry, but absolute terror of the starvation that crowds in against the borders of the camp. This man has tried to make a toilet by digging a hole in the ground near his paper house and surrounding it with an old piece of burlap. But he will only do things like that this year.

He is a newcomer and his spirit and his decency and his sense of his own dignity have not been quite wiped out. Next year he will be like his next-door neighbor.

This is a family of six; a man, his wife and four children. They live in a tent the color of the ground. Rot has set in on the canvas so that the flaps and the sides hang in tatters and are held together with bits of rusty baling wire. There is one bed in the family and that is a big tick lying on the ground inside the tent.

They have one quilt and a piece of canvas for bedding. The sleeping arrangement is clever. Mother and father lie down together and two children lie between them. Then, heading the other way, the other two children lie, the littler ones. If the mother and father sleep with their legs spread wide, there is room for the legs of the children.

And this father will not be able to make a maximum of $400 a year anymore because he is no longer alert; he isn't quick at piecework, and he is not able to fight clear of the dullness that has settled on him. His spirit is losing caste rapidly.

The dullness shows in the faces of this family, and in addition there is a sullenness that makes them taciturn. Sometimes they still start the older children off to school, but the ragged little things will not go; they hide themselves in ditches or wander off by themselves until it is time to go back to the tent, because they are scorned in the school.

The better-dressed children shout and jeer, the teachers are quite often impatient with these additions to their duties, and the parents of the "nice" children do not want to have disease carriers in the schools.

The father of this family once had a little grocery store and his family lived in back of it so that even the children could wait on the counter. When the drouth set in there was no trade for the store anymore.

This is the middle class of the squatters' camp. In a few months this family will slip down to the lower class.

Dignity is all gone, and spirit has turned to sullen anger before it dies.

The next-door-neighbor family, of man, wife and three children of from three to nine years of age, have built a house by driving willow branches into the ground and wattling weeds, tin, old paper and strips of carpet against them.

A few branches are placed over the top to keep out the noonday sun. It would not turn water at all. There is no bed.

Somewhere the family has found a big piece of old carpet. It is on the ground. To go to bed the members of the family lie on the ground and fold the carpet up over them.

The three-year-old child has a gunny sack tied about his middle for clothing. He has the swollen belly caused by malnutrition.

He sits on the ground in the sun in front of the house, and the little black fruit flies buzz in circles and land on his closed eyes and crawl up his nose until he weakly brushes them away.

They try to get at the mucus in the eye corners. This child seems to have the reactions of a baby much younger. The first year he had a little milk, but he has had none since.

He will die in a very short time. The older children may survive. Four nights ago the mother had a baby in the tent, on the dirty carpet. It was born dead, which was just as well because she could not have fed it at the breast; her own diet will not produce milk.

After it was born and she had seen that it was dead, the mother rolled over and lay still for two days. She is up today, tottering around. The last baby, born less than a year ago, lived a week. This woman's eyes have the glazed, faraway look of a sleepwalker's eyes.

She does not wash clothes anymore. The drive that makes for cleanliness has been drained out of her and she hasn't the energy. The husband was a sharecropper once, but he couldn't make it go. Now he has lost even the desire to talk.

He will not look directly at you, for that requires will, and will needs strength. He is a bad field worker for the same reason. It takes him a long time to make up his mind, so he is always late in moving and late in arriving in the fields. His top wage, when he can find work now, which isn't often, is $1 a day.

The children do not even go to the willow clump anymore. They squat where they are and kick a little dirt. The father is vaguely aware that there is a culture of hookworm in the mud along the riverbank. He knows the children will get it on their bare feet.

But he hasn't the will nor the energy to resist. Too many things have happened to him. This is the lower class of the camp.

This is what the man in the tent will be in six months; what the man in the paper house with its peaked roof will be in a year, after his house has washed down and his children have sickened or died, after the loss of dignity and spirit have cut him down to a kind of subhumanity.

Helpful strangers are not well received in this camp. The local sheriff makes a raid now and then for a wanted man, and if there is labor trouble the vigilantes may burn the poor houses. Social workers have taken case histories.

They are filed and open for inspection. These families have been questioned over and over about their origins, number of children living and dead.

The information is taken down and filed. That is that. It has been done so often, and so little has come of it.

And there is another way for them to get attention. Let an epidemic break out, say typhoid or scarlet fever, and the county doctor will come to the camp and hurry the infected cases to the pesthouse. But malnutrition is not infectious, nor is dysentery, which is almost the rule among the children.

The county hospital has no room for measles, mumps, whooping cough; and yet these are often deadly to hunger-weakened children. And although we hear much about the free clinics for the poor, these people do not know how to get the aid and they do not get it. Also, since most of their dealings with authority are painful to them, they prefer not to take the chance.

This is the squatters' camp. Some are a little better, some much worse. I have described three typical families. In some of the camps there are as many as three hundred families like these. Some are so far from water that it must be bought at five cents a bucket.

And if these men steal, if there is developing among them a suspicion and hatred of well-dressed, satisfied people, the reason is not to be sought in their origin nor in any tendency to weakness in their character.

Starvation
Under the Orange Trees

THE SPRING is rich and green in California this year. In the fields the wild grass is ten inches high, and in the orchards and vineyards the grass is deep and nearly ready to be plowed under to enrich the soil. Already the flowers are starting to bloom. Very shortly one of the oil companies will be broadcasting the locations of the wild-flower masses. It is a beautiful spring.

There has been no war in California, no plague, no bombing of open towns and roads, no shelling of cities. It is a beautiful year. And thousands of families are starving in California. In the county seats the coroners are filling in "malnutrition" in the spaces left for "causes of death." For some reason, a coroner shrinks from writing "starvation" when a thin child is dead in a tent.

For it's in the tents you see along the roads and in the shacks built from dump heap material that the hunger is, and it isn't malnutrition. It is starvation. Malnutrition means you go without certain food essentials and take a long time to die, but starvation means no food at all. The green grass spreads right into the tent doorways and the orange trees are loaded. In the cotton fields, a few wisps of the old crop cling to the black stems. But the people who picked the cotton, and cut the peaches and apricots, who crawled all day in the rows of lettuce and beans, are hungry. The men who harvested the crops of California, the women and girls who stood all day and half the night in the canneries, are starving.

It was so two years ago in Nipomo, it is so now, it will continue to be so until the rich produce of California can be grown and harvested on some other basis than that of stupidity and greed.

What is to be done about it? The Federal Government is trying to feed and give direct relief, but it is difficult to do quickly for there are forms to fill out, questions to ask, for fear someone who isn't actually starving may get something. The state relief organizations are trying to send those who haven't been in the state for a year back to the states they came from. The Associated Farmers, which presumes to speak for the farms of California and which is made up of such earth-stained toilers as chain banks, public utilities, railroad companies and those huge corporations called land companies, this financial organization in the face of the crisis is conducting Americanism meetings and bawling about reds and foreign agitators. It has been invariably true in the past that when such a close-knit financial group as the Associated Farmers becomes excited about our ancient liberties and foreign agitators, someone is about to lose something.

A wage cut has invariably followed such a campaign of pure Americanism. And of course any resentment of such a wage cut is set down as the work of foreign agitators. Anyway that is the Associated Farmers contribution to the hunger of the men and women who harvest their crops.

The small farmers, who do not belong to the Associated Farmers and cannot make use of the slop chest, are helpless to do anything about it. The little storekeepers at crossroads and in small towns have carried the accounts of the working people until they are near to bankruptcy.

And there are one thousand families in Tulare County, and two thousand families in Kings, fifteen hundred families in Kern, and so on. The families average three persons, by the way. With the exception of a little pea picking, there isn't going to be any work for nearly three months.

There is sickness in the tents, pneumonia and measles, tuberculosis. Measles in a tent, with no way to protect the eyes, means a child with weakened eyes for life. And there are varied diseases attributable to hunger, rickets and the beginning of pellagra.

The nurses in the county, and there aren't one-tenth enough of them, are working their heads off, doing a magnificent job, and they can only begin to do the work. The corps includes nurses assigned by the federal and state public health services, school nurses and county health nurses, and a few nurses furnished by the Council of Women for Home Missions, a national church organization. I've seen them, red-eyed, weary from far too many hours, and seeming to make no impression in the illness about them.

It may be of interest to reiterate the reasons why these people are in the state and the reason they must go hungry. They are here because we need them. Before the white American migrants were here, it was the custom in California to import great numbers of Mexicans, Filipinos, Japanese, to keep them segregated, to herd them about like animals, and, if there were any complaints, to deport or to imprison the leaders. This system of labor was a dream of heaven to such employers as those who now fear foreign agitators so much.

But then the dust and the tractors began displacing the sharecroppers of Oklahoma, Texas, Kansas and Arkansas. Families who had lived for many years on the little "cropper lands" were dispossessed because the land was in the hands of the banks and finance companies, and because these owners found that one man with a tractor could do the work of ten sharecropper families.

Faced with the question of starving or moving, these dispossessed families came west. To a certain extent they were actuated by advertisements and handbills distributed by labor contractors from California. It is to the advantage of the corporate farmer to have too much labor, for then wages can be cut. Then people who are hungry will fight each other for a job rather than the employer for a living wage.

It is possible to make money for food and gasoline for at least nine months of the year if you are quick on the getaway, if your wife and children work in the fields. But then the dead three months strikes, and what can you do then? The migrant cannot save anything. It takes everything he can make to feed his family and buy gasoline to go to the next job. If you don't believe this, go out in the cotton fields next year. Work all day and see if you have made thirty-five cents. A good picker makes more, of course, but you can't.

The method of concentrating labor for one of the great crops is this. Handbills are distributed, advertisements are printed. You've seen them. Cotton pickers wanted in Bakersfield or Fresno or Imperial Valley. Then all the available migrants rush to the scene. They arrive with no money and little food. The reserve has been spent getting there.

If wages happen to drop a little, they must take them anyway. The moment the crop is picked, the locals begin to try to get rid of the people who have harvested their crops. They want to run them out, move them on.

The county hospitals are closed to them. They are not eligible to relief. You must be eligible to eat. That particular locality is through with them until another crop comes in.

It will be remembered that two years ago some so-called agitators were tarred and feathered. The population of migrants left the locality just as the hops were ripe. Then the howling of the locals was terrible to hear. They even tried to get the army and the CCC ordered to pick their crops.

About the 15th of January the dead time sets in. There is no work. First the gasoline gives out. And without gasoline a man cannot go to a job even if he could get one. Then the food goes. And then in the rains, with insufficient food, the children develop colds because the ground in the tents is wet.

I talked to a man last week who lost two children in ten days with pneumonia. His face was hard and fierce and he didn't talk much.

I talked to a girl with a baby and offered her a cigarette. She took two puffs and vomited in the street. She was ashamed. She shouldn't have tried to smoke, she said, for she hadn't eaten for two days.

I heard a man whimpering that the baby was sucking but nothing came out of the breast. I heard a man explain very shyly that his little girl couldn't go to school because she was too weak to walk to school and besides the school lunches of the other children made her unhappy.

I heard a man tell in a monotone how he couldn't get a doctor while his oldest boy died of pneumonia but that a doctor came right away after it was dead. It is easy to get a doctor to look at a corpse, not so easy to get one for a live person. It is easy to get a body buried. A truck comes right out and takes it away. The state is much more interested in how you die than in how you live. The man who was telling about it had just found that out. He didn't want to believe it.

Next year the hunger will come again and the year after that and so on until we come out of this coma and realize that our agriculture for all its great produce is a failure.

If you buy a farm horse and only feed him when you work him, the horse will die. No one complains of the necessity of feeding the horse when he is not working. But we complain about feeding the men and women who work our lands. Is it possible that this state is so stupid, so vicious and so greedy that it cannot feed and clothe the men and women who help to make it the richest area in the world? Must the hunger become anger and the anger fury before anything will be done?

From *Writers Take Sides*

J UST RETURNED from a little tour in the agricultural fields of California. We have our own fascist groups out here. They haven't bombed open towns yet but in Salinas last year tear gas was thrown in a Union Hall and through the windows of workingmen's houses. That's rather close, isn't it?

Your question as to whether I am for Franco is rather insulting. Have you seen anyone not actuated by greed who was for Franco? No, I'm not for Franco and his Moors and Italians and Germans. But some Americans are. Some Americans were for the Hessians England sent against our own revolutionary army. They were for the Hessians because they were selling things to them. The descendants of some of these Americans are still very rich and still touchy concerning the American Way, and our "ancient liberties." I am treasonable enough not to believe in the liberty of a man or a group to exploit, torment, or slaughter other men or groups. I believe in the despotism of human life and happiness against the liberty of money and possessions.

I Am a Revolutionary

I READ A PIECE about myself recently written to reassure my readers that I am not a revolutionary. At the same time the Communist Party denounces me in the same terms. I hasten to inform both the extreme right and that pseudo right which calls itself left that they are both wrong. I am a very dangerous revolutionary.

The Communists of our day are about as revolutionary as the Daughters of the American Revolution. Having accomplished their coup and established their empire, revolution is their nightmare. They have had to hunt down and eliminate everyone with the slightest revolutionary tendency, even those who helped accomplish their own. Where they have absolute power they have established the most reactionary governments in the world, governments so fearful of revolt that they must make every man an informer against his fellows, and layer their society with secret police. And like most insecure organizations, they must constantly enlarge to cover the fact that they are unsound. Any other group following their pattern they would call imperialistic.

Me and my work they do not like and have eliminated where they have had the power. My books are forbidden entrance to Soviet centers not because they are not revolutionary but because they are. Indeed any criticism is construed as revolt by the two great wings of reaction.

The bait of the Marxist movement was that once free of bourgeois control the masses would cease to be masses and would emerge as individuals. Authority and power would then melt away. This dream has long since been abandoned except in the baited areas. Far from disappearing, power and oppression have increased. The so-called masses are more lumpen than ever. Any semblance of the emergence of the individual is instantly crushed and the doctrine of party and state above everything has taken the place of the theory of liberated men.

The victim of this savagely applied system is the individual. Individuality must be destroyed because it is dangerous to all reactionary plans because the individual is creative and creativeness outside the narrow pattern of status quo cannot be tolerated. Creativeness has its foundation in inspection, criticism and rearrangement, and all of these are anathema to reaction. Thought, which is the exclusive property of the individual, must be stamped out. The individual human brain working alone is the only creative organ in nature. The group creates nothing although it sometimes carries out the creation of the individual. Reaction must make its choice—it must eliminate question and criticism as dangerous since such systems must protect themselves from close scrutiny. But by eliminating the individual, they must also give up the work of the individual. They must give up literature, music, art. But they must also give up versatility. They must bring into being a true lumpen human who accepts without question, who works without personal purpose, who does not conceive of improvisation. Such systems, by the very nature of their self-protection, destroy any possibility of either greatness or permanence.

Herein is my revolt. I believe in and will fight for the right of the individual to function as an individual without pressure from any direction. I am unalterably opposed to any interference with the creative mind. It may be wrong but out of it have come the only rights we know. I am opposed to these pressures and constrictions no matter where they arise in my own country or in any other. This is true revolt, not the robot chanting of brain-washed zombies. I realize the necessity for washing brains. Thought must be washed out, for thought is the present danger to and the inevitable destroyer of reaction.

The greatest and most permanent revolution we knew took place when all men finally discovered that they had individual souls, individually important. This concept permanently changed the face of the world. But it has another step to go. The release of the individual mind to a sense not only of its value but of its preciousness will cause an even greater change. Such a revolution is on the way. No system of policing and conditioning can long survive. And I place myself at the service of this revolutionary cause. The minds of individual men must and will be free.

Duel Without Pistols

W E WERE in Italy, my wife and I, churching and antiquitying, and gathering material for a book, part of which will, I hope, appear in *Collier's* from time to time.

A man in Florence explained to me that antiquities are just about the best product a country can have. He made sense. First, you don't have a shipping problem; tourists come to you. Second, the tourists don't take them away—at least if you watch them. Third, your product just keeps getting antiquer all the time. You just sit in the sun and take the profits. That gives you plenty of time to complain about so many tourists spoiling the country. It's a nice business.

Neither my wife nor I can speak Italian. But we took up tourist sign language, which consists of one gesture. If you are explaining something in English to a man who understands only Italian, you speak very loudly and slowly, grimacing as you speak. At the same time, you put your forefinger and thumb together and make a gentle, downward, pulling motion as though you were milking a mouse into the palm of your hand. I don't know what this signifies, but everybody does it.

We drove from Florence to Rome in a Citroën—sturdy, intelligent, cheap, a truly French automobile. It has great power and dash, until it comes to a hill, and it has individuality. Sometimes it smokes, sometimes it speeds up when I haven't touched the throttle and sometimes it just refuses to run at all. There's no good then in tinkering with it or even with swearing at it. You must just walk away and ignore it. In a little while it starts running again.

Rome is a confusing city, and I am an easily confused man. When we got into the outskirts, those two confusions got together, and we really had something. I can't rightly say I got lost, because I didn't have any place to get lost from. I never knew where I was. It was late on a hot after-noon, and the Roman traffic was a feebly squirming mess of motor scoot-ers, bicycles, automobiles, pedestrians and horse-drawn carriages. At street intersections, beautiful policemen stood on boxes and executed ballet movements which had no effect on the traffic, except to slow it down a little.

When we finally found out where our hotel was, it took us more than an hour to get there. I didn't have to turn off the ignition key; the car groaned and stopped, and later they had to push it away to a garage. I think it had a nervous breakdown. The bill was 50,000 lire, and I can't see that anything was done to it, except maybe to soothe it.

Our nerves were shattered, too. We were cuffing weakly at each other with tired ill temper. I dripped out of the car and flowed like syrup into the hotel to find a bellboy. As I came out, a photographer was asking my wife if he could take a picture of me. "At this point, I think he'd kill you," she said. He took the picture anyway. I was too tired to kill him.

The square in front of the hotel was crawling with soldiers of many nations, all heavily armed. And it was while we were trying to find out the reason for the soldiers that we finally learned what had caused the traffic. General Ridgway, in Europe to take command of the NATO military forces, had just arrived in Rome. The Communists had prepared a riot in his honor; it did not come off, but everybody in Italy had gathered to watch, just in case it did.

Furthermore, General and Mrs. Ridgway were staying at our hotel. My wife (in Italy, a wife is known as a *moglie*, and in some of the newspa-pers mine has been referred to as my elegant *moglie*, which seems to please her for some reason) lost no time in making social contact with Mrs. Ridgway. They went down in the elevator together. Mrs. Ridgway said wearily, "Hello."

"Hi!" said my *moglie*.

"Hot, isn't it?" said the general's *moglie*.

"Sure is," said my *moglie*, and at that moment the elevator grounded.

My wife reported, "She's very nice, and she's very pretty, and she looked *cool*." This was a good trick, because nobody else was looking cool that day.

I am a great window-looker-outer, and we had a window right over the square. I took my post there with a glass of beer, and there I stayed the rest of the day. The hotel was surrounded by layers and layers of soldiers, mostly Italians assigned to protect General Ridgway from being shot at by Communists. I have never felt safer in my life. It was like walking in a downpour, surreptitiously sharing an umbrella with a person ahead of you.

I stuck to my post until late in the night, and I guess there must have been some American soldiers among the troops, because very late I heard as horrible a rendition of "Down by the Old Mill Stream" as it is possible to imagine. The tenor should be shot.

At about four o'clock in the morning, there was an explosion in the square. I leaped from my bed to the window in time to see fourteen Italian soldiers begin to change a tire.

General Ridgway left that next day without a single riot. When he had got to Paris, earlier, there had been a big, successful riot in his honor, but the French government had acted in a surprising and brutal way. They not only put a lot of rioters in jail, but they put the bosses who had dreamed up the riot in jail, too. This was considered unorthodox and ungentlemanly. Ordinarily, only a lot of poor people and some policemen get hurt in a riot, and the leaders sit back and count up the score and take bows. The action of the French government had a chilling effect on the planned riots in Italy. The Communists just didn't riot, and they couldn't get anybody to riot for them. It was a great disappointment.

On the drive down from France, I had found that I was well known in Italy. By that I mean that my books have been translated and published and read by a great many people, and that the motion pictures made from my books were known to many more. I found the notice very pleasant. People were kind to me; I could get credit if I ran out of money; waiters and bellhops brought their copies of my books and asked me to sign them. It was a nice feeling.

Writers are taken seriously in Italy and are accorded the same respect that Lana Turner's legs get in our country. This is a shock at first, and I hope I don't grow to love it, because I certainly am not going to get it at home. I remember coming out of a club in New York one night. Two autograph-hunting kids were standing at the curb. One said, "Who's he?" and the other replied, "He ain't nobody. Gregory Peck's in there." Come to think of it, I must say I like that too.

Anyway, the friendliness in Italy had made me feel good. There had been nice pieces about me and about my work in the newspapers in Venice and Florence; so I was not surprised in Rome when a friend brought in a newspaper named *L'Unità* and showed me a large piece in which my name occurred very often. I can't read Italian, but I could make out from the headline that it was An Open Letter to John Steinbeck. I felt pleased, and flattered that they should do this for me.

I said so to my friend, and he looked at me in amazement. "Are you kidding?" he said. "This is the biggest Red paper in Italy. And this is no compliment." Then he translated the letter.

The letter writer, by name Ezio Taddei, addressed me as Dear Steinbeck and then proceeded to take me to pieces. Not only me, either. He used me to call General Ridgway a murderer, to bring up the moldy propaganda about germ warfare and to describe the degeneracy and brutality of American soldiers. He painted a picture of Korea as a place where our troops regularly use the bodies of little children as roadways for tanks. He told of American soldiers creeping out in the night to drop infected spiders and flies on the faces of Korean babies, and he ended up by telling me that if I didn't do something about it and denounce my own country, nobody was ever going to like me as a writer anymore.

"The news that has seeped through (about Korea)," he wrote, "has been enough to arouse the disgust and indignation of the whole civilized world. It is not a case of isolated crimes committed by a few individuals, in which case the responsibilities would be limited, but of organized crimes, ordered and directed by a general and commander in chief."

Well, at first I was amused by the complete nonsense of this letter. I've never answered criticism in my life. That's a losing game. You can answer a columnist once, but he has a column every day. I was just about to decide not to dignify the letter with an answer when I found that I was getting mad. This Taddei had used my name not merely for an attack on me, but to get the attention of his readers for what I considered a foul purpose.

I made some inquiries and found that *L'Unità* has a circulation of 300,000. Taking into account what the newspapers and magazines call "secondary readers," that circulation meant that roughly 1,000,000 people, and maybe more, would be reading Taddei's attack on America.

Then some other thoughts occurred to me. I've done some newspaper work. I know that the average reader does not read very closely. In a week, a good part of that million would believe *I* had said these things. If I did not answer, I was positive that the Reds would noisily claim either that I was afraid or that my silence indicated I agreed with them. It has been my experience that they are pretty dirty fighters.

I was getting madder and madder. My anger took the form of kindness and gentle treatment of my wife. This reaction startled her considerably. She thought I was crazy or sick. She alternately soothed me and offered me medicine.

I answered the open letter. The answer was not dictated by noble motives. I was simply sore at the guy for trying to use me for dirty politics. I wrote ten pages, in which I took Taddei's letter apart paragraph by paragraph; he had made the mistake of using misstatements of fact which were easy to refute by reference to public record.

"I wonder," I wrote, "whether you believe your own accounts of children ground up under our tanks, of huts blown up and refugees machine-gunned. But perhaps you believe anything you are instructed to believe. And so I will ask your readers who are not instructed: Why, if we are so brutal to refugees, do they always come to us, never to the Communists? People in trouble do not run toward brutality. They run away from it."

I dealt at length with his germ-warfare charges, pointing out that the first mention of this weapon by any nation occurred during World War II, when Russia announced officially that it was fully prepared to "use bacteriological warfare in retaliation against any enemy." Then I said:

"The germs the United Nations are dropping in Korea are little pamphlets. These papers contain the most dangerous and communicable germs in the world, the truth. This is the germ the Soviet fears more than any other single thing. . . . These truth germs we admit we are dropping in Korea. We are proud to drop them."

Finally, in dealing with his scathing references to American soldiers, I abandoned the fact-versus-lie approach. It simply wasn't enough.

"Taddei," I said, "do you know what American soldiers are? They are our sons, our beloved sons drawn from our hearts in the time of our nation's need. They are the dear children of our farmers and our miners, our factory workers, our tradesmen, bankers, writers, artists. I myself have two little sons of six and eight. When they are old enough, they will be American soldiers if my nation needs them.

"Now, if you, you personally, have meant to say or indicate or suggest that American soldiers are wicked, degenerate or brutish—you, Ezio Taddei, are a liar."

Finally, I abandoned even this approach and simply called him a liar in so many words.

My wife began laying out bandages, being convinced that I would be challenged to a duel. By that time I was angry enough to welcome such an idea. (In this respect, my more reasonable—or, as some would call it, cowardly—nature was functioning very nicely. My thinking went like this: If he challenges me, I will naturally have the choice of weapons. And I remembered the story of how Abraham Lincoln was once challenged and chose cow manure at five paces. I decided to borrow this weapon, with full credit to Lincoln.)

At the end of my reply to Taddei I said that I was giving L'Unità the right to publish it—but that if they did not, or if they cut or tampered with it in any way, I would try to publish it elsewhere, and as widely as possible. I had my letter translated into Italian and sent it to L'Unità.

My wife and I spent the weekend churching and antiquitying. We looked over the Colosseum and brought our schoolbook memories to the Roman Forum. In Ciceronian tones and bad Latin, we denounced Catiline on the floor of the Roman senate. Also, we looked at bones; I guess next to broken marble and beheaded statues, bones constitute Rome's greatest single asset. We went to St. Peter's and the Sistine Chapel, too. We were getting to be such experts in churches and antiquities that we were able to break into bitter arguments about dates and events and materials. My sweetness disappeared, and my *moglie* was happy, reassured that I was neither crazy nor sick.

On Monday morning, the *Unità* people phoned, routing me out of bed. The conversation, both on their part and on mine, was carried on with gentility and hypocrisy.

They said they were glad to have my letter. I said I was glad they were glad. They said they wanted to publish it. I found that very pleasing. They said that due to space limitations they felt it might be necessary to make some cuts—but only because of its length, understand.

I found this attitude downright gentlemanly. But I assured them that I was not a verbose writer. I was heartbroken, but I could not accept their space limitations.

Did I, they asked, then intend to publish it elsewhere? I did.

On this note of false courtesy, we broke off. I went back to sleep. Half an hour later, they called again and said they would like to call on me. I assured them that nothing would gratify me more.

The moment I hung up, I began to worry about this meeting. If they followed the Russian technique, no one who came would speak English. Also, no one would come alone. As a result, everything would be done through an interpreter and I would never know what went on.

Then a welcome thought: Reynolds Packard was covering Rome for the New York *Daily News*. You can't get a sketch of Packard on a thumbnail. He's big and quiet and Irish-looking, and he has what I always think of as an ominous calm and a dangerous innocence. As comrades in arms, we had fought the battle of the Aletti Hotel in Algiers during the war. We had stormed up beaches together under fire, and sometimes under water. We knew enough about each other so that we are likely to be mutually gentle and considerate for life. Packard is an American newspaperman in the best sense. And he speaks Italian well. I phoned him and asked if he would sit in. He said, "Yop!" which is a lot of talk from Packard.

Our meeting was decorous. Communists always seem to travel in pairs, like cops in Los Angeles. On this occasion, there was one who spoke English and one who said he didn't. Then there was Packard, who always gives the deceptive impression of being half asleep, and, of course, myself.

We got down to business. They opened; they had to, because I didn't say anything. The letter written by Taddei, the spokesman said, had not been written for the reasons I thought. It had been addressed to me as a token of respect.

I bowed and smiled. Packard closed his eyes and gently scratched his stomach with his index finger. The spokesman went on. Since I had unfortunately misunderstood the intent of the open letter, the newspaper, again out of respect, wanted to print my reply. Again I bowed, waiting for the catch. It came right away. They were embarrassed by the length of my reply. It was a matter of paper shortages. Times were hard in Italy. Newspapers had to limit the length of their stories. Therefore, they wanted me to cut my reply to perhaps half its present length. They knew I would do it best.

I said that I deeply appreciated their concern for me, but I wanted to reveal to them my own difficulties. I had not wanted to answer Taddei's letter; I hadn't wanted him to write it in the first place. But once written, it could not be recalled. My answer, I said, was as short as I could possibly write it. I was not known for wasting words. Cutting was the most difficult of writing jobs. I had already spent far too much time with this matter. To cut would keep me out of churches and museums for two more days, and, besides, I could not recall anything I felt I *could* cut—out of respect for Mr. Taddei, of course.

Now a little edge crept into the conversation. Did I know that under Italian law an editor had the legal right to cut anything he wished?

No, I did not, but if that was the law, I could do nothing about it. If they felt they must cut, I said, then they must cut.

They were glad I felt that way. And if they did a careful and tasteful job of cutting, then naturally I would not carry out my unjustified threat to publish my letter elsewhere.

It was not a threat, I assured them. It was an inevitability.

"But your letter is twice as long as Taddei's."

"That is a matter of sorrow to me. It took, I think, much more than twice as long to write."

It would take three columns to print my letter. No paper in Italy would consider printing so long a piece in one issue.

"About that, I suppose we must wait and see," I said. I did not inform them that practically every non-Communist paper in Italy had asked for the letter, complete, unchanged.

The man who did not speak English said something in fast Italian, and his companion answered with several seconds of rapid talk. Packard's eyes opened a trifle and then closed again.

We all stood up. They found my attitude unreasonable. I found that I didn't have a choice. Would it not be considered strange, I asked, if I said publicly I would do a thing and then did not do it?

There was a real coldness in the room. We all shook hands and murmured how great our pleasure had been at the meeting, and they went out, walking very straight. They were not pleased with me.

Packard opened his eyes a little. "That other guy knows English," he said.

The next morning *L'Unità* printed my reply, Communistically cut. Which is to say that every bit of information was deleted, and the paragraphs were rearranged so that the piece didn't make sense. It was a deadly job. But to top it, Taddei had written an answer to my cut answer. His letter ran more than three columns. With alacrity and pleasure, I sent my original piece over to *Il Tempo,* which is a Rome newspaper of excellent reputation. *Il Tempo* did not find any space difficulties. It used my letter in full.

The next day was a little hectic. *L'Unità* announced that I was a Fascist and in the pay of a Fascist publication. The Communists also said that *Collier's* was part of a well-known Nazi-Fascist-Imperialist-Wall Street cannibalistic group which had organized to destroy the working classes. Further, they had re-examined my books and had found that they were no damn good.

For the rest of my stay in Rome, my phone never stopped ringing. Everybody wanted a statement; all I wanted was to get back to my churching and antiquitying.

There is only one last part of the incident which is amusing. My wife, who covers for me with a camera, had an idea that it would be good to get a picture of Taddei for this piece. She called *L'Unità,* got a girl who spoke English, and asked to take a picture of Taddei. The girl said the office was closed and would not be open until five-thirty.

At five-thirty, my wife called again and got a man who did not speak English. But he spoke a lot of rapid Italian, and what he said must have been good, because over the phone she could hear people killing themselves with laughter. She hung up and in five minutes called again. This time, she got a man who admitted that he spoke a little English. It seemed to her he had the same voice as the man who a moment before could not speak English. She explained who she was and said she wanted to photograph Taddei for *Collier's.* The man said he would have to ask Mr. Taddei. Unfortunately, Mr. Taddei was not at that moment available; he would call back.

He never did.

Well, that was the end of that, and I hope it's the end of the whole mess. I wasn't meant to get into things like this. I wish I wouldn't get mad. I get mad at some things in my own country sometimes, too, and I can't keep my big mouth shut. I don't think I'll ever learn to do that.

Someday I'll go back to Italy and finish looking at old bones, old churches and old ruins. I also want to get down to Positano, and look at fish and people. Besides, I have an anniversary to keep there.

One time during the war, I was on a PT boat off the Italian shore, right near Positano. One of our enlisted men went ashore to reconnoiter a brunette of excellent modern architecture. During this tour of duty, he was accosted by a big black chicken with a German accent. Naturally, he arrested the chicken for questioning. Under arrest, that chicken suddenly drew a knife, and our man was forced to defend himself. In the ensuing fight, the bird suffered wounds which resulted in his death.

Those of us in the PT boat had been living on wet sandwiches for a long time. We found a little beach and prepared to cremate the casualty. At that moment, some evil men opened fire on us with 88-millimeter guns, and we had to run to sea. The next day, we tried again to give that chicken a decent burial—with exactly the same results. The third day it was too late. The chicken had spoiled.

Someday I'm going down to that beach again, and I'm going to build a little memorial fire and sit beside it. Who knows what dangerous poultry might stroll by? My elegant *moglie* makes an elegant barbecue sauce.

The Trial of Arthur Miller

THE TRIAL of Arthur Miller for contempt of Congress brings close to all of us one of the strangest and most frightening dilemmas that a people and a government has ever faced. It is not the first trial of its kind, nor will it in all probability be the last. But Arthur Miller is a writer—one of our very best. What has happened to him could happen to any writer; could happen to me. We are face to face with a problem by no means easy of solution. "Is a puzzlement!"

No man knows what he might do in a given situation, and surely many men must wonder how they would act if they were in Arthur Miller's shoes. I wonder what I would do.

Let me suppose that I were going to trial for contempt of Congress as he is. I might be thinking somewhat as follows:

There is no doubt that Congress has the right, under the law, to ask me any question it wishes and to punish my refusal to answer with a contempt charge. The Congress has the right to do nearly anything conceivable. It has only to define a situation or an action as a "clear and present danger" to public safety, public morals, or public health. The selling or eating of mince pie could be made a crime if Congress determined that mince pie was a danger to public health—which it probably is. Since many parents raise their children badly, mother love could be defined as a danger to the general welfare.

Surely, Congress has this right to ask me anything on any subject. The question is: Should the Congress take advantage of that right?

Let us say that the Congressional Committee feels that the Communist Party and many groups which have been linked with it—sometimes arbitrarily—constitute a clear and present danger to the nation. Now actually it is neither virtue nor good judgment on my part that has kept me from joining things. I am simply not a joiner by nature. Outside of the Boy Scouts and the Episcopal choir, I have never had an impulse to belong to things. But suppose I had. And suppose I have admitted my association with one or more of these groups posted as dangerous. As a writer, I must have been interested in everything, have felt it part of my profession to know and understand all kinds of people and groups. Having admitted these associations, I am now asked by the Committee to name individuals I have seen at meetings of such groups. I hope my reasoning then would go as follows:

The people I knew were not and are not, in my estimation, traitors to the nation. If they were, I would turn them in instantly. If I give names, it is reasonably certain that the persons named will be called up and questioned. In some cases they will lose their jobs, and in any case their reputations and standing in the community will suffer. And remember that these are persons who I honestly believe are innocent of any wrongdoing. Perhaps I do not feel that I have that right; that to name them would not only be disloyal but actually immoral. The Committee then is asking me to commit an immorality in the name of public virtue.

If I agree, I have outraged one of our basic codes of conduct, and if I refuse I am guilty of contempt of Congress, sentenced to prison and fined. One way outrages my sense of decency and the other brands me as a felon. And this brand does not fade out.

Now suppose I have children, a little property, a stake in the community. The threat of the contempt charge jeopardizes everything I love. Suppose, from worry or cowardice, I agree to what is asked. My deep and wounding shame will be with me always.

I cannot be reassured by the past performance of the Committee. I have read daily for a number of years the testimony of admitted liars and perjurers whose charges have been used to destroy the peace and happiness of people I do not know, and many of whom were destroyed without being tried.

Which path am I to choose? Either way I am caught. It may occur to me that a man who is disloyal to his friends could not be expected to be loyal to his country. You can't slice up morals. Our virtues begin at home. They do not change in a courtroom unless the pressure of fear is put upon us.

But if I am caught between two horrors, so is the Congress caught. Law, to survive, must be moral. To force personal immorality on a man, to wound his private virtue, undermines his public virtue. If the Committee frightens me enough, it is even possible that I may make up things to satisfy the questioners. This has been known to happen. A law which is immoral does not survive and a government which condones or fosters immorality is truly in clear and present danger.

The Congress had a perfect right to pass the Alien and Sedition Act. This law was repealed because of public revulsion. The Escaped Slave laws had to be removed because the people of free states found them immoral. The Prohibition laws were so generally flouted that all law suffered as a consequence.

We have seen and been revolted by the Soviet Union's encouragement of spying and telling, children reporting their parents, wives informing on their husbands. In Hitler's Germany, it was considered patriotic to report your friends and relations to the authorities. And we in America have felt safe from and superior to these things. But are we so safe or superior?

The men in Congress must be conscious of their terrible choice. Their legal right is clearly established, but should they not think of their moral responsibility also? In their attempts to save the nation from attack, they could well undermine the deep personal morality which is the nation's final defense. The Congress is truly on trial along with Arthur Miller.

Again let me change places with Arthur Miller. I have refused to name people. I am indicted, convicted, sent to prison. If the charge were murder or theft or extortion I would be subject to punishment, because I and all men know that these things are wrong. But if I am imprisoned for something I have been taught from birth is a good thing, then I go to jail with a deep sense of injustice and the rings of that injustice are bound to spread out like an infection. If I am brave enough to suffer for my principle, rather than to save myself by hurting other people I believe to be innocent, it seems to me that the law suffers more than I, and that contempt of the law and of the Congress is a real contempt rather than a legalistic one.

Under the law, Arthur Miller is guilty. But he seems also to be brave.

Congress feels that it must press the charge against him, to keep its prerogative alive. But can we not hope that our representatives will inspect their dilemma? Respect for law can be kept high only if the law is respectable. There is a clear and present danger here, not to Arthur Miller, but to our changing and evolving way of life.

If I were in Arthur Miller's shoes, I do not know what I would do, but I could wish, for myself and for my children, that I would be brave enough to fortify and defend my private morality as he has. I feel profoundly that our country is better served by individual courage and morals than by the safe and public patriotism which Dr. Johnson called "the last refuge of scoundrels."

My father was a great man, as any lucky man's father must be. He taught me rules I do not think are abrogated by our nervous and hysterical times. These laws have not been annulled; these rules of attitudes. He taught me—glory to God, honor to my family, loyalty to my friends, respect for the law, love of country and instant and open revolt against tyranny, whether it come from the bully in the schoolyard, the foreign dictator, or the local demagogue.

And if this be treason, gentlemen, make the most of it.

Atque Vale

I AM CONSTANTLY amazed at the qualities we expect in Negroes. No race has ever offered another such high regard. We expect Negroes to be wiser than we are, more tolerant than we are, braver, more dignified than we, more self-controlled and self-disciplined. We even demand more talent from them than from ourselves. A Negro must be ten times as gifted as a white to receive equal recognition. We expect Negroes to have more endurance than we in athletics, more courage in defeat, more rhythm and versatility in music and dancing, more controlled emotion in theater. We expect them to obey rules of conduct we flout, to be more courteous, more gallant, more proud, more steadfast. In a word, while maintaining that Negroes are inferior to us, by our unquestioning faith in them we prove our conviction that they are superior in many fields, even fields we are presumed to be trained and conditioned in and they are not.

Let me give a few examples.

In the Alabama bus boycott we knew there would be no Negro violence—and there wasn't. The only violence was white violence.

In the streets we expect courtesy from Negroes even when we are ugly and overbearing.

In the prize ring we know a Negro will be game and will not complain at a decision.

In Little Rock we knew that any brutality would originate among the whites.

For a long time whites would not compete against Negroes for fear they might lose. It was said that their coordination—it was called animal coordination—was better and their physical responses quicker.

If there is racial trouble, we are convinced that Negroes will not strike the first blow, will not attack in the night, will not set off bombs, and our belief is borne out by events.

We expect Negroes to be good-tempered and self-controlled under all circumstances.

But our greatest expectation is that they will be honest, honorable, and decent. This is the most profound compliment we can pay any man or group. And the proof of this shows in our outrage when a Negro does not live up to the picture we ordinarily have of him.

With thousands of burglaries, muggings, embezzlements reported every day, we are upset when a Negro is found doing what so many whites do regularly.

In New York, with its daily reports of public thefts, deceits, and assorted political and fiscal raids on public money and treason against public trust, one Negro who succumbs to the temptation to do what many white people do fills us with dismay and the papers are full of it. What greater compliment can we pay to a people?

Finally, let me bring it down to cases.

I have children, as many of you whites who read this have. Do you think your children would have the guts, the dignity, and the responsibility to go to school in Little Rock knowing they would be insulted, shoved, hated, sneered at, even spat upon day after day, and do it quietly without showing anger, petulance, or complaint? And even if they could take it, would they also get good grades?

Now I am a grown, fairly well-educated—I hope intelligent—white man. I know that violence can produce no good effect of any kind. And yet if my child were spat on and insulted, I couldn't trust myself not to get a ball bat and knock out a few brains. But I trust Negroes not to, and they haven't.

I think so much of those school children in Little Rock—a small handful who carry the will and conscience, the hopes and futures of millions in their arms. They have not let their people down. I think, what quiet pride their grandchildren can have in them knowing they came of such stock.

And then I think of the faces of the mob that tried to keep them out, faces drooling hatred, cursing and accursed faces, brave only in numbers, spitting their venom at children. And some of those faces, masked, sneaking in the night to plant a bomb—the final weapon of a coward.

What pride can their descendants take in their ancestry? But of course they will forget, or lie, or both.

When Martin Luther King was stabbed by a hysterical woman, he might well have felt some anger or hurt or despair. But his first words on coming out of the anesthetic were: "Don't let them hurt her. She needs help."

Perhaps some of the anger against Negroes stems from a profound sense of their superiority, and perhaps their superiority is rooted in having a cause and an unanswerable method composed of courage, restraint, and a sense of direction.

Dear Adlai

Dear Adlai:

Back from Camelot, and, reading the papers, not at all sure it was wise. Two first impressions. First, a creeping, all pervading, nerve-gas of immorality which starts in the nursery and does not stop before it reaches the highest offices both corporate and governmental. Two, a nervous restlessness, a hunger, a thirst, a yearning for something unknown—perhaps morality. Then there's the violence, cruelty and hypocrisy symptomatic of a people which has too much, and last, the surly ill temper which only shows up in humans when they are frightened.

Adlai, do you remember two kinds of Christmases? There is one kind in a house where there is little and a present represents not only love but sacrifice. The one single package is opened with a kind of slow wonder, almost reverence. Once I gave my youngest boy, who loves all living things, a dwarf, peach-faced parrot for Christmas. He removed the paper and then retreated a little shyly and looked at the little bird for a long time. And finally he said in a whisper, "Now who would have ever thought that I would have a peach-faced parrot?" Then there is the other kind of Christmas with presents piled high, the gifts of guilty parents as bribes because they have nothing else to give. The wrappings are ripped off and the presents thrown down and at the end the child says—"Is that all?" Well, it seems to me that America now is like that second kind of Christmas. Having too many THINGS they spend their hours and money on the couch searching for a soul. A strange species we are. We can stand anything God and nature can throw at us save only plenty. . . . If I wanted to destroy a nation, I would give it too much and I would have it on its knees, miserable, greedy and sick. . . . And then I think of our "Daily" in Somerset, who served your lunch. She made a teddy bear with her own hands for our grandchild. Made it out of an old bath towel dyed brown and it is beautiful. She said, "Sometimes when I have a bit of rabbit fur, they come out lovelier." Now there is a present. And that obviously male teddy bear is going to be called for all time MIZ Hicks.

When I left Bruton, I checked out with Officer 'Arris, the lone policeman who kept the peace in five villages, unarmed and on a bicycle. He had been very kind to us and I took him a bottle of Bourbon whisky. But I felt it necessary to say—"It's a touch of Christmas cheer, officer, and you can't consider it a bribe because I don't want anything and I am going away. . . ." He blushed and said, "Thank you, sir, but there was no need." To which I replied—"If there had been, I would not have brought it."

Mainly, Adlai, I am troubled by the cynical immorality of my country. I do not think it can survive on this basis and unless some kind of catastrophe strikes us, we are lost. But by our very attitudes we are drawing catastrophe to ourselves. What we have beaten in nature, we cannot conquer in ourselves.

Someone has to reinspect our system and that soon. We can't expect to raise our children to be good and honorable men when the city, the state, the government, the corporations all offer higher rewards for chicanery and deceit than probity and truth. On all levels it is rigged, Adlai. Maybe nothing can be done about it, but I am stupid enough and naively hopeful enough to want to try. How about you?

Yours,
John

G.O.P. Delegates
Have Bigger, Better Badges

SAN FRANCISCO, AUG. 20—Here we go again.

The cows are out and the delegates in. San Francisco streets are crawling. Chinatown hasn't been so lively since the tong wars.

A great many relatives are going to get "genuine Chinese kimonos," made in the New York garment district.

The Republicans have much better and bigger badges than the Democrats. In Chicago, I had a little old plastic card to pin to my lapel.

Here in San Francisco they have given me a glorious bronze medal on a white ribbon, a combination of sharpshooter's medal and the Order of the Golden Fleece. I may wear this permanently and pass it on to my children.

So far, no trouble. The G.O.P. public-relations people have treated me royally. I don't have to bum a floor pass from television.

This convention is on wheels—as controlled and pretty as a spectacular. The best entertainers are performing here at the Cow Palace.

The script is written and the lines have been learned. The invocation indicates that the Deity is a Republican. This will disappoint a host of Democrats.

The main issue seems to be Richard Nixon. From what I've picked up, both parties are passionate for his nomination. I listened in on a Democratic bull session where the feeling was that Nixon, Dulles, and Benson are Democratic assets. Naturally, the Republicans have other ideas.

Honest Len Hall has just ascertained that everybody is happy. The ways are greased and the Ship of State is sliding down to the political sea.

I was prophetic in my guess that courage and virtue were going to be pretty much in evidence here, just as they were in Chicago. But last night I had a little time with a mug, so I guess I can take it for a few more days.

Honest George Christopher, Mayor of San Francisco, is now making a welcoming speech that in any other place would be considered real-estate talk.

It is said that Honest Ethel Merman is going to sing pretty soon. That is parlaying Perle Mesta across the board.

This hasn't been a very interesting convention so far. It is so well run that there aren't even any lost kids. I haven't seen a hot-dog stand. I hate to criticize but this kind of thing could destroy the institution of the convention.

No fights, no hot dogs—who wants it?

The Republicans have learned one thing from the Kremlin. On the back wall are pictures of Eisenhower and Nixon three stories high. There haven't been such huge portraits since Stalin was downgraded.

At this moment, Honest Goodwin Knight, Governor of California, has come out fearlessly for good government.

You can see that newspapermen in general and I in particular, who thrive and delight in turbulence and difference of opinion, seem doomed to four days of boredom unless something breaks loose. Something could—but isn't very likely to.

I may have to organize a splinter group myself just to keep the ball rolling. There can be too much peace and prosperity.

I may be forced to begin to make up my copy, and I so warn my readers. You can only report a vacuum so long.

It would be unfair to blame me for this copy—there is a gas of boredom over this gathering that grips the brain and slows the typewriter to a stop.

Tomorrow, I will file some news if I have to create it. Maybe something is happening in Skid Row. I'm going to see.

Can you imagine? No hot dogs.

L'Envoi

T HIS NARRATIVE opened with a storm, the hurricane Donna, far and away the greatest sendoff an expedition ever had and I thought at the time a little overboard. And by rights it should end with a storm, and it did. But again I am troubled by matters of proportion. My travels with Charley were a simple, almost humble undertaking. They caused no flurry and piled up a limited heap of information. Thinking back, I don't know what, if anything, I learned. Therefore the storm at the end may seem a very big stage, set for a very small drama. Of course I could whomp up a medium storm or a small earthquake in good taste and proper proportion, but in this account I have clung tenaciously, perhaps foolishly, to the truth. The storm I must use is the only storm I have.

My lady wife lowered the *New York Times* and gazed at me so long that I inspected any recent deeds and impulses.

"You've been invited to the inauguration," she said.

"You made the rule about no jokes in the morning."

"It says here you've been invited to the inauguration."

"By whom, for God's sakes?"

"By the President, who else?"

"But I don't know him. What is this?"

"Four painters, four poets and four novelists. You're one of the novelists."

"That's crazy," I said. "Everybody knows what the government thinks of artists. They're good for questioning about overcoming the government by force and violence. I'm not sure the invitation isn't unconstitutional. That new guy had better watch his step. Aren't westerns good enough for him? Who does he think he is?"

"I've never seen an inauguration," she said.

"Neither have I."

And there we were.

In one trait I am predictable. I dislike being late. I arrive at the theater while they are sweeping out from the matinee. I haunt a ship hours before it has any intention of sailing. Reluctantly accepting a cocktail invitation, I usually arrive before my hostess is out of the tub.

The historic snowstorm of the Kennedy inauguration caused endless trouble. Some heads of state were long late and some didn't get there at all. It was not so with us. We had arrived and were billeted in a lovely house in Georgetown and were having a tall cool drink when the first snow fell and we watched it flake by flake as it slowed, and finally brought the city to a standstill, covered stalled cars with a soft white blanket. It may have inconvenienced some charging bellowing officials but for us it made of Washington the most beautiful city in the world, a quiet place. In cities, the muffled under-sound of motors is so constant that we consider it silence. When it is removed the effect is startling, almost shocking. It was very well for us sitting comfortably watching through the window while the heavy businesslike flakes settled with every intention of remaining. And the depth built up. Every statue wore a tall white cap and every marble nose was tipped with a horn like that of a rhinoceros. The streets were tangles of abandoned cars and the sidewalks narrow paths between high shoveled walls. Men and women moved with high tiptoe leaps as though speed and posture might keep the snow from their shoes. I thought of the grand preparations, the hours of ladies in beauty parlors, the hundreds of thousands of new and delicate ball gowns, the spike-heeled satin shoes a passing out might sully. What despair there must be in thousands of feminine breasts. It is true the inauguration concerned only one man who by one short oath would renounce the world he knew and could never regain it. But it is also true that if the last judgment were announced, the first and proper thought of all ladies would be "What shall I wear?" And while the archangels are preparing the courtroom and the blessed tune their harps and certain others lie hunching under their fires, the ladies will be dashing hysterically in and out of fitting rooms.

And then, as the snow piled deeper and deeper and movement became impossible and then ridiculous—people changed. A kind of hell-for-leather gaiety invaded the city. Tragedy became a holiday. Even Republicans who had seen in the weather Divine wrath at a Democratic victory began to have fun.

Our blessings held. The cocktail parties to which we were assigned were all in easy walking distance.

The morning was like the Christmas song—"where the snow lay all about, deep and soft and even." And the sun turned it glittering. In the night the Army had been out plowing the main thoroughfares. And true to form, I got us to our seats below the rostrum at the Capitol long before the ceremony, so long before that we nearly froze. Mark Twain defined women as lovely creatures with a backache. I wonder how he omitted the only other safe generality—goddesses with cold feet. A warm-footed woman would be a monstrosity.

I think I was the only man there who heard the inauguration while holding his wife's feet in his lap, rubbing vigorously. With every sentence of the interminable prayers, I rubbed. And the prayers were interesting, if long. One sounded like general orders to the deity issued in a parade-ground voice. One prayer brought God up to date on current events with a view to their revision. In the midst of one prayer, smoke issued from the lectern and I thought we had gone too far but it turned out to be a short circuit.

How startling then to hear the simple stark oath of office offered and accepted. How moving. How deeply moving. I had never seen the ceremony before and it was good and I was glad.

Only one episode remains to be told and then my travels with Charley are finished. And we have never admitted this scene although we haven't out and out lied about it. Remember when you have visited some foreign area and some other traveler has asked, "Did you see such and such?" If you say no he screams, "What? Why that was the best. Don't see why you went at all if you didn't see such and such." We have learned to reply to the question, "Wonderful." Or "Remarkable!" That doesn't say we did or didn't see it and saves the argument.

Well, we were invited to the Inaugural Ball, the biggest and most desirable one where thousands of people would gather, where all the new dresses and satin shoes and hairdos would be. In the house of our hostess, other guests were ready, fingers moving restlessly in filmy cloth or tucking in hair that had never escaped, and every mirror was a place for sidelong glances. Dress ties were patted reassuringly every few seconds. The radio said that traffic conditions were impossible. Mobs of people, beautifully dressed, were floundering through snowdrifts and the great black official cars chugged through streets clanking chains. We drank together a last glass of champagne. And then everyone was gone and the house was quiet and the low lights were soft and the room a cushion of warm comfort. It was automatic. We didn't plan it. We drank another glass of wine looking out at the mountains of snow and then we crept up to our room and put on dressing gowns. In the kitchen we made sandwiches and arranged trays. Then I stood the great and important tickets of invitation to the ball on top of the television and turned on the set. We saw the President and his lady right up close and we saw the packed thousands below in crushed and snow-dabbled ball gowns. We nibbled our sandwiches and had a tall drink. And afterwards, when asked how we liked the Inaugural Ball, we have said, "Loved it. Remarkable. Wonderful!" And so it was. And we saw much more of it than the ones who were there. I guess it was the best ball I was ever invited to, and I enjoyed it the most, too.

And in the morning the snow was past and so was the journey.

I do know this—the big and mysterious America is bigger than I thought. And more mysterious.

III.

OCCASIONAL PIECES

JOHN STEINBECK was willing, indeed eager, to write on nearly any subject—and that is both an engaging and a highly revealing fact of his career. As a writer of fiction he experimented ceaselessly. Although he's seldom mentioned in the same breath as the high modernists, Steinbeck shared their restless need to "make it new," to experiment with form, to mine mythic contexts, to chart the contours of modern times. Born too late to be an expatriate—six years after F. Scott Fitzgerald, three after Ernest Hemingway—and to see action in World War I, Steinbeck was, as he muses in "The Golden Handcuff" (reprinted in Part I), a part of "the Unfortunate Generation, because we didn't have a Generation nor the sense to invent one. The Lost Generation, which preceded us, had become solvent and was no longer lost. The Beat Generation was far in the future." He playfully notes that he was born on liminal turf, and that terrain would, in fact, define him. Realist, naturalist, symbolist, fabulist. Dramatist, novelist, journalist. Writer of hard-hitting realism and musical comedy. Steinbeck refuses to be pigeonholed. *Of Mice and Men, The Moon Is Down,* and *Burning Bright* are all "play-novelettes," a form he invented. *The Grapes of Wrath* mimics documentary films with its sweeping interchapters and focused Joad narrative. The self-reflective quality of *East of Eden,* as recent critics have noted, anticipates metafiction. Steinbeck, self-declared citizen of the "Unfortunate Generation," used that kind of artistic indeterminacy to his advantage. In his fiction he insisted repeatedly on his right to experiment; in his nonfiction he claimed the right to explore any subject that caught his fancy, as he notes in "Letters to Alicia":

> In the past I have been soundly spanked by some of our talmudic critics for failure to pick out one ant-hill and stay with it. It is a permanent

failing. Thirteenth-century manuscripts and modern automobiles are separately but equally interesting to me. I love processes and am perhaps the world's greatest pushover as an audience.

A girl in a department store demonstrating a tool for carving roses from radishes has got me and gone with me. Let a man open a suitcase on the pavement and begin his pitch "Tell you what I'm gonna do!" and I will be there until he closes. (*Daily Mail*, 7 Jan. 1966)

Highly representative of Steinbeck's "scattered" and "unorthodox" interests is "Then My Arm Glassed Up," an article written for *Sports Illustrated* in response to the magazine's request for an article about sports. It's an epistolary piece, addressed to senior editor Ray Cave. Passionate correspondent, keeper of journals, Steinbeck loved to address his prose to a particular audience—usually a friend—whether he was composing a book, a play, or, quite often, an essay. A letter gave him free rein to range from idea to idea, as here, where the writer begins with a memory from Salinas days; cites a definition from the *Oxford English Dictionary* (the most essential book he owned); notes the sporting habits of hunters and fishermen and baseball players (fishing was a favorite escape, as the *Le Figaro* piece "On Fishing" suggests); gives a brief historical context, followed by a fanciful, decidedly silly suggestion for competitive seed growing; and concludes seriously, thoughtfully, on bullfighting, from which he draws insights about the meaning of courage. That's Steinbeck's range, serious to silly, historical to moral, reflective to didactic. And beneath it all there may be another, altogether typical, Steinbeckian "level." Asked to write for a sporting magazine, Steinbeck takes on the consummate writer-sportsman and playfully spars with Ernest Hemingway, bullfight aficionado, hunter and fisher, and Steinbeck's artistic rival, in a way, since the early 1930s.

No subject was off limits. In 1954, at the request of Henry Ringling North, who had been with Steinbeck and Navy Task Group 80.6 off the Italian coast during World War II, Steinbeck wrote a winsome piece for the Barnum and Bailey Circus program. Indeed, with great frequency and ferocity, he defended his artistic freedom to write about whatever caught his fancy, as did the subject of dogs; or snared his intellect, as did the march of history; or sparked his passion for improvement, as did any kind of project to improve something.

He wrote frequently, affectionately, often whimsically about dogs—Pirate's loyal band in *Tortilla Flat;* the Joads' dog, killed on the road; the stately walks of the banker's dog, Red Baker, in *The Winter of Our Discontent,* "who moved with slow dignity, pausing occasionally to sniff the passenger list on the elm trunks." And of course Charley. There's something endearing about Steinbeck's taking notice of dogs of "ambiguous breed" belonging to bomber crews in World War II. Or about his devoting one of the "Letters to Alicia" to the topic of guard dogs and scout dogs working the Saigon airport (19 January 1967). His best writing about dogs, however, is grounded—like so much that he wrote—in personal anecdote, sprinkled throughout letters and his journalism. In 1935, for example, he wrote Wilbur Needham, a friend, describing a particular Mexican dog he'd been watching, vintage Steinbeck:

> In the village of Tamazunchale there was a dog lying on a doorstep. In his family there were two pigs and four chickens. And all up and down the cobbled street lived other pigs and other dogs and other chickens. Now our dog whom we shall call Corazón del San Pedro Martín de Gonzáles y Montalba was content when his own pigs ate garbage in the street in front of his house, but let any outland pig, say from next door, come into his zone, and out charged Corazón etc. and bit that pig. There would be screams and a scuffle and in a moment Corazón would trot back to his doorway, having satisfied his sense of propriety and private ownership. But one morning when I sat in one doorway and Corazón sat in his—a completely foreign pig from a half a block down trespassed on half a rotten cabbage. And this was a very big old pig. Up jumped Corazón del San Pedro Martín de Gonzáles y Montalba. He made a slash at that pig's buttocks but that pig turned and took off a piece of Corazón's ear. Corazón, after one howl, walked sheepishly back to his doorway. He glanced over to see whether I had noticed, and when he saw that I had, he bit hell out of one of his own chickens. (Benson 322)

Toby, the English setter described in "Random Thoughts on Random Dogs," could be equally fierce, generate equally playful prose. In 1936 when Steinbeck was working on *Of Mice and Men,* the puppy Toby, "left alone one night, made confetti of about half my mss book. Two months' work to do over again. It sets me back. There was no other draft. I was pretty mad but the poor little fellow may have been acting critically" (Benson 327). And his last dog, Angel, "just about perfect of his breed," was an English bull terrier. He came to Steinbeck as a puppy in 1965 and sat quietly through "a run-through of Frank Loesser's new musical, the only dog who ever saw a run-through" (*SLL* 814–15).

Steinbeck read history and science more voraciously than many twentieth-century writers—a fact made clear in the constant references to historical figures and episodes throughout his nonfiction. In the late 1940s and 1950s, in particular, he was drawn to historical topics, and he thought of working on films or plays about compelling figures, admonitory pieces focused on heroic or exemplary lives. In 1946, finishing work with Elia Kazan on the film *Viva Zapata!* he mentioned a wish to do "one more film—the life of Christ from the four Gospels" (*SLL* 343), a film never completed; nor was a 1946 synopsis for a picture called "The Witches of Salem" brought to fruition; nor did a play about Columbus or one about the Vikings (a revision of an early Ibsen play, "The Vikings at Helgoland") ever make it to the boards. An aborted manuscript called "The Last Joan," as Burgess Meredith described it, had "to do with witchcraft. And that in a modern sense we better heed what the present Joan tells us of the atom bomb, because it's the last time that we'll have a Joan to tell us what to do" (Benson 588). Joan of Arc's story, in particular, fascinated him—as is clear from "The Joan in All of Us" (first written in 1954 for *Le Figaro*)—because from her life he could tease out something significant about his own will to believe. Indeed, Steinbeck couldn't shake a fundamental respect for conscience, wherever he found it: Tom and Ma Joad, "Doc," the Chinese Lee in *East of Eden,* or Sam Hamilton, "one of those pillars of fire by whom little and frightened men are guided through the darkness," Steinbeck writes in *Journal of a Novel.* "The writers of today, even I, have a tendency to celebrate the destruction of the spirit and god knows it is destroyed often enough. But the beacon thing is that sometimes it is not . . . the great ones, Plato, Lao Tze, Buddha, Christ, Paul, and the great Hebrew prophets are not remembered for negation or denial. . . . It is the duty of the writer to lift up, to extend, to encourage" (*JN* 115). Joan's life as soldier, politician, theologian was, quite simply, one of those beacons he sought in history, a "miracle" that,

Steinbeck concludes, might live "in all of us." Rather like the Puritans poring over the Old Testament to seek parallels with the New, Steinbeck sought "types" in history to adumbrate contemporary issues. This penchant for typology explains much about his interest in the Arthurian tales late in his life; their stories contained our own.

And like a latter-day Ben Franklin, Steinbeck offered up a number of proposals and projects in his nonfiction and in letters, some serious, many whimsical. Inventions are charming, especially several he described to Mrs. Richard Rodgers, also an inventor: a "plastic jar made like an hour glass" (*SLL* 489), into which went water, scented soap, and women's undergarments, to be shaken "like a cocktail shaker" (*SLL* 489) (an idea later adapted for washing clothes in his trailer while crossing the country in *Travels with Charley*), or he invented "silk slip covers for the lapels of a dark suit to make it a dinner jacket," or "stirrups for long nightgowns to keep them from climbing" (*SLL* 493). Golfomation was proposed in an article for the Louisville *Courier-Journal*, Steinbeck at his silliest:

It is a contraption which bolts to the side of a golfmobile—a set of arms to which are fixed various woods and irons. It has vacuum tubes and a presetting device. All you do is to feed into Univac or one of the larger IBM calculating machines your medical history, blood count, psychiatric report, clubs, and college degrees, domestic difficulties, most recent blood pressure and incidence of anger plus your police record and cheating standard.

On the report of Univac you preset your Golfomation, start the golfmobile and go back to the deep chair and shallow lady. And the darned thing plays your game for you, slices when you would slice, hooks just as you would hook, lies about the number of strokes getting out of the rough, and even in simulated rage breaks the clubs against the fenders of the golfmobile.

Then it brings you your score and its engine shuts off until you want to play again. It is push-button golf at its very best. (17 Apr. 1957)

Steinbeck was often simply having fun writing, a notion many find troublesome. Why didn't this lionized writer more carefully guard his reputation, corral his little essays, offer up only the very best? Ever the westerner, Steinbeck claimed the right to range over what intellectual turf he discovered.

He was also a tinkerer, lover of things mechanical like cars and weapons. "Give me a box of odds and ends of metal and wood and I can build dam [sic] near anything," he wrote in 1951 (Benson 674). Inventions for his house fell into that category. "Someone once said of me that if I bought the Washington Monument, I would start covering it with leather" ("Letters to Alicia," 11 Dec. 1965). He carved wood and planned to do an article on the artisans of Florence. Steinbeck was ever drawn to men who knew machines, like Al Joad, who is "one with his engine" and keeps the "ancient overloaded Hudson" running; or Gay, "the little mechanic of god, the St. Francis of all things that turn and twist and explode," who repairs the Model T in *Cannery Row*. The "Hansen Sea Cow," demonic engine in *Sea of Cortez*, is a major character. Grace notes throughout this journalism make reference to Steinbeck's cars, usually bestowing the inanimate with very human quirks. A rented Land Rover is "a heavy, ugly, high standing truck-like creature with four-wheel traction and a will toward immortality" (*Daily Mail*, 7 Jan. 1966:6). A Citroën is "sturdy, intelligent, cheap, a truly French automobile. It has great dash, until it comes to a hill, and it has individuality" ("Duel Without Pistols," reprinted in Part II). And an old Rolls-Royce is "of sneering gentility, a little younger than Stonehenge and in a little better condition" (Benson 728). That affection for cars is clearly in evidence in "A Model T Named 'It.' "

Throughout his nonfiction, a sense of fun and humor is displayed pervasively; even in his most "serious" fiction, one can find comic moments as well as elements of wit, humor, and parody.

For decades, largely because of his humor, Mark Twain was not taken seriously. Steinbeck mentions Twain so often that it is almost certain the older writer was something of a model for the younger. They both were essentially westerners who spent the last years of their lives in the East but kept a western sense of irreverence throughout. During their lives, both were often dismissed as "popular" writers, which is to say they deliberately tried to communicate with the ordinary reader and succeeded—each wrote many books that sold very well. As a result of their success, they became national figures who, by laughter and lament, brought conscience to bear on corruption, irrationality, and bigotry. While moralists, both were iconoclasts who liked to poke fun at the rich and powerful, and particularly at those who took themselves too seriously. They opposed conventional morality, which they found to be too rigid, humorless, and often self-righteous. They wrote, frequently humorously, about the "rascal" figure, the person like Huck Finn or Mack in *Cannery Row*, who defies society and operates by a moral code of his own that is more humane and reasonable. And both Twain and Steinbeck could stand back and make fun of themselves, something that endears them to us.

Writing about his friend a few months after Steinbeck's death, Nathaniel Benchley articulates, perhaps better than anyone, the quality of Steinbeck's quirky humor:

Reading through his obituaries, I found a good deal of analytical writing about his work, and one rewrite man ventured the personal note that he was considered shy, but nowhere did I see a word about one of the most glorious facets of his character, which was his humor. All good humor defies analysis (E. B. White likened it to a frog, which dies under dissection) and John's defied it more than most, because it was not gag-type humor but was the result of his wildly imaginative mind, his remarkable store of knowledge, and his precision with words. This respect for and precision with words led him to avoid almost every form of profanity; where most people would let their rage spill out the threadbare obscenities, he would concoct some diatribe that let off the steam and was at the same time mildly diverting. One example should suffice: At Easter about three years ago we were visiting the Steinbecks at Sag Harbor, and John and I arose before the ladies to make breakfast. He hummed and puttered about the kitchen with the air of a man who was inventing a new form of toaster, and suddenly the coffeepot boiled over, sending torrents of coffee grounds over the stove and clouds of vapor into the air. John leaped for the switch, shouting, "Nuts!

No wonder I'm a failure! No wonder nobody ever asks for my hand in marriage! Nuts!" By that time both he and the coffee had simmered down, and he started a new pot. I think that this was the day he stoutly denied having a hangover, and after a moment of reflection added, "Of course, I do have a headache that starts at the base of my spine. . . ." He spent the rest of the morning painting an Easter egg black, as a protest. (*Paris Review* 164)

Then My Arm
Glassed Up

Dear Ray Cave:

I HAVE your letter of August 29, and it pleased me to know that you
think of me as a sportsman, albeit perhaps an unorthodox one. As you
must know, I get many requests for articles, such as, "You got to rite
my term paper for my second yer english or they wun't leave me play on
the teem." Here is a crisis. If I don't rite his term paper I may set sports
back irreparably. On the other hand, I don't think I am a good enough
writer to rite his term paper in his stile well enough to get by his teacher.
I remember one time when a professor in one of our sports-oriented col-
leges had in his English composition class a football player whose excellence on the playing field exhausted his capabilities, and yet a tyrannical
scholasticism demanded that he write an essay. Well, he did, and the professor, who was a friend of mine, was utterly charmed by it. It was one of
Emerson's best, and such was the purity of approach on the part of the
football player that he had even spelled the words correctly. And he was
astounded that the professor could tell that it was not all his own work.

Early on I had a shattering experience in ghostwriting that has left its
mark on me. In the fourth grade in Salinas, Calif., my best friend was a
boy named Pickles Moffet. He was an almost perfect little boy, for he
could throw rocks harder and more accurately than anyone, he was brave
beyond belief in stealing apples or raiding the cake section in the basement of the Episcopal church, a gifted boy at marbles and tops and sub-
limely endowed at infighting. Pickles had only one worm in him. The
writing of a simple English sentence could put him in a state of shock
very like that condition which we now call battle fatigue. Imagine to
yourself, as the French say, a burgeoning spring in Salinas, the streets

glorious with puddles, grass and wildflowers and toadstools in full chorus, and the dense adobe mud of just the proper consistency to be molded into balls and flung against white walls—an activity at which Pickles Moffet excelled. It was a time of ecstasy, like the birth of a sweet and sinless world.

And just at this time our fourth-grade teacher hurled the lightning. She assigned us our homework. We were to write a quatrain in iambic pentameter with an a b a b rhyme scheme.

Well, I thought Pickles was done for. His eyes rolled up. His palms grew sweaty, and a series of jerky spasms went through his rigid body. I soothed him and gentled him, but to show you the state Pickles was in— he threw a mud ball at Mrs. Warnock's newly painted white residence. *And he missed the whole house.*

I think I saved Pickles' life. I promised to write two quatrains and give one to him. I'm sure there is a moral in this story somewhere, but where? The verse I gave to Pickles got him an A while the one I turned in for myself brought a C.

You will understand that the injustice of this bugged me pretty badly. Neither poem was any great shucks, but at least they were equally bad. And I guess my sense of injustice outweighed my caution, for I went to the teacher and complained: "How come Pickles got an A and I only got a C?"

Her answer has stayed with me all my life. She said, "What Pickles wrote was remarkable for Pickles. What you wrote was inferior for you." You see? Sports get into everything, even into verse-writing, and I tell this story to myself every time I think I am getting away with something.

As I started to say, I get many requests for articles, and sometimes the letter of refusal is longer than the article would have been.

I have always been interested in sports, but more as an observer than as a participant. It seems to me that any sport is a kind of practice, perhaps unconscious, for the life-and-death struggle for survival. Our team sports simulate war, with its strategy, tactics, logistics, heroism and/or cowardice. Individual competition of all kinds has surely ingredients of single combat, which was for millions of years the means of going on living. The Greeks, who invented realism and pretty much cornered the market, began the training of a soldier by teaching him dancing. The rhythm, precision and coordination of the dance made the hoplite one hell of a lot better trooper. In this connection, it is interesting that the hill men of Crete in their all-male dancing go through the motions of using shield and spear, of defense and dodge and parry, of attack, thrust and retreat. I don't imagine they know this, but it is what they do.

The very word "sport" is interesting. It is a shortening of "disport" (OED: "disportare, to carry away, hence to amuse or to entertain"). From earliest times people played lightly at the deadly and serious things so that they could stand them at all—all, that is, except the Greeks, who in their competitions were offering the gift of their endurance, their strength and their spirits to the gods. Perhaps our values and our gods have changed.

My own participation in sports has been completely undistinguished. I once threw the javelin rather promisingly until my arm glassed up. Once I was fairly good at boxing, mainly because I hated it and wanted to get it over with and to get out. This is not boxing but fighting.

My feeling about hunting has made me pretty unpopular. I have nothing against the killing of animals if there is any need. I did, can and always will kill anything I need or want to eat, including relatives. But the killing of large animals just to prove we can does not indicate to me that we are superior to animals but arouses a kind of deep-down feeling that we are not. A room full of stuffed and glass-eyed heads always gives me a feeling of sadness for the man so unsure of himself that he has constantly to prove himself and to keep the evidence for others to see. What I do admire and respect is our memory of a time when hunting was a large part of our economy. We preserve this memory intact even though we now have a larger mortality in hunters than in game.

I must admit that I have enjoyed two stuffed specimens on public display. They were in Moscow in Red Square and thousands of people went by to see them. Since then the more dangerous of the two has been removed from public view, but for the wrong reason.

I find the so-called blood sports like fox hunting charming and sometimes ravishingly beautiful. Besides, fox hunting serves the useful purpose of preventing population explosion in the gentry and increasing the number of fine horses. The fox population doesn't seem affected one way or another.

I love a certain kind of fishing above all other so-called sports. It is almost the last remaining way for a man to be alone without being suspected of some secret sin. By fishing without bait it is even possible to avoid being disturbed by fish. I am surprised that the dour brotherhood of psychoanalysts has not attacked fishing, since it seems to me it is in competition. Two hours with a fishing rod is worth ten hours on the couch and very much less expensive.

My passion for fishing does not extend to big-game fishing. While I admire the strength, skill and endurance of the men who do it well, I have found that after a time the cranking in of sea monsters becomes damned hard work. And many a man who would resist to the death carrying a bucket of coal up to a second-floor fireplace will break his heart struggling with a fish he is going to kill, photograph and throw away. I have studied fish both zoologically and ecologically, and once long ago I worked for the California Fish and Game Commission, where I helped at the birth and raising of a good many millions of trout. At that time I learned to admire them but not greatly to respect their intelligence. And it has seemed to me that a man who can outthink fish may have a great future, but it will be limited to fish. His acquired knowledge will do him little good at a Sunday-school picnic or a board meeting.

Nearly all sports as we know them seem to be memories and in a way ceremonial reenactments of situations that were once of paramount importance to our survival. For example, jousting in the sixteenth century was an expensive and mannered playback of the tactics of the heavy armed cavalry of the late Roman Empire. Our own once-noble cavalry, which was eliminated by the machine gun and the armored car, became the tank corps. It is interesting how symbols persist. Tank officers, at least until a few years ago, still wore spurs with their dress uniforms.

Not only are our former triumphs remembered in sports, but some of our ancient fears. The hatred and terror of sharks familiar to all sailors in history have made shark hunting very popular. There is almost a feeling of glory and sacrificial punishment in the shark hunter. He kills these great and interesting animals not only with glee but with a sense of administering justice to a cruel and hated enemy. The carcasses are usually thrown away after photographing. There is utterly no understanding that sharks may well be factors in an intricate ecological balance. Edible sharks, such as the leopards, the whites and the makos, are rarely eaten, and it is never considered that the increase in the shark population has not to do with a shark dynamism but rather that we are dumping more and more shark-edible garbage at sea.

You see, my interest in sports is catholic but cool. I don't expect you will believe that I once sent for a mail order course in alligator wrestling complete with a practice alligator, so I will not tell you this.

Yes, my interest in sports is quiet but deep. I am particularly drawn to the game of rounders, which we call baseball. I would be wrong to call it a sport. I don't think the players have a real sporting attitude toward it. Mostly they want to win because if they win they get more money. In baseball I like the audience almost better than the game. I guess that is why I am a Met fan. But for many years our household was torn to pieces emotionally every year. My wife was a Dodger fan born and bred in Fort Worth, which is, or was, a Dodger farm. Every year, she went through the fervency, the hope, the prayer, the shining eyes and the loud and raucous voice and, finally, after the season the dark and deadly gloom and despair that lasted clear into spring-training time. I guess our family devoted more pure spiritual energy to the Dodgers than to any other religious organization. This, of course, was before they defected to the West. Any kind of skulduggery and ineptness my wife could forgive and even defend, but treason she could not take. She is a Met fan now, and our house is whole again.

Early on, to save arguments, I became an Oriole fan and even bought a little stock in that club. If you were for anyone else you got an argument, but if you said you were an Oriole fan people just laughed and let you alone. I thought I had a guarantee that they would stay on the bottom, but now they have doublecrossed me by climbing up. I nearly went to the Senators, because there is a federal law which forbids them to win. Then the Mets happened, and I was stuck.

Baseball brings out a kind of pugnacious frustration in foreigners. Once as guests of a very old and dear friend in London, we were at Lord's watching a sedate and important cricket match. When a player let a fast ball go by, my wife yelled, "Git it! What ya got, lead in ya pants?" A deathly silence fell on the section around us, and it was apparent that our host would have to resign from all his clubs. Afterward he lectured her gently. "My dear," he said, "we don't do it."

"Peewee Reese would of got it," said my elegant *moglie*.

"Don't tell me about baseball," said our host. "It's only rounders, and I know all about it. Don't forget, I, too, have been to *Egbert's Field*." There is no way to explain that baseball is not a sport or a game or a contest. It is a state of mind, and you can't learn it.

You will be aware by now of my reasons for not being able to write a piece about sports for *Sports Illustrated*. My interests are too scattered and too unorthodox. But I do find the American cult of youth, violence and coronaries a little unreasonable. It does seem to me that "as life's shadows lengthen" our so-called senior citizens should have competitive sports, but that the pace should be reduced. Turtle racing won't do, because it is dull. But, being lazy, I invented some years ago a sport which satisfied my ego and my sense of competition and matched my inclination. It is called vine racing. Each contestant plants a seed beside a pole of specified height, and the first vine to reach the top wins. There are, however, some furious vines which have been known to grow ten inches a day—which might in some owner-managers raise the blood pressure. For those passionate ones, among whom am I, I have laid out the ground rules for an even more sedate and healthful contest. This is oak-tree racing. Each of the eager players plants an acorn. The obvious advantage of this contest is that, depending on the agreed finishing height, it may go on for generations. At the cry "They're off!" the fancy could enjoy all semblance of growth and renewal until the checkered flag came down three hundred years later. By that time the original contestants should be represented by large numbers of descendants, for tree racing allows one the leisure to indulge in other sports, the darlings.

I should like to mention one more activity which only the Anglo-Saxons consider a sport and hate and attend in droves. That is bullfighting. In this I have gone full course, read, studied, watched and shared. From the first horror I went to the mortal beauty, the form and exquisiteness from *Verónica* to *faena*. I have seen a great many bullfights (it is only called a fight in English). I even saw Manolete fight a number of times, which is more than Ernest Hemingway did. And I have seen a few great and beautiful things in the bullring. There are only a few, and you must see very many fights to see the great one. But I suppose there are very few great anythings in the world. How many great sonnets are there? How many great plays? For that matter, how many great vines?

I think I have been through most of the possible feelings about tauromachy, rising eventually to the sublime conception that the incomparable bravery of the matador somehow doled out courage to the audience. Oh! this was not blind and ignorant celebration. I hung around the rings. I knew about the underweight bulls, the sandbags on the kidneys, the shaved horns and sometimes the needle of barbiturate in the shoulder as the gate swung open. But there was also that moment of what they call truth, a sublimity, a halo of the invincible human spirit and unspeakable, beautiful courage.

And then doubt began to creep in. The matadors I knew had souls of Toledo steel for the bull, but they were terrified of their impresarios, pulp in the hands of their critics and avaricious beyond belief. Perhaps they gave the audience a little courage of a certain kind, but not the kind the audience and the world needed and needs. I have yet to hear of a bullfighter who has taken a dangerous political stand, who has fought a moral battle unless its horns were shaved. It began to seem to me that his superb courage could be put to better uses than the ritual slaughter of bulls in the afternoon. One Ed Murrow standing up to take the charge of an enraged McCarthy, one little chicken-necked Negro going into a voting booth in Alabama, one Dag Hammarskjold flying to his death and knowing it—this is the kind of courage we need, because in the end it is not the bulls that will defeat us, I am afraid, but our own miserable, craven and covetous selves.

So you see, Ray Cave, it was a mistake to ask me to write an essay about sports. Hell, I don't even know the batting average of Eddie Kranepool.

John Steinbeck

On Fishing

I AM ONE of the world's foremost observers of other people's fishing. I believe that certain national characteristics emerge in fishing and attitudes toward fishing. With this in view I have for many years studied the relationship of fisherman to fish. It is therefore natural that I am drawn to the Oise on a Sunday afternoon in the summer where one may observe Parisian fishing at its very best.

Perhaps I should set down some American and British attitudes and methods in order that my conclusions about French fishing may stand out by contrast.

Fishing in America has several faces, of which I shall only mention two. First, all Americans believe that they are born fishermen. For a man to admit a distaste for fishing would be like denouncing mother love or hating moonlight.

The American conceives of fishing as more than a sport: it is his personal contest against nature. He buys mountains of equipment: reels, lines, rods, lures, all vastly expensive. Indeed the manufacture and sale of fishing equipment is one of America's very large businesses. But equipment does not finish it. The fisherman must clothe himself for the fish with special and again expensive costumes. Then, if he can afford it, he buys or charters a boat as specialized for fishing as an operating theater is for surgery. He is now ready to challenge the forces of nature in their fishy manifestations.

The fisherman prefers to travel many thousands of miles, to put himself through powerful disciplines, to learn a special vocabulary and to enter a kind of piscatorial religion all for the purpose of demonstrating his superiority over fish. He prefers the huge and powerful denizens of the sea which have great nuisance and little food value. Once fastened to his enemy, the fisherman subjects himself to physical torture while strapped into a chrome barber's chair, and resists for hours having his arms torn off. But he has proved that he is better than fish. Or he may celebrate the fighting quality of the bone fish which has no value except for the photographs of the antagonists. The fisherman endows the fish with great intelligence and fabulous strength to the end that in defeating it he is even more intelligent and powerful.

It has always been my private conviction that any man who pits his intelligence against a fish and loses has it coming, but this is a highly un-American thought. I hope I will not be denounced.

A secondary but important place of fishing in America is political. No candidate would think of running for public office without first catching and being photographed with a fish. A nonfisherman could not be elected President. This may explain to my French readers why our politicians spend so much time on rivers and streams. Golf has nowhere near the political importance that fishing has, but maybe that is changing.

The British fisherman has quite a different approach, one that brings out all the raw sentiment he can permit himself. The English passion for private property rises to its greatest glory in the ownership and negotiability of exclusive fishing rights in rivers and streams. The ideal British fishing story would go something like this. . . .

Under a submerged log in a stream through a beautiful meadow lies an ancient and brilliant trout which for years has resisted and outwitted the best that can be brought against him. The whole countryside knows him. He even has a name. He is called Old George or Old Gwyndolyn, as the case may be. The fact that Old George has lived so long can be ascribed to the gentlemanly rules of conduct set up between trout and Englishmen. Under these rules, the fisherman must use improbable tackle and a bait Old George is known to find distasteful. Of course a small boy with a worm or anyone with a half stick of dynamite could do for Old George, but that would be as un-British as shooting a chicken-stealing fox instead of setting twenty-five horsemen and fifty socially eligible dogs after the fox, whom we will call Old Wilbur. The English use "Old" as a term of endearment verging on the sloppy. A British wife who truly loves her husband to distraction adds the word "poor" so that he becomes Poor Old Charley, but this is affection verging on the distasteful.

In our ideal fish story, the fisherman rereads Izaak Walton to brush up his philosophic background, smokes many pipes, reduces all language to a series of grunts and finally sets out of an evening to have a go at Old George.

He creeps near to the sunken log and drops his badly tied dry fly upstream of the log so that it will float practically into Old George's mouth. This has been happening to Old George every evening for ten or fifteen years. But one evening perhaps Old George is sleeping with his mouth open or maybe he is bored. The hook gets entangled in his mouth. Then the fisherman, with tears streaming from his eyes, pulls Poor Old George out on the grassy bank. There with full military honors and a deep sense of sorrow from the whole community, Old George flops to his death. The fisherman eats George boiled with brussels sprouts, sews a black band on his arm and gains the power of speech sufficiently to bore the hell out of the local pub for years to come.

Now consider the banks of the lovely Oise on a summer Sunday afternoon. This is very different fishing. Each man has his place and does not move from it, sometimes a boat permanently moored between poles, sometimes his little station on the bank allotted and loved. Since the fishermen do not move it is conceivable that neither do the fish. The status quo must be universal. I have seen a man in his niche on the bank, a great umbrella over him, a camp chair under him, a bottle of wine beside him and in front, the reeds clipped to a neat low hedge and a row of geraniums planted.

The fishing equipment is simple but invariable. The pole is of bamboo, not expensive but often adorned, painted blue or red or sometimes in stripes of many colors. The tackle is as delicate and transparent as a spiderweb. On a hook about the size of a pinhead is fixed a tiny bread pellet. The Parisian is now ready for the fishing.

Here is no sentiment, no contest, no grandeur, no economics. Now and then a silly baby fish may be caught but most of the time there seems to be a courteous understanding by which fish and fishermen let each other strictly alone. Apparently there is also a rule about conversation. The fisherman's eyes get a dreaming look and he turns inward on his own thoughts, inspecting himself and his world in quiet. Because he is fishing, he is safe from interruption. He can rest detached from the stresses and pressures of his life or anybody's life. In America it is said that it takes three weeks to rest from the rigors of a two-week vacation. Not so on the Oise.

I find that I approve very highly of Parisian fishing. From the sanctity of this occupation, a man may emerge refreshed and in control of his own soul. He is not idle. He is fishing.

I can't wait to buy a bamboo pole and a filament of line and a tube of bread crumbs. I want to participate in this practice which allows a man to be alone with himself in dignity and peace. It seems a very precious thing to me.

Circus

O H! WE HAD plenty of good holidays in Salinas when I was growing up, Christmas and May Day and the like, but none of them
could compete for quiet violence with a certain day in the late
spring. Marble season would be over and top season well along toward
boredom when suddenly in a night the roadside barn walls would blos-
som with tigers and elephants, with clowns and lovely equestriennes.

Our insides would begin to churn and we would put our tops away
and stare into space. Then our parents were likely to give us a spring
tonic, not knowing that we were simply trying to remember how a circus
was. And we could not because the old year's circus was as vague as a
dream.

We didn't sleep the night before the DAY. It was the rule that we
could not get up before we heard the train. The circus train blew a different whistle than ordinary trains, a WHEE-OO—Whee-oo WHEE-OO!
sound in the first dawn.

Before the third repeat we had leaped fully clothed from bed and
slammed out of the house and were pounding down Stone Street toward
the Depot. As we ran, streams and eddies of kids joined us. By the time
we reached the Catholic Church we were a river of kids and as we broke
around Castroville Street we had become a torrent. And there it was on
the siding, flat cars of cages and Calliopes and baggage and ticket wagons, stock cars of horses and elephants, passenger cars for performers and
all painted in heady circus colors, yellows and blues and reds.

How they ever got the big tops up with us underfoot I will never
know. I remember the rings of hammer men and the waterfall of sledges
raining down so that the stakes seemed to swim into the ground. I remember the smells of lion and goat and wolf and torn grass and the smell

of coffee from the cookhouse tent. Some of us, the lucky ones, were allowed to help, water carrying, horse holding and even leading certain of the more amiable animals in the parade, and as though just doing it weren't enough, we were rewarded with breakfast in the cookhouse and a free pass to the show. No honor since has compared with that pass held high to the ticket taker, held so everyone could see.

I had a pony in those days, part Shetland and part Cayuse and no great shucks for looks as I realize now, and every year those lovely circus men tried to buy my pony from me and offered fantastic prices. This would be whispered about for weeks and conferred a kind of holiness on both the pony and on me. Kids would pay a small sum just to stroke my pony on the neck. I have often wondered what those circus men would have done if I had consented to sell.

The circus itself was a dream that afterwards went in and out of memory. When we came home in the evening green-faced and swollen with hot dogs and cotton candy, our parents automatically gave us a physic and put us to bed, and we were too hypnotized to resist.

But that didn't end it. In the weeks that followed our dogs got a stretch of training that nearly killed them. It was a smart tomcat that was not put in a bird cage for display. My pony wearily resisted my attempts to make her kneel. It took a long time to get over the circus. We couldn't decide whether to be clowns or equestrians or acrobats but there was not any question that we were called. The circus was our future. Any other profession was a tacky substitute.

Well, that's the way the circus got into our blood as individuals.

But the circus is a mass emotion and has been for longer than any single thing we know. The circus was old when Rome was new. Elephants and lions and trained Thessaly horses in silver harness moved through the narrow streets of Carthage and Nîmes and Arles and Rome before the birth of things we consider ancient.

In the procession of the Roman Triumph, after the glory of the conqueror and the slaves and the spoils and the rare and beautiful animals, the clowns tumbled, making fun of everything that had gone before. Even then the little dog wore an elephant's head and the house cat a lion's mane. The acts so funny now were funny then, the huge man in a tiny chariot, the stilt man, the unaware clown with water spurting from his ears, the parodies of kings and heroes all designed to say: "Don't get too big, because you're very close to funny."

The circus may have been more brutal then than now but it was essentially the same circus. It has changed very little because people do not want it to change. It is our oldest and deepest-rooted entertainment.

And the reason is that the circus is change of pace—beauty against our daily ugliness, excitement against our boredom. The lion tamer and the acrobat are brave and clever against our cowardice and clumsiness and the clowns make our selfish tragedy seem funny. Every man and woman and child comes from the circus refreshed and renewed and ready to survive. What doctor can do as much?

Random Thoughts
on Random Dogs

A VERY WISE MAN writing recently about the emergence and development of our species suggests that the domestication of the dog was of equal importance with the use of fire to first man. Through association with a dog, man doubled his perceptions, and besides this the dog—sleeping at dawn-man's feet—let him get a little rest undisturbed by creeping animals. The uses of the dog change. One of the first treatises on dogs in English was written by an abbess or a prioress in a great religious house. She lists the ban dog, the harrier, the dog from Spain called spaniel and used for reclaiming wounded birds, the dogs of "venerie," etc., and finally she says, "There been those smalle whyte dogges carried by ladys to draw the fleas away to theirselves." What wisdom was here. The lap dog was not a decoration but a necessity.

A dog has, in our day, changed his function. Of course, we still have hounds used for the chase and greyhounds for racing, and the pointers, setters, and spaniels for their intricate professions, but in our total dog population these are the minority. Many dogs are used as decorations but by far the greatest number are a sop for loneliness. A man's or a woman's confidant. An audience for the shy. A child to the childless. In the streets of New York between seven and nine in the morning you will see the slow procession of dog and owner proceeding from street to tree to hydrant to trashbasket. They are apartment dogs. They are taken out twice a day and, while it is cliché, it is truly amazing how owner and dog resemble each other. They grow to walk alike, have the same set of head.

In America styles and dogs change. A few years ago the Airedale was most popular. Now it is the Cocker, but the Poodle is coming up. A thousand years ago I can remember when the Pug was everywhere.

In America we tend to breed out nonworking dogs to extremes. We breed Collies with their heads so long and narrow that they can no longer find their way home. The ideal Dachshund is so long and low that his spine sags. Our Dobermen are paranoid. We have developed a Boston Bull with a head so large that the pups can only be born by Caesareans.

It is not wise to mourn for the apartment dog. His lifespan is nearly twice that of the country dog. His boredom is probably many times greater. One day I got in a cab and gave the address of an animal store. The driver asked, "Is it a dog you're after? Because I can let you have a dog. I got dogs."

"It's not a dog, but how is it you have dogs?"

"It's this way," the cabbie said. "It's Saturday night in an apartment and a man and his wife were lapping up a scoop of gin. About midnight they get to arguing. She says, 'Your damn dog. Who has to clean up after him and walk him and feed him, and you just come home and pat him on the head.' And the guy says, 'Don't you run down my dog.' 'I hate him,' she says. 'O.K., pal,' he says, 'if that's the way you want it. Come on, Spot,' and he and the dog hit the street. The guy sits on a bench and holds the mutt in his arms and cries and then the two of them go to a bar and the guy tells everybody there no dame could treat his pal that way. Well, pretty soon they close the bar and it's late and the liquor begins to wear off and the guy wants to go home. So he gets in the cab and gives the dog to the cabbie. It happens to me every Saturday night."

I have owned some astonishing dogs. One I remember with pleasure was a very large English Setter. He saw things unknowable. He would bark at a tree by the hour, but only at one tree. In grape season he ate nothing but grapes which he picked off the vine, one grape at a time. In pear season he subsisted on windfall pears, but he would not touch an apple. Over the years he became more and more otherworldly. I think he finally came to disbelieve in people. He thought he dreamed them. He gathered all the dogs in the neighborhood and gave them silent lectures or sermons, and one day he focused his attention on me for a full five minutes and then he walked away. I heard of him from different parts of the state. People tried to get him to stay, but in a day or so he would wander on. It is my opinion that he was a seer and that he had become a missionary. His name was T-Dog. Long later, and a hundred miles away, I saw a sign painted on a fence which said "T-God." I am convinced that he had transposed the letters of his last name and gone out into the world to carry his message to all the dogs thereof.

I have owned all kinds of dogs but there is one I have always wanted and never had. I wonder if he still exists. There used to be in the world a white, English Bull Terrier. He was stocky, but quick. His muzzle was pointed and his eyes triangular so that his expression was that of cynical laughter. He was friendly and not quarrelsome, but forced into a fight he was very good at it. He had a fine, decent sense of himself and was never craven. He was a thoughtful, inward dog, and yet he had enormous curiosity. He was heavy of bone and shoulder. Had a fine arch to his neck. His ears were sometimes cropped, but his tail never. He was a good dog for a walk. An excellent dog to sleep beside a man's bed. He showed a delicacy of sentiment. I have always wanted one of him. I wonder whether he still exists in the world.

...like captured fireflies

M Y ELEVEN-YEAR-OLD son came to me recently and in a tone of patient suffering, asked, "How much longer do I have to go to school?"

"About fifteen years," I said.

"Oh! Lord," he said despondently. "Do I have to?"

"I'm afraid so. It's terrible and I'm not going to try to tell you it isn't. But I can tell you this—if you are very lucky, you may find a teacher and that is a wonderful thing."

"Did you find one?"

"I found three," I said.

It is customary for adults to forget how hard and dull and long school is. The learning by memory all the basic things one must know is the most incredible and unending effort. Learning to read is probably the most difficult and revolutionary thing that happens to the human brain and if you don't believe that, watch an illiterate adult try to do it. School is not easy and it is not for the most part very much fun, but then, if you are very lucky, you may find a teacher. Three real teachers in a lifetime is the very best of luck. My first was a science and math teacher in high school, my second a professor of creative writing at Stanford and my third was my friend and partner, Ed Ricketts.

I have come to believe that a great teacher is a great artist and that there are as few as there are any other great artists. It might even be the greatest of the arts since the medium is the human mind and spirit.

My three had these things in common—They all loved what they were doing. They did not tell—they catalyzed a burning desire to know. Under their influence, the horizons sprung wide and fear went away and the unknown became knowable. But most important of all, the truth, that dangerous stuff, became beautiful and very precious.

I shall speak only of my first teacher because in addition to the other things, she brought discovery.

She aroused us to shouting, bookwaving discussions. She had the noisiest class in school and she didn't even seem to know it. We could never stick to the subject, geometry or the chanted recitation of the memorized phyla. Our speculation ranged the world. She breathed curiosity into us so that we brought in facts or truths shielded in our hands like captured fireflies.

She was fired and perhaps rightly so, for failing to teach the fundamentals. Such things must be learned. But she left a passion in us for the pure knowable world and me she inflamed with a curiosity which has never left me. I could not do simple arithmetic but through her I sensed that abstract mathematics was very like music. When she was removed, a sadness came over us but the light did not go out. She left her signature on us, the literature of the teacher who writes on minds. I have had many teachers who told me soon-forgotten facts but only three who created in me a new thing, a new attitude and a new hunger. I suppose that to a large extent I am the unsigned manuscript of that high school teacher. What deathless power lies in the hands of such a person.

I can tell my son who looks forward with horror to fifteen years of drudgery that somewhere in the dusty dark a magic may happen that will light up the years . . . if he is very lucky.

The Joan in All of Us

I T IS a rare writer in any language who has not thought long and long-
ingly of Joan of Arc as a subject. At any given time there are four new
plays about her. There are any number of approaches to the story.
One man is concerned with whether her voices were real voices or the
inwardness of a pubescent girl; another writer becomes concerned with
her confession and retraction, her choice between her conviction and orthodoxy.

I have read most of the histories, testimonies, novels, and plays
which concern Joan and her times, and I think I know why writers in all
times find her story such a magnetic theme. There is of course the factor
of universality. Anyone can find some part of himself in Joan's story,
some corroboration of his convictions, no matter what they may be. The
tremendous and disparate literature proves this. But I wonder whether
there is not another and more basic quality which has not been stated because it is perhaps too obvious.

The story of Joan could not possibly have happened—and did. This
is the miracle, the worrisome nagging fact. Joan is a fairy tale so improbable that, without the most complete historical record and evidence, it
could not be believed. If a writer were to make it up the story would be
howled down as an insult to credulity. No reasonable man would waste
time on such an outrageous, sentimental romance, every moment of
which is contrived, unnatural, and untrue.

Critics of the story would have no difficulty with the voices. Many
sensitive children hear voices in their daydreaming—but from there on
the historical nonsense begins.

A peasant girl of Joan's time was considered little more than an animal. She could not have got a hearing from the most obscure of local

gentry. Politics was not a field open to people of her class; indeed only the highest in the social scale had access to political ideas. And the ideas she advanced were simple. How could they be valid to men who had spent their lives in the subtleties of the power drives of Europe?

This girl, illiterate and of a class which politically did not exist, went up through a kind of chain of command to a Dauphin torn with subtleties and indecisions and convinced him in spite of all the knowledge and experience of his professional advisers. This is ridiculous, but it happened.

But this is only the first miracle. Military science as practiced in her day was the most jealously select of activities. To command at all required not only an accepted bloodline, but training from childhood. A soldier began to learn his trade when he left the cradle. Look at the suits of armor for boys who could barely walk. War was as carefully systematized and formal as ballet. Assault and defense were known movements set and invariable. War was no business for amateurs. Command was no business for peasants. A girl leading an army, directing its movements, putting forward revolutionary tactics, is not the least improbable part of the story—a girl whose experience was limited to commanding a small herd of sheep.

But having taken the command, and having set the tactics—she won. She anticipated the change of wind, pushed aside military prejudices, and won her victory. What consternation must have arisen in the minds of commanders . . . so it might have been if a Parisian laundress had suggested that Ardennes was unprotected, and a general staff had listened to her. So it would be now if a farm girl bringing a barrow of carrots to Les Halles left her cart, went to the National Assembly and persuaded the professionals their partisanship should take a secondary place in their minds. It could not happen now any more than then.

The end of Joan is perhaps the most incredible part of all. It was not enough that without training she should be soldier and politician—she must also become theologian with her own life as the wager and sainthood as the hidden prize. Who then could have conceived that this troublesome, tiresome child would become the dream and the miracle?

Here I think is the reason writers are drawn to Joan, although their sense of reality is outraged by her story. We know what can and must happen, given the ingredients of life. But there is not one among us who does not dream that the rules may sometime be set aside—and the dream come true. We have the traditions of many miracles—but usually the witnesses were few, the records sparse and uncertain, and the truth obscured by time and the wishful recording of "after the fact." But to the miracle of Joan the witnesses were legion, the records exact, and the fact established. This is a miracle that *did* happen, and rules that *were* set aside. There is in our minds, because of Joan, the conviction that if it could happen then—it can happen again.

This is perhaps the greatest miracle of all—the little bit of Joan living in all of us.

A Model T Named "It"

I GUESS MODEL TS would run forever, if you would let them. I was well gone in adolescence before I came by one at a price I could afford to pay—fifty dollars. It was almost as old as I was, and it had been around a helluva lot more than I had and was probably smarter to begin with. Its gear and brake pedals were polished like silver and the oaken floorboards had deep grooves made by the heels of former owners, and they must have been legion.

There was no coil box cover on it. It was known as a touring car and it could not even remember when it had had a top. The seats were pretty well gone, but four or five gunnysacks laid down not only kept the seat springs from corkscrewing into you but also covered up the incontrovertible evidence that generations of chickens had roosted on the steering column. It had a lovely odor—I still remember it—a smell of oil-soaked wood and sunbaked paint, of gasoline, of exhaust gases and ozone from the coil box.

The car was not safe to drive at night, but we did it anyway. Having no battery and taking your lights from a generator, you had to go very fast to get enough light to see by, but then you were going too fast to avoid anything you saw, having no brakes.

I think I loved that car more than any I have ever had. It understood me. It had an intelligence not exactly malicious, but it did love a practical joke. It knew, for instance, exactly how long it could keep me spinning the crank and cursing it before I would start kicking its radiator in. It ran perfectly when I was in blue jeans, but let me put on my best suit and a white shirt, and maybe a girl beside me, and that car invariably broke down in the greasiest possible manner.

I never gave it a name. I called it IT.

The problem of starting the motor of the Model T was complicated. I have dealt with it in another work. But once the motor was started, you came in contact with the Model T Ford transmission, called the planetary system.

There were always emergencies in the gearbox of the planetary system. Let's say you had a date, fifty cents and three quarts of gasoline. This would be the time when the high-low band wore through to the metal. Your problem then was to move the reverse band to the low-high section and get along without a reverse for the time being. The process of change was invariable. You removed the top plate and took off the bands. The metal was not only very oily but very springy, and the forks were held together by curious wedge-shaped bolts and nuts. Now, just when you had the forks pinched close and were trying to get the bolt back in place, you dropped the nut. It fell into the black oil pool beneath the assembly where no hand could reach it. So you got a piece of wire out of the back seat and bent one end of it to make a fishhook. Sometimes it took two or three hours to locate the fallen nut by the touch system, to get the hook through it and to lift it out. It was a most delicate operation and it should have developed some great safecrackers.

There were certain standard practices in the repair of the Model T. For instance, if the radiator sprung a leak, you dropped a handful of corn or oatmeal into the water. The heat of the water cooked the mush which coated the tubes and sealed the leak. Once, years later, I had a car of another make of great age and dignity. My mother was coming to visit me and I was to meet her at the railroad station. My radiator was leaking pretty badly, so, automatically, I put in a handful of oatmeal, forgetting that times had changed. You see, the Model T circulated its water by a principle, part magic, part accident, and part physics, but this other car had a water pump—a needless and stupid innovation. This car ran so cool that it took a long time for the mush to cook. I got to the station, installed my dignified mother in the front seat and started home. Naturally there was no radiator cap; we considered such things a nuisance, since we were always losing them anyway. Suddenly there was a sloppy explosion and a Bikini mushroom of oatmeal rose into the air. Part of it splashed on the windshield, but the larger part on my mother's beflowered hat.

We drove through downtown Los Angeles erupting mush, my mother scraping it out of her eyes. I never saw so much mush. I never saw my mother so mad. It goes to show the kind of habits you got into from driving the Model T.

The attitude of girls toward IT was supercilious, but realistic. They would have preferred to go in something else, but mainly they wanted to go. I think they must have known that a swain's attention was split; he might be saying with a kind of worldliness, "I think you're pretty," but in his mind it was "I wonder what that sound is? Lord God, has she kicked out another bearing?" A girl starting out in a Model T never knew whether love or mechanics would be the result, and if it happened to be both, well, crankcase oil looks very bad on a white dress. The Model T was as important to romance as the girl was. We never quite eliminated her.

The American restlessness took on new force. No one was satisfied with where he was; he was on his way someplace else; just as soon as he got that timer adjusted. No doorbell dry cells were ever safe. And all of these things were important, but most important of all was the spiritual association of kids and motors.

When I consider how much time it took to keep IT running, I wonder if there was time for anything else, and maybe there wasn't. The Model T was not a car as we know them now—it was a person—crotchety and mean, frolicsome and full of jokes—just when you were ready to kill yourself, it would run five miles with no gasoline whatever. I understood IT, but as I said before, IT understood me, too. It magnified some of my faults, corrected others. It worked on the sin of impatience; it destroyed the sin of vanity. And it helped to establish an almost Oriental philosophy of acceptance.

In the years I had IT, no mechanic ever touched it, no shadow of a garage ever passed over it. I do not recall any new part ever being bought for it. It's a sentimental memory with me. I know, of course, that things do not cease to exist in some form. Metal may change its composition through rust or blast furnace, but all of its atoms remain somewhere, and I have wondered sadly about IT. Maybe its essence was blasted gloriously in a bomb or a shell. Perhaps it lies humbly on the cross-ties while streamlined trains roll over it. It might be a girder of a bridge, or even something to support a tiny piece of the UN building in New York. And just perhaps, in the corner of some field, the grass and the yellow mustard may grow taller and greener than elsewhere and, if you were to dig down, you might find the red of rust under the roots, and that might be IT, enriching the soil, going home to its mother, the earth.

IV.

ON WRITING

BEING A WRITER WAS, for Steinbeck, not just an occupation; it was his passion, his life, his joy. Although he often worried about his work and suffered misgivings, he was happiest when he was writing. "My basic rationale might be that I like to write," he said in "Rationale." "I feel good when I am doing it—better than when I am not. I find joy in the texture and tone and rhythms of words and sentences." Indeed, his relation to his writing at times approached a kind of reverent fascination: "Writing to me is a deeply personal, even a secret function and when the product is turned loose it is cut off from me and I have no sense of its being mine. It is like a woman trying to remember what childbirth is like. She never can" (*SLL* 360).

He commonly used journal entries and letters in the morning to warm up to his work, and in extensive journals (two have been published, *Journal of a Novel: The "East of Eden" Letters* [1969] and *Working Days: The Journals of "The Grapes of Wrath"* [1989]) he speaks in a variety of voices, confessional to notational; muses on the processes and problems of writing; reflects on what he wrote the previous day and will write on the day to come; and notes his physical and emotional state in connection with whatever he was working on. While working on *The Grapes of Wrath*, he recorded both the exhilaration and despair of writing: "This must be a good book. It simply must. I haven't any choice. It must be far and away the best thing I have ever attempted—slow but sure, piling detail on detail until a picture and an experience emerge. Until the whole throbbing thing emerges. And I can do it. I feel very strong to do it. Today for instance into the picture is the evening and the cooking of the rabbits . . ." (*WD* 25). His imagination was strongly visual, and when writing at his most concentrated, he wrote in a tiny scrawl, sometimes in pen, later in pencil, seldom deleting words, caught up in the intensity of his craft. Writing also drained him, filled him with self-doubt: "This book has become a misery to me because of my inadequacy," he wrote later in his *Grapes* journal. "And I'm frightened that I'm losing this book in the welter of other things" (*WD* 76, 77). But there are many more passages in both the journals and his voluminous letters that are contemplative and philosophical, insisting again and again on the significance of the written word.

Perhaps because he was always working at the impossible, always modest about his accomplishments, forever nursing his own insecurities, he was extremely sensitive to criticism, even buffering himself by anticipating negative critical responses. "The critics will scream shame at me . . ." he wrote in his notebook after receiving galleys for an early book, *To a God Unknown*. One problem for Steinbeck throughout his career was that he was an experimenter, and he doubted that critics would appreciate what he was doing. "My experience in writing has followed an almost invariable pattern," he observes in "Critics, Critics, Burning Bright." "Since by the process of writing a book I have outgrown that book, and since I like to write, I have not written two books alike." This "endless experiment with his medium," as he calls it, conflicted with the tendency—which he complained about frequently—of critics to pigeonhole authors and to continue always to judge them on that basis. The straitjacket that *The Grapes of Wrath* forced him into was that of a social and political activist. Six years after the publication of *Grapes,* he published *Cannery Row* (1945), and critics like Edmund Wilson were disappointed that it wasn't serious enough: "When this watcher of life should exalt us to the vision of art, he simply sings 'Mother Machree' " (McElrath 278). Orville Prescott in the *New York Times* concurred: "Ever since his triumph with *The Grapes of Wrath* Mr. Steinbeck has been coasting. He still is" (McElrath 277).

In 1950, five years after *Cannery Row,* reviewers came down hard on him for the play *Burning Bright,* which was probably the most experimental piece of writing he ever attempted. By this time he was fed up by the unwillingness of the critics to examine this new thing with any objectivity, and in response he wrote "Critics, Critics Burning Bright," a fairly levelheaded response to what he believed were wrongheaded reactions to his play. Then in 1955 Pascal Covici gave Steinbeck a scrapbook "of all or nearly all the criticisms of a volume of mine" ("Critics—from a Writer's Viewpoint" 20), and he was prompted to reflect, once again, on criticism and critics in general. Steinbeck's sensitivity to criticism did not lead him very often to react to specific critics and their attacks—probably a wiser course to take, as his wife Elaine always advised him. But when he did respond, it was in part out of anger, in part out of fun. "There was a time, a lustier time, when critics were answered and everyone had fun." Besides, he added, "I like a good fight. I find it healthy" (quoted in Benson 814). The truth of the matter is that most of Steinbeck's novels received largely positive reviews, and even the least popular books had their champions. And on the rare occasion when Steinbeck himself wrote criticism, he did so with fairness and verve.

One thing that Steinbeck was particularly proud of was his invention of the play-novelette form, which he used on three occasions: *Of Mice and Men, The Moon Is Down,* and *Burning Bright.* "The work I am doing now," he wrote to his agents in April 1936 as he was composing *Of Mice and Men,* "is neither a novel nor a play but it is a kind of playable novel. Written in novel form but so scened and set that it can be played as it stands. It wouldn't be like other plays since it does not follow the formal acts but uses chapter for curtains. . . . Plays are hard to read so this will make both a novel and play as it stands" (Shillinglaw xv–xvi). He expanded on the virtues of this form twice, in 1938 for *Stage* magazine (in a piece originally titled "The Novel Might Benefit . . . ," reprinted here as "The Play-Novelette") and again in his "Author's Foreword" to the novelette publication of *Burning Bright.*

Like all writers, Steinbeck was fond of books, "one of the very few authentic magics our species has created." He did not think that the book would disappear, be replaced by "the quick, cheap, easy forms of entertainment," for as he says in "Some Random and Randy Thoughts on Books," "No television show is a friend as a book is a friend. And no other form, save . . . music, invites the participation of the receiver as a book does." He was not, however, a collector of books for their physical selves. "I have never asked for nor wanted an autographed book." Indeed, he marveled at those willing to pay premiums for rare books or special editions, a willingness that seemed to have little to do with their contents. Pascal Covici, his editor, loved the physical book, and on several occasions during Steinbeck's career he talked the author into letting him publish special editions. In a letter to librarian-critic Lawrence Clark Powell, Steinbeck noted:

> I was expecting a howl about the price of *The Red Pony*. I wouldn't pay ten dollars for a Gutenberg Bible. In this case, I look at it this way. Covici loves beautiful books. These are old stories reprinted and they don't amount to much anyway, so if he wants to make a pretty book, why not? The funny thing is that they're over-subscribed, about five hundred. I didn't know there were that many damn fools in the world—with 10 bucks, I mean. I don't let Covici dictate one word about how I write and I try never to make a suggestion about publishing to him. (*SLL* 139)

Steinbeck comes out squarely for the cheap paperback, the "twenty-five-cent book."

The Play-Novelette

THE BOOK *Of Mice and Men* was an experiment and, in what it set out to do, it was a failure. The purpose of this article is to set forth the nature of the experiment and to consider whether it might not, with greater care and experience, succeed.

Simply stated, *Of Mice and Men* was an attempt to write a novel that could be played from the lines, or a play that could be read. The reading of plays is a specialized kind of reading, and the technique of reading plays must be acquired with some difficulty. The tools are a visual imagination and an unconscious awareness of dramatic symbols so complete that the reaction to them is automatic. These two implements are not very widely possessed; or, if they are developable, are not widely developed. The small distribution of plays intended to be read indicates the almost aversion most people have for reading them.

A play written in the physical technique of the novel would have a number of advantages. Being more persuasive than the play form, it would go a great way toward making the play easy to read for people who cannot and will not learn to absorb the play symbols. It is much easier for the average reader to absorb without difficulty the easy "he said" manner of the novel than the "character, colon, parenthesis, adverb, close parenthesis, dialogue" manner of the play.

In the second place the novel's ability to describe scene and people in detail would not only make for a better visual picture to the reader, but would be of value to director, stage designer, and actor, for these latter would know more about the set and characters. More than this, it would be possible for the playwright by this method to set his tone much more powerfully than he can in the limited *time, place, scene* method of the play. And this tone is vastly important. Shaw, to a certain extent, uses the introduction for this purpose. But the novel form would integrate tone and play in one entity, would allow the reader, whether actor, director or lay reader, a sense of the whole much more complete than he can get from the present play form.

So much for the value of such a method for the drama. But the novel itself would be interfered with by such a method in only one way, and that is that it would be short. Actually the discipline, the necessity of sticking to the theme (in fact of knowing what the theme is), the brevity and necessity of holding an audience could influence the novel only for the better. In a play, sloppy writing is impossible, for an audience will not sit through it. Wandering, discussion, and essay are impossible because an audience becomes restless. It must not be supposed that I am advocating this method for the whole field of the novel. I am not. The novel of contemplation, of characterization through analysis, of philosophic discussion is not affected at all by this form.

The problem is rendered very easy of approach at the present time. For some years the novel has increasingly taken on the attributes of the drama. Thus the hard-finish, objective form which is the direction of the modern novel not only points in the direction of the drama, but seems unconsciously to have aimed at it. To read an objective novel is to see a little play in your head. All right, why not make it so you can see it on a stage? This experiment, then, is really only a conclusion toward which the novel has been unconsciously heading for some time.

The final argument in favor of such a form is a little more difficult to state. For whatever reason, and to state a reason would be to start an argument, the recent tendency of writers has been to deal in those themes and those scenes which are best understood and appreciated by groups of people. There are many experiences which cannot be understood in solitude. War cannot be understood by an individual, nor can many forms of religious experience. A mob cannot be understood by a person sitting alone in an armchair, but it can be understood by that same person in the mob. You rarely see a man listening to a radio broadcast of a prizefight jump yelling to his feet, but he would be doing just that if he were at the prizefight. All the sounds are there, but the thing that is missing is the close, almost physical contact with the other people at the prizefight. A man alone under a reading light simply cannot experience *Waiting for*

Lefty on anywhere near the same plane as he can when the whole audience around him is caught in the force of that play. I remember seeing the Theatre Union in San Francisco improvising. To have read the thing would have been absurd, for it would have consisted of grunts, little cries, and half sentences; but to see it, with other people about you seeing it too, was to feel your skin crawl, and to feel yourself drawn into the group that was playing.

Now if it is true, and I believe it is, that the preoccupation of the modern novelist lies in these themes which are most poignantly understood by a group, that novelist limits the possibility of being understood by making it impossible for groups to be exposed to his work. In the reading of a novel there are involved only the author, the novel, and the reader; but in the seeing of a play there are the author, the play, the players, and the whole audience, and each one of these contributes a vital part to the whole effect.

On such plans, thoughts, and premises the book *Of Men and Mice* was written. It was a failure because it wouldn't play; and it wouldn't play because I had not sufficient experience and knowledge in stagecraft. The timing was out, the curtains were badly chosen, some of the scenes got off the line, and many of the methods ordinarily used in the novel, and which I used in the book, do not get over on the stage. The book had to be rewritten to play, and I don't know yet whether it will play.

The fact that this experiment was a failure, however, is no proof that such a book as I had wished to write cannot be written. I thoroughly intend to try it again. If it could be successful, certainly there would be an increased interest in the theater among those people who now prefer novels. And if such an experiment could go further than experiment and become a practiced, valid form, then it is not beyond contemplation that not only might the novel benefit by the discipline, the terseness of the drama, but the drama itself might achieve increased openness, freedom and versatility.

My Short Novels

I HAVE NEVER written a preface to one of my books before, believing that the work should stand on its own feet, even if the ankles were slightly wobbly. When I was asked to comment on the six short novels of this volume, my first impulse was to refuse. And then, thinking over the things that have happened to these stories since they were written, I was taken with the idea that what happens to a book is very like what happens to a man.

These stories cover a long period of my life. As each was finished, that part of me was finished. It is true that while a work is in progress, the writer and his book are one. When a book is finished, it is a kind of death, a matter of pain and sorrow to the writer. Then he starts a new book, and a new life, and if he is growing and changing, a whole new life starts. The writer, like a fickle lover, forgets his old love. It is no longer his own: the intimacy and the surprise are gone. So much I knew, but I had not thought of the little stories thrust out into an unfriendly world to make their way. They have experiences, too—they grow and change or wane and die, just as everyone does. They make friends or enemies, and sometimes they waste away from neglect.

The Red Pony was written a long time ago, when there was desolation in my family. The first death had occurred. And the family, which every child believes to be immortal, was shattered. Perhaps this is the first adulthood of any man or woman. The first tortured question "Why?" and then acceptance, and then the child becomes a man. *The Red Pony* was an attempt, an experiment if you wish, to set down this loss and acceptance and growth. At that time I had had three books published and none of them had come anywhere near selling their first editions. *The Red Pony* could not find a publisher. It came back over and over again, until at last a brave editor bought it for *The North American Review* and paid ninety dollars for it, more money than I thought the world contained. What a great party we had in celebration!

It takes only the tiniest pinch of encouragement to keep a writer going, and if he gets none, he sometimes learns to feed even on the acid of failure.

Tortilla Flat grew out of my study of the Arthurian cycle. I wanted to take the stories of my town of Monterey and cast them into a kind of folklore. The result was *Tortilla Flat*. It followed the usual pattern. Publisher after publisher rejected it, until finally Pascal Covici published it. But it did have one distinction the others had not: it was not ignored. Indeed, the Chamber of Commerce of Monterey, fearing for its tourist business, issued a statement that the book was a lie and that certainly no such disreputable people lived in that neighborhood. But perhaps the Chamber of Commerce did me a good service, for the book sold two editions, and this was almost more encouragement than I could stand. I was afraid that I might get used to such profligacy on the part of the public, and I knew it couldn't last. A moving-picture company bought *Tortilla Flat* and paid four thousand dollars for it. Thirty-six hundred came to me. It was a fortune. And when, a few years later, the same company fired its editor, one of the reasons was that he had bought *Tortilla Flat*. So he bought it from the company for the original four thousand dollars and several years later sold it to M-G-M for ninety thousand dollars. A kind of justification for me, and a triumph for the editor.

Of Mice and Men was an attempt to write a novel in three acts to be played from the lines. I had nearly finished it when my setter pup ate it one night, literally made confetti of it! I don't know how close the first and second versions would prove to be. This book had some success, but as usual it found its enemies. With rewriting, however, it did become a play and had some success.

There were long books between these little novels. I think the little ones were exercises for the long ones. The war came on, and I wrote *The Moon Is Down* as a kind of celebration of the durability of democracy. I couldn't conceive that the book would be denounced. I had written of Germans as men, not supermen, and this was considered a very weak attitude to take. I couldn't make much sense out of this, and it seems absurd now that we know the Germans were men, and thus fallible, even defeatable. It was said that I didn't know anything about war, and this was perfectly true, though how Park Avenue commandos found me out I can't conceive.

Subsequently I saw a piece of war as a correspondent, and following that wrote *Cannery Row*. This was a kind of nostalgic thing, written for a group of soldiers who had said to me, "Write something funny that isn't about the war. Write something for us to read—we're sick of war." When *Cannery Row* came out, it got the usual critical treatment. I was wasting my time in flippancy when I should be writing about the war. But half a million copies were distributed to troops, and they didn't complain. We had some very warlike critics then, much more bellicose than the soldiers.

In Mexico I heard a story and made a long jump back to the *Tortilla Flat* time. I tried to write it as folklore, to give it that set-aside, raised-up feeling that all folk stories have. I called it *The Pearl*. It didn't do so well at first either, but it seems to be gathering some friends, or at least acquaintances. And that's the list in this volume. It is strange to me that I have lived so many lives. Thinking back, it seems an endless time and yet only a moment.

Rationale

RECENTLY I was asked by a University for a Rationale of the corpus of my work. I didn't know the word.

The *Oxford Dictionary* defines a "Rationale" as: 1. A reasoned exposition of principles, an explanation or statement of reasons, a set of reasoned rules or directions; and 2. The fundamental reason, the logical or rational basis for anything. Or in simpler words—what did you write and why did you write it?

There may be writers who before the fact of writing may have been able to do this. In my own case, I fear that a *rationale* might well be a rationalization, undertaken after the fact—a critic's rather than a writer's approach. It is like asking a prisoner, "Why did you commit murder?" His reply might be, "Let me think. I guess I didn't like the guy, and—well I was mad." He can work out why he did it but he can't really remember the emotional pressure which drifted his hand toward the knife.

So in my work I can say, "It must have been this way or this"—but I am not at all sure that I remember. I can say of one book, "I suppose I saw things which made me angry." Of another, "It was just an idea which amused me and I wrote it." Of another, "It is possible that I was trying to explain something—something that was not clear to me. I may have felt that writing it would make me understand it better."

My basic rationale might be that I like to write. I feel good when I am doing it—better than when I am not. I find joy in the texture and tone and rhythms of words and sentences, and when these happily combine in a "thing" that has texture and tone and emotion and design and architecture, there comes a fine feeling—a satisfaction like that which follows good and shared love. If there have been difficulties and failures overcome, these may even add to the satisfaction. . . .

As for my "reasoned exposition of principles," I suspect that they are no different from those of any man living out his life. Like everyone, I want to be good and strong and virtuous and wise and loved. I think that writing may be simply a method or technique for communication with other individuals; and its stimulus, the loneliness we are born to. In writing, perhaps we hope to achieve companionship. What some people find in religion, a writer may find in his craft or whatever it is—absorption of the small and frightened and lonely into the whole and complete, a kind of breaking through to glory.

A lady of my acquaintance was asked by her young daughters where babies came from, and after making certain that they really wanted to know, she told them. They listened solemnly and at the end, the mother asked, "Now are you sure you understand?"

The oldest girl said, "Yes, we understand what you do—but *why* do you do it?"

The mother thought for a moment and then replied, "Because it's *fun!*"

And that could well be my rationale. My work is and has been fun. Within myself, I find no hunger to inquire further.

Critics–from a Writer's Viewpoint

RECENTLY my publisher, with the best intention in the world, gave me a scrapbook of all or nearly all the criticisms of a volume of mine. On first reading this compendium was confusing. In many cases one critic canceled out another; while the exponents of the new criticism wrote a parochial language which was completely obscure to me. I became depressed after first looking into this scrapbook, for it seemed to me that there were no laws of criticism. Read all together one had an appalling sense of anarchy.

It is the convention that a writer should never answer a critic, no matter how violent or seemingly unfair the review. For example, when a *New Yorker* critic attacked a play of mine on the basis of parts and lines which had been removed in rehearsal I knew that he had not looked very carefully at the play and had refreshed his memory from a script which had been abandoned during production. It did not occur to me to protest. This piece is not a protest. It is rather an attempt to scrutinize and perhaps understand present-day American criticism as it is seen by a writer.

One thing we are prone to forget is that the critic is primarily a writer himself and that his first interest lies in his own career. This being so, is it surprising that he is prone to warp his piece in favor of his own cleverness? The critic is nearly always a creative writer or wants to be. Thus, we find him invariably with a novel or play in process or in mind and the critical process can by no means carry over into the creative process. A reviewer who hates dullness is quite capable of writing a dull book. A drama critic of inexorable standards can write, and within our memory has, a play which violated every standard his critical pattern set up.

We are likely also to forget that critics are people with all of the frailties and attitudes of people. One critic explained to me after the fact that he had given me a ferocious beating because he had a hangover. Another, with a reputation for blistering anything he touched, suddenly went enthusiastically appreciative of almost everything. The explanation was not hard to find. He had published three novels which failed and his fourth was well received and his whole approach changed. Another reviewer uses a neurosis stemming from his birth under unusual circumstances and from unusual parents as the gall in which he dips his pen. Still another critic of personal indecision, reviewing a novel with a homosexual theme, attacked it hysterically on points of grammar.

Here is a thing we are most likely to forget. A man's writing is himself. A kind man writes kindly. A mean man writes meanly. A sick man writes sickly. And a wise man writes wisely. There is no reason to suppose that this rule does not apply to critics as well as to other writers.

One might go farther into the effects of personal life on criticism. It is reasonable to suppose that the reviewer privately unloved will take a dim view of love; that the childless critic will be intolerant of children; that the failure will hate success; a bachelor be cynical of marriage; the tired and old find youth and enthusiasm intolerable; and the conservative be outraged by experiment.

In inspecting present-day American reviewers, one should also take into consideration the fact that the critic very rarely intended criticism as his career. It is in many cases a means of surviving until he can become novelist, playwright, or poet and if, in the course of years, he should become none of these he must, no matter how much he may resist, develop an anger against those who do.

Another thought that comes to me is that people get tired of their jobs, no matter what they are. I can well imagine that a man who is compelled for his living to read book after book after book might well grow to detest books; that a drama critic forced to go to plays, when he might rather have some private evening social life, could develop a fierce animosity toward the theater. This is more than a conjecture.

But let us consider success within criticism itself. It consists in building up a large body of readers, as large as possible. To do this the critic must attract attention, just as people are more interested in violence than in quiet, in murder and in accidents than in uneventfulness, in divorce than in marriage, so they read destructive attack with greater avidity than praise. Indeed, one critic made his whole reputation by denouncing Dante, Goethe, and Shakespeare as literary hacks. He lived on that one for years. He was considered original.

There are generalized tendencies which emerge after much reading of notices.

A reviewer is prone to like the previous book or play of a writer better than the present one, but the previous one he didn't like as well as the one previous to that. Reading a course of reviews of a critic over a period gives a writer the idea that he started with nothing and got nowhere. In fact, is in a continual state of slipping back. Drama critics have apparently great power in determining whether a play shall survive or not. Book critics, on the other hand, seem to have little to do with the success or failure of a book. Some years ago a publisher placed a self-addressed postcard with checkboxes in every book sent out. The response indicated that 3 percent bought the book because of advertising, 2 percent because of reviews, and 95 percent because of word-of-mouth. A national magazine review section has, over a period of ten years or more, torn into every book of mine with a vehemence far beyond the call of duty or even of hatred. This magazine has enormous circulation, yet its campaign has had no appreciable effect on the sale of my books.

I have spoken to some extent of unfavorable reviews. I think a writer squirms much more at a favorable notice if the reviewer has missed the point. I remember some overwhelmingly flattering reviews which gave me great sadness because the critic had not understood one thing I was talking about.

What, from a writer's standpoint, is the function of a critic? Some critics seem to feel that they are the directors of writers. They show them the path they should take and punish them if they fall to take it. This has little value to a writer since he is not likely to repeat the book in question.

Should the critic, then, be a kind of intermediary between writer and reader? I don't know, but I suspect that if a writer cannot make himself clear to a reader a critic has little chance of making him clearer. Is the critic a kind of traffic cop of literature? Is he a separator of sheep from goats? Is he an interpreter? Perhaps different reviewers assume different roles. One dramatic critic who apparently must have had a fine time in Germany before the turn of the century has found no pleasure since. Another reviewer for a magazine prefers anything first written in French.

It is amusing to me how many critics are deeply involved with immortality. They threaten the writer with mortality. They have even convinced some of our best living authors that the immortality of their work is important so that they quarrel like children over the billing on a tombstone. A sad state for otherwise brilliant men who should know that literary immortality is a relative matter subject to unforeseen futures. It has occurred in the past too often not to be possible in the future that the writer most read fifty years after his death was unknown or unacceptable during his life. Our immortal of the future may be someone the present critics do not know about or do not consider important.

It would be very interesting for a good and intelligent critic to exercise his craft on a body of work of his fellow critics. If this should happen I think it would be found that the product of a reviewer is not objective at all, but subject to all of the virtues and vices of other writers in other fields. I don't think critics should change; only our attitude toward them. Poor things, nobody reviews them.

Some Random and Randy
Thoughts on Books

THIS IS THE AGE of the package. Everything from dressed and stuffed fleas to locomotives is packaged. And by a slow and steady process, the package is becoming more important than its contents. And why not, since your modern purchaser buys by package?

American books constitute packages and I imagine that the same rules which apply to pillboxes and canned food must apply to books. It seems to be true that if you put identical pills in yellow boxes and in white boxes, purchasers will buy the yellow boxes.

We have three kinds of packages for books—those which attract as flowers attract insects, those which establish their profundity with stern, dull covers (since profundity is generally believed to be dull), and finally, those which by illustration on their jackets indicate or lie about the contents. All of it is a fly-catching process.

It is generally understood by publishers that if a one-pound book is offered beside a two-pound book, the heavier, thicker article is more desirable. The same instinct applies which makes every child at some time or other trade his dime for a nickel. Thick heavy books are more in demand than light, thin books, regardless of the content.

This last fact once caused me to make two suggestions to my publishers which they have stupidly failed to follow. If leaden covers were used, the weight problem would have been overcome. And if the book were printed on rye bread it would be very much thicker. Further, your bread book would solve two problems. The reader would never lose his place since he would eat each page as he finished it; also the lost profit of the borrowed book would be eliminated. And people do like to read while they eat. A few years ago, a public librarian in Birmingham, England, earnestly requested the subscribers not to use bacon or kippers as bookmarks because the grease soaked through the pages and the odor might repel future readers. I feel that bookmaking is far from completely exploited—cellophane bags of marmalade or liver paste glued to the inside of the front cover, for example.

But I shall return to the business as it is practical. Recently some translations of my own work came in from France. The covers were not of cloth but of a black cardboard and the designs were bright and fresh and charming. One's first impulse is to say, "Why can't we do this in America?" The answer is that no one would buy them. We have conditioned our people to look for other values in their purchases.

Original manufacturing costs have increased so greatly that only a temporary publisher can or will take a chance with innovations. Volume is necessary in publishing. This alone will keep our publishers from undertaking any violent experiment. The book clubs, whether they admit it or not, must not go out on a limb. They have entered into a kind of contract with their millions of subscribers not to shock or startle them with great departure from mediocrity. And finally the cost of a book alone will keep innovation out. To buy a book you must have three-fifty or four dollars. If you have four dollars, after taxes and necessities, to spend on a book, you are solvent at least temporarily. If you are solvent for any length of time you are likely to be conservative, and if you are conservative you damn well do not trust newfangled ideas or experiments. The French books mentioned above did not look like other books. They were obviously unsound.

I do not believe that any change can take place quickly. Your historical novel must have jacket blurbs and illustration to indicate that sex was better and more prevalent in those days. Your "sound" novel must be dressed in dour colors with no gaiety to draw the reader away from the solid chore of reading. Your humorous books should have a man, woman or cat laughing on its jacket. This indicates that H. Allen Smith is funny and if you know it is funny, you will laugh.

Perhaps the blurb does set the book. I remember a book which had the following line in the text: "Then they went to bed together." However, the blurb said "a night of tempestuous love." The time may come when one will not have to read books. If the blurbs were on sale separately it might be a good and profitable venture and if the blurbs were then digested we would have the ultimate.

I myself am a hater of jackets. My impulse is to get them off and thrown away quickly. They crease and get in the way. I suppose they were originally put on as a wrapping and also to keep the dirty hands of prospective customers from spoiling new books. Why could there not be a display copy in a cellophane jacket? Does the jacket contribute anything to a book beyond adding to the cost? It would be interesting to see. And why is cloth necessary? I have heard that it adds greatly to the cost of manufacturing. Would not a treated board be as durable and much cheaper? Is not the increasing cost of books an actual selling deterrent? The two-fifty book is now four dollars.

It has happened that when I have thrown away the jacket because it was in the way, that I wanted to go back to the account of the author. Could this not be bound in the book so that it is a permanent part of the volume?

For myself, I like the whole theory of the twenty-five-cent book. For one thing the very cost of a trade edition encourages a degree of selfishness. Such a book must be hoarded and put on the shelves. It becomes property and property must be protected. I must know who borrows the book and I must see that it is returned and many friendships have been crushed on the rocks of the unreturned book. With the cheap editions the opposite is true. You load your friends' arms with books. You say, "When you are through with them, pass them on." This is a very fine thing.

I don't know how many writers have the feeling I have about books. I do not love books for themselves. I like to have certain books about me to refer to but only because of the text. I have never collected books for their physical selves. I have never asked for nor wanted an autographed book. Sure I love to see a library walled with the lovely backs of finely bound books, but this is decoration to me, not literature. The prettiest volumes have not been opened, the most valuable firsts have not been cut. I would for myself much rather have thousands of cheap, dog-eared volumes filed in closed cabinets like phonograph records. It is much easier to browse through filing cards than to climb on the arms of a chair looking for a certain book which you remember was green. You think it is on the top shelf. The book turns out to be brown and after you have lost interest, you find it on the bottom shelf behind a bent copy of the *London Illustrated* you had always intended to go back to. No, for real accessibility, I like the card index.

The book itself took on its magical, sacrosanct and authoritative character at a time when there were very few books and those possessed by the very rich or the very learned. Then the book was the only release of the mind into distant places and into golden thinking. There was no other way of going outside one's self except through the talisman of the book. And it is wonderful that even today with all competition of records, of radio, of television, of motion pictures, the book has kept its precious character. A book is somehow sacred. A dictator can kill and maim people, can sink to any kind of tyranny and only be hated, but when books are burned, the ultimate in tyranny has happened. This we cannot forgive. The use of the book as propaganda is more powerful and effective than any other medium. A broadcast has little authority but a book does not lie. People automatically distrust newspapers. They automatically believe in books. This is strange but it is so. Messages come from behind the controlled and censored areas of the world and they do not ask for radios, for papers and pamphlets. They invariably ask for books. They believe books when they believe nothing else. This being true, I wonder that governments do not use books more often than they do. A book is protected and passed on. It is the rarest of things for a man to destroy a book unless he truly hates it. Book destruction is a kind of murder. And in the growing tendency to censor and control for the problematical good of the people, books have escaped more than any form. A picture can be cut to ribbons, but any restraint laid on a book is fought to a finish.

I wonder very much about the future of books. Can they continue to compete with the quick, cheap, easy forms which do not require either reading or thinking? I must say they do, or some of them are trying to do just that. So many books now are written with motion pictures in view. It is said that some publishers will not print a book if there is not a possibility of a motion-picture sale. And even the writer in many cases is concerned as part writer and part salesman. He should stand in a bookstore labeling his product with his name. He should go on television shows and become a performing ape. He should subject his private life, his sex life and his muscle, even his body hair, to the adenoidal stares of his prospective readers. He is said to be letting the book down if he does not do these things. He is being antisocial if he will not permit one of the picture magazines to record his breakfast and his wife or wives on slick paper.

I do not believe that a book can compete with its rivals on their terms. On the other hand, they cannot compete with the book on its terms. No other form save music can so "invite the mind and the emotions." One cannot conceive of a motion picture as being personal as a beloved book is personal. No television show is a friend as a book is a friend. And no other form, save again music, invites the participation of the receiver as a book does.

What a long way to get around to the subject of format. I do not know much about manufacturing. It seems to me that your physical book should be as like the abstract book as possible. There should be warm books and cool books, gay books and somber books. If a book is full of pain, let it be painful in color and design, if it is beautiful and sharp, these should design its clothing. Just as a title should catch the essence of a book, so should its format.

The yellow-pillbox theory will in the long run contribute little to books for books must be true in one sense or another and merchandising must be largely untrue. The yellow box will subtly force a customer to eat a bread pill and perhaps take some good from it. And perhaps a book can be forced to do this job, but I doubt it. A book is a naked article. A book is only read when you are alone. No group audience starts the laughter or the tears for you. It is a communion of two and as such it is unique.

And so I think that a book should feel good in the hand and gladden the eye. Its shape and size should be designed so that it is not clumsy to hold nor difficult to see. Its price should be low enough so that no crime against economics is committed in buying it. I am not speaking now of the books which are simply pauses on the way to motion pictures but of the books that were written to be books and nothing else but books. There is something untranslatable about a book. It is itself—one of the very few authentic magics our species has created.

Nobel Prize
Acceptance Speech

I THANK the Swedish Academy for finding my work worthy of this highest honor. In my heart there may be doubt that I deserve the Nobel Award over other men of letters whom I hold in respect and reverence—but there is no question of my pleasure and pride in having it for myself.

It is customary for the recipient of this award to offer scholarly or personal comment on the nature and the direction of literature. However, I think it would be well at this particular time to consider the high duties and the responsibilities of the makers of literature.

Such is the prestige of the Nobel Award and of this place where I stand that I am impelled, not to squeak like a grateful and apologetic mouse, but to roar like a lion out of pride in my profession and in the great and good men who have practiced it through the ages.

Literature was not promulgated by a pale and emasculated critical priesthood singing their litanies in empty churches—nor is it a game for the cloistered elect, the tin-horn mendicants of low-calorie despair.

Literature is as old as speech. It grew out of human need for it and it has not changed except to become more needed. The skalds, the bards, the writers are not separate and exclusive. From the beginning, their functions, their duties, their responsibilities have been decreed by our species.

Humanity has been passing through a gray and desolate time of confusion. My great predecessor William Faulkner, speaking here, referred to it as a tragedy of universal physical fear, so long sustained that there were no longer problems of the spirit, so that only the human heart in conflict with itself seemed worth writing about. Faulkner, more than most men, was aware of human strength as well as of human weakness.

He knew that the understanding and the resolution of fear are a large part of the writer's reason for being.

This is not new. The ancient commission of the writer has not changed. He is charged with exposing our many grievous faults and failures, with dredging up to the light our dark and dangerous dreams for the purpose of improvement.

Furthermore, the writer is delegated to declare and to celebrate man's proven capacity for greatness of heart and spirit—for gallantry in defeat, for courage, compassion and love. In the endless war against weakness and despair, these are the bright rally flags of hope and of emulation. I hold that a writer who does not passionately believe in the perfectibility of man has no dedication nor any membership in literature.

The present universal fear has been the result of a forward surge in our knowledge and manipulation of certain dangerous factors in the physical world. It is true that other phases of understanding have not yet caught up with this great step, but there is no reason to presume that they cannot or will not draw abreast. Indeed, it is a part of the writer's responsibility to make sure that they do. With humanity's long, proud history of standing firm against all of its natural enemies, sometimes in the face of almost certain defeat and extinction, we would be cowardly and stupid to leave the field on the eve of our greatest potential victory.

Understandably, I have been reading the life of Alfred Nobel; a solitary man, the books say, a thoughtful man. He perfected the release of explosive forces capable of creative good or of destructive evil, but lacking choice, ungoverned by conscience or judgment.

Nobel saw some of the cruel and bloody misuses of his inventions. He may even have foreseen the end result of his probing—access to ultimate violence, to final destruction. Some say that he became cynical, but I do not believe this. I think he strove to invent a control—a safety valve. I think he found it finally only in the human mind and the human spirit.

To me, his thinking is clearly indicated in the categories of these awards. They are offered for increased and continuing knowledge of man and of his world—for *understanding* and *communication*, which are the functions of literature. And they are offered for demonstrations of the capacity for peace—the culmination of all the others.

Less than fifty years after his death, the door of nature was unlocked and we were offered the dreadful burden of choice. We have usurped many of the powers we once ascribed to God. Fearful and unprepared, we have assumed lordship over the life and death of the whole world of all living things. The danger and the glory and the choice rest finally in man. The test of his perfectibility is at hand.

Having taken Godlike power, we must seek in ourselves for the responsibility and the wisdom we once prayed some deity might have. Man himself has become our greatest hazard and our only hope. So that today, Saint John the Apostle may well be paraphrased: In the end is the *word*, and the word is *man*, and the word is *with* man.

V.

FRIENDS

JOHN STEINBECK had many, many friends. He was drawn to ordinary people, and relished the company of the extraordinary people in his life like Edward Ricketts and Robert Capa and Arthur Miller. He wrote letters to friends daily, and because he was a writer, he was drawn to their stories in return. Although he spent a lot of time writing, "the loneliest job in the world," he relished company and conversation.

The writer's loneliest period may have been his high school years, when he spent much of his time in his bedroom reading and working on stories. But college was another matter. He made numerous friends at Stanford, and kept in touch with many through letters for years—roommate Carlton Sheffield, English majors Webster Street and A. Grove Day. A few faculty members helped shape his thinking and writing, particularly Edith Mirrielees, who taught a course in writing the short story. A tough taskmaster, Mirrielees didn't coddle the young Steinbeck, as he wrote in a preface to her book *Story Writing*: "If I had expected to be discovered in a full bloom of excellence, the grades you gave my efforts quickly disillusioned me" (vii). He had expected some kind of formula, some secret ingredient, but got none from her. Instead, what he got was frank criticism and encouragement—something he would, in turn, give to young writers who sought his opinion. One of Steinbeck's friends who also took courses from Mirrielees remembered her as "one of these odd, prissy, little old-fashioned women who you couldn't imagine John getting along with, and yet he had the greatest admiration for her, and he would take whatever she told him about what he wrote" (Benson 58).

Not until after college, however, did Steinbeck meet the man who became the closest, most influential friend of his life, Edward Flanders Ricketts. It was Ricketts who inspired the writer's many accounts of friendship, for that was the relationship that Steinbeck explored most consistently in his fiction: Lenny and George, Mack and Jim, Tom and Casy, Mack and the boys, Adam Trask and Lee. In all of these stories of male bonding, there was, either as one of the friends or as a sage looking on, a figure of serene demeanor and broad understanding. That character was always modeled on Edward Flanders Ricketts. He was a natural object for Steinbeck's interest. He was self-contained without being arrogant; extremely competent at his work as a marine biologist; knew things that Steinbeck didn't know well enough, like music and science and poetry and philosophy; was quiet and yet loved parties and conversation and ideas; and was a nonconformist with broad enthusiasms. "His mind had no horizons," Steinbeck writes in "About Ed Ricketts," one of the most heartfelt essays that he ever composed, written a few years after Ed's untimely death in 1948.

Other friends, others he admired, inspired shorter pieces. Tom Collins was the migrant camp manager he met while doing research for his newspaper series on the Dust Bowl migrants, "The Harvest Gypsies" (1936). Collins, like Ricketts, was a thoughtful nonconformist, the kind of creative, unusual person who always attracted Steinbeck. Both Ricketts and Collins were frustrated writers, and Steinbeck attempted to get various works of his two friends published; for Collins he wrote the piece reprinted here, a foreword to the autobiographical novel *Bringing in the Sheaves* (by Windsor Drake, the pen name that Collins adopted). His words about Woody Guthrie and Henry Fonda also grew out of his work on *The Grapes of Wrath*. Singer of Dust Bowl ballads, Woody sang "The Ballad of Tom Joad" at a New York benefit. And Fonda's early and defining film role as Tom Joad began a long friendship between the actor and the writer.

When he moved to New York City, first with his second wife, Gwyn, in 1941, later with Elaine in 1950, he became closer to his agents at McIntosh and Otis and to his lifelong editor, Pascal Covici. But he never wrote much about the loyal women who were his agents, Elizabeth Otis, with him from the beginning; Mavis McIntosh, who handled all film adaptations; or Shirley Fisher, whose husband flew the bomber *Mary Ruth* out of England in World War II and who herself became a Sag Harbor fishing buddy. But once, giving Elizabeth part of the proceeds from the musical *Pipe Dream,* he wrote her a letter that suggests much about the quality of his deep friendship and loyalty, to her, to others:

> As for the percent in P.D.—let us never mention it again. I love you very dearly and I have never been able to demonstrate it—perhaps due to a curious embarrassed stiffness on the part of each of us. Also I remember everything—*EVERYTHING* and I am thankful for all of it and all of you. And now I will draw back into the little house of shyness in which we both live. (Benson 779)

From that "little house" he made gestures to his closest friends. To Pascal Covici he gave the manuscript of *East of Eden,* in a wooden box he had carved himself. "The dedication is to you with all the admiration and affection that have been distilled from our singularly blessed association of many years" (*SLL* 437), he wrote to Covici. And on his death, he wrote him a short tribute: "Pat Covici was much more than my friend. Only a writer can understand how a great editor is father, mother, teacher, personal devil and personal god" ("In Memoriam" 19).

For the most part, Steinbeck kept to his "little house" and wrote publicly about only a few of his closest friends. But the accounts share a certain depth of feeling that is characteristically Steinbeck, a writer often accused of being sentimental who could with words express what he often could not in person. When photographer and collaborator Robert Capa died in 1954, Steinbeck was in Paris, and, shocked and numb, he walked the city for hours, an account recorded in a piece for *Le Figaro.* He later wrote a short piece on Capa for *Photography* magazine (1954), included here. Another friendship first forged during the war was with the indefatigable journalist Ernie Pyle, a bond built on admiration for the quality of his commitment to reporting: "Ernie Pyle was a poet." When they first met at a hotel in Algiers in 1943, they "acted like a couple of lovebirds courting each other," reported journalist Quentin Reynolds, a correspondent for *Collier's.* Pyle was about to be sent home for a rest, "not out of the kindness of editors," Steinbeck writes, "but because they were afraid he would melt and run down over himself from pure weariness" ("Letters to Alicia," 21 May 1966).

One man Steinbeck cared about a great deal was Adlai Stevenson, two-time Democratic candidate for the Presidency in 1952 and 1956. Stevenson had the enormous handicap of running against a hero that everyone loved, Dwight D. Eisenhower, while he, Stevenson, was the relatively unknown governor of Illinois. Steinbeck started out in the first campaign as an Eisenhower supporter—he had known about him, as did all Americans, during the war and had admired him. Yet, as he says in his foreword, reprinted here, to a collection of Stevenson speeches, he changed his mind "entirely because of the speeches," entirely because of Stevenson's ideas and his clear, unambiguous expression of those ideas. In 1956, Steinbeck was enlisted by Alan Jay Lerner, the musical comedy composer, to contribute ideas and drafts for speeches to the Stevenson campaign. At the Democratic convention that year he was able to meet and talk at some length to Stevenson, and they became friends.

From *About Ed Ricketts*

J UST ABOUT DUSK one day in April 1948, Ed Ricketts stopped work in the laboratory in Cannery Row. He covered his instruments and put away his papers and filing cards. He rolled down the sleeves of his wool shirt and put on the brown coat which was slightly small for him and frayed at the elbows.

He wanted a steak for dinner and he knew just the market in New Monterey where he could get a fine one, well hung and tender.

He went out into the street that is officially named Ocean View Avenue and is known as Cannery Row. His old car stood at the gutter, a beat-up sedan. The car was tricky and hard to start. He needed a new one but could not afford it at the expense of other things.

Ed tinkered away at the primer until the ancient rusty motor coughed and broke into a bronchial chatter which indicated that it was running. Ed meshed the jagged gears and moved away up the street.

He turned up the hill where the road crosses the Southern Pacific Railways track. It was almost dark, or rather that kind of mixed light and dark which makes it very difficult to see. Just before the crossing the road takes a sharp climb. Ed shifted to second gear, the noisiest gear, to get up the hill. The sound of his motor and gears blotted out every other sound. A corrugated iron warehouse was on his left, obscuring any sight of the right of way.

The Del Monte Express, the evening train from San Francisco, slipped around from behind the warehouse and crashed into the old car. The cowcatcher buckled in the side of the automobile and pushed and ground and mangled it a hundred yards up the track before the train stopped.

Ed was conscious when they got him out of the car and laid him on the grass. A crowd had collected of course—people from the train and more from the little houses that hug the track.

In almost no time a doctor was there. Ed's skull had a crooked look and his eyes were crossed. There was blood around his mouth, and his body was twisted, distorted—wrong, as though seen under an untrue lens.

The doctor got down on one knee and leaned over. The ring of people was silent.

Ed asked, "How bad is it?"

"I don't know," the doctor said. "How do you feel?"

"I don't feel much of anything," Ed said.

Because the doctor knew him and knew what kind of a man he was, he said, "That's shock, of course."

"Of course!" Ed said, and his eyes began to glaze.

They edged him onto a stretcher and took him to the hospital. Section hands pried his old car off the cowcatcher and pushed it aside, and the Del Monte Express moved slowly into the station at Pacific Grove, which is the end of the line.

Several doctors had come in and more were phoning, wanting to help because they all loved him. The doctors knew it was very serious, so they gave him ether and opened him up to see how bad it was. When they finished they knew it was hopeless. Ed was all messed up—spleen broken, ribs shattered, lungs punctured, concussion of the skull. It might have been better to let him go out under the ether, but the doctors could not give up, any more than could the people gathered in the waiting room of the hospital. Men who knew better began talking about miracles and how anything could happen. They reminded each other of cases of people who had got well when there was no reason to suppose they could. The surgeons cleaned Ed's insides as well as possible and closed him up. Every now and then one of the doctors would go out to the waiting room, and it was like facing a jury. There were lots of people out there, sitting waiting, and their eyes all held a stone question.

The doctors said things like "Doing as well as can be expected" and "We won't be able to tell for some time but he seems to be making progress." They talked more than was necessary, and the people sitting there didn't talk at all. They just stared, trying to get adjusted.

The switchboard was loaded with calls from people who wanted to give blood.

The next morning Ed was conscious but very tired and groggy from ether and morphine. His eyes were washed out and he spoke with great difficulty. But he did repeat his first question.

"How bad is it?"

The doctor who was in the room caught himself just as he was going to say some soothing nonsense, remembering that Ed was his friend and that Ed loved true things and knew a lot of true things too, so the doctor said, "Very bad."

Ed didn't ask again. He hung on for a couple of days because his vitality was very great. In fact he hung on so long that some of the doctors began to believe the things they had said about miracles when they knew such a chance to be nonsense. They noted a stronger heartbeat. They saw improved color in his cheeks below the bandages. Ed hung on so long that some people from the waiting room dared to go home to get some sleep.

And then, as happens so often with men of large vitality, the energy and the color and the pulse and the breathing went away silently and quickly, and he died.

By that time the shock in Monterey had turned to dullness. He was dead and had to be got rid of. People wanted to get rid of him quickly and with dignity so they could think about him and restore him again.

On a small rise not far from the Great Tide Pool near Lighthouse Point there is a small chapel and crematory. Ed's closed coffin was put in that chapel for part of an afternoon.

Naturally no one wanted flowers, but the greatest fear was that someone might say a speech or make a remark about him—good or bad. Luckily it was all over so quickly that the people who ordinarily make speeches were caught unprepared.

A large number of people drifted into the chapel, looked for a few moments at the coffin, and then walked away. No one wanted company. Everyone wanted to be alone. Some went to the beach by the Great Tide Pool and sat in the coarse sand and blindly watched the incoming tide creeping around the rocks and tumbling in over the seaweed.

A kind of anesthesia settled on the people who knew Ed Ricketts.

There was not sorrow really but rather puzzled questions—what are we going to do? how can we rearrange our lives now? Everyone who knew him turned inward. It was a strange thing—quiet and strange. We were lost and could not find ourselves.

It is going to be difficult to write down the things about Ed Ricketts that must be written, hard to separate entities. And anyone who knew him would find it difficult. Maybe some of the events are imagined. And perhaps some very small happenings may have grown out of all proportion in the mind. And then there is the personal impact. I am sure that many people, seeing this account, will be sure to say, "Why, that's not true. That's not the way he was at all. He was this way and this." And the speaker may go on to describe a person this writer did not know at all. But no one who knew him will deny the force and influence of Ed Ricketts. Everyone near him was influenced by him, deeply and permanently. Some he taught how to think, others how to see or hear. Children on the beach he taught how to look for and find beautiful animals in worlds they had not suspected were there at all. He taught everyone without seeming to.

Nearly everyone who knew him has tried to define him. Such things were said of him as "He was half-Christ and half-goat." He was a great teacher and a great lecher—an immortal who loved women. Surely he was an original and his character was unique, but in such a way that everyone was related to him, one in this way and another in some different way. He was gentle but capable of ferocity, small and slight but strong as an ox, loyal and yet untrustworthy, generous but gave little and received much. His thinking was as paradoxical as his life. He thought in mystical terms and hated and distrusted mysticism. He was an individualist who studied colonial animals with satisfaction.

We have all tried to define Ed Ricketts with little success. Perhaps it would be better to put down the mass of material from our memories, anecdotes, quotations, events. Of course some of the things will cancel others, but that is the way he was. The essence lies somewhere. There must be some way of finding it.

Finally there is another reason to put Ed Ricketts down on paper. He will not die. He haunts the people who knew him. He is always present even in the moments when we feel his loss the most.

One night soon after his death a number of us were drinking beer in the laboratory. We laughed and told stories about Ed, and suddenly one of us said in pain, "We'll have to let him go! We'll have to release him and let him go." And that was true not for Ed but for ourselves. We can't keep him, and still he will not go away.

Maybe if I write down everything I can remember about him, that will lay the ghost. It is worth trying anyway. It will have to be true or it can't work. It must be no celebration of his virtues, because, as was said of another man, he had the faults of his virtues. There can be no formula. The simplest and best way will be just to remember—as much as I can.

The statistics on Ed Ricketts would read: Born in Chicago, played in the streets, went to public school, studied biology at the University of Chicago. Opened a small commercial laboratory in Pacific Grove, California. Moved to Cannery Row in Monterey. Degrees—Bachelor of Science only; clubs, none; honors, none. Army service—both World Wars. Killed by a train at the age of fifty-two. Within that frame he went a long way and burned a deep scar.

I was sitting in a dentist's waiting room in New Monterey, hoping the dentist had died. I had a badly aching tooth and not enough money to have a good job done on it. My main hope was that the dentist could stop the ache without charging too much and without finding too many other things wrong.

The door to the slaughterhouse opened and a slight man with a beard came out. I didn't look at him closely because of what he held in his hand, a bloody molar with a surprisingly large piece of jawbone sticking to it. He was cursing gently as he came through the door. He held the reeking relic out to me and said, "Look at that god-damned thing." I was already looking at it. "That came out of me," he said.

"Seems to be more jaw than tooth," I said.

"He got impatient, I guess. I'm Ed Ricketts."

"I'm John Steinbeck. Does it hurt?"

"Not much. I've heard of you."

"I've heard of you, too. Let's have a drink."

That was the first time I ever saw him. I had heard that there was an interesting man in town who ran a commercial laboratory, had a library of good music, and interests wider than invertebratology. I had wanted to come across him for some time.

We did not think of ourselves as poor then. We simply had no money. Our food was fairly plentiful, what with fishing and planning and a minimum of theft. Entertainment had to be improvised without benefit of currency. Our pleasures consisted in conversation, walks, games, and parties with people of our own financial nonexistence. A real party was dressed with a gallon of thirty-nine-cent wine, and we could have a hell of a time on that. We did not know any rich people, and for that reason we did not like them and were proud and glad we didn't live *that* way.

We had been timid about meeting Ed Ricketts because he was rich people by our standards. This meant that he could depend on a hundred to a hundred and fifty dollars a month and he had an automobile. To us this was fancy, and we didn't see how anyone could go through that kind of money. But we learned.

Knowing Ed Ricketts was instant. After the first moment I knew him, and for the next eighteen years I knew him better than I knew anyone, and perhaps I did not know him at all. Maybe it was that way with all of his friends. He was different from anyone and yet so like that everyone found himself in Ed, and that might be one of the reasons his death had such an impact. It wasn't Ed who had died but a large and important part of oneself.

When I first knew him, his laboratory was an old house in Cannery Row which he had bought and transformed to his purposes. The entrance was a kind of showroom with mounted marine specimens in glass jars on shelves around the walls. Next to this room was a small office, where for some reason the rattlesnakes were kept in cages between the safe and the filing cabinets. The top of the safe was piled high with stationery and filing cards. Ed loved paper and cards. He never ordered small amounts but huge supplies of it.

On the side of the building toward the ocean were two more rooms, one with cages for white rats—hundreds of white rats, and reproducing furiously. This room used to get pretty smelly if it was not cleaned with great regularity—which it never was. The other rear room was set up with microscopes and slides and the equipment for making and mounting and baking the delicate microorganisms which were so much a part of the laboratory income. In the basement there was a big stockroom with jars and tanks for preserving the larger animals, and also the equipment for embalming and injecting the cats, dogfish, frogs, and other animals that were used by dissection classes.

This little house was called Pacific Biological Laboratories, Inc., as strange an operation as ever outraged the corporate laws of California. When, after Ed's death, the corporation had to be liquidated, it was impossible to find out who owned the stock, how much of it there was, or what it was worth. Ed kept the most careful collecting notes on record, but sometimes he would not open a business letter for weeks.

How the business ran for twenty years no one knows, but it did run even though it staggered a little sometimes. At times it would spurt ahead with system and efficiency and then wearily collapse for several months. Orders would pile up on the desk. Once during a weary period someone sent Ed a cheesecake by parcel post. He thought it was preserved material of some kind, and when he finally opened it three months later we could not have identified it had it not been that a note was enclosed which said, "Eat this cheesecake at once. It's very delicate."

Often the desk was piled so high with unopened letters that they slid tiredly to the floor. Ed believed completely in the theory that a letter unanswered for a week usually requires no answer, but he went even farther. A letter unopened for a month does not require opening.

Every time some definite statement like that above is set down I think of exceptions. Ed carried on a large and varied correspondence with a number of people. He answered letters quickly and at length, using a typewriter with elite type to save space. The purchase of a typewriter was a long process with him, for much of the type had to be changed from business signs to biologic signs, and he also liked to have some foreign-language signs on his typewriter, tilde for Spanish, accents and cedilla for French, umlaut for German. He rarely used them but he liked to have them.

The days of the laboratory can be split into two periods. The era before the fire and that afterwards. The fire was interesting in many respects.

One night something went wrong with the electric current on the whole waterfront. Where 220 volts were expected and prepared for, something like two thousand volts suddenly came through. Since in the subsequent suits the electric company was found blameless by the courts, this must be set down to an act of God. What happened was that a large part of Cannery Row burst into flames in a moment. By the time Ed awakened, the laboratory was a sheet of fire. He grabbed his typewriter, rushed to the basement, and got his car out just in time, and just before the building was about ready to crash into its own basement. He had no pants but he had transportation and printing. He always admired his choice. The scientific library, accumulated with such patience and some of it irreplaceable, was gone. All the fine equipment, the microscopes, the museum jars, the stock—everything was gone. Besides typewriter and automobile, only one thing was saved.

Ed had a remarkably fine safe. It was so good that he worried for fear some misguided and romantic burglar might think there was something of value in it and, trying to open it, might abuse and injure its beautiful mechanism. Consequently he not only never locked the safe but contrived a wood block so that it could not be locked. Also, he pasted a note above the combination, assuring all persons that the safe was not locked. Then it developed that there was nothing to put in the safe anyway. Thus the safe became the repository of foods which might attract the flies of Cannery Row, and there were clouds of them drawn to the refuse of the fish canneries but willing to come to other foods. And it must be said that no fly was ever able to negotiate the safe.

But to get back to the fire. After the ashes had cooled, there was the safe lying on its side in the basement where it had fallen when the floor above gave way. It must have been an excellent safe, for when we opened it we found half a pineapple pie, a quarter of a pound of Gorgonzola cheese, and an open can of sardines—all of them except the sardines in good condition. The sardines were a little dry. Ed admired that safe and used to refer to it with affection. He would say that if there *had* been valuable things in the safe it would surely have protected them. "Think how delicate Gorgonzola is," he said. "It couldn't have been very hot inside that safe. The cheese is still delicious."

In spite of a great erudition, or perhaps because of it, Ed had some naive qualities. After the fire there were a number of suits against the electric company, based on the theory, later proved wrong, that if the fires were caused by error or negligence on the part of the company, the company should pay for the damage.

Pacific Biological Laboratories, Inc., was one of the plaintiffs in this suit. Ed went over to Superior Court in Salinas to testify. He told the truth as clearly and as fully as he could. He loved true things and believed in them. Then he became fascinated by the trial and the jury and he spent much time in court, inspecting the legal system with the same objective care he would have lavished on a new species of marine animal.

Afterwards he said calmly and with a certain wonder, "You see how easy it is to be completely wrong about a simple matter. It was always my conviction—or better, my impression—that the legal system was designed to arrive at the truth in matters of human and property relationships. You see, I had forgotten or never considered one thing. Each side wants to win, and that factor warps any original intent to the extent that the objective truth of the matter disappears in emphasis. Now you take the case of this fire," he went on. "Both sides wanted to win, and neither had any interest in, indeed both sides seemed to have a kind of abhorrence for, the truth." It was an amazing discovery to him and one that required thinking out. Because he loved true things, he thought everyone did. The fact that it was otherwise did not sadden him. It simply interested him. And he set about rebuilding his laboratory and replacing his books with an antlike methodicalness.

Ed's use of words was unorthodox and, until you knew him, somewhat startling. Once, in getting a catalogue ready, he wanted to advise the trade that he had plenty of hagfish available. Now the hagfish is a most disgusting animal both in appearance and texture, and some of its habits are nauseating. It is a perfect animal horror. But Ed did not feel this, because the hagfish has certain functions which he found fascinating. In his catalogue he wrote, "Available in some quantities, delightful and beautiful hagfish."

He admired worms of all kinds and found them so desirable that, searching around for a pet name for a girl he loved, he called her "Wormy." She was a little huffy until she realized that he was using not the adjective but a diminutive of the noun. His use of this word meant that he found her pretty, interesting, and desirable. But still it always sounded to the girl like an adjective.

Ed loved food, and many of the words he used were eating words. I have heard him refer to a girl, a marine animal, and a plain song as "delicious."

His mind had no horizons. He was interested in everything. And there were very few things he did not like. Perhaps it would be well to set down the things he did not like. Maybe they would be some kind of key to his personality, although it is my conviction that there is no such key.

Chief among his hatreds was old age. He hated it in other people and did not even conceive of it in himself. He hated old women and would not stay in a room with them. He said he could smell them. He had a remarkable sense of smell. He could smell a mouse in a room, and I have seen him locate a rattlesnake in the brush by smell.

He hated women with thin lips. "If the lips are thin—where will there be any fullness?" he would say. His observation was certainly physical and open to verification, and he seemed to believe in its accuracy and so do I, but with less vehemence.

He loved women too much to take any nonsense from the thin-lipped ones. But if a girl with thin lips painted on fuller ones with lipstick, he was satisfied. "Her intentions are correct," he said. "There is a psychic fullness, and sometimes that can be very fine."

He hated hot soup and would pour cold water into the most beautifully prepared bisque.

He unequivocally hated to get his head wet. Collecting animals in the tide pools, he would be soaked by the waves to his eyebrows, but his head was invariably covered and safe. In the shower he wore an oilskin sou'wester—a ridiculous sight.

He hated one professor whom he referred to as "old jingle ballicks." It never developed why he hated "old jingle ballicks."

He hated pain inflicted without good reason. Driving through the streets one night, he saw a man beating a red setter with a rake handle. Ed stopped the car and attacked the man with a monkey wrench and would have killed him if the man had not run away.

Although slight in build, when he was angry Ed had no fear and could be really dangerous. On an occasion one of our cops was pistol-whipping a drunk in the middle of the night. Ed attacked the cop with his bare hands, and his fury was so great that the cop released the drunk.

This hatred was only for reasonless cruelty. When the infliction of pain was necessary, he had little feeling about it. Once during the depression we found we could buy a live sheep for three dollars. This may seem incredible now but it was so. It was a great deal of food and even for those days a great bargain. Then we had the sheep and none of us could kill it. But Ed cut its throat with no emotion whatever, and even explained to the rest of us who were upset that bleeding to death is quite painless if there is no fear involved. The pain of opening a vein is slight if the instrument is sharp, and he had opened the jugular with a scalpel and had not frightened the animal, so that our secondary or empathic pain was probably much greater than that of the sheep.

His feeling for psychic pain in normal people also was philosophic. He would say that nearly everything that can happen to people not only does happen but has happened for a million years. "Therefore," he would say, "for everything that can happen there is a channel or mechanism in the human to take care of it—a channel worn down in prehistory and transmitted in the genes."

He disliked time intensely unless it was part of an observation or an experiment. He was invariably and consciously late for appointments. He said he had once worked for a railroad where his whole life had been regulated by a second hand and that he had then conceived his disgust, a disgust for exactness in time. To my knowledge, that is the only time he ever spoke of the railroad experience. If you asked him to dinner at seven, he might get there at nine. On the other hand, if a good low collecting tide was at 6:53, he would be in the tide pool at 6:52.

The farther I get into this the more apparent it becomes to me that no rule was final. He himself was not conscious of any rules of behavior in himself, although he observed behavior patterns in other people with delight.

For many years he wore a beard, not large, and slightly pointed, which accentuated his half-goat, half-Christ appearance. He had started wearing the beard because some girl he wanted thought he had a weak chin. He didn't have a weak chin, but as long as she thought so he cultivated his beard. This was probably during the period of the prognathous Arrow Collar men in the advertising pages. Many girls later he was still wearing the beard because he was used to it. He kept it until the Army made him shave it off in the Second World War. His beard sometimes caused a disturbance. Small boys often followed Ed, baaing like sheep. He developed a perfect defense against this. He would turn and baa back at them, which invariably so embarrassed the boys that they slipped shyly away.

Ed had a strange and courteous relationship with dogs, although he never owned one or wanted to. Passing a dog on the street, he greeted it with dignity and, when driving, often tipped his hat and smiled and waved at dogs on the sidewalk. And damned if they didn't smile back at him. Cats, on the other hand, did not arouse any enthusiasm in him. However, he always remembered one cat with admiration. It was in the old days before the fire when Ed's father was still alive and doing odd jobs about the laboratory. The cat in question took a dislike to Ed's father and developed a spite tactic which charmed Ed. The cat would climb up on a shelf and pee on Ed's father when he went by—the cat did it not once but many times.

Ed regarded his father with affection. "He has one quality of genius," Ed would say. "He is always wrong. If a man makes a million decisions and judgments at random, it is perhaps mathematically tenable to suppose that he will be right half the time and wrong half the time. But you take my father—he is wrong all of the time about everything. That is a matter not of luck but of selection. That requires genius."

Ed's father was a rather silent, shy, but genial man who took so many aspirins for headaches that he had developed a chronic acetanilide poisoning and the quaint dullness that goes with it. For many years he worked in the basement stockroom, packing specimens to be shipped and even mounting some of the larger and less delicate forms. His chief pride, however, was a human fetus which he had mounted in a museum jar. It was to have been the lone child of a Negress and a Chinese. When the mother succumbed to a lovers' quarrel and a large dose of arsenic administered by person or persons unknown, the autopsy revealed her secret, and her secret was acquired by Pacific Biological. It was much too far advanced to be of much value for study so Ed's father inherited it. He crossed its little legs in a Buddha pose, arranged its hands in an attitude of semi-prayer, and fastened it securely upright in the museum jar. It was rather a startling figure, for while it had negroid features, the preservative had turned it to a pale ivory color. It was Dad Ricketts' great pride. Children and many adults made pilgrimages to the basement to see it. It became famous in Cannery Row.

One day an Italian woman blundered into the basement. Although she did not speak any English, Dad Ricketts naturally thought she had come to see his prize. He showed it to her; whereupon, to his amazement and embarrassment, she instantly undressed to show him her fine scar from a Caesarian section.

Cats were a not inconsiderable source of income to Pacific Biological Laboratories, Inc. They were chloroformed, the blood drained, and embalming fluid and color mass injected in the venous and arterial systems. These finished cats were sold to schools for study of anatomy.

When an order came in for, say, twenty-five cats, there was only one way to get them, since the ASPCA will not allow the raising of cats for laboratory purposes. Ed would circulate the word among the small boys of the neighborhood that twenty-five cents apiece would be paid for cats. It saddened Ed a little to see how venially warped the cat-loving small boys of Monterey were. They sold their own cats, their aunts' cats, their neighbors' cats. For a few days there would be scurrying footsteps and soft thumps as cats in gunny sacks were secretly deposited in the basement. Then guileless and innocent-faced little catacides would collect their quarters and rush for Wing Chong's grocery for pop and cap pistols. No matter what happened, Wing Chong made some small profit.

Once a lady who liked cats very much, if they were the better sort of cats, remarked to Ed, "Of course I realize that these things are necessary. I am very broad-minded. But, thank heaven, you do not get pedigreed cats."

Ed reassured her by saying, "Madam, that's about the only kind I do get. Alley cats are too quick and intelligent. I get the sluggish stupid cats of the rich and indulgent. You can look through the basement and see whether I have yours—yet." That friendship based on broad-mindedness did not flourish.

If there were a complaint and a recognition Ed always gave the cat back. Once two small boys who had obviously read about the oldest cheat in the world worked it twice on Ed before he realized it. One of them sold the cat and collected, the other came in crying and got the cat back. They should have got another cat the third time. If they had been clever and patient they would have made a fortune, but even Ed recognized a bright yellow cat with a broken tail the third time he bought it.

.   .   .   .

Life on Cannery Row was curious and dear and outrageous. Across the street from Pacific Biological was Monterey's largest, most genteel and respected whorehouse. It was owned and operated by a very great woman who was beloved and trusted by all who came in contact with her except those few whose judgment was twisted by a limited virtue. She was a large-hearted woman and a law-abiding citizen in every way except one—she did violate the nebulous laws against prostitution. But since the police didn't seem to care, she felt all right about it and even made little presents in various directions.

During the depression Madam paid the grocery bills for most of the destitute families on Cannery Row. When the Chamber of Commerce collected money for any cause and businessmen were assessed at ten dollars, Madam was always nicked for a hundred. The same was true for any mendicant charity. She halfway paid for the widows and orphans of policemen and firemen. She was expected to and did contribute ten times the ordinary amount toward any civic brainstorm of citizens who pretended she did not exist. Also, she was a wise and tolerant pushover for any hard-luck story. Everyone put the bee on her. Even when she knew it was a fake she dug down.

Ed Ricketts maintained relations of respect and friendliness with Madam. He did not patronize the house. His sex life was far too complicated for that. But Madam brought many of her problems to him, and he gave her the best of his thinking and his knowledge, both scientific and profane.

There seems to be a tendency toward hysteria among girls in such a house. I do not know whether hysterically inclined types enter the business or whether the business produces hysteria. But often Madam would send a girl over to the laboratory to talk to Ed. He would listen with great care and concern to her troubles, which were rarely complicated, and then he would talk soothingly to her and play some of his favorite music to her on his phonograph. The girl usually went back reinforced with his strength. He never moralized in any way. He would be more likely to examine the problem carefully, with calm and clarity, and to lift the horrors out of it by easy examination. Suddenly the girl would discover that she was not alone, that many other people had the same problems—in a word that her misery was not unique. And then she usually felt better about it.

There was a tacit but strong affection between Ed and Madam. She did not have a license to sell liquor to be taken out. Quite often Ed would run out of beer so late at night that everything except Madam's house was closed. There followed a ritual which was thoroughly enjoyed by both parties. Ed would cross the street and ask Madam to sell him some beer. She invariably refused, explaining every time that she did not have a license. Ed would shrug his shoulders, apologize for asking, and go back to the lab. Ten minutes later there would be soft footsteps on the stairs and a little thump in front of the door and then running slippered steps down again. Ed would wait a decent interval and then go to the door. And on his doorstep, in a paper bag, would be six bottles of ice-cold beer. He would never mention it to Madam. That would have been breaking the rules of the game. But he repaid her with hours of his time when she needed his help. And his help was not inconsiderable.

Sometimes, as happens even in the soundest whorehouse, there would be a fight on a Saturday night—one of those things which are likely to occur when love and wine come together. It was only sensible that Madam would not want to bother the police or a doctor with her little problem. Then her good friend Ed would patch up cut faces and torn ears and split mouths. He was a good operator and there were never any complaints. And naturally no one ever mentioned the matter since he was not a doctor of medicine and had no license to practice anything except philanthropy. Madam and Ed had the greatest respect for each other. "She's one hell of a woman," he said. "I wish good people could be as good."

Just as Madam was the target for every tired heist, so Ed was the fall guy for any illicit scheme that could be concocted by the hustling instincts of some of the inhabitants of Cannery Row. The people of the Row really loved Ed, but this affection did not forbid them from subjecting him to any outrageous scheming that occurred to them. In nearly all cases he knew the game before the play had even started and his hand would be in his pocket before the intricate gambit had come to a request. But he would cautiously wait out the pitch before he brought out the money. "It gives them so much pleasure to earn it," he would say.

He never gave much. He never *had* much. But in spite of his wide experience in chicanery, now and then he would be startled into admiration by some particularly audacious or imaginative approach to the problem of a touch.

One evening while he was injecting small dogfish in the basement, one of his well-known clients came to him with a face of joy.

"I am a happy man," the hustler proclaimed, and went on to explain how he had arrived at the true philosophy of rest and pleasure.

"You think I've got nothing, Eddie," the man lectured him. "But you don't know from my simple outsides what I've got inside."

Ed moved restlessly, waiting for the trap.

"I've got peace of mind, Eddie. I've got a place to sleep, not a palace but comfortable. I'm not hungry very often. And best of all I've got friends. I guess I'm gladdest of all for my friends."

Ed braced himself. Here it comes, he thought.

"Why, Ed," the client continued, "some nights I just lay in my bed and thank God for my blessings. What does a man need, Eddie—a few things like food and shelter and a few little tiny vices, like liquor and women—and tobacco—"

Ed could feel it moving in on him. "No liquor," he said.

"I ain't drinking," the client said with dignity, "didn't you hear?"

"How much?" Ed asked.

"Only a dime, Eddie boy. I need a couple of sacks of tobacco. I don't mind using the brown papers on the sacks. I *like* the brown papers."

Ed gave him a quarter. He was delighted. "Where else in the world could you find a man who would lavish care and thought and art and emotion on a lousy dime?" he said. He felt that it had been worth more than a quarter, but he did not tell his client so.

On another occasion Ed was on his way across the street to Wing Chong's grocery for a couple of quarts of beer. Another of his clients was sitting comfortably in the gutter in front of the store. He glanced casually at the empty quart bottles Ed carried in his hand.

"Say Doc," he said, "I'm having a little trouble peeing. What's a good diuretic?"

Ed fell into that hole. "I never needed to think beyond beer," he said.

The man looked at the bottles in Ed's hand and raised his shoulders in a gesture of helplessness. And only then did Ed realize that he had been had. "Oh, come on in," he said, and he bought beer for both of them.

Afterward he said admiringly, "Can you imagine the trouble he went to for that beer? He had to look up the word diuretic, and then he had to plan to be there just when I went over for beer. And he had to read my mind quite a bit. If any part of his plan failed, it all failed. I think it is remarkable."

The only part of it that was not remarkable was planning to be there when Ed went for beer. He went for beer pretty often. Sometimes when he overbought and the beer got warm, he took it back and Wing Chong exchanged it for cold beer.

The various hustlers who lived by their wits and some work in the canneries when they had time were an amazing crew. Ed never got over his admiration for them.

"They have worked out my personality and my resistances to a fine mathematical point," he would say. "They know me better than I know myself, and I am not uncomplicated. Over and over, their analysis of my possible reaction is accurate."

He was usually delighted when one of these minor triumphs took place. It never cost him much. He always tried to figure out in advance what the attack on his pocket would be. At least he always knew the end. Every now and then the audacity and freedom of thought and invention of his loving enemy would leave him with a sense of wonder.

Now and then he hired some of the boys to collect animals for him and paid them a fixed price, so much for frogs, so much for snakes or cats.

One of his collectors we will call Al. That was not his name. An early experience with Al gave Ed a liking for his inventiveness. Ed needed cats and needed them quickly. And Al got them and got them quickly—all fine mature cats and, only at the end of the operation did Ed discover, all tomcats. For a long time Al held out his method but finally he divulged it in secret. Since Al has long since gone to his maker and will need no more cats, his secret can be told.

"I made a double trap," he said, "a little cage inside a big cage. Then in the little cage I put a nice lady cat in a loving condition. And, Eddie, sometimes I'd catch as many as ten tomcats in one night. Why, hell, Ed, that exact same kind of trap catches me every Saturday night. That's where I got the idea."

Al was such a good collector that after a while he began to do odd jobs around the lab. Ed taught him to inject dogfish and to work the ball mill for mixing color mass and to preserve some of the less delicate animals. Al became inordinately proud of his work and began to use a mispronounced scientific vocabulary and put on a professorial air that delighted Ed. He got to trusting Al although he knew Al's persistent alcoholic history.

Once when a large number of dogfish came in Ed left them for Al to inject while he went to a party. It was a late party. Ed returned to find all the lights on in the basement. The place was a wreck. Broken glass littered the floor, a barrel of formaldehyde was tipped over and spilled, museum jars were stripped from the shelves and broken. A whirlwind had gone through. Al was not there but Al's pants were, and also an automobile seat which was never explained.

In a white fury Ed began to sweep up the broken glass. He was well along when Al entered, wearing a long overcoat and a pair of high rubber boots. Ed's rage was terrible. He advanced on Al.

"You son of a bitch!" he cried. "I should think you could stay sober until you finished work!"

Al held up his hand with senatorial dignity. "You go right ahead, Eddie," he said. "You call me anything you want, and I forgive you."

"Forgive me?" Ed screamed. He was near to murder.

Al silenced him with a sad and superior gesture. "I deserve it, Eddie," he said. "Go ahead—call me lots of names. I only regret that they will not hurt my feelings."

"What in hell are you talking about?" Ed demanded uneasily.

Al turned and parted the tails of his overcoat. He was completely naked except for the rubber boots.

"Eddie boy," he said, "I have been out calling socially in this condition. Now, Eddie, if I could do that, I must be pretty insensitive. Nothing you can call me is likely to get under my thick skin. And I forgive you."

Ed's anger disappeared in pure wonder. And afterward he said, "If that Al had turned the pure genius of his unique mind to fields other than cadging drinks, there is no limit to what he might have done." And then he continued, "But no. He has chosen a difficult and crowded field and he is a success in it. Any other career, international banking for instance, might have been too easy for Al."

Al was married, but his wife and family did not exercise a restraining influence on him. His wife finally used the expedient of putting Al in jail when he was on one of his beauties.

Al said one time, "When they hire a new cop in Monterey they give him a test. They send him down Cannery Row, and if he can't pick me up he don't get the job."

Al detested the old red stone Salinas jail. It was gloomy and unsanitary, he said. But then the county built a beautiful new jail, and the first time Al made sixty days he was gone seventy-five. He came back to Monterey enthusiastic.

"Eddie," he said, "they got radios in the cells. And that new sheriff's a pushover at euchre. When my time was up the sheriff owed me eighty-six bucks. I couldn't run out on the game. A sheriff can make it tough on a man. It took me fifteen days to lose it back so it wouldn't look too obvious. But you can't win from a sheriff, Eddie—not if you expect to go back."

Al went back often until his wife finally tumbled to the fact that Al preferred jail to home life. She visited Ed for advice. She was a red-eyed, unkempt little woman with a runny nose.

"I work hard and try to make ends meet," she said bitterly. "And all the time Al's over in Salinas taking his ease in the new jail. I can't let him go to jail anymore. He likes it." She was all frayed from having Al's children and supporting them.

For once Ed had no answer. "I don't know what you can do," he said. "I'm stumped. You could kill him—but then you wouldn't have any fun anymore."

This account of Ed Ricketts goes seesawing back and forth chronologically and in every other way. I did not intend when I started to departmentalize him, but now that seems to be a good method. He was so complex and many-faceted that perhaps the best method will be to go from one facet of him to another so that from all the bits a whole picture may build itself for me as well as for others.

Ed had more fun than nearly anyone I have ever known, and he had deep sorrows also, which will be treated later. As long as we are on the subject of drinking I will complete that department.

Ed loved to drink, and he loved to drink just about anything. I don't think I ever saw him in the state called drunkenness, but twice he told me he had no memory of getting home to the laboratory at all. And even on those nights one would have had to know him well to be aware that he was affected at all. Evidences of drinking were subtle. He smiled a little more broadly. His voice became a little higher in pitch, and he would dance a few steps on tiptoe, a curious pigeon-footed mouse step. He liked every drink that contained alcohol and, except for coffee, which he often laced with whisky, he disliked every drink that did not contain alcohol. He once estimated that it had been twelve years since he had tasted water without some benign addition.

At one time when bad teeth and a troublesome love affair were running concurrently, he got a series of stomachaches which were diagnosed as a developing ulcer. The doctor put him on a milk diet and ordered him off all alcohol. A sullen sadness fell on the laboratory. It was a horrid time. For a few days Ed was in a state of dismayed shock. Then his anger rose at the cruelty of a fate that could do this to him. He merely disliked and distrusted water, but he had an active and fierce hatred for milk. He found the color unpleasant and the taste ugly. He detested its connotations.

For a few days he forced a little milk into his stomach, complaining bitterly the while, and then he went back to see the doctor. He explained his dislike for the taste of milk, giving as its basis some pre-memory shock amounting to a trauma. He thought this dislike for milk might have driven him into the field of marine biology since no marine animals but whales and their family of sea cows give milk and he had never had the least interest in any of the Cetaceans. He said that he was afraid the cure for his stomachaches was worse than the disease and finally he asked if it would be all right to add a few drops of aged rum to the milk just to kill its ugly taste. The doctor perhaps knew he was fighting a losing battle. He gave in on the few drops of rum.

We watched the cure with fascination as day by day the ratio changed until at the end of a month Ed was adding a few drops of milk to the rum. But his stomachaches had disappeared. He never liked milk, but after this he always spoke of it with admiration as a specific for ulcers.

There were great parties at the laboratory, some of which went on for days. There would come a time in our poverty when we needed a party. Then we would gather together the spare pennies. It didn't take very many of them. There was a wine sold in Monterey for thirty-nine cents a gallon. It was not a delicate-tasting wine and sometimes curious things were found in the sludge on the bottom of the jug, but it was adequate. It added a gaiety to a party and it never killed anyone. If four couples got together and each brought a gallon, the party could go on for some time and toward the end of it Ed would be smiling and doing his tippy-toe mouse dance.

Later, when we were not so poor, we drank beer or, as Ed preferred it, a sip of whisky and a gulp of beer. The flavors, he said, complemented each other.

Once on my birthday there was a party at the laboratory that lasted four days. We really needed a party. It was fairly large, and no one went to bed except for romantic purposes. Early in the morning at the end of the fourth day a benign exhaustion had settled on the happy group. We spoke in whispers because our vocal cords had long since been burned out in song.

Ed carefully placed half a quart of beer on the floor beside his bed and sank back for a nap. In a moment he was asleep. He had consumed perhaps five gallons since the beginning of the party. He slept for about twenty minutes, then stirred, and without opening his eyes groped with his hand for the beer bottle. He found it, sat up, and took a deep drink of it. He smiled sweetly and waved two fingers in the air in a kind of benediction.

"There's nothing like that first taste of beer," he said.

Not only did Ed love liquor. He went further. He had a deep suspicion of anyone who did not. If a nondrinker shut up and minded his own business and did not make an issue of his failing, Ed could be kind to him. But alas, a laissez-faire attitude is very uncommon in teetotalers. The moment one began to spread his poison Ed experienced a searing flame of scorn and rage. He believed that anyone who did not like to drink was either sick and/or crazy or had in him some obscure viciousness. He believed that the soul of a nondrinker was dried-up and shrunken, that the virtuous pose of the nondrinker was a cover for some nameless and disgusting practice.

He had somewhat the same feeling for those who did not or pretended they did not love sex, but this field will be explored later.

If pressed, Ed would name you the great men, great minds, great hearts and imaginations in the history of the world, and he could not discover one of them who was a teetotaler. He would even try to recall one single man or woman of much ability who did not drink and like liquor, and he could never light on a single name. In all such discussions the name of Shaw was offered, and in answer Ed would simply laugh, but in his laughter there would be no admiration for that abstemious old gentleman.

Ed's interest in music was passionate and profound. He thought of it as deeply akin to creative mathematics. His taste in music was not strange but very logical. He loved the chants of the Gregorian mode and the whole library of the plainsong with their angelic intricacies. He loved the masses of William Byrd and Palestrina. He listened raptly to Buxtehude, and he once told me that he thought the *Art of the Fugue* of Bach might be the greatest of all music up to our time. Always "up to our time." He never considered anything finished or completed but always continuing, one thing growing on and out of another. It is probable that his critical method was the outgrowth of his biologic training and observation.

He loved the secular passion of Monteverde, and the sharpness of Scarlatti. His was a very broad appreciation and a curiosity that dug for music as he dug for his delicious worms in a mud flat. He listened to music with his mouth open as though he wanted to receive the tones even in his throat. His forefinger moved secretly at his side in rhythm.

He could not sing, could not carry a tune or reproduce a true note with his voice, but he could hear true notes. It was a matter of sorrow to him that he could not sing.

Once we bought sets of tuning forks and set them in rubber to try to reteach ourselves the forgotten mathematical scale. And Ed's ear was very aware in recognition although he could not make his voice come even near to imitating the pitch. I never heard him whistle. I wonder whether he could. He would try to hum melodies, stumbling over the notes, and then he would smile helplessly when his ear told him how badly he was doing it.

He thought of music as something incomparably concrete and dear. Once, when I had suffered an overwhelming emotional upset, I went to the laboratory to stay with him. I was dull and speechless with shock and pain. He used music on me like medicine. Late in the night when he should have been asleep, he played music for me on his great phonograph—even when I was asleep he played it, knowing that its soothing would get into my dark confusion. He played the curing and reassuring plainsongs, remote and cool and separate, and then gradually he played the sure patterns of Bach, until I was ready for more personal thought and feeling again, until I could bear to come back to myself. And when that time came, he gave me Mozart. I think it was as careful and loving medication as has ever been administered.

Ed's reading was very broad. Of course he read greatly in his own field of marine invertebratology. But he read hugely otherwise. I do not know where he found the time. I can judge his liking only by the things he went back to—translations of Li Po and Tu Fu, that greatest of all love poetry, the *Black Marigolds*—and *Faust*, most of all *Faust*. Just as he thought the *Art of the Fugue* might be the greatest music up to our time, he considered *Faust* the greatest writing that had been done. He enlarged his scientific German so that he could read Faust and hear the sounds of the words as they were written and taste their meanings. Ed's mind seems to me to have been a timeless mind, not modern and not ancient. He loved to read Layamon aloud and Beowulf, making the words sound as fresh as though they had been written yesterday.

He had no religion in the sense of creed or dogma. In fact he distrusted all formal religions, suspecting them of having been fouled with economics and power and politics. He did not believe in any God as recognized by any group or cult. Probably his God could have been expressed by the mathematical symbol for an expanding universe. Surely he did not believe in an afterlife in any sense other than chemical. He was suspicious of promises of an afterlife, believing them to be sops to our fear or hope artificially supplied.

.   .   .   .

Very many conclusions Ed and I worked out together through endless discussion and reading and observation and experiment. We worked together, and so closely that I do not now know in some cases who started which line of speculation since the end thought was the product of both minds. I do not know whose thought it was.

We had a game which we playfully called speculative metaphysics. It was a sport consisting of lopping off a piece of observed reality and letting it move up through the speculative process like a tree growing tall and bushy. We observed with pleasure how the branches of thought grew away from the trunk of external reality. We believed, as we must, that the laws of thought parallel the laws of things. In our game there was no stricture of rightness. It was an enjoyable exercise on the instruments of our minds, improvisations and variations on a theme, and it gave the same delight and interest that discovered music does. No one can say, "This music is the only music," nor would we say, "This thought is the only thought," but rather, "This is a thought, perhaps well or ill formed, but a thought which is a real thing in nature."

Once a theme was established we subjected observable nature to it. The following is an example of our game—one developed quite a long time ago.

We thought that perhaps our species thrives best and most creatively in a state of semi-anarchy, governed by loose rules and half-practiced mores. To this we added the premise that over-integration in human groups might parallel the law in paleontology that over-armor or over-ornamentation are symptoms of decay and disappearance. Indeed, we thought, over-integration *might be* the symptom of human decay. We thought: there is no creative unit in the human save the individual working alone. In pure creativeness, in art, in music, in mathematics, there are no true collaborations. The creative principle is a lonely and an individual matter. Groups can correlate, investigate, and build, but we could not think of any group that has ever created or invented anything. Indeed, the first impulse of the group seems to be to destroy the creation and the creator. But integration, or the designed group, seems to be highly vulnerable.

Now with this structure of speculation we would slip examples on the squares of the speculative graphing paper.

Consider, we would say, the Third Reich or the Politburo-controlled Soviet. The sudden removal of twenty-five key men from either system could cripple it so thoroughly that it would take a long time to recover, if it ever could. To preserve itself in safety such a system must destroy or remove all opposition as a danger to itself. But opposition is creative and restriction is noncreative. The force that feeds growth is therefore cut off. Now, the tendency to integration must constantly increase. And this process of integration must destroy all tendencies toward improvisation, must destroy the habit of creation, since this is sand in the bearings of the system. The system then must, if our speculation is accurate, grind to a slow and heavy stop. Thought and art must be forced to disappear and a weighty traditionalism take its place. Thus we would play with thinking. A too greatly integrated system or society is in danger of destruction since the removal of one unit may cripple the whole.

Consider the blundering anarchic system of the United States, the stupidity of some of its lawmakers, the violent reaction, the slowness of its ability to change. Twenty-five key men destroyed could make the Soviet Union stagger, but we could lose our Congress, our President, and our general staff and nothing much would have happened. We would go right on. In fact we might be better for it.

That is an example of the game we played. Always our thinking was prefaced with "It might be so!" Often a whole night would draw down to a moment while we pursued the fireflies of our thinking.

. . . .

Ed's scientific notebooks were very interesting. Among his collecting notes and zoological observations there would be the most outspoken and indelicate observation from another kind of collecting. After his death I had to go through these notebooks before turning them over to Hopkins Marine Station, a branch of Stanford University, as Ed's will directed. I was sorry I had to remove a number, a great number, of the entries from the notebooks. I did not do this because they lacked interest, but it occurred to me that a student delving into Ed's notes for information on invertebratology could emerge with blackmail material on half the female population of Monterey. Ed simply had no reticence about such things. I removed the notes but did not destroy them. They have an interest, I think, above the personalities mentioned. In some future time the women involved may lovingly remember the incidents.

In the back of his car Ed carried an ancient blanket that once had been red but that had faded to a salmon pink from use and exposure. It was a battle-scarred old blanket, veteran of many spreadings on hill and beach. Grass seeds and bits of seaweed were pounded and absorbed into the wool itself. I do not think Ed would have started his car in the evening without his blanket in the back seat.

Before love struck and roiled his vision like a stirred pool, Ed had a fine and appraising eye for a woman. He would note with enthusiasm a well-lipped mouth, a swelling breast, a firm yet cushioned bottom, but he also inquired into other subtleties—the padded thumb, shape of foot, length and structure of finger and toe, plump-lobed ear and angle of teeth, thigh and set of hip and movement in walking too. He regarded these things with joy and thanksgiving. He always was pleased that love and women were what they were or what he imagined them.

But for all of Ed's pleasures and honesties there was a transcendent sadness in his love—something he missed or wanted, a searching that sometimes approached panic. I don't know what it was he wanted that was never there, but I know he always looked for it and never found it. He sought for it and listened for it and looked for it and smelled for it in love. I think he found some of it in music. It was like a deep and endless nostalgia—a thirst and passion for "going home."

He was walled off a little, so that he worked at his philosophy of "breaking through," of coming out through the back of the mirror into some kind of reality which would make the day world dreamlike. This thought obsessed him. He found the symbols of "breaking through" in *Faust*, in Gregorian music, and in the sad, drunken poetry of Li Po. Of the *Art of the Fugue* he would say, "Bach nearly made it. Hear now how close he comes, and hear his anger when he cannot. Every time I hear it

I believe that this time he will come crashing through into the light. And he never does—not quite."

And of course it was he himself who wanted so desperately to break through into the light.

We worked and thought together very closely for a number of years so that I grew to depend on his knowledge and on his patience in research. And then I went away to another part of the country but it didn't make any difference. Once a week or once a month would come a fine long letter so much in the style of his speech that I could hear his voice over the neat page full of small elite type. It was as though I hadn't been away at all. And sometimes now when the postman comes I look before I think for that small type on an envelope.

Ed was deeply pleased with the little voyage which is described in the latter part of this book [*The Log from the "Sea of Cortez"*], and he was pleased with the manner of setting it down. Often he would read it to remember a mood or a joke.

His scientific interest was essentially ecological and holistic. His mind always tried to enlarge the smallest picture. I remember his saying, "You know, at first view you would think the rattlesnake and the kangaroo rat were the greatest of enemies since the snake hunts and feeds on the rat. But in a larger sense they must be the best of friends. The rat feeds the snake and the snake selects out the slow and weak and generally thins the rat people so that both species can survive. It is quite possible that neither species could exist without the other." He was pleased with commensal animals, particularly with groups of several species contributing to the survival of all. He seemed as pleased with such things as though they had been created for him.

With any new food or animal he looked, felt, smelled, and tasted. Once in a tide pool we were discussing the interesting fact that nudibranchs, although beautiful and brightly colored and tasty-looking and soft and unweaponed, are never eaten by other animals which should have found them irresistible. He reached underwater and picked up a lovely orange-colored nudibranch and put it in his mouth. And instantly he made a horrible face and spat and retched, but he had found out why fishes let these living tidbits completely alone.

On another occasion he tasted a species of free-swimming anemone and got his tongue so badly stung by its nettle cells that he could hardly close his mouth for twenty-four hours. But he would have done the same thing the next day if he had wanted to know.

Although small and rather slight, Ed was capable of prodigies of strength and endurance. He could drive for many hours to arrive at a good collecting ground for a favorable low tide, then work like a fury turning over rocks while the tide was out, then drive back to preserve his catch. He could carry heavy burdens over soft and unstable sand with no show of weariness. He had enormous resistance. It took a train to kill him. I think nothing less could have done it.

His sense of smell was very highly developed. He smelled all food before he ate it, not only the whole dish but each forkful. He invariably smelled each animal as he took it from the tide pool. He spoke of the smells of different animals, and some moods and even thoughts had characteristic odors to him—undoubtedly conditioned by some experience good or bad. He referred often to the smells of people, how individual each one was, and how it was subject to change. He delighted in his sense of smell in love.

With his delicate olfactory equipment, one would have thought that he would be disgusted by so-called ugly odors, but this was not true. He could pick over decayed tissue or lean close to the fetid viscera of a cat with no repulsion. I have seen him literally crawl into the carcass of a basking shark to take its liver in the dark of its own body so that no light might touch it. And this is as horrid an odor as I know.

Ed loved fine tools and instruments, and conversely he had a bitter dislike for bad ones. Often he spoke with contempt of "consumer goods"—things made to catch the eye, to delight the first impression with paint and polish, things made to sell rather than to use. On the other hand, the honest workmanship of a good microscope gave him great pleasure. Once I brought him from Sweden a set of the finest scalpels, surgical scissors, and delicate forceps. I remember his joy in them.

His laboratory practice was immaculate and his living quarters were not clean. It was his custom to say that most people paid too much for things they didn't really want, paid too much in effort and time and thought. "If a swept floor gives you enough pleasure and reward to pay for sweeping it, then sweep it," he said. "But if you do not see it dirty or clean, then it is paying too much to sweep it."

I think he set down his whole code or procedure once in a time of stress. He found himself quite poor and with three children to take care of. In a very scholarly manner, he told the children how they must proceed.

"We must remember three things," he said to them. "I will tell them to you in the order of their importance. Number one and first in importance, we must have as much fun as we can with what we have. Number two, we must eat as well as we can, because if we don't we won't have the health and strength to have as much fun as we might. And number three and third and last in importance, we must keep the house reasonably in order, wash the dishes, and such things. But we will not let the last interfere with the other two."

Ed's feeling for clothes was interesting. He wore Bass moccasins, buckskin-colored and quite expensive. He loved thick soft wool socks and wool shirts that would scratch the hell out of anyone else. But outside of those he had no interest. His clothing was fairly ragged, particularly at elbows and knees. He had one necktie hanging in his closet, a wrinkled old devil of a yellow tint, but no one ever saw him wear it. His clothes he just came by, and the coats were not likely to fit him at all. He was not in the least embarrassed by his clothes. He went everywhere in the same costume. And always he seemed strangely neat. Such was his sense of inner security that he did not seem ill dressed. Often people around him appeared overdressed. The only time he ever wore a hat was when there was some chance of getting his head wet, and then it was likely to be an oilskin sou'wester. But whatever else he wore or did not wear, there was invariably pinned to his shirt pocket a twenty-power Bausch and Lomb magnifying glass on a little roller chain. He used the glass constantly. It was a very close part of him—one of his techniques of seeing.

Always the paradox is there. He loved nice things and did not care about them. He loved to bathe and yet when the water heater in the laboratory broke down he bathed in cold water for over a year before he got around to having it fixed. I finally mended his leaking toilet tank with a piece of chewing gum which I imagine is still there. A broken window was stuffed with newspaper for several years and never was repaired.

He liked comfort and the chairs in the lab were stiff and miserable. His bed was a redwood box laced with hemp rope on which a thin mattress was thrown. And this bed was not big enough for two. Ladies complained bitterly about his bed, which was not only narrow and uncomfortable but gave out shrieks of protest at the slightest movement.

I used the laboratory and Ed himself in a book called *Cannery Row*. I took it to him in typescript to see whether he would resent it and to offer to make any changes he would suggest. He read it through carefully, smiling, and when he had finished he said, "Let it go that way. It is written in kindness. Such a thing can't be bad."

But it was bad in several ways neither of us foresaw. As the book began to be read, tourists began coming to the laboratory, first a few and then in droves. People stopped their cars and stared at Ed with that glassy look that is used on movie stars. Hundreds of people came into the lab to ask questions and peer around. It became a nuisance to him. But in a way he liked it too. For as he said, "Some of the callers were women and some of the women were very nice-looking." However, he was glad when the little flurry of publicity or notoriety was over.

It never occurred to me to ask Ed much about his family background or his life as a boy. I suppose it would be easy to find out. When he was alive there were too many other things to talk about, and now—it doesn't matter. Of course I have heard him asked the usual question about his name. Ricketts. He said, "No, I was not named after the disease—one of my relatives is responsible for its naming."

When the book *Studs Lonigan* came out, Ed read it twice very quickly. "This is a true book," he said. "I was born and grew up in this part of Chicago. I played in these streets. I know them all. I know the people. This is a true book." And, of course, to Ed a thing that was true was beautiful. He followed the whole series of Farrell's books after that and only after the locale moved to New York did he lose interest. He did not know true things about New York.

. . . .

I became associated in the business of the laboratory in the simplest of ways. A number of years ago Ed had gradually got into debt until the interest on his loan from the bank was bleeding the laboratory like a cat in the basement. Rather sadly he prepared to liquidate the little business and give up his independence—the right to sleep late and work late, the right to make his own decisions. While the lab was not run efficiently, it could make enough to support him, but it could not also pay the bank interest.

At that time I had some money put away and I took up the bank loans and lowered the interest to a vanishing point. I knew the money would vanish anyway. To secure the loan I received stock in the corporation—the most beautiful stock, and the mortgage on the property. I didn't understand much of the transaction but it allowed the laboratory to operate for another ten years. Thus I became a partner in the improbable business. I must say I brought no efficiency to bear on it. The fact that the institution survived at all is a matter that must be put down to magic. I can find no other reasonable explanation. It had no right to survive. A board of directors' meeting differed from any other party only in that there was more beer. A stern business discussion had a way of slipping into a consideration of a unified field hypothesis.

Our trip to the Gulf of Lower California was a marvel of bumbling efficiency. We went where we intended, got what we wanted, and did the work on it. It had been our intention to continue the work with a survey of the Aleutian chain of islands when the war closed that area to us.

At the time of Ed's death our plans were completed, tickets bought, containers and collecting equipment ready for a long collecting trip to the Queen Charlotte Islands, which reach so deep into the Pacific Ocean. There was one deep bay with a long and narrow opening where we thought we might observe some changes in animal forms due to a specialized life and a long period of isolation. Ed was to have started within a month and I was to have joined him there. Maybe someone else will study that little island sea. The light has gone out of it for me.

Now I am coming near to the close of this account. I have not put down Ed's relations with his wives or with his three children. There isn't time, and besides I did not know much about these things.

As I have said, no one who knew Ed will be satisfied with this account. They will have known innumerable other Eds. I imagine that there were as many Eds as there were friends of Ed. And I wonder whether there can be any parallel thinking on his nature and the reason for his impact on the people who knew him. I wonder whether I can make any kind of generalization that would be satisfactory.

I have tried to isolate and inspect the great talent that was in Ed Ricketts, that made him so loved and needed and makes him so missed now that he is dead. Certainly he was an interesting and charming man, but there was some other quality which far exceeded these. I have thought that it might be his ability to receive, to receive anything from anyone, to receive gracefully and thankfully and to make the gift seem very fine. Because of this everyone felt good in giving to Ed—a present, a thought, anything.

Perhaps the most overrated virtue in our list of shoddy virtues is that of giving. Giving builds up the ego of the giver, makes him superior and higher and larger than the receiver. Nearly always, giving is a selfish pleasure, and in many cases it is a downright destructive and evil thing. One has only to remember some of our wolfish financiers who spend two-thirds of their lives clawing fortunes out of the guts of society and the latter third pushing it back. It is not enough to suppose that their philanthropy is a kind of frightened restitution, or that their natures change when they have enough. Such a nature never has enough and natures do not change that readily. I think that the impulse is the same in both cases. For giving can bring the same sense of superiority as getting does, and philanthropy may be another kind of spiritual avarice.

It is so easy to give, so exquisitely rewarding. Receiving, on the other hand, if it be well done, requires a fine balance of self-knowledge and kindness. It requires humility and tact and great understanding of relationships. In receiving you cannot appear, even to yourself, better or stronger or wiser than the giver, although you must be wiser to do it well.

It requires a self-esteem to receive—not self-love but just a pleasant acquaintance and liking for oneself.

Once Ed said to me, "For a very long time I didn't like myself." It was not said in self-pity but simply as an unfortunate fact. "It was a very difficult time," he said, "and very painful. I did not like myself for a number of reasons, some of them valid and some of them pure fancy. I would hate to have to go back to that. Then gradually," he said, "I discovered with surprise and pleasure that a number of people did like me. And I thought, if they can like me, why cannot I like myself? Just thinking it did not do it, but slowly I learned to like myself and then it was all right."

This was not said in self-love in its bad connotation but in self-knowledge. He meant literally that he had learned to accept and like the person "Ed" as he liked other people. It gave him a great advantage. Most people do not like themselves at all. They distrust themselves, put on masks and pomposities. They quarrel and boast and pretend and are jealous because they do not like themselves. But mostly they do not even know themselves well enough to form a true liking. They cannot see themselves well enough to form a true liking, and since we automatically fear and dislike strangers, we fear and dislike our stranger-selves.

Once Ed was able to like himself he was released from the secret prison of self-contempt. Then he did not have to prove superiority any more by any of the ordinary methods, including giving. He could receive and understand and be truly glad, not competitively glad.

Ed's gift for receiving made him a great teacher. Children brought shells to him and gave him information about the shells. And they had to learn before they could tell him.

In conversation you found yourself telling him things—thoughts, conjectures, hypotheses—and you found a pleased surprise at yourself for having arrived at something you were not aware that you could think or know. It gave you such a good sense of participation with him that you could present him with this wonder.

Then Ed would say, "Yes, that's so. That's the way it might be and besides—" and he would illuminate it but not so that he took it away from you. He simply accepted it.

Although his creativeness lay in receiving, that does not mean that he kept things as property. When you had something from him it was not something that was his that he tore away from himself. When you had a thought from him or a piece of music or twenty dollars or a steak dinner, it was not his—it was yours already, and his was only the head and hand that steadied it in position toward you. For this reason no one was ever cut off from him. Association with him was deep participation with him, never competition.

I wish we could all be so. If we could learn even a little to like our-selves, maybe our cruelties and angers might melt away. Maybe we would not have to hurt one another just to keep our ego-chins above water.

There it is. That's all I can set down about Ed Ricketts. I don't know whether any clear picture has emerged. Thinking back and remember-ing has not done what I hoped it might. It has not laid the ghost.

The picture that remains is a haunting one. It is the time just before dusk. I can see Ed finishing his work in the laboratory. He covers his in-struments and puts his papers away. He rolls down the sleeves of his wool shirt and puts on his old brown coat. I see him go out and get in his beat-up old car and slowly drive away in the evening.

I guess I'll have that with me all my life.

Ernie Pyle

I T'S A HARD THING to write about a dead man who doesn't seem dead to you. Ernie Pyle didn't want to go back to the war. When he left France, he set down his disgust and fear and weariness. He thought he could rest a little, but he couldn't. People told him what to do and what he should do. He could have overcome that but he couldn't overcome his own sense of responsibility. He had become identified with every soldier in the army. Ernie died every time a man was killed, and his little body shriveled every time a man was wounded. He'd done it so often, it is probable that his own death was just a repetition. In Africa he said, "The percentage is pulling down on me. You stand in the line of fire long enough and you're going to get hit. It's in the figures." And after that he went through Italy and France. And his percentage grew smaller and smaller. In San Francisco before he went to the Pacific he seemed a little numb. The rest hadn't rested him. His eyes were deep and tired and restless. He sat with a glass of whiskey in his hand and his jaw muscles were tight. He looked sick. The phone rang all the time. He must speak, he must write this and this. And he was utterly weary. "I don't know why I have to go back but I do," he said. "It's my business." He was wearing a new uniform and cap. "These are a waste of money," he said, "I won't need them." His percentage had disappeared and he knew it. And he didn't resent it. He had done everything else with the soldiers except this last thing. "I don't know whether I can write anymore," he said. "I thought I'd get rested but I didn't. Anyway, it will be warm in the Philippines." He had made his usual neat arrangements—old friends, written to or telephoned. Gifts sent or delivered. He was always like that. When he got back from France, he came in excitedly with a scarf. "A real French silk handkerchief. I bought it in Paris right after the city was taken." The scarf was bad rayon. The French salesman had started early. "It's beautiful, Ernie."

"There was a soldier with only one leg, on the hospital ship," Ernie said. "He was hopping about like a cricket—up and down stairs. It was wonderful. I can't stand hurt men," he said. "I'm going to Albuquerque and forget the whole damn thing. There's nothing to write about. It's the same thing over and over. I'm through. Maybe I'll start going around the country the way I used to.

"It's just piled up dead men," he said, "millions of them. And it's crazy because the war is over. They can't win. All they can do is kill more people. Jesus I'm tired." Then he saw the President and Stevenson and Forrestal and lots of congressmen. Everyone expected him to go back. Everyone except Ernie thought Ernie was imperishable. But he knew his time was up. It's in his letters and in his last articles. He was so tired and disgusted that he almost welcomed it. In the San Francisco Hotel he poured himself a good stiff drink. "Got to go now," he said. "They're going to give me some new shots. I'm half blood and half serum already." He went out of the hotel and a woman shouted—"There's Ernie Pyle!" A crowd collected about him and he worked his way slowly through the milling group—a tired little man with his percentage all run out—going to toss his carcass on the great heap.

Tom Collins

THE FIRST TIME I saw Windsor Drake it was evening, and it was raining. I drove into the migrant camp, the wheels of my car throwing muddy water. The lines of sodden, dripping tents stretched away from me in the darkness. The temporary office was crowded with damp men and women, just standing under a roof, and sitting at a littered table was Windsor Drake, a little man in a damp, frayed white suit. The crowding people looked at him all the time. Just stood and looked at him. He had a small moustache, his graying, black hair stood up on his head like the quills of a frightened porcupine, and his large, dark eyes, tired beyond sleepiness, the kind of tired that won't let you sleep even if you have the time and a bed.

I had a letter to Windsor Drake. It was passed on to him by the crowding people, since moving through them was out of the question. He read the letter, stood up and said, "Let's go to my shack and make some coffee."

The crowd parted and let him through, and we walked through the rain to his little shack. The coffee got made all right, but never quite drunk, for reports began coming in from the dripping tents. There was an epidemic in the camp,—in the muddy, flooded camp. In that camp of two thousand souls, every kind of winter disease had developed; measles and whooping cough; mumps; pneumonia and throat infections. And this little man was trying to do everything. He had to. There was no one else but the people in the camp. Even if they wanted to help they couldn't for want of knowledge.

We tried to drink the coffee. A man ran up. Riot in the sewing room. Over we splashed. The sewing room was the measles room. Forty speckled children lying on blankets on the floor. Cloth tacked over the windows to protect children's eyes from the daylight. In the doorway, a huge, bare-armed woman stood, while a little assault developed in the mud in front of her. She had instructions from Windsor to keep uninfected visitors out and she was doing it to the outrage of families and neighbors who always visited with sick people. The riot was settled, infections explained. We went back to our coffee, reheated it, poured the cups full. But hell broke loose in a sanitary unit. A new-come woman, contrary to regulations, was standing on the toilet seat besieged by a furious group of women who only recently learned not to stand on the seats. And Windsor Drake settled that.

We went back to our coffee, heated it again. And all evening it went on. A man beat his wife. New children came down with the measles and had to be separated from their parents and taken to the sewing room. Nerves were on edge in the pouring rain. Fights started out of nothing and sometimes ended bloodily. And Windsor Drake trotted back and forth explaining, coaxing, now and then threatening, trying to keep peace in the miserable, wet slum until daylight should come. His white trousers were splashed mud to the knees, and his big eyes had that burning tiredness beyond sleep. Near midnight the camp gradually quieted out of sheer exhaustion. Then Windsor put a battered skillet on the little stove and dropped some bacon in it.

I dropped to sleep in my chair. A baby's crying near at hand awakened me. Windsor was gone. He came back in a few moments and stood turning the burnt bacon.

"What happened?" I asked.

"Baby lost the breast. Mother was too tired to wake up."

"What did you do?"

"Found the breast and gave it back to the baby."

"Didn't the mother wake up then?"

"No—too tired. Been working all day in the rain."

Later in the year Windsor and I traveled together, sat in the ditches with the migrant workers, lived and ate with them. We heard a thousand miseries and a thousand jokes. We ate fried dough and sow belly, worked with the sick and the hungry, listened to complaints and little triumphs.

But when I think of Windsor Drake, I remembered first the tired eyes, and I think of the baby that lost the breast in the night, and the mother too tired to wake up.

Robert Capa

I KNOW NOTHING about photography. What I have to say about Capa's work is strictly from the point of view of a layman, and the specialists must bear with me. It does seem to me that Capa has proved beyond all doubt that the camera need not be a cold mechanical device. Like the pen, it is as good as the man who uses it. It can be the extension of mind and heart.

Capa's pictures were made in his brain—the camera only completed them. You can no more mistake his work than you can the canvas of a fine painter. Capa knew what to look for and what to do with it when he found it. He knew, for example, that you cannot photograph war because it is largely an emotion. But he did photograph that emotion by shooting beside it. He could show the horror of a whole people in the face of a child. His camera caught and held emotion.

Capa's work is itself the picture of a great heart and an overwhelming compassion. No one can take his place. No one can take the place of any fine artist, but we are fortunate to have in his pictures the quality of the man.

I worked and traveled with Capa a great deal. He may have had closer friends but he had none who loved him more. It was his pleasure to seem casual and careless about his work. He was not. His pictures are not accidents. The emotion in them did not come by chance. He could photograph motion and gaiety and heartbreak. He could photograph thought. He made a world and it was Capa's world. Note how he captures the endlessness of the Russian landscape with one long road and one single human. See how his lens could peer through the eyes into the mind of a man.

Capa for all his casualness was a worrier. In Russia he had to send his film to be developed by the Soviet Government. He fidgeted and fried until the negatives came back. And then nothing was right. They were over- or underdeveloped. The grain was wrong. He would clasp his brow and yell with anguish. He cared all right. He cared very much.

The greatness of Capa is twofold. We have his pictures, a true and vital record of our time—ugly and beautiful, set down by the mind of an artist. But Capa had another work which may be even more important. He gathered young men about him, encouraged, instructed, even fed and clothed them, but best he taught them respect for their art and integrity in its performance. He proved to them that a man can live by this medium and still be true to himself. And never once did he try to get them to take his kind of picture. Thus the effect of Capa will be found in the men who worked with him. They will carry a little part of Capa all their lives and perhaps hand him on to their young men.

It is very hard to think of being without Capa. I don't think I have accepted that fact yet. But I suppose we should be thankful that there is so much of him with us still.

Adlai Stevenson

W HEN I FIRST MET Mr. Roosevelt he had been President for
some time. I said, "Mr. President, I'm one American who
doesn't want a Government job."

He laughed and said, "In my experience, you're the only one."

Mr. Stevenson, I still don't want a Government job.

A year and a half ago, I had never heard of Mr. Stevenson. A year ago
I knew his name and only remembered it because of the unusual first
name. Until the convention I had never heard nor read a Stevensonian
word. And now we hurry through dinner to hear him on radio or to see
him on television. We fight over the morning paper with the "full text."
And I can't remember ever reading a political speech with pleasure—
sometimes with admiration, yes, but never with pleasure.

I was in Europe at convention time. Europe was, as nearly as we
could tell, pretty solidly behind Eisenhower. So was I, as solid as possible. Then gradually the newspapers in France and England and Italy
began to print remarks by a man named Stevenson, first a phrase, then a
sentence, then a paragraph. When I left England very recently nearly
every newspaper was printing a daily Stevenson box on the front page.
Europe has switched to Stevenson. So have I. And I have been drawn
only by his speeches. They are unique in my experience and from the reaction of the audiences—and I have only seen them on television—the
speeches are a new experience to everyone. The listeners set up no hulla-
baloo. The speaker is never canceled out by emotional roars of inatten-
tive applause. People seem to resent applause because in the noise they
might miss something. I've read that the meetings are quiet because the
audiences are not moved. Then I've watched them leaning forward, their
eyes never leaving the speaker's face and turning irritably toward any dis-

traction. They're listening, all right, listening as an audience does to fine theater or fine music or fine thinking.

It is one of our less admirable traits that we always underrate the intelligence of the "people." The speaker never includes himself as one of the "people." It is always those others. The story is told of a movie producer who argued that people would not understand a part of a film he was previewing. His nine-year-old boy spoke up, saying, "Dad, I understand it."

The producer whirled on him and shouted, "We are not making pictures for nine-year-old boys."

Now I read in the opposition press that Stevenson is talking over the heads of the people. I have read the speeches not once but several times. The words are small and direct, the ideas are clear. I can understand them and I don't think I am more intelligent than the so-called "people." I have come to the conclusion that the fear in Stevenson's opponents is not that the people don't understand him, but that they do.

Throughout our whole history we have been in favor of humor. To be against humor was like being against mother love. But I read now that humor has been made an official sin. Anything effective is a sin to your opponent. Traditionally, political humor has followed a pattern. The speaker made a joke which had been carefully inspected to see that it had nothing whatever to do with the subject he intended to discuss. The flat little joke got a titter of laughter and the speaker knew that his audience was warmed up. He flopped without transition into the body of his speech, hoping that for a few sentences his listeners would still be listening for another joke. Audiences are pretty clever, though, and they rarely fall for this method.

Stevenson has changed the technique. He draws his humor from his subject. His jokes, far from obscuring his message, enlighten it. This makes him doubly dangerous to an opponent, for his listeners not only listen, they remember and they repeat. I don't recall any other speeches that have made people unsatisfied with a digest. We want the thing in the man's own words.

Being a writer, I have had a bit of trouble here and there, and it has been my experience that when I have been accused of some particularly gaudy sin, my accuser has felt some kind of knife and is striking back. I can understand why the opposition hates Mr. Stevenson's humor. They are very busy licking their wounds. In our whole political history I can recall only one man who used humor effectively. That was Abraham Lincoln and he, too, was excoriated by his opponents. In his time also humor was a sin.

There is a further devastating effect of the Stevensonian speech, which his opponents cannot admit. He makes their efforts sound so ill-conceived, clumsily thought-out and dull. The weighty sarcasms, moral indignations, the flaggy patriotisms and dingy platitudes which have been perfectly good in other elections are covered with gray dust in this year. It is very hard to follow a great act with a Minsky blackout.

Now and then in a group the question arises, Does Stevenson write his own speeches? I don't know, but as a writer I know that only one man writes those speeches. There may be people working on ideas and organization and so forth, but I am sure that either Stevenson writes every word of the speeches or some other one man writes every word of them. Individuality is in every line. I don't think it could be imitated.

I have dwelt only on Mr. Stevenson's speeches because that is all I know about the man. There are only four approaches in knowing a man. What does he look like? What has he done? What does he say—in other words think—and, last and most important, as a conditioner—what has he done to or for me?

I know Mr. Stevenson only from pictures of him, from reading his history and from his speeches. I was for Eisenhower, knew about him and liked him. I did not switch to Stevenson because of physical appearance, surely. Neither candidate is any great shucks in that department. I could not have changed on a basis of past achievements because Eisenhower's contribution is second to none in the world and certainly overshadows the record of the Governor of Illinois, no matter how good it may have been. I have switched entirely because of the speeches.

A man cannot think muddled and write clear. Day by day it has seemed to me that Eisenhower's speeches have become more formless and mixed up and uncertain. I don't know why this is. Maybe he is being worried and mauled by too many dissident advisers who in fighting each other are destroying their candidate. Eisenhower seems like a punch-drunk fighter who comes out of his corner on wavery legs and throws his first punch at the referee. Again, Eisenhower seems to have lost the ability to take any kind of stand on any subject. We're pretty sure that he still favors children or dogs but that maybe he would like the states to take them over, too—anything to avoid making a decision. He is rather firm on those issues which are still handled by the Deity and he has a sense of relief that this is so.

Stevenson, on the other hand, has touched no political, economic, or moral subject on which he has not taken a clear and open stand even to the point of bearding selfish groups to their faces.

I do not know, but I can imagine the pressures on candidates for the Presidency. They must be dreadful, but they must be equally dreadful for both candidates. With equal pressures we have seen in a pitiful few months the Eisenhower mind crumble into uncertainty, retire into generalities, fumble with friendships and juggle alliances. At the same time Stevenson has moved serenely on, clarifying his position, holding to his line and never being drawn nor driven from his nongeneralized ideals.

And if the pressures on a candidate are powerful, how much more so must they be on a President? I find I am for the man I think can take the pressures best and can handle them without split loyalties, expedient friendships or dead animals—cats or albatrosses. In a word I think Stevenson is more durable, socially, politically and morally. Neither candidate has or is likely to do anything to or for me personally. And I can't hurt or help either of them. As a writer I love the clear, clean writing of Stevenson. As a man I like his intelligent, humorous, logical, civilized mind. And I strongly suspect what we can't possibly know until November. Americans are real mean when they go behind that voting-booth curtain. But I suspect there are millions just like me who have switched to Stevenson as the greater man and as potentially the greater President.

Henry Fonda

AFTER I SO BLITHELY agreed to write a piece about Hank Fonda, and after it was too late to withdraw, I realized, with a certain chagrin, that I don't know any of the things expected in such a piece—the personal, insulting, warm and malicious material columnists thrive on and readers have grown to expect. What I know about Fonda anyone can know simply by hearing and seeing him on stage or on film.

Certainly I have heard the gossip by which people reassure themselves that if not better than the subject, they are at least no worse. I have heard that he is moody, introspective, difficult and brooding. But, hell! I've heard the same things about myself and I know for a fact that I am easygoing, open, kindly and perhaps a little beautiful, so why should I believe things about Hank I know to be false about myself?

I know Henry Fonda as an actor, a devoted, hardworking, responsible one with a harsh urge toward perfection. Not long ago a friend loaned me a sixteen-millimeter print of the film *The Grapes of Wrath*, made well over twenty years ago. I was greatly reluctant to look at it. Times pass: we change; the urgency departs, and this is called "dating." But I did thread the thing on my home projector and sat back to weather it out. Then a lean, stringy, dark-faced piece of electricity walked out on the screen, and he had me. I believed my own story again. It was fresh and happening and good. Hank can do that. He carries with him that excitement which cannot be learned—as many an actor has found to his sorrow—but he backs up his gift with grueling, conscientious work and agony of self-doubt.

Another thing about Fonda that should be obvious is the care he has exercised to keep from being typed. When his name is on the playbill, you have no way of knowing what it will be about. He could go without apparent effort from *The Grapes of Wrath* to *Mister Roberts* to *Point of No Return*. I said apparent effort by design because I know the enormous effort and care and study that go into his easy and relaxed performances.

Once I was working on a short, to me amusing little novel designed to be translated to the stage. I discussed it with Hank, and he said he would like to play it. "But it's a musical and I can't sing," he said. "Never mind, I'll take singing lessons." And he did, for a year. Meanwhile, I was praying that he might not learn to sing too well, because I remembered that Walter Huston, who couldn't sing, did "September Song" better than anyone has ever done it since. And Harrison couldn't sing in *My Fair Lady* either.

At the end of a year of singing lessons, Hank auditioned for the part and was turned down by the composer, who was understandably interested in the music. The show flopped dismally and we will never know whether the Fonda kind of magic would have brought it to life. One thing I do know. It would certainly have been believable and consequently better.

I suppose one human never really knows much about another. My impressions of Hank are of a man reaching but unreachable, gentle but capable of sudden wild and dangerous violence, sharply critical of others but equally self-critical, caged and fighting the bars but timid of the light, viciously opposed to external restraint, imposing an iron slavery on himself. His face is a picture of opposites in conflict.

Woody Guthrie

THE SONGS of the working people have always been their sharpest statement and the one statement which cannot be destroyed. You can burn books, buy newspapers, you can guard against handbills and pamphlets, but you cannot prevent singing.

For some reason it has always been lightly thought that singing people are happy people. Nothing could be more untrue. The greatest and most enduring folk songs are wrung from unhappy people—the spirituals of the slaves which say, in effect, "It is hopeless here, maybe in heaven it will be nicer." We have the grunting songs of the weight-lifting stevedores which tell of a little pleasure on Saturday night. The cowboy songs are wails of loneliness.

Working people sing of their hopes and of their troubles, but the rhythms have the beat of work—the long and short bawls of the sea shanties with tempos of capstan or sheets, the lifting rhythms, the swinging rhythms and the slow, rolling songs of the Southwest built on the hoofbeats of a walking horse. The work is the song and the song is the people.

There is great relief in saying a thing that hurts—I remember a very little boy who was going to the barber for his first time. He was terrified and his eyes were filled with tears. He stood very stiffly on the curb and sang—

> *"They think I will be scared,*
> *They all think I will be scared,*
> *But I will not,*
> *But I will not cry,*
> *Oh! No! I will not cry."*

Songs are the statements of a people. You can learn more about people by listening to their songs than in any other way, for into the songs go all the hopes and hurts, the angers, fears, the wants and aspirations.

A few years ago when I sat in the camps of the people from the Dust Bowl when hunger was everywhere, I heard the singing and I knew that this was a great race, for, while there was loneliness and trouble in their singing, there was also fierceness and the will to fight. A man might sing "Goin' down this road a-feelin' bad," but his next line was "Cause I aint gonna be treated that-a-way."

In a cotton strike a woman spoke and her voice chanted a song—

> "My man is in jail for striking—
> It aint agin' th' law,
> My boy is in jail for striking—
> It aint agin' th' law.
> I say—Plead Not Guilty!
> An' rot they dam jails down!"

And that for a statement of survival has not often been equaled.

It would be a good idea to listen very closely to these songs, to listen for the rhythms of work, and over them, the words of anger and survival.

Woody is just Woody. Thousands of people do not know he has any other name. He is just a voice and a guitar. He sings the songs of a people and I suspect that he is, in a way, that people. Harsh-voiced and nasal, his guitar hanging like a tire iron on a rusty rim, there is nothing sweet about Woody, and there is nothing sweet about the songs he sings. But there is something more important for those who will listen. There is the will of a people to endure and fight against oppression. I think we call this the American Spirit.

VI.

JOURNALIST ABROAD

JOHN STEINBECK was a restless man long before he traveled with Charley. Growing up, he did not identify with his stolid hometown of Salinas, but rode forth on his pony, Jill, to explore the hills surrounding the gray little town of 2,500. At eighteen he left for Stanford University, returning home only for brief family visits. Never intending to complete degree requirements, he dropped in and out of the university, at one point attempting to sail to China on a merchant sailing ship. In 1925, he left Stanford for good and sailed to New York City and freedom, only to return to California broke a few months later. The first time he made real money on a book, *Tortilla Flat,* he and his first wife, Carol, took off for Mexico, a country he came to love and visit with some regularity: "There's an illogic there I need," he insisted in an unpublished letter to Monterey friends, the Lovejoys. Two years after their first trip—establishing a pattern he would maintain for decades, a long trip about every other year—the couple went to Scandinavia and Russia. In the 1940s, he traveled with greater frequency—to the Sea of Cortez; overseas as a war correspondent; to Mexico to film *The Pearl* and then to research Emiliano Zapata's life; to postwar Russia with photographer Robert Capa. When, in December 1950, he married his third wife, the plucky, intelligent, and equally peripatetic Elaine Steinbeck, he spent months in Europe, England, the Caribbean, Asia. Indeed from the mid-1940s to 1967—his final trip abroad—John Steinbeck was, in truth, a citizen of the world, both because his books were read in nearly every country and because he spent about as much time out of the United States as in it. "You said that this [Pacific Grove cottage] was my home but I have thought about it deeply," he wrote to Elaine in 1949, months before the two married. "I think I have no 'place' home. Home is people and where you work well.

I have homes everywhere and many I have not even seen yet. That is perhaps why I am restless. I haven't seen all of my homes" (*SLL* 382).

This restlessness may be the least understood, least appreciated aspect of Steinbeck's career. Assuming Thoreau's perspective, some readers wish that Steinbeck "traveled much in California" and cultivated always the land and people of his birthplace. But unlike William Faulkner, at home only in Mississippi, or Ernest Hemingway, at home wherever the stakes were high, Steinbeck was both rooted and rootless. Whimsical self-portraits capture that inner tension, as in his first letter to Elaine: "This has been my tragedy—with the soul to wear a scarlet-lined opera cape and small sword I have the physical misfortune always to be handed a hod" (*SLL* 357). His personal rubber stamp, used at the end of letters or in books he inscribed, was "Pigasus," a winged pig, below which was written in Latin, "To the stars on the wings of a pig." Steinbeck was ever the man in khaki, tinkering with a screwdriver, digging in the garden, his mind on St. Peter's and the Peloponnesian War. "Your life sounds good to me," he wrote to his reclusive, scholarly college roommate, Carlton Sheffield. "I have the indolence for it but have never been able to practice it. Too jittery and nervous. And yet every instinct aims toward just such a life. I guess I inherited from my mother the desire to do four things at once" (*SLL* 457). It may be that this California novelist had to reverse direction, and, like Fitzgerald's Nick Carraway, lay claim to a new frontier, the East Coast and beyond. Perhaps Steinbeck didn't so much abandon his native state as reenact the "westering" spirit he describes in his fiction—freedom and movement and self-determination. He may well be the quintessential Westerner, the maverick.

In 1952, having written the book that gave closure to his California upbringing, *East of Eden,* he took Elaine on their first trip to Europe, she as photographer, he as writer. To help finance their six-month stay, he had his agents contact *Collier's,* a popular magazine appealing to a middle-class audience. With the advent of television, *Collier's* was struggling to retain its readership and welcomed the chance to run brief essays by a famous author. And Steinbeck, worried about paying alimony, child support, and his own expenses, welcomed the chance to write for pay. The work did not go well, however. After his first two pieces were rejected, he wrote to Elizabeth Otis in dismay: ". . . in writing for someone you must first, during and after, keep an invisible editor sitting on the typewriter shaking an admonitory finger in your face" (*SLL* 447). He had voiced the same frustration before—concern over meeting fixed dead-lines that weren't his own: "I was going to do some articles for the [*Herald*] *Tribune* but just haven't wanted to," he had written Pascal Covici in 1944 during a trip to Mexico. "Can't get coagulated. Newspaper work isn't natural to me. And while I could turn out the wordage, it wouldn't be worth printing, like so much of my work overseas" (Benson 534).

For a man who wrote scores of articles for newspapers and maga-zines, it seems an odd position to take. In fact, writing to order some-times came more readily—during the war he had met newspaper deadlines without complaint, and he did eventually submit three superb articles on Europe to *Collier's*, "The Soul and Guts of France," "Duel Without Pistols" (reprinted in Part II), and "I Go Back to Ireland." And as he gradually found a more personal voice, the articles seemingly became less of a chore. In the late 1950s and 1960s he often wrote newspaper ar-ticles as letters, and that gave him even greater creative license. The writer who honed an objective stance throughout the 1930s and during the war, who never mentioned that his wife Carol accompanied the crew on the Sea of Cortez trip and said little about himself, would, with greater frequency, include references to his own actions and those of Elaine, his "elegant *moglie*" as an Italian paper described her. They were a team, as were he and Capa, as were he and Charley. Elaine's actions and opin-ions, her charm and her flair—all noted with humor and affection—serve as a foil for his own reflections. Steinbeck's journalism of the 1950s re-flects his growing comfort with self in the world.

Some of his best overseas nonfiction is about France—particularly Paris, where he spent the bulk of his time. Steinbeck's little-known 1954 series of seventeen articles written for *Le Figaro*, a stylish morning paper featuring the arts, offered French readers a "tourist's" perspective on the city: "I will offer you Paris perhaps not as it is, but as I see it," he wrote in the manuscript for his first article of the series he called "One American in Paris," translated into French for publication. The articles range freely over what he saw in the city, what he did with his two young sons, what happened to him, and what he thought at the time. His was the "unin-structed eye," he insists, "which sees things the expert doesn't notice. . . .

Mine is a completely naïve eye on Paris—but it is an eye of delight." In fact, he had set forth his writerly terrain two years earlier when he wrote one of his most engaging travel articles, "The Soul and Guts of France": "I do not know what the people of France are thinking, but I do know to a certain extent what the farmers, winegrowers, teachers and kids of the little village of Poligny are thinking and talking about. This seems important to me. People like these are the soul and guts of France."

Not only did Steinbeck write best about ordinary people and their daily lives, but he also wrote best when he narrowed his scope, found a slice of life that appealed. "I find I have to write about little things," he wrote Covici in 1952. "I can't write about big things. It never comes out good" (Benson 724). The *Le Figaro* series is, in fact, somewhat uneven, in part because he doesn't always stick to the "little things" that appeal—his Paris neighborhood, fishing on the Ile de la Cité, sites that struck his fancy. Furthermore, he insists a bit too stridently, perhaps, that underneath it all, humans are the same. It's a note he often struck in his travel writing: "the ends" that girded national identities are similar—generosity of spirit, courage, despair, and hope. The Joads and the Russian peasants and the French teacher in Poligny are, in fact, one in spirit. It's Steinbeck's perpetual message of hope and belief that "men and ideas are eternal."

"Positano," about the Italian coastal village, is one of his finest travel articles and is Steinbeck's most characteristic brew—a bit of solid description of coast, hotel, and convent; a tale or two from the town's "remarkable past"; a couple of Steinbeckian eccentrics, Signor Bassano, the exuberant "Experienced Guide," and the mayor of Positano, who "dresses in tired slacks, a sweatshirt and sandals"; concluding with the irresistible vignette that can't quite be, often certainly isn't, true. In the whole of Steinbeck's creative nonfiction, there are several of these little fantasies: two or three ghost stories, a couple of accounts of disappearing buildings, a report of an elf who visited his hotel room in Algiers. Indeed, even in a daylight mood, Steinbeck was a bit of the Irish storyteller, weaving fancy into narratives. Could the McKnights' Thanksgiving turkey, given Grand Marnier to steady it before the slaughter, have given a "hiccuping gobble" and "screaming triumphantly" flown to sea from their Positano garden? Perhaps. As both writer of fiction and nonfiction, Steinbeck richly enjoyed tugging the reader's leg a bit. Sometimes the journalistic soufflé fell, but often air kept it aloft. His breezy travel series on Italy, France, and England for the Louisville *Courier-Journal* in 1956 (following the success of his popular 1956 series on the conventions) included liberal dollops of froth and whimsy, "reports on Europe comprised of lies, inaccuracies and whoppers" (14 Apr. 1957). Included here is "Florence: The Explosion of the Chariot."

Accounts of a 1965–66 trip to England, Ireland, and Israel were published in the Long Island newspaper *Newsday* as "Letters to Alicia." A second series in 1966–67 covered his and Elaine's trip to Vietnam. His association with the paper actually began a decade earlier when he met publishers Alicia Patterson and Harry F. Guggenheim at the Kentucky Derby, where both had been invited by the editor of the *Courier-Journal,* Mark Ethridge. Steinbeck's first piece for *Newsday* was published in May 1956, a description of the author's first Derby, and in the next four years, he would write only a handful of articles for *Newsday.* The publisher, Alicia Patterson, liked to have important writers published in her paper—Aldous Huxley on the dangers of subliminal advertising ("Tyranny over the Mind," 1958) and Erskine Caldwell ("U.S.A. Today," an account of a cross-country tour in the early 1960s). When her husband took over editorship of the paper after her death in 1963, he continued the practice, hiring John O'Hara to write a weekly column. In 1965 Guggenheim asked Steinbeck to write a weekly column; the writer was initially reluctant to accept Guggenheim's request, but when the publisher insisted and gave Steinbeck the freedom to write "things . . . of any length" that "could have the casualness of letters," he began "Letters to Alicia," seventy-seven published letters. Each was addressed "Dear Alicia," because he had greatly admired Alicia Patterson to whom he had once "sold" an article for the "verbally agreed price of one red rose a year in perpetuity," as he wrote to her husband. As he explained to Guggenheim, having a deceased woman as his audience

is not mawkish or sentimental. The letters would not be to someone who is dead but rather to a living mind and a huge curiosity. That is why she was such a great newspaper woman. She wanted to know everything. But she also had respect for her readers. . . . If I write these letters intending to amuse, inform and illuminate (Plato?) Ali-

cia they will do the same to great numbers of people. There should
be in them (the letters) everything there is—truth insofar as I can see
it, hatred, love and a great deal of quiet laughter. . . . The last reason
for writing these to Alicia is that it gives me a focal point, a person
to address. I can't write to everybody. You end up writing to nobody.
(14 Aug. 1965)

He felt called upon, then and later, however, to defend his choice of audience. Some staff members of the paper found Steinbeck's references to
Alicia "mawkish" and "cumbersome"; many papers syndicating the column simply left the salutation off. But Steinbeck, with Guggenheim's full
support, kept Alicia as his muse—although he suggested to Guggenheim
that papers objecting strongly might omit her name or substitute the
name of the local editor. "The fact of a letter changes the whole style of
any writing, makes it intimate and very different from the essay. I think it
also arouses the peeping Tom in many people. They love to read other
people's mail . . ." (17 Nov. 1965).

In the first series of "Letters to Alicia," Steinbeck tells about the
Christmas of 1965 with John Huston at his house at St. Cleran's, Ireland:
"We did this last year and I fell in love with the west of Ireland," he had
written to Guggenheim while planning the trip, "perhaps because a part
of my own blood line comes from thereabouts. While there last year I
came upon a piece of local folk lore which fascinated me. I plan to write
it in a new technique and on the spot and John Huston plans to make a
film of it in the place where it happened" (Sept. 1965). Such is the gene-
sis of one of Steinbeck's best pieces in the first series, "The Ghost of Anthony Daly." It is more winsome than his earlier piece on Ireland, "I Go
Back to Ireland," but both capture his fondness for a country that was his
mother's ancestral home: ". . . nearly all the Irish I know are pretty much
like my uncles in complexion and character—talented, contentious and
lonely," he wrote in one letter to Guggenheim. "I feel related in Ireland"
(12 Feb. 1966).

The Soul and Guts
of France

AN AMERICAN politician, running for reelection, reads the newspapers, cons the columnists, meets with his party organization— and then, if he is intelligent, goes into the country and listens to what the farmers are saying. The newspapers are not enough; if a candidate heeds them alone, he is likely to be very badly fooled.

French newspapers are more distant from the people than our own, if that is possible. One day of reading the Paris journals can bring on a state of confusion that may last for weeks.

I do not know what the people of France are thinking, but I do know to a certain extent what the farmers, winegrowers, teachers and kids of the little village of Poligny are thinking and talking about. This seems important to me. People like these are the soul and guts of France. They continued to fight the Germans after their government and armies were gone. It should not be surprising that they are as tough and individualistic as our own farmers. I believe that the future of Europe will be decided by people such as these. I think that it is a good thing to hear what they have to say.

Poligny is in the Jura, the rich, rising lap of the great mountains which separate France from Switzerland. Some of the best wines of France come from this district.

The people are hardy and hardworking. During the war, a good number of the men were wounded in their unrelenting war against the occupation forces, and lots of them bear the marks of the concentration camps. They were not broken. They remain incorrigible individuals, no two holding opinions exactly alike.

We were invited to visit by Louis Gibey, a teacher who raises grapes. Louis and his wife and his three little daughters live in a very old house on a dirt street in Poligny. His neighbors are the peasant farmers of the district. The street swarms with children, with dogs, and, morning and evening, with cows strolling to and from their pasturage. A hundred yards away, the vineyards begin their climb up the hills. The village lies in the pass that leads upward to Switzerland. It is a town of great age. Probably it was here when the Romans came. A tower and part of a city wall recall the Middle Ages, and its churches date from the twelfth century.

Louis' house is innocent of plumbing, but he does have a hand pump in the kitchen, a wonderful luxury. Most of the houses in the street get their water from the municipal fountain. With the Gibey family live one white rabbit, one Siamese cat with a crooked tail, known as Tail-tail, a lady hound-dog called Diane to indicate her hunting ability, and a reasonable facsimile of a basset hound, named Miro, also a great hunter, who can open doors. This remarkable dog can also slip up beside you, as you sit at table, and get your dinner from under your raised fork.

The peasants of the street love to hunt. Every family owns at least one hunting dog, and one dog named Ticot is so famous that the birth of his son, which occurred while we were there, aroused the whole street. The men hunt rabbits, hares, small deer, foxes and several kinds of game birds. They are crack shots, a characteristic which gave the occupying Germans no comfort.

By our standards, the peasant houses are not immaculate, and there is little physical luxury, but the food is good and plentiful, the wine superb.

We were given the best room in the house, newly plastered by our host. The children had new shoes for the occasion, but the shoes had been bought for glory rather than comfort and hurt the little girls' feet. Mostly the shoes were left off but kept on display, thus preserving both grandeur and comfort.

Once settled in Poligny, we promptly became involved in the three important activities of the Rue de Charcigny—and, indeed, the whole town: wine, hunting and politics.

Wine is by far the most important of these matters to the townspeople. Each man has his own cellar, besides belonging to the cooperative which ferments, bottles and markets his grapes.

You visit a man in his house, and he brings a crusty bottle up from below ground. His wife rushes wonderful cheese to the table. A little girl lugs in a loaf of bread approximately as big as she is. The bread has a fine crisp crust and the sour taste of great French bread. Now you are ready for business.

Your host handles the dusty bottle as tenderly as he might move a flask of nitroglycerin. A silence falls on the room as he slowly twists the corkscrew in. There is a tiny squeak as the cork comes out. Your host looks at the cork, turns it over, smells it and then passes it to his guests. The quality of the cork is the first clue to the quality of the wine. This bottle is of the year 1947, one of the greatest years the district has ever known.

The host pours off a few drops, to get rid of the bits of cork. Then he fills the glasses. Now all glasses are clicked together and each man drinks. There is silence for a moment, and then the host says, "I detect a little harshness."

A neighbor sitting on his left is staring at the amber wine. "Have you forgotten the season?" he asks. "The vines are in flower."

"Of course they are," says the host and he explains to us.

In the spring, when the flowers are on the vines and before the new grapes are set, the wine in barrels and in bottles remembers the time of its own flowering. Then there is a little stir in the wine and a small amount of refermentation takes place. The flavor changes a little; it has a restless taste. And then after the flowering, the wine settles down again. But whatever the reason for it, be it memory, or the warming spring air, or pure magic—it is literally true that the wine does grow uneasy and a little harsh during the vines' flowering.

Now the glasses are refilled and perhaps a neighbor slips out and returns with a dusty bottle from his own cellar. And the talk is of wine. For perhaps a thousand years, the ancestors of these men have raised their vines on the slopes behind the town, and the slow knowledge, or feeling, or instinct, has accumulated. Wine is the greatest single thing in their lives.

They are like all country people. They boast that their wine is the finest in France and yet they find fault with every bottle they open. This bottle is corky, this one is not cool enough, this one too cool. This bottle was shaken while being carried to the table. It is exactly like my Aunt

Mamie, who is a great cook. She serves a wonderful dinner, perfect in every detail, and she complains the whole time—the oven wasn't right, the eggs not fresh enough, the chicken too tough, the yeast in the high, lovely biscuits was a traitor. I guess it is a quality all perfectionists have, never to admit their work is perfect.

We sat long at the table, eating the hunks of bread and nibbling the soft country cheese and slicing the firm Gruyère, which we call domestic Swiss cheese. A dairyman tasted the cheese with the same application the wine makers have devoted to the wine.

"In some places in the world," he said, "I have heard that people think the best cheese should have large holes. This is not true. The very best cheese has few holes and those very small and perfectly round."

"Remark the bread," our host said. "See, it is not white. This is a sadness. It is late in the season. French flour is getting low, and at the bottom of the barrel the flour is not white."

Do not think that this process of eating and tasting has been eventless in other directions. Children have rushed in and out, carrying bread and cheese, sipping wine from their fathers' glasses. A minor dogfight has started and been settled. Our hostess is on her knees ironing clothes on a blanket on the floor. A cow has looked in and then withdrawn to chew and ponder. A mother duck has strolled through, followed by five yellow ducklings. Miro, the great hunter, has been licking the white rabbit all over from head to foot. Diane has been tromped, has howled and has gone away to feminine brooding. Three little girls have arrived with gifts, one a basket of fresh-picked cherries, one an apronful of tiny wild strawberries hardly bigger than beans and very sweet, and the third with a garland of wild flowers intricately braided together to make a kind of crown.

And now the time has come, by general consent, for politics, a game the French play with their own ground rules.

During the wine tasting we had gradually increased in numbers. A fierce, good-looking young man stood in the doorway. He had been a great *maquis* fighter against the Germans. I remarked that the trousers he wore looked like those worn by our airborne soldiers.

He laughed and said, "You know, your army sold many kinds of things after the war, clothes and blankets and pants like these. And then they were all sold, so we French are making them." He gazed at his trousers. "I don't think they are as good," he said.

A thin man with a pinched face took the ball then. He had been captured during the war and sent to Buchenwald. He still limped on the leg the Nazis had shattered with an iron bar. He said:

"I should think you could have made a better choice than Ridgway to take Eisenhower's place."

We had been in Paris during the Communist rioting over Ridgway's arrival, and we were still a little sore about it. "Why?" I asked. "He's a good man. He did a good job in the East. He's a good soldier and a good administrator. And I should think you French would like him. He was the first big American general to land in France for the liberation. What have you got against him?"

A white-haired man, vice-president of the wine cooperative, spoke. "Well, with all the talk about Korea—it makes a bad impression to send Ridgway."

"With all what talk?" I demanded. "Do you mean to say you seriously consider that we are using germs?"

"One never knows," the vice-president of the wine co-operative said gently. "There's so much talk. How can we tell?"

I found that I was getting angry—a tactical error—and I said, "Look! Suppose you were a Communist general and your men were really ignorant, and suppose your enemy was dropping propaganda leaflets that disturbed your men and made them ask questions. Wouldn't you find it easy to tell your people the leaflets carried germs so they wouldn't pick them up? And if you had some epidemics anyway, wouldn't such a campaign do two things—excuse your bad medical service and also keep people from reading the propaganda?"

"How do we know?" the white-haired man said. "We hear so many things."

"Whom do you hear them from? I can understand a half-literate, completely dominated people believing this germ story, but I can't understand a modern Frenchman believing it."

Louis Gibey, the vintner-teacher, said nervously, "Who will be your next President?"

"I don't know."

"Can Eisenhower be elected?"

"I don't know," I said. "Do you like him?"

An old peasant said, "We like him very much. He understands us. He said we must not rearm so fast that our living standard falls. We like that. We are just now beginning to get enough to eat."

"Suppose the time is too short."

The old man said, "We knew starvation under the Germans. We are afraid of hunger. We don't want to spend our little gains for guns."

"Well, if you had to choose between a little hunger and being taken over by the Kremlin, which would you choose?" I asked him.

"We don't think the danger is as great as you do. We don't want to spend our little gains."

"I don't either," I said. "Have you thought that a good part of the taxes I pay and all Americans pay is going to help Europe rearm? Think of the howls of rage that would go up if part of your taxes had to go to us. Would you like it?"

A jovial man, who wore a gigantic cummerbund of wool, smiled into his glass. "We wouldn't like it. But surely you don't think you are doing it for us. You are doing it for yourselves. You are using us to defend you."

"That is more or less true," I said, "and as realistic Frenchmen who do not believe in pure charity, you should be reassured by that. And if we go down, can you survive?"

"We don't want war," Cummerbund said. "I was wounded in 1916 and wounded again in 1943. No, we don't want any war."

"You didn't want it when Hitler came in—but not wanting it didn't stop him. Do you think prayer will stop the Russians? You may not like us here, but if we hadn't come you would still be under the Nazis."

"There were the Russians," the white-haired man said. "The Russians fought very well."

"I've thought about this quite a bit," I said. "I want you to imagine something. Suppose we had not come into the war, and suppose the British had not. Imagine that the Russians had beaten the Germans all alone. Do you really think you would have your free wine cooperative now, your elections, your schools, even your churches? Do you really believe you would? Or would you have been like Poland, like Romania, like East Germany? Do you know any time when the Russians have not taken over when they could? Just think about it. And where they have taken over, has any freedom remained?"

A man in a ragged hat spoke—thickly, because his front teeth had been knocked out. "It is very confusing," he said. "But sometimes we think it might be better if you left us alone."

"You mean you do not want ECA money?"

Gibey said, "It is badly done. You don't know what happened. The money is given only to big companies. They use it to drive small companies out of business. The big companies are growing and the little ones are disappearing. It is very dangerous. The politicians are in it. We don't trust politicians."

I said, "I don't know the details, but it occurs to me the little companies cannot build heavier military equipment unless they get together. Have your little companies done that?"

"We think most of the money goes to the rich," Gibey said.

"And yet you say that you are getting on your feet. Don't you think our help had anything to do with that? We don't believe all politicians are bad."

The young man in the airborne pants said, "You have had your scandals. We read about them."

"Sure we have. And also we have our thousands of honest men, and they are the ones who matter in the long run. The proof is that we function. The American government is not about to fall to pieces."

"We are cynical about politicians," Gibey said. "We remember what the politicians did during the last war."

There was a stir at the door. A woman came in, saying, "Ticot's son is crying."

The argument stopped instantly. Everyone got up from the table. We walked rapidly down the street among the homecoming cows, then up a flight of stairs and into a peasant kitchen. Beside the stove in a big wooden box was chained a nondescript bitch, snarling with fear and rage. From under her heavy body came a thin squealing. Three men grabbed the snapping bitch and held her down, while a fourth reached under her and brought out a tiny white pup with brown markings. Its face was deeply wrinkled, and its eyes were navy blue and sightless.

They carried the pup to the light while it cried and sneezed. An end of straw stuck out of one nostril. The man who held Ticot's son pulled a long straw out of the puppy's nose. Ticot's son yawned widely and went to sleep in his hand. The circle of men admired the little sleeping puppy.

"He is indeed Ticot's son," they said. "See the brown triangle between the eyes. Ticot has the same mark. See those two round spots on the back. Ticot has them, and Ticot is the greatest—the greatest hunter in the whole Jura."

"Where is Ticot now?" I asked.

"Oh, you see, no one has hunted for a week. Ticot became disgusted. He has gone hunting by himself."

One man said excitedly: "I can tell by the sound of Ticot's voice whether he is hunting rabbits or hares or deer. He has a different voice for each."

"Who owns Ticot?" I asked.

"Why, everyone. Everyone who goes hunting. Ticot is of this street. He is a free dog."

"And Ticot's wife?"

"Oh! That one!" they said, and dropped the subject so quickly that I understood Ticot's wife was not above reproach.

The puppy was dropped back into the box, and Mrs. Ticot gently licked him all over without awakening him.

"Now we must go to the cave," the white-haired man said. "You will want to see where the beautiful wine is made."

Our party tromped down the stairs and into the ancient street. In a narrow, grass-grown road that was well traveled when the Romans came, Daniele and Lena Gibey had dressed their little sister Jenny in trailing vines and had put a crown of wild flowers on her head.

Little Jenny was pulling the petals from a white daisy, reciting as she did:

"I love you (petal), I love you a little (petal), I love you passionately (petal), I love you not too much (petal), I love you to the point of insanity (petal), I love you not at all (petal)." The last petal fell, and as Jenny looked up in triumph at her sisters, the flower crown fell rakishly over one hoyden eye.

The wine cave turned out to be a twelfth-century church of the purest Gothic architecture. It was attacked and despoiled during the French Revolution. Church authorities look at it now and then, but it would take many millions of francs to restore it, and no one has them. The round place where the rose window once was is bricked up. Inside, the triple columns rise cleanly to the groined ceiling. Under the pointed arches at the sides, the great wine barrels lay; they did not seem out of place in the cool, dusky church.

"It is cool in here," the men said. "It is better not to waste such a good place. When the church wants it, it is here, and meanwhile we keep the roof in repair."

The walls and columns were black with the dirt of centuries, and the sweet smell of working wine made an incense in the air.

Parachute Pants said, "The floor fell in over there and underneath we found nearly two hundred skeletons. In some of the skulls were the arrowheads that had killed them. Soldiers, they must have been, from some old time."

An electric pump was moving wine from one great cask to another so that the sediment could be cleared.

The white-haired man said, "How can you be sure that germs were not used in Korea?"

I said, "Because we are not like that. If we wished only to kill, we could do it better with other weapons. But we have not used those weapons. We would be stupid to use germs."

"But you dropped the atomic bomb on Hiroshima."

"Yes, we did, and we believe that millions of lives were saved at the cost of thousands."

The white-haired man said, "It is so hard to know." And he went outside.

The man with the cummerbund said, kindly, "You see, he is a Communist. He finds it very hard to change."

"You mean he is a member of the party?"

"I don't think so. The leaders are members of the party. He is not a leader. Most of us have changed here in Poligny, but he finds it very hard to change. He is an idealist."

"Tell me about the change in the rest of you."

"Well, when the Germans were here, the Communists had the best

242   JOHN STEINBECK

and most effective resistance. So most of us joined them, and we thought of ourselves as Communists. We were fighting to liberate France. We even thought of the Communist Party as a French party. Then the war was over, and the leaders made a very bad mistake. Maybe you remember it. They told us we must swear never to fight against the Red Army. Then we knew it was not a French party at all, and we left it. You see, we are Frenchmen, and we would fight against any army that invaded us, Red or Blue or Green. It was a very bad mistake the leaders made."

"And the white-haired man?" I asked.

"It was his dream that men would be kind to one another and would share their goods and their work. It was a kind of heaven to him, and the Communists promised they would bring that about. He finds it very hard to give up his dream of heaven." The man smiled. "But I'm afraid he is weakening. The leaders of the Communists are making too many mistakes. When they are trained in Moscow, they forget what Frenchmen are like. They forget that first of all they are Frenchmen. The leaders are so full of hatred. They preach nothing but hatred. And our friend there has no hatred for anyone. It is a sadness to him."

"If what you say is true all over France, how do you account for the large Communist vote?"

Gibey said, "I think that millions of Frenchmen vote Communist as a way of protesting against the government. We think we should always protest against government. I think your own Thomas Jefferson advocated this as a way to keep governments from forgetting their purpose."

The wine pump gagged and gasped and had to be primed. Then we drew little glasses of wine from some of the older casks and sipped the unfinished wine, not perfect but aging into excellence.

An old man with a fine, fierce, bristling mustache said, "Maybe you Americans don't understand the French, either. You must learn that first of all we are French. That is the basic thing to remember. We will not be anybody's colony, even America's."

"What do you mean by that?"

"Our government says 'We are for America. Vote for us or you will get no American money.' That is a pressure, and we resent it. It makes us feel that our government is under the thumb of the Americans and that we have become an American colony. Frenchmen do not like this. Many vote for the Communists because of this. I do myself."

I said, "Perhaps you are caught between two historical forces, and you must choose between them. Maybe there isn't any third way. But consider this: We do not tell you how to plant your land, what to read or not read, whom to vote for. Your borders are not closed. You can travel in France or even leave France. You are not drafted for labor. Your crops are not taken away. There are no concentration camps, no secret executions, no secret police to listen in on your talk. You do not disappear in the night. Is Poland so lucky, or Romania or Czechoslovakia or Bulgaria? How long is it since you have seen a Hungarian tourist? All of these countries protested by letting the Communists in. But once in, the Communists do not listen to protests. You must think about this."

The man with the missing front teeth said passionately, "All we want is peace. We have peace now, and we want to keep it. We do not want to do anything—and we do not want you to do anything for us—that will lead to war. We are tired of war! We are bitterly tired of war! That's all we think about."

"Do you think that is the attitude of all Frenchmen?"

"I think so. Of course, I am not sure."

"Can you tell us the attitude of the Americans?" Louis Gibey asked.

"Not on many things, because we have as many ideas as we are people, but in some general things I think I can. We don't want war any more than you do. But America has no America to protect it. We want to keep our institutions. If they are to change, we want to change them ourselves and in our own time and by our own methods. We think the rest of the free world feels the same, but by an accident in time and economics it has fallen to us, whether we want it or not, to lead, to prod, to organize and to direct the opposition to the forces which would reduce all of us. If we do not do it, who will? Will you? Will the British? Will Italy or Scandinavia?

"Sure, you would *defend* yourselves. And the enemy would like nothing better than to pick off one at a time the ripe fruits of dissension and national pride.

"Do you think we really like to spend most of our income on

weapons when that same money could build dams, plant parks, build symphony orchestras, set up schools such as the world has never known? Do you think we like to defraud ourselves of these things? We could do it, too. Don't think we couldn't. We could retire into our hemisphere and close our eyes to the rest of the world.

"And then, little by little, Europe would stagger and fall. And one day we would be faced with war, and do you know who would do the fighting against us? Your sons, drilled and lied to, figures moving and fighting on the end of a string manipulated from the Kremlin.

"Just remember that leadership is not chosen by a people. It is forced on them. We don't want it, but we have it. And thank Heaven we are not too tired nor too confused nor too cynical to use it. When you are grousing about our help, just think a little of that. Our farmers don't want it, either, but we will not go down without trying. That's my speech."

The wine peasants of Poligny sipped from their glasses, and their eyes had the French look, cynical and critical and humorous and contentious and very tough and individual. I couldn't tell whether I had got through or not.

Louis Gibey said, "I want to tell you about a paradox. You see, we have always thought of the Catholic Church as the symbol of reaction—the arm of the extreme right. But do you know, there is a whole crop of young priests in France now working for the social changes which are supposed to be the projects of the extreme left. Yes, it is a paradox. The Communists have become the reactionaries, rigid, formalistic, unchanging and unchangeable. It is the clergy now that leads to the left; maybe not the archbishops and cardinals, but the young, tough priests."

The hard-handed peasants of Poligny sipped their wine and chuckled. They love a paradox.

Through the open door came the shrill voice of Jenny chanting monotonously, "I love you, I love you a little, I love you passionately."

And I remembered reading in Albert Guérard's beautiful little history of France the poem:

She alone has received the conquered into her bosom.
She alone has tended all mankind under a common name;
A mother rather than a queen, she has turned her subjects into citizens;

She binds together the remotest lands by ties of pious reverence.
Thanks to her yoke of peace, the stranger believes himself in his own country;
We have become a single people.

It sounds like a hymn to America, but it was written by Rutilius Namatianus, a Gaul, in the fifth century A.D. And he wrote it about Rome. And Rome was falling.

Then Guérard quotes Virgil's great call to Rome four centuries earlier—"Thy fate it is to rule nations." If you change the word "rule" to "lead," it might be said of America today.

It was cool and peaceful in the ancient church and the battered faces of the peasants showed dimly in the semidarkness.

From far up on the mountain behind the town came the belling of a hound on track.

"Ticot," said Parachute Pants softly.

"I love you to insanity," shrieked Jenny in the road outside the church.

One American in Paris

(fourth piece)

IT WOULD BE ridiculous for me to try to write anything new or original about Paris. In all the world no city has been so loved and so celebrated. Indeed the traveler comes soon to feel that he is received into the arms of this city which is so much more than a city. I imagine that many Americans come to Paris for its restaurants, its gaiety, its beauty. For myself, when I come back to Paris I feel always that I am coming home. I love the good food too and the beauty but I invariably find myself drawn to the Ile de la Cité, that stone ship of the Seine whose cargo has gone to the whole world. I love this island, I love the music in stone which is Notre Dame. I rejoice in the little streets and houses which are material memories of another time. But the relationship goes farther than this. The Ile is holy ground. Here the thinking of the Western world was born—the brave thinking arduously rising out of the noble ruins of Rome and Greece. Here the great ones sorted over the pieces of the past, chose the valid, cast aside the gross, added their own new ingredient and drew a cold world to warm itself at the new fire. And surely the Ile spilled over to the banks and coursed out, but here, right here, physically under my feet, the miracle happened—not quickly but with the incredible labor of birth and growth. I have read of the French Gothic that it draws the eyes to heaven, that it defies or seems to the laws of weight, and the limitations of stone. It seems to me that Notre Dame and its brothers are the symbols of that exuberant thought.

But the great churches are only one symbol—my own thinking, my own conceptions, are no less the products of this tiny island, when the fabric of man's relation to man was picked apart and rewoven with the new thread of responsibility. Here the conception of liberty was born—not only political liberty but the enormous conception that the individual mind of man had not only the right but the duty to rove the world and dig into the heavens. This island raised the heavy sky and kicked out the close horizons. This is indeed holy ground.

My sons are too little for abstractions but I can take them to the Ile and raise for their delight the lovely ghosts. Here where you stand Caesar stood; here Richard of the Lion Heart trotted his heavy charger over the cobbles. Right here Francis the First walked with perhaps Leonardo at his side and here Abelard pushed back his hood and raised his voice. My boys love this pageantry. And later we walk down to the river and sit on the stone and let our feet dangle over the water. We wait patiently for some of the many fishermen to catch a fish and when some tiny thing is hooked we run to examine and to congratulate. This minnow is a triumph beyond which the big game fisherman cannot rise. Kicking our heels against the stone we watch the barges moving by, the laundry drying on the deck and the seeming sweet, slow life of the barge men. Sometimes we can smell the soup cooking in the galley and through a window see the sturdy wife, her sleeves rolled up, stirring the pot. Then there is excitement, another fisherman has landed a fierce fish as big as his little finger.

Sitting there I had a horrid thought, a mean and malicious thought, and I told it to a French friend.

"What would happen," I asked, "if I should go to an aquarium and buy alive a trout of thirty centimeters—then bring it concealed to the embankment, put a hook in its mouth and throw it living in the river. I would then play it with courage and finally land the beauty."

"Oh! my friend," my companion cried. "Put this thought from your mind. Promise you will never do it."

"But what would happen?"

My friend said seriously, "Fifty fishermen, the flower of Seine fishermen, men of integrity and seriousness, would commit suicide."

We walk past the bird market. We are always just about to buy a bird— only our inability to decide which bird deters us. We want them all. . . .

How this island, this magic ship, calls to me when I am away from it. How it reassures me that the world is not about to disappear, and that men and ideas are eternal. And this island set in its timeless river proves to me that I am small but reassures me that I am important.

And I will not catch the trout.

One American in Paris

(thirteenth piece)

NOW I HAVE more than passed the halfway mark in these little pieces for *Figaro Littéraire*. I have enjoyed the writing of them and also I have enjoyed the generous response to them from the readers. I began the series with timidity because I did not know the fabric of the French mind, I was too ignorant of recent French history. I felt a kind of shyness about writing to Parisians. This shyness has now disappeared because of the generosity of the reception. I knew historically the French genius for fairness and receptiveness but it is quite a different thing to have it proved to me personally. I have even received letters which say I write in the French manner. This cannot be true. I write in my own manner, but the letters further prove that the French, who are renowned throughout the world as the greatest of individualists, have maintained that diagnostic of the individual: tolerance.

How seldom do our most carefully considered plans materialize! I had thought to make all Paris my field. I should have known better. Here, as in New York, my district has become my city. I visit other districts but the place where I buy bread and wine for my family is my village. The gendarme on my corner is no longer police but my gendarme—an individual. The neighborhood people have become my neighbors. I am no longer strange to them nor they to me.

One sees first the broad picture, the design complete but the details undeveloped. Then gradually the outlines of the details become clear and the larger picture fades. I suppose that this is inevitable. I am sure it is good. Paris is becoming a city of units to me, and the units are people. As in a foreign language, words gradually begin to stand out of sentences, so in a foreign city individuals begin to stand out of crowds.

Around the corner from where I live a barrow man has his post. He cleans the street and picks up papers in the park. He lives a comfortable and successful life. At night he sleeps under his barrow and when it rains he drapes a waterproof cover over the handles to make a shelter. His friends visit him under his barrow and sometimes they play cards. The postman delivers mail to the barrow. He has always a bottle of wine uncorked in his shoulder bag and a piece of bread and cheese for his friends. His eye is merry and his nose is not pale. In the great world he would be considered a failure and something of a rascal, for the world of property considers it a sin to be content without things. But from watching him, and I now have a bowing acquaintance with him, I think he is a more successful organism than those worried men with briefcases and feverish eyes who race to work driven by the pressures of things. My man has apparently given up things he can do without for other things to him more important. I admire him.

We learn so many things. This cold unfriendly people, full of self-interest—described by Descartes as a people of unsentimental reason. What utter nonsense! Madame tells my wife not to buy from her but to go a few blocks over where the same thing may be had more cheaply. The kiosk saves for us the papers we want. Just as they have been sorted out to us so we have to them. We are no longer the mass tourists but individuals. It is a lesson we must learn over and over, that people and person are two very different things. We are helped and our way is made easy for us by the kindness of our neighbors. Perhaps this is because we like them very much.

I know that it is considered unseemly for a modern writer to find anything good in his time. I also know, because I have seen it, that there is terrible poverty in Paris, that there are areas of despair and want, that there are groups of anger and also that there are other groups of cynical disdain and selfishness. In spite of this I want to draw to the attention of Parisians some things they may have forgotten perhaps because of the pressures of daily life and perhaps because they are too close and ordinary to be remembered.

Do you know how unique is your respect for the individual no matter what his position? Are you aware of the courtesy and kindness of person to person? The genius for allowing a man to be himself without interference makes a great impression on me. I had always heard of the disagreeableness of the Parisian taxi drivers. What an error. A cigarette exchanged, a few words concerning weather and the world, and this so-called sullenness disappears; one finds a man of incisiveness and intelligence and moreover a member of the best-informed group in the city. The cab drivers know everything and sit like brooding gods on their knowledge.

I wonder whether you Parisians know how kindly you are to the stranger who asks for help. When I've asked directions of a stranger in the street, he has more often than not gone out of his way to direct me and even conducted me to my destination. When I dine in a bistro strange to me, it is my custom to ask the waiter or sommelier to suggest a wine out of the conviction that he knows his cellar better than I. Invariably the result is delicious and by no means the most expensive. When I've shopped for one of the innumerable small items necessary in running a house, the shopkeeper, if he does not have the article, has either sent out for it or conducted me to a shop which had it.

From my window I have seen my small sons returning from play in the park. The gendarme who directs traffic knows them. He stops traffic and makes sure that they arrive safely through the roaring river of motors, then smiles and waves his white stick at them.

These are the cold and selfish French of our experience. What dear people they are!

Before very long I must go away, first to Italy and to Greece and then to New York. But I strongly suspect that the elastic string of Paris is tied to me and that for all my life I will not visit Paris. It is other places I will be visiting, while Paris will be a very special home to me.

Positano

I FIRST HEARD of Positano from Alberto Moravia. It was very hot in Rome. He said, "Why don't you go down to Positano on the Amalfi coast? It is one of the fine places of Italy." Later John McKnight of the United States Information Service told me the same thing. He had spent a year there working on a book. Half a dozen people echoed this. Positano kind of moved in on us and we found ourselves driving down to Naples on our way.

To an American, Italian traffic is at first just downright nonsense. It seems hysterical, it follows no rule. You cannot figure what the driver ahead or behind or beside you is going to do next, and he usually does it. But there are other hazards besides the driving technique. There are the motor scooters, thousands of them, which buzz at you like mosquitoes. There is a tiny little automobile called "topolino" or "mouse" which hides in front of larger cars; there are gigantic trucks and tanks in which most of Italy's goods are moved; and finally there are assorted livestock, hay wagons, bicycles, lone horses and mules out for a stroll, and to top it all there are the pedestrians who walk blissfully on the highways never looking about. To give this madness more color, everyone blows the horn all the time. This deafening, screaming, milling, tire-screeching mess is ordinary Italian highway traffic. My drive from Venice to Rome had given me a horror of it amounting to cowardice.

I hired a driver to take me to Positano. He was a registered driver in good standing. His card read: "Signor Bassani Bassano, Experienced Guide—all Italy—and Throt Europe." It was the "Throt Europe" that won me.

Well, we had accomplished one thing. We had imported a little piece of Italian traffic right into our own front seat. Signor Bassano was a remarkable man. He was capable of driving at a hundred kilometers an hour, blowing the horn, screeching the brakes, driving mules up trees, and at the same time turning around in the seat and using both hands to gesticulate, describing in loud tones the beauties and antiquities of Italy and Throt Europe. It was amazing. It damn near killed us. And in spite of that he never hit anybody or anything. The only casualties were our quivering, bleeding nerves. I want to recommend Signor Bassano to travelers. You may not hear much of what he tells you, but you will not be bored.

We squirmed and twisted through Naples, past Pompeii, whirled and flashed into the mountains behind Sorrento. We hummed "Come Back to Sorrento" dismally. We did not believe we could get back to Sorrento. Flaming like a meteor, we hit the coast, a road, high, high above the blue sea, that hooked and corkscrewed on the edge of nothing, a road carefully designed to be a little narrower than two cars side by side. And on this road, the buses, the trucks, the motor scooters and the assorted livestock. We didn't see much of the road. In the back seat my wife and I lay clutched in each other's arms, weeping hysterically, while in the front seat Signor Bassano gestured with both hands and happily instructed us: "Ina da terd sieglo da Hamperor Hamgousternos coming tru wit Leeegeceons." (Our car hit and killed a chicken.) "Izz molto lot old heestory here. I know. I tall." Thus he whirled us "Throt Italy." And below us, and it seemed sometimes under us, a thousand feet below lay the blue Tyrrhenian licking its lips for us.

And yet he brought us at last, safe but limp, to Positano.

Positano bites deep. It is a dream place that isn't quite real when you are there and becomes beckoningly real after you have gone. Its houses climb a hill so steep it would be a cliff except that stairs are cut in it. I believe that whereas most house foundations are vertical, in Positano they are horizontal. The small curving bay of unbelievably blue and green water lips gently on a beach of small pebbles. There is only one narrow street and it does not come down to the water. Everything else is stairs. You do not walk to visit a friend, you either climb or slide.

Nearly always when you find a place as beautiful as Positano, your impulse is to conceal it. You think, "If I tell, it will be crowded with tourists and they will ruin it, turn it into a honky-tonk, and then the local people will get touristy and there's your lovely place gone to hell." There isn't the slightest chance of this in Positano. In the first place, there is no room. There are about two thousand inhabitants in Positano and there is room for about five hundred visitors, no more. The cliffs are all taken. Except for the half-ruinous houses very high up, all space is utilized. And the Positanese invariably refuse to sell.

Again, Positano is never likely to attract the organdy-and-white-linen tourist. It would be impossible to dress as a languid tourist-lady and climb the Positano stairs for a cocktail. She will arrive looking like a washcloth at a boys' camp. There is no way for her to get anywhere except by climbing. This alone eliminates one kind of tourist, the show tourist. The third deterrent to a great influx of tourists lies in the nature of the Positanese themselves. They just don't give a damn. They have been living here since before recorded history and they don't intend to change now. They don't have much, but they like what they have and will not move over.

We went to the Sirenuse, an old family house converted into a first-class hotel, spotless and cool, with grape arbors over its outside dining rooms. Every room has its little balcony and looks out over the blue sea to the islands of the sirens from which those ladies sang so sweetly. The owner of the Hotel Sirenuse is an Italian nobleman, Marquis Paolo Sursale. He is also the mayor of Positano, a strong, handsome man of about fifty who dresses mostly like a beachcomber and works very hard at his job as mayor. How he got the job is an amusing story.

Positano elects a town council of fifteen members. The council then elects one of its members as mayor. The people of Positano are almost to a man royalist in their politics. This is largely true of much of the South of Italy, but it is vastly true of Positano. The fishermen and shoemakers, the carpenters and truck drivers favor a king, and particularly a king from the House of Savoy. This was true when the present mayor was elected. The Marquis Paolo Sursale was elected because he was a Communist, the only one in town. It was his distinction in a whole electorate of royalists. One of Sursale's ancestors commanded a galley of war at the Battle of Lepanto in 1571 when the power of the Moslem was finally broken and Christian control of Europe assured. He does not say why he became a Communist. But he does say that he left the party in 1947 not in anger but in a kind of disgust. The township was a little sad about his losing his distinction, but they have elected him ever since, in spite of that.

The mayor of Positano is an archaeologist, a philosopher and an administrator. He has one policeman to keep order and there isn't much for his force to do. He says, "Nearly all Positanese are related. If there is any trouble, it is like a family fight and I never knew any good to come of interfering in a family quarrel." The mayor wanders about the town upstairs and downstairs. He dresses in tired slacks, a sweatshirt and sandals. He holds court anywhere he is, sitting on a stone wall overlooking the sea, leaning against the edge of a bar, swimming in the sea or curled up on the beach. Very little business gets done in the City Hall. The police force has so much time free that he takes odd jobs to make a little extra money.

The history of Positano is rich, long and a little crazy. But one thing is certain: it has been around a long time. When the Emperor Tiberius moved to Capri because he was detested in Rome, he didn't trust anyone. He thought people were trying to poison him, and he was probably right. He would not eat bread made with the flour of his part of the country. His galley instead crept down the coast to Positano and got the flour from a mill which still stands against the mountain side. This mill has been improved and kept up, of course, but it still grinds flour for the Positanese.

This little town of Positano has had a remarkable past. As part of the Republic of Amalfi in the ninth, tenth and eleventh centuries, it helped to write the first maritime laws we know in which the rights of sailors were set down. In the tenth century it was one of the most important mercantile cities of the world, rivaling Venice. Having no harbor, its great galleys were pulled bodily up on the beach by the townspeople.

Like most Italian towns, Positano has its miraculous picture. It is a Byzantine representation of the Virgin Mary. Once long ago, the story goes, the Saracenic pirates raided the town and among other things carried away this picture. But they had no sooner put to sea than a vision came to them which so stunned them that they returned the picture. Every year on August 15, this incident is reenacted with great fury and some bloodshed. In the night the half-naked pirates attack the town, which is defended by Positanese men-at-arms dressed in armor. Some of this fighting gets pretty serious. The pirates then go to the church and carry the holy picture off into the night. Now comes the big moment. As soon as they have disappeared into the darkness, a bright and flaming image of an angel appears in the sky. At present General Mark Clark is the sponsor of this miracle. He gave the town a surplus Air Force barrage balloon. Then very soon the pirates return in their boats and restore the picture to the church and everybody marches and sings and has a good time.

In the sixteenth and seventeenth centuries Positano became very rich. Its ships went everywhere, trading in the Near and Middle East, carrying the spices and silks and precious woods the West craved. Then the large and beautiful baroque houses that stand against the mountain were built and decorated with the loot of the world.

About a hundred years ago a tragedy came to the town. Steamships began to ply the ocean. Positano could not compete; year by year it grew poorer and more desperate. At that time there were about eight thousand citizens. Between 1860 and 1870 about six thousand of the townsmen emigrated to America and the great houses stood vacant; their walls crumbled; the painted designs paled out and the roofs fell in. The population has never got much above two thousand since.

About ten years ago a Moslem came to Positano, liked it and settled. For a time he was self-supporting, but gradually he ran out of assets and still he stayed. The town supported him and took care of him. Just as the mayor was their only Communist, this was their only Moslem. They felt that he belonged to them. Finally he died, and his only request was that he might be buried with his feet towards Mecca. And this, so Positano thought, was done. Four years later some curious meddler made a discovery. The Moslem had been buried by dead reckoning and either the compass was off or the map was faulty. He had been buried 28 degrees off course. This was outrageous to a seafaring town. The whole population gathered, dug the Moslem up, put him on course and covered him up again.

Positano does not have much of any industry. At night the fishing boats put out with powerful lights on their bows. They fish all night for anchovies and squids, and the bow lights of the boats litter the sea to sight's edge. But in fishing, Positano has a rival—the little town of Praiano, a few miles down the coast. The rivalry has been so great that a fishing code has been long established. When a school of fish is sighted, the lampara boats run for it. The first boat to reach it puts out its net and makes its circling run. Meanwhile other boats from the other town have raced for the school. If the first boat completes its circle before the others arrive, the school belongs to it. If not, both the towns share in the catch.

On shore there is a little shoemaking, some carpentry and a few arts and crafts. It would be difficult to consider tourists an industry because there are not enough of them. They do, however, provide a bit of luxury for the villagers.

Far up the mountain a convent looks down on the sea, and here little girls are taught the delicate and dying art of lacemaking by the sisters. The girls are paid and the lace sold to support the school and incidentally the children. The flying fingers of the little girls working with the hundreds of bobbins make the eye dizzy, and the children look up and laugh and talk as though they were not even aware of the magic of their flashing fingers. Some of the work is unbelievable. We saw a great tablecloth, a spiderweb, intricate as a thought. It was the work of fifty girls for one year.

A number of writers have gone to Positano to do their work. Some of these are Americans and some are British. Nothing in the little town is designed to disturb your thoughts, provided you have a thought. Such a recluse was John McKnight, now of the United States Foreign Service, but then in process of writing *The Papacy*, a long and careful study of the history of the Vatican.

He and his wife lived for a year in a little house with a garden right over the water in the southern part of the town. The McKnights come from North Carolina and they settled into the life of Positano as naturally as they had settled into Chapel Hill. Then the year turned and Thanksgiving began looming.

Now an American living long abroad may become completely expatriate, but let Christmas or Fourth of July or Thanksgiving come around and something begins to squirm inside him and he finds he has to do something about it.

Johnny and Liz McKnight speak Italian fluently, read, eat and live Italian. But when Thanksgiving came near in Positano, the McKnights found themselves dreaming of roast turkey and dressing, of cranberry sauce and plum pudding, of mint juleps. They got to waking up in the night and thinking about it.

The turkey arrived in a crate tied to the top of a bus. It was a fine, vigorous but slightly hysterical bird and for a week it gobbled and strutted in the one-bird turkey yard built for it in the garden until gradually its nerves got back to normal.

Johnny remembered a bit of wisdom imparted to him by his grandfather, in North Carolina. Violent death, his grandfather said, be it to man or to turkey, is a nervous and discouraging experience. The muscles are likely to go hard and certain unhappy juices are released into the system. His grandfather did not know how that affected the flavor of man but in a turkey it had a tendency to make the meat tough and a little bitter. But there was a way to avoid that. If about two hours before the execution, the turkey is given a couple of shots of good brandy, the nervous tension relaxes, the turkey's state of mind is clear and healthy and he goes to the block happy and even gratefully. Then when he is served, instead of bitter juices of fear and shock, there is likely to be a delicious hint of cognac in the meat.

Johnny decided to follow the custom of North Carolina. Then he found that he did not have any brandy; the only thing he had was a bottle of Grand Marnier. It was better than brandy. It would give not only solace to the turkey but an orangey flavor to the meat.

The turkey fought the idea at first. But finally Johnny got him held firmly under his arm and held the beak open while Liz put four or five eyedroppers of Grand Marnier down the bird's throat. At first the turkey gagged a little, but in a moment or two its head dropped, a sweet but wild look came in its eyes and it waved its head in rhythm with some gentle but not quite sober thought that went through its head. Johnny carried it gently to the pen. It wobbled a bit and then settled down comfortably and went to sleep.

"I'll do for it in its sleep," Johnny thought. "That turkey will never know what happened." And he went to the refrigerator to see how the mint juleps were doing.

They were doing fine. He brought two of them back to the garden, and he and Liz sat down to begin the Thanksgiving.

The McKnights do not know what happened. Johnny thinks the turkey may have had a bad dream. They heard a hiccuping gobble. The turkey rose straight up in the air, and screaming triumphantly flew out to sea.

Now we must go back to the sea laws of the Amalfi coast. In the hills above the towns of Positano and its rival Praiano, watchers are usually posted. They not only keep watch for schools of fish but for anything which may be considered flotsam, jetsam or salvage. These watchers saw the McKnights' seagoing turkey fly to sea and they also saw it crash into the water a couple of miles offshore.

Immediately boats put off from both Positano and Praiano. The race was on and they arrived at about the same time. But the turkey, alas, had drowned. The fishermen brought it tenderly back, arguing softly about whether it was a matter for salvage court. The turkey was obviously out of command. Johnny McKnight easily settled the problem with the rest of the bottle of Grand Marnier.

They cooked the turkey that afternoon and sat down to dinner about eight in the evening. And they say that not even an extra dose of sage in the dressing completely removed the taste of seawater.

Florence:
The Explosion of the Chariot

THEY DO Easter week big in Florence; and now that it is over, it leaves a strange and exotic memory. Everything here breathes of the past, not a general past—a Florentine past, which means that it is really part of the present. History seeps out like groundwater, and the Middle Ages merge with the now.

All week there were services almost continuously in the old churches. We walked from one to another in a growing hypnosis of color—the chanting of great choirs, the magnificent robes of the clergy, the medieval costumes of the city and the thousands of boys in white surplices, with the voices of angels and the faces of street urchins; the music, the Gregorian chanting climbed like vines up the tall Gothic columns and mushroomed back from the vaults of the domes. It is a haunting experience.

It was a week of gift giving; small, thoughtful presents, baskets of gold-wrapped chocolate eggs and many flowers. We went nowhere without carrying some small gift, an embroidered handkerchief or a potted flowering shrub. And our apartment is overflowing with the gifts our friends have brought to us. It is a gentle, pleasant custom.

The high point of the week as every Florentine knows is the Scopio del Carro, the explosion of the chariot. I had never seen it before. Once it took place at midday of Saturday before Easter, but now it is at nine in the evening and the country people for miles around come in to see it.

At seven in the evening, the carro is brought out, a huge wooden tower on wheels. It is about three stories high, painted with crosses and coats of arms, and on its top a golden crown supported on the tails of four gold dolphins.

Furthermore, this tower is loaded down with fireworks. It is drawn through the streets by four pure-white oxen, their horns and hooves gilded and garlands of flowers on their heads. People by the thousands follow it until it arrives in the space between the Duomo, the great cathedral of Arnolfo and Brunelleschi, and the domed sacristy near by.

The carro is escorted by a troop of men in the clothing and armor of the Middle Ages, shining steel breastplates and helmets and the red-and-white cloaks of old Florence. The guard is armed with swords and long, steel-tipped spears.

Once in the square, the oxen are unyoked, and a wire is attached to the tower, thence stretched through the open doors of the cathedral and up the long nave to the high altar. At the altar, an artificial dove hangs from the wire, but such a dove as you can't imagine—a jet-propelled dove.

Meanwhile, the square fills with people, but filled does not describe it. It is jam-packed with people. We watched it from a window over the square and saw this mass of people get to swaying and weaving like wheat under a strong wind. The cathedral is packed, too, and the streets as far as you can see, a field of swaying faces and the mood is happy and excited.

In the cathedral, the service continues, moving toward its climax at nine o'clock. Then the archbishop takes the holy fire from an ancient urn and ignites the fuse of the dove.

Actually, the dove is a kind of rocket. It whooshes along the wire, giving off smoke and flame; darts out the great doors, and strikes the tower, which erupts with fireworks exploding upward until finally they ignite a large Catherine wheel on the very top, which whirls with a screaming sound, spinning colored fire centrifugally in a great circle.

If all goes well, the dove is supposed to strike the tower and then by a second explosion to be propelled back to the high altar. If he gets there, good crops will result. If he does not, everyone forgets the whole thing. Our dove didn't make it, but the crops look great so far.

As the tower erupts with fireworks, the cathedral erupts with music, a thousand voices singing triumphantly the Gloria in Excelsis. It is an exciting and beautiful thing, and it occurs only in Florence.

As in all such ceremonies there is a story, a legend, a history—take your pick. And the story of this is as follows:

At the time of the first Crusade, one of the greatest and most noble houses of Florence was that of the Pazzi family. A member of this family, one Pazzolino Pazzi, led the Florentine forces to the Crusade, and he was the first man to plant the flag of the Cross on the walls of Jerusalem.

He was rewarded with three pieces of flint stone from the Holy Sepulcher and the right to add five crosses to the family crest. On his return to Florence, he was given a triumphal welcome, and his family received the honor of distributing the new holy fire of Easter to all of the hearths and candles of the city.

The new fire was and is struck from the three flint stones from the Holy Sepulcher. The Pazzi family built the painted tower with its arms and crown, and maintained it, and got a good deal of honor from the whole thing until they got into political trouble with Lorenzo di Medici.

Political trouble at that time included assassination, and the Pazzi lost both the bout and the privilege, as well as a considerable number of their kinsmen. But to this day, their arms are on the exploding tower. This is not the original tower, however. Several others have burned, and one exploded in the streets, killing quite a few people. The present tower was built in 1725, which in this country is considered yesterday.

I like this legend, and I intend to believe it. I won't go along with the spoilsport historians who write that Pazzolino Pazzi died a hundred years before the first Crusade, and that the Holy Sepulcher is of calcareous stone with no vestige of flint in it.

They even say that the relighting of the holy fire at Easter is a direct steal from the Roman custom of relighting the fires from the Temple of the Vestal Virgins. But to me, the explosion of the chariot is a pure and vital and moving spectacle.

I Go Back to Ireland

THERE MUST BE a kind of apprehension in the sleepy little villages of Italy, Germany, England and Ireland in the summer, when the descendant of the native comes back to discover the seat of his culture. I suppose Ireland suffers more from this than any other land. Every Irishman—and that means anyone with one drop of Irish blood—sooner or later makes a pilgrimage to the home of his ancestors. There he crows and squeals over the wee cot or the houseen, pats mossy rocks, goes into ecstasies over the quaint furniture, and finds it charming that the livestock lives with the family.

He wouldn't live there if you gave him the place. And the locals don't think they're quaint—they think they're perfectly normal. To them, it's the American descendant whose speech sounds outlandish, particularly when he puts on a nostalgic brogue, which he usually does. The natives must think the pilgrims are crazy.

I have just made such a pilgrimage. I am half Irish, the rest of my blood being watered down with German and Massachusetts English. But Irish blood doesn't water down very well; the strain must be very strong.

I guess the people of my family thought of Ireland as a green paradise, mother of heroes, where golden people sprang full-flowered from the sod. I don't remember my mother actually telling me these things, but she must have given me such an impression of delight. Only kings and heroes came from this Holy Island, and at the very top of the glittering pyramid was our family, the Hamiltons.

My grandfather, who had come from there carrying the sacred name, was really a great man, a man of sweet speech and sweet courtesy. He died when I was quite young, but it is remarkable how much I remember about him. His little bog-trotting wife, I am told, put out milk for the leprechauns in the hills behind King City, California, and when a groundling neighbor suggested the cats drank it, she gave that neighbor a look that burned off his nose.

Anyway, we grew up feeling singularly favored because of even our demi-Irishness. There was very little running back to Ireland for a look; there was none, in fact. My grandparents never went home to visit. I can recall only two relatives who did. One was a cousin of my mother's who was a judge of the Supreme Court in California. He went back, I guess, mostly to impress the Irish relatives with the importance of the American branch. They must have cut him down to size, because he rarely spoke of his visit.

Later, one of my uncles made the trip. He reported that he had wept out of pure sentiment the whole time. He also reported that the family was just about played out; there remained two sisters and a brother— Katherine, Elizabeth and Thomas—children of my grandfather's brother, all old and all unmarried. They lived in the "new house" (the old house had burned down several hundred years ago).

After my uncle's return, we had an occasional letter from Elizabeth. She wrote a thin, elegant hand, and her English had an exquisite quality, reminiscent of the eighteenth-century writers. We felt good about that; we didn't really believe any dull or illiterate Irish existed—in Ireland, at least. We knew plenty of that kind in this country, but perhaps we thought they had degenerated here.

I should have gone to visit long ago, but I didn't. During the war, I landed at various Irish airports and could have gone, but some curious, powerful reluctance always came over me when I got close to the home place. Meanwhile, the letters had stopped and we heard nothing more.

Last summer, my wife and I finally went there.

It's green, all right—but so is Scotland. It seemed to me a different green, but I wouldn't submit the two greens to a color test. We rented an automobile to cross from Belfast to Londonderry—an extravagance which outraged even the man who owned the car, a Rolls-Royce of sneering gentility, a little younger than Stonehenge and in a little better condition. Summer was full-blown in Ireland and the grain was bowing golden-headed, ready for the cutting.

Then we crossed and came to Derry, and it's a dour, cold city to an outsider—dark, angular buildings and uncrowded streets, waiting for something—a city of protest against the rolling green of County Derry and the lovely hills of Donegal across Lough Foyle.

There was no home feeling in the bleak hotel, that carried its own darkness with it. The girl behind the desk would not smile nor pass a cordial word, no matter how much we tried to trap her. In the bar there was no gaiety. I don't know whether laughter was there before we went in for a drink or after we left, but none was offered for us to share, and curtains of rules brushed against us.

A drink in our room? Not permitted. Two minutes late to the dining room? Not permitted to serve after hours. A London paper, then. All taken. There was a hush on the people like the hush on the city, and the feeling that eyes brushed over you and dropped when you looked up. We were strangers.

The porter—not the real porter, he hastened to tell us, the real porter was away—said he would get us a man to drive us into the country the next day, a man who knew the countryside.

This not-the-real-porter was nice to us. He was sorry he couldn't have some clothes pressed for us; it was after hours. He wanted to bring a drink to us. He looked sadly at the bribe in his hand. He would try.

In a while he came back. The liquor was locked up, the manager had the key, and the manager was gone. A sandwich? The pantry was locked up. I don't know who had that key. A copy of the London *Times* in the morning? They were all ordered and it was too late to order another one. He looked as though he wanted to return the bribe; he was a young, dark, sad-looking man. I found myself trying to explain to him.

"Does the young lady at the desk never smile?" I asked.

"Rarely," he said.

"Is no rule ever broken at all?"

"I don't understand," he said.

"Look," I said, "my people came from hereabouts. They were law-abiding people, but there was a filament of illegality in them. My mother wasn't above putting too much catsup on her plate and sopping it up with a piece of bread in a restaurant."

"Catsup?" he asked.

I said, "One of my uncles had a major difficulty in college for stealing chickens. Another of my uncles had to be disarmed when he had murder in his heart, and I, myself . . ."

I stopped, because the not-the-real-porter was looking at me helplessly, trying to make out my meaning. My voice was rising against a wall of frustration.

"What I am trying to say is this," I said. "Has all illegality gone out of this rebellious island in three generations?"

"Sir?" he asked.

"I mean, if I should give you in your hand more than enough—twice more than enough—to buy a bottle of whisky, a loaf of bread and a sausage, couldn't you find some lawbreaker to sell them to you?"

"The rules are very strict," he said, "I'm sorry. I wish I could help you."

My heart broke for him.

"I'm not the real porter," he said. "Good night, sir, I'm sorry."

We sat in the window, looking across the street at the angry stone buildings and the small, locked-up shops. The street was deserted and a desolation came over us. I told my wife how brave and open my ancestors were, how full of lust and courtesy and fine laughter. I lied about them some—I guess I had to. The Sunday dark fell on that city which is somber even on weekdays and in sunlight.

Now my reluctance came on me tenfold and I wanted to give up the pilgrimage and go away quickly and forget it, because reality was violating every inherited memory and I was saying to myself that if the old folks went away from here, maybe they had good reason.

I put on a bathrobe and took the long, deserted, green-carpeted hall to the bathroom. From a room on the corridor came an old woman carrying a broom and a long-handled dustpan. I said good evening to her and her face wrinkled up into a smile that lighted the dark corners of that desolate corridor.

"Good evening, sir," she said.

I stopped in front of her, because this was a tone I had not heard. "I know before I ask that the irons are locked up," I said, "but can you steal an iron and take the wrinkles out of a pair of pants for me?"

"What room?" she asked, and then, "You'll have smooth pants."

The front was broken. In an hour she had the trousers back, still steaming a little, and I tipped her until she begged for mercy. We slept better because of her.

In the morning, we had our driver, all right—he who knew the countryside—a rakish man in a torn cap, who assured us that he knew every nubbin of a hill in all directions. He didn't, but he was willing. His car was so old that it churned and clattered, and a blue, suffocating smoke came from it. We were looking for a place called Mulkeraugh. You can spell it half a dozen ways and it isn't on any map. I knew from half-memory that it was near to Ballykelly, which is near to Limavady, and I knew that from Mulkeraugh you could look across the lough to the hills of Donegal.

We clattered and smoked along eighteen miles from Londonderry, past thatched cottages and hedged little fields where the black bundles of the flax lay waiting to be taken in. The countryside was rolling and lovely and the blackness of the city went out of us. The Donegal hills were remote and sunny across the broad water of the lough.

We drove right through Ballykelly without knowing it was there, but at Limavady they turned us back. I guess I had thought of Ballykelly as a town; it isn't—it's what they call in Texas a wide place in the road. Except for two churches, it wasn't different from the cottage-lined highway we had been driving on. An old man stood in front of one of the churches. "Mulkeraugh?" he said. "Second turning to the left—a quarter of a mile."

"Do you know any Hamiltons there?" I asked.

"They're all dead," he said. "Miss Elizabeth died two years ago. You'll find Mr. Richey, her cousin, on the hill, though."

Mulkeraugh isn't a place at all. It's a hill and three or four farms near about. Mr. Richey came to the door of the house on the hill and he looked like some of our breed—the pink cheeks, the light blue sparkling eyes.

He said, "The Hamilton place is sold, sold to the ground. You can find out about it at the lawyer's office in Limavady."

I said, "I'm the grandson of Samuel; he left here a long time ago."

"I have heard there was a brother," he said; "went away to America. But wasn't his name Joseph?"

It was the same everywhere we asked—my grandfather did not exist. So far as Ireland was concerned, there was no Samuel Hamilton. Why should they remember? The tree of our culture had no roots. Maybe I'd known that unconsciously, and that was why I had been reluctant to go back. My grandfather's brother, he who stayed, that was different. And his children, they were different. And how much land they had, that was different. And how improved it was and how much it brought when it was sold. These were immediate things, and who could remember an old, old fact like my grandfather?

Everyone knew the three children of my grandfather's brother, Miss Katherine, Miss Elizabeth and Mr. Tom. It was a good farm they had— about two hundred acres—and a good house of two stories. These children never married, the two sisters and the brother; why? No one knew why. They were well-endowed, well-educated people, and they had more land than most. They had silver spoons and fine china and little coffee cups, so thin you could see through them, and all the collected things of the family for hundreds of years, pictures and books and records and furniture, to make them envied all over the countryside. But they never married. They were well known, well liked. They grew old together.

Miss Katherine was the efficient one, almost like Tommy's mother, and Tommy did just what she said about the farm. He plowed when she said and he sowed when she said and he harvested when she said.

Miss Elizabeth was more for reading and writing things, and she had a rose garden. She spent a great deal of her time cultivating her flowers. Tommy was a silent man, but good, and well liked everywhere. The three grew older on the farm and they never married.

Then, about twelve years ago, Miss Katherine died. The directing head was gone. The farm went to pieces little by little and month by month, so slowly that it was hardly noticeable. Tommy, with no one to tell him what to do, when to plow and when to sow, began to neglect the land, and he sold some of the cows and didn't replace them. When the roof leaked, he didn't mend it. The hedges began to creep into the fields. When his friends remonstrated, he smiled and agreed that he should keep up the land, but the directing head was gone and there was no one to tell him.

Elizabeth, the neighbors said, had her head in a book. She tended the roses and she and Tommy grew ever closer together. And then, about seven years ago, Tommy died. He got a scratch on his side from a nail and did nothing about it, because nobody told him to, and he died of blood poisoning.

People who told us about what happened next did so reluctantly, as though they didn't want to be gossiping. Miss Elizabeth, they said, grew strange after Tommy died—"strange" was the word they used. She'd be smart and clever as always, but there'd be things like this: she would be talking to a neighbor and at the same time listening to something far away. And right in the middle of a perfectly normal conversation, she would say, "Tom is going to take out that tree stump in the lane. We need a new tree there."

And when neighbor women were having tea with her from those thin little cups you could almost see through, Elizabeth would say, "I'll have to ask you to excuse me now, Tom's coming in and he'll be very tired." And she would usher them out of the house.

And then in the night they'd hear Miss Elizabeth walking in the lanes between the hedgerows and she'd be calling her brother, telling him it was late and his supper was waiting. And several times she was seen in the night, searching through the fields. She was in a nightgown and her feet were bare, but she wasn't sleepwalking, they said—she wasn't asleep at all. She'd just turned strange, they said.

It wasn't as though she was crazy. Except for that, she talked as good sense as anybody, but she just could not bring herself to believe that her brother was dead. And she did another strange thing that was unlike her, they said. She got herself a cause. She joined the party which resisted with all its strength the joining of the northern counties to Eire. She worked for her cause and she made a will in which she ordered everything she possessed sold on her death and every penny turned over to the party that resisted the joining of Ulster to Eire, and then she died.

The neighbors said it was a sorrow to see the house torn apart. It was well known that the Hamiltons had beautiful things. On the day of the auction, the automobiles and the carriages came by the hundred, and people bought pictures just for the frames: and the beautiful silver went, and the fine china, and the books, bought for the binding only—and all by strangers. Strangers bought the farmhouse. It was a sorrow, the neighbors said.

. . .

I went to see the house and there was nothing of us there. The rose garden was overgrown with weeds and only the whips of the rosebushes showed above the grass, with haws still on from the last year. The ivy had nearly covered the stone paths. The new owners were kind. But they were strangers, and, what was even worse, we were strangers.

The sexton of the church at Ballykelly is an old, old man, lean and dry, and his speech is like my grandfather's speech.

I asked, "Did you know the Hamiltons?"

"Hamiltons?" he said. "I ought to—I dug their graves. I buried them, all of them. Miss Elizabeth was the last, two years ago. She was a bright one."

We looked at the graves, with the new cement coping around the plot. "Miss Elizabeth put it in her will about coping," the sexton said. He didn't ask, but we felt that he wanted to know. I said, "My grandfather was William's brother." He nodded slowly. "I've heard," he said. "Went away—I forget where."

"California," I said.

"What was his name again?" the sexton asked.

The rain was beginning to fall. He left us for a moment and came back, carrying a full-blown red rose. "Would you like to have it?" he asked.

I took it. And that's the seat of my culture and the origin of my being and the soil of my background, the one full-blown evidence of a thousand years of family. I have it pressed in a book.

The Ghost of Anthony Daly

Galway, Ireland

Dear Alicia:

I'VE EDGED OFF from writing you about the ghost of Anthony Daly, not because it is a complicated story, but because every sentence I write can and will be challenged by any number, who will swear it wasn't that way at all. I have heard a half-dozen versions and there must be more. Meanwhile, I am sleeping and working in the Grey Room at St. Cleran's and that's the room Daly haunts. He has been often seen and felt and heard in this room, but so far unfortunately not by me, although he would be welcome. But maybe I'm not the kind he likes to haunt. And I do feel slighted because the ghost of Daly has walked this house and especially this room for 146 years, and he has every right to, as you shall hear.

In 1820 this house and the surrounding countryside was owned by the Burkes, once Burgos. They came to England with William the Conqueror and later held large parts of Ireland by English grant and English military power, to the hatred and pain of the Irish, who, like the American Indians, thought they had a right to the land because they were here first, a long time first.

One evening in the spring of 1820, James Hardiman Burke was returning to this house from the holdings at Laughrea when he was fired at from the bushes beside the road. He put spurs to his horse and escaped and immediately called for the military commander of the district, because shooting at a landlord was not regarded kindly by landlords. The soldiery combed the neighborhood and came up with a candidate for vengeance, a young and handsome and athletic Irishman named Anthony Daly, who was known to be a troublemaker and an organizer of rebellious attitudes among the subject Irish. There are some that say he had also found romantic congress with one or more of the St. Cleran's ladies, which, if true, put two handles on his coffin.

Daly was brought to trial for his life on evidence either bought with money or threats, while other evidence to the effect that he was otherwhere and probably equally untrue was rejected by the judge, who sat alone since the Irish did not rate jury trial by their peers because, if they had, there would not have been a conviction in a thousand years. Daly's defense was clear and reasonable to everyone but the judge. He swore that he was a crack shot and that the proof of his innocence was that Burke was alive. This logic was rejected and Daly was condemned to death by hanging.

It has always been the conviction of tyrants right down to our own time that terror is an effective weapon against a subject people. Daly's hanging must be impressive enough to be remembered by any future malcontent who might take it into his head to shoot a landlord.

The story now splits seven ways from breakfast. Some say the local hangman refused to do the job and then got sick when he was ordered to do it, that one after another refused the duty so that Burke himself had to do the hanging. Others hold that one of the informers against Daly, knowing his life was in short demand, agreed to do it.

The gallows was at Seefin's hill, a high point in the country and about a mile from where I sit now at St. Cleran's. To make the occasion particularly bitter, a coffin was placed in Daly's own cart, pulled by his own horse, and he was paraded about the neighborhood surrounded by soldiers to prevent the gathering Irish from rescuing him. And, last, he was taken to St. Cleran's so the ladies could have a shuddering last look at him. One story is that a special window had been knocked in the house wall facing Seefin's hill so that the ladies could watch the hanging through their spyglasses, that afterwards the window was bricked up again. And whether or not it proves anything, when several years ago John Huston was repairing this house, he came on a bricked-up window facing the direction of Seefin's hill.

To give the whole ceremony added meaning, it was carried out on

Good Friday of 1820 and if that was an early Easter and the leaves were not on the trees, the ladies could have seen the hanging.

But the nature of the story makes me jump back and forth. When the cart was drawn through one of the stone and iron gates of St. Cleran's, Daly rose up and struck his manacles on the iron to try to break free. But the manacles held and his hand, impaled on an iron spike, splashed blood on the stone gate post. And Daly, looking at the blood, cried out, "When I am dead, draw my blood and put it on the Dunsandle gate as well, so no peace may ever enter this house."

There are many stories of the progress—how the people gathered to rescue him and were persuaded that it was hopeless by the attending priest. How, at one time, with a changing guard, Daly was left alone with the hangman for half an hour. In this version the hangman is the informer. At a public house, the colonel halted the escort and took Daly from the cart and bought him a drink, and Daly satirically bought the hangman a drink and offered his horse in payment.

After hours of slow progress, they came at last to Seefin's hill where the gallows was set up. There was no drop. The cart was backed under the rope and Daly was intended to strangle slowly for the instruction of the onlookers.

Now the colonel approached and said, "I am empowered to save your life if you will give me the names of your fellow conspirators." Then Daly's mother cried out, "Anthony, my son, you were born a man." And Daly shouted, "And I will die a man."

The story is full of strange twists and quirks, and so it should be. All hope of reprieve being gone, the colonel asked if the prisoner had any last request. And Daly said, "I have. I used of old times to come to Seefin's hill to practice my broad jump. I want to jump once more before I die."

And this did not seem strange because Daly was famous as a jumper. He was helped down from the cart and the irons removed from his wrists and ankles, but he was so cramped that he had to rub up the circulation. Then with the soldiers standing alert, he took his run and made a tremendous broad jump, and, having done so, indicated that he was ready. His pregnant wife was brought forward and he kissed her, saying, "If we have a son, I charge him as a sacred duty to avenge his father," and, with that, he leaped into the cart, his wrists were manacled and the rope was put about his neck. Suddenly he aimed a kick at the hangman, knocking him off the cart. Then Daly took two steps and leaped and his neck snapped and he was dead.

And Blind Rafftery was among the watchers and he made a poem about Daly that is still sung and part of it carved in this memorial on Seefin's hill.

You can see the quality of the man whose ghost is said to haunt this Grey Room where a turf fire is burning now.

But that's not all. They cut him down and drew his blood and splashed it on the gates of the manor. And his pregnant wife put a widow's curse on the place and that's as hard a curse as there is. The grass would never grow where the gallows stood, she said. And I've seen the holes and no grass is there. The rooks would never roost nor rest in St. Cleran's wood—and they do not. They will not ever fly over it. And she said, no Burke would ever die in bed in the manor nor, living, know any peace. And this also seems to be true. They died in other places and, before very long, they moved away and left the house vacant, and it was half ruinous when John Huston bought it and restored it, until now it is perhaps the most beautiful Georgian house anywhere.

There is the story and, as I promised you early in, Alicia, every part of it but the last will be argued over and refuted and added to in any public house in Galway on any Saturday night.

I've waited this week to see Daly in the Grey Room. Two nights ago I thought I felt him, but it is more likely that the frosting breeze through the open window did it.

Anthony Daly is welcome if he wants to come haunting, but maybe that very welcome will give his poor soul leave to rest. I don't think I'll see him. Maybe no one will again.

You can see from all this that Ireland is still Ireland, and you don't have to dig down for it, either.

Yours,
John Steinbeck

VII.

WAR CORRESPONDENT

EVEN BEFORE America declared war in 1941, John Steinbeck was attuned to German aggression. While filming *The Forgotten Village* in Mexico during the summer of 1940, he wrote a worried letter to his uncle in Washington, D.C.: ". . . the life of an Indian village is tied up with the life of the Republic. The Germans have absolutely outclassed the allies in propaganda. If it continues, they will completely win Central and South America away from the United States" (*SLL* 205). A few days later he wrote to request an audience with President Roosevelt and, granted twenty minutes, flew to Washington to propose to him that "a propaganda office be set up which, through radio and motion pictures, attempts to get this side of the world together. Its method would be to make for understanding rather than friction" (*SLL* 207). That gesture explains much about Steinbeck's involvement in war, both World War II and, some twenty years later, the Vietnam War. He wanted to be involved, to offer advice, and to cultivate what was, for him, the highest calling of the artist—helping people understand one another. All his subsequent involvement with the Office of War Information in World War II, as well as his own publications about both wars, was directed toward those ends.

Although he lent his services to write propaganda immediately after the United States entered World War II, what John Steinbeck really craved was action at the battlefront. "I want a job with a big reactionary paper like the *Herald-Tribune* because I think I could get places that way I couldn't otherwise" (Benson 512). With the help of the *Herald Tribune*'s literary critic, Lewis Gannett, Steinbeck got a job as overseas correspondent for what was a conservative but highly respected newspaper. He sailed from New York about June 3, 1943—only two months after his second marriage. Posted first in England, he was to "see the war through the eyes of the Common Man," as London's *Daily Express* reported (Simmonds 172). His first dispatches about the troopship crossing delighted his *Tribune* editor, who wrote in a private memorandum that the articles were "even better than we had hoped. In fact, I haven't read anything better about the war—anything to equal them in graphic description or in beauty of writing" (Simmonds 173).

These and later dispatches from England tell about things correspondents had, for the most part, overlooked: waiting bomber crews whose "care of the guns is slow and tender, almost motherly" (*New York Herald Tribune*, 30 June 1943). And "girls" who watched for German planes on the south coast of England, "girls" who have been "bombed and strafed, who have shot enemies out of the sky and then gone back to mending socks" (*OWW* 55–56). And he records the conversations of enlisted men in pubs; of people in a bus queue on Piccadilly, talking of Mussolini's resignation; of a maimed pilot in a restaurant, face collapsed, hands reduced to two fingers, scheming about how to fly missions again. Steinbeck wrote about the ordinariness of life on the edge of the war: the "complicated and carefully tended vegetable gardens" (*OWW* 71) or the "quality in the people of Dover that may well be the key to the coming German disaster. They are incorrigibly, incorruptibly unimpressed" (*OWW* 47). To some extent, the rhythm of these dispatches mirrors that of *The Grapes of Wrath*, as Steinbeck records the intimacies of conversation and then pans to the broader vision of the war effort in England— bomber crews preparing to fly or London recovering from the siege or the cultural impact of Bob Hope. He wrote well. And, for the most part, he wrote quickly, sending dispatches to New York nearly every day.

Half of these dispatches are sent from his two months in England. By late August, Steinbeck was in North Africa, where he found little to engage him—a hapless congressman who posed woodenly in a cemetery, himself never having seen combat; a deserter named Slog getting home to Brooklyn amid Italian prisoners. With the invasion of Italy, Steinbeck finally witnessed action at the front; he was assigned to a force commanded by Douglas Fairbanks, Jr., and with that unit went to Palermo, Sicily, and, on September 9, to capture the small island of Ventotene off the Italian coast. Here and at Red Beach near Salerno he participated in the action he craved, and he did not flinch: "I do know those things about myself that I had to know," he tells his wife, Gwyn. "I know that I can take it as well as most and better than some and that is a reassuring thing to know. And there is no way of knowing it until it happens" (18 Sept. 1943). His dispatches about the Italian invasion are among the best he wrote.

Among seasoned war correspondents, there had initially been some resistance to a popular novelist in their midst. "To this hard-bitten bunch of professionals I arrived as a Johnny-come-lately, a sacred cow, a kind of tourist," Steinbeck writes in his introduction to *Once There Was a War*. "I think they felt that I was muscling in on their hard-gained territory. When, however, they found that I was not duplicating their work, was not reporting straight news, they were very kind to me and went out of their way to help me and to instruct me in the things I didn't know. For example, it was [Robert] Capa who gave me the best combat advice I ever heard. It was 'Stay where you are. If they haven't hit you, they haven't seen you' " (*OWW* xvi). And he recalls the restrictions placed on the correspondent: "We edited ourselves much more than we were edited. We felt responsible to what was called the home front. There was a general feeling that unless the home front was carefully protected from the whole account of what war was like, it might panic. Also we felt we had to protect the armed services from criticism, or they might retire to their tents to sulk like Achilles" (*OWW* xvii).

In his four and a half months overseas, Steinbeck wrote eighty-six dispatches, published first in the *Herald Tribune* between 21 June and 15 December 1943; twenty-three were published simultaneously under different titles in London's *Daily Express*. The dispatches were also syndicated in more than forty leading newspapers, evidence of Steinbeck's status as a hugely popular writer; *The Ladies' Home Journal* and *Reader's Digest* also ran a few of the pieces in 1944. In 1958, Covici urged Steinbeck to publish his dispatches with an introduction, and the writer selected sixty-eight—omitting from the selection one on the importance of letters to soldiers:

> And a man feels trapped. If something is wrong, there is nothing in
> the world that he can do about it. He cannot go to a sick wife, nor
> can he revenge himself on a creeper. He is here and helpless and

one good letter can make the difference between a good soldier and
a sick man. . . . Good food can be given to a man, and entertainment and hard work, but nothing in the world can take the place of
the letters. They are the single strings and when they are cut the
morale of that man is shattered. (3 Aug. 1943)

Although Steinbeck's World War II journalism is written with complete
anonymity, complete detachment, this dispatch suggests the agony Steinbeck himself felt while on assignment. Because he heard so infrequently
and unsatisfactorily from his own young wife, he left Europe early and
when offered an assignment in the Pacific turned it down. Battered by his
near escape from a German bomb on Red Beach, both eardrums broken,
he'd had enough of war.

Twenty-three years later, Steinbeck wrote about another war. The
second series of "Letters to Alicia," begun in December 1966, includes
letters about Vietnam—a trip that Lyndon Johnson had earlier wanted
Steinbeck and other writers to make and that, a year later, both Harry
Guggenheim, publisher of *Newsday,* and Lyndon Johnson urged upon
Steinbeck. The Vietnam pieces are, without a doubt, the most controversial writing of Steinbeck's career. They were so when published in
1966–67. They are so now. Covering a war that polarized America, John
Steinbeck took a side not congenial with the politics of the left—or, many
thought, with his own liberal perspective. "These newly come harbingers
of peace say we don't belong in Vietnam and we can't win. Well, we do
belong there and we never wanted to win. But I believe we intend to
make sure that Peking doesn't win, either. That's why we belong there"
(18 Dec. 1965). Suddenly the people's bard was mouthing hawkish senti-
ments, denouncing protesters, writing jingoistic prose in support of
American policy in South Vietnam, and slathering on details about the
machinery of war. Photos of a gun-toting Steinbeck in fatigues ran in
many newspapers. Americans gagged on this new Steinbeck, seemingly
a traitor to the downtrodden.

Protecting South Vietnam was a position taken by Lyndon Johnson's
administration as the bombing began in earnest in 1965; and one
backed, of course, by other prominent literary figures, among them
Vladimir Nabokov, John Updike, Ralph Ellison, James T. Farrell, and John

Dos Passos (Brinkley 27). But Steinbeck was perhaps the most vocal and most frequently denounced—and the one who went to Vietnam to see for himself. For a man who was sixty-four years old, not terribly fit, and in poor health, it was a courageous trip to take, and he spared himself no discomfort in his mission to witness this new kind of war, a "drifting phantasm of a war" (14 Jan. 1967), where you couldn't chart progress on a map, "a feeling war with no fronts and no rear" (14 Jan. 1967). A new kind of soldier was called for, Steinbeck asserts, one who "must think for himself, must exercise judgment to survive and often enough when casualties indicate, must assume command" (14 Jan. 1967). With these soldiers, he spent five weeks of his six-week stay "in the field." He ventured into battle on a Huey chopper with the 10th Cavalry; he visited the 23rd Artillery Group guarding Saigon; he went on River Patrol Boat 37 covering the Bassac River; and with Elaine he was fired at while leaving the Delta hamlet of Tan An. At the end of it all, he wrote Guggenheim that he'd been in all but three of the American machines of war. All in order to report the facts as he saw them.

Several points need to be kept in mind while reading these accounts. First, Steinbeck hated communism, as is clear from all he wrote about the numbing effects of totalitarianism on the individual. After two decades of Cold War standoff, he shared with many Americans the belief that the engagement had shifted to the Third World, where "the great plan has been frustrated and staggered" by U.S. involvement. He was convinced that Peking and Moscow, selling arms to the North Vietnamese, were behind the North Vietnamese front; was certain that Asia could fall to the Communists; believed that the people of South Vietnam—like the Joads or "the people" in *The Moon Is Down*—needed to stand firm against the threat of political oppression. Second, Lyndon Johnson was a friend, Lady Bird one of Elaine's schoolmates at the University of Texas, and John himself fiercely loyal to friends and even more stalwart when it came to his President and to the ideal of American democracy. Third, his shrill words about war protesters in America came from a man who felt keenly a sense of individual responsibility and accountability—he drove himself to produce throughout his life, and he lacked tolerance for objectors who whined about peace, as he saw it, without offering some solution. More than fifteen years earlier, writing about James Dean, he noted in a 1958 interview that "any young man or any man who isn't angry at one time or another is a waste of time. No, no. Anger is a symbol of thought and evaluation and reaction." But James Dean, he continued, "symbolizes the angry young man against, but not towards something. He's against things, but not *for* things" (Fench 66). That was precisely Steinbeck's position in the mid-1960s. Any conscientious objector to war could and should, in his mind, volunteer to help in hospitals—engage in humanitarian action. Fourth, these letters were written in 1966 and early 1967, before the antiwar movement gained momentum and attracted scores of students and intellectuals. In addition, Steinbeck waxed enthusiastic about war machinery because he had long been fascinated by weapons—odd weapons, the history of warfare, target practice with his sons. The belletristic prose is, in part, sheer enthusiasm for technological progress.

Finally, and perhaps most importantly, John Steinbeck's reasons for witnessing the war were deeply personal. He'd seen war; he hated war; he had the highest respect both in 1943 and 1966 for the ordinary soldier—and at the time his son John IV was serving as an ordinary soldier in Vietnam. Patriotic, ideological, and familial bonds coalesced. Signing on in November 1965, John IV wrote to his father that he would send letters back recording "our (the soldiers') impression" to read and pass on, perhaps to publish, "to do with as you see fit." In declaring his intention to write letters to his father that he wished to be made public, in selecting precisely his father's grassroots perspective on war, John IV wanted respect and recognition from the writer-father from whom he'd had nineteen stumbling years of love. If his words rang true, John IV wrote, "it will be true for an Era, a mileu [*sic*], a conscience, and America; a static one at best, but it is ours" (25 Nov. 1965). What father, burdened with guilt about his sons and his fatherhood, could resist the appeal made here? In going to Vietnam, Steinbeck made his final, and perhaps ineffective, effort to be a good and conscientious father. "And do you know the best thing," he wrote in his introduction to the series. "We hope to see our boy in Vietnam. Wouldn't that be a joy?" (3 Dec. 1966).

In assessing Steinbeck's writing on the Vietnam War, it must be kept in mind that the writer did have reservations about war, most expressed privately. To Harry Guggenheim he wrote in August 1966 that it was America's "sloppy position" on the war—which was not then called a war, of course—that caused much of the "dissident uproar." "How can a country negotiate for peace when by its own telling, it has never been at war?" (22 Aug. 1966). Coming out of Vietnam to Bangkok in January 1967, he wrote Guggenheim that he was disappointed in Johnson's State of the Union speech, for "a lack of clarity has made people wonder exactly what our policy is: 'We want to defeat the North VN but not destroy their nation.' That's bloody nonsense. Unless we get rid of Ho Chi Minh, we have a war. If he makes peace, he's out of a job" (19 Jan. 1967). Later, he confided in Guggenheim that he was sure that a cease-fire would come soon, by summer he imagined. As Elaine Steinbeck has sadly noted, however, "John changed his mind totally about Vietnam while there, and he came home to write it and spent all the rest of the time dying. That's not just an apology for John. That is true."

Troopship

Somewhere in England, June 20, 1943—

THE TROOPS in their thousands sit on their equipment on the dock. It is evening, and the first of the dimout lights come on. The men wear their helmets, which made them all look alike, make them look like long rows of mushrooms. Their rifles are leaning against their knees. They have no identity, no personality. The men are units in an army. The numbers chalked on their helmets are almost like the license numbers on robots. Equipment is piled neatly—bedding rolls and half-shelters and barracks bags. Some of the men are armed with Springfield or Enfield rifles from the First World War, some with M-1s, or Garands, and some with the neat, light clever little carbines everyone wants to have after the war for hunting rifles.

Above the pier the troopship rears high and thick as an office building. You have to crane your neck upward to see where the portholes stop and the open decks begin. She is a nameless ship and will be while the war lasts. Her destination is known to very few men and her route to even fewer, and the burden of the men who command her must be almost unendurable, for the master who loses her and her cargo will never sleep comfortably again. He probably doesn't sleep at all now. The cargo holds are loaded and the ship waits to take on her tonnage of men.

On the dock the soldiers are quiet. There is little talking, no singing, and as dusk settles to dark you cannot tell one man from another. The heads bend forward with weariness. Some of these men have been all day, some many days, getting to this starting point.

There are several ways of wearing a hat or a cap. A man may express himself in the pitch or tilt of his hat, but not with a helmet. There is only one way to wear a helmet. It won't go on any other way. It sits level on the head, low over eyes and ears, low on the back of the neck. With your helmet on you are a mushroom in a bed of mushrooms.

Four gangways are open now and the units get wearily to their feet and shuffle along in line. The men lean forward against the weight of their equipment. Feet drag against the incline of the gangways. The soldiers disappear one by one into the great doors in the side of the troopship.

Inside the checkers tabulate them. The numbers chalked on the helmets are checked again against a list. Places have been assigned. Half of the men will sleep on the decks and the other half inside in ballrooms, in dining rooms where once a very different kind of people sat and found very important things that have disappeared. Some of the men will sleep in bunks, in hammocks, on the deck, in passages. Tomorrow they will shift. The men from the deck will come in to sleep and those from inside will go out. They will change every night until they land. They will not take off their clothes until they land. This is no cruise ship.

On the decks, dimmed to a faint blue dusk by the blackout lights, the men sink down and fall asleep. They are asleep almost as soon as they are settled. Many of them do not even take off their helmets. It has been a weary day. The rifles are beside them, held in their hands.

On the gangways the lines still feed into the troopship—a regiment of colored troops, a hundred Army nurses, neat in their helmets and field packs. The nurses at least will have staterooms, however crowded they may be in them. Up No. 1 Gangway comes the headquarters complement of a bombardment wing and a company of military police. All are equally tired. They find their places and go to sleep.

Embarkation is in progress. No smoking is allowed anywhere. Everyone entering the ship is triply checked, to make sure he belongs there, and the loading is very quiet. There is only the shuffle of tired feet on the stairways and quiet orders. The permanent crew of military police know every move. They have handled this problem of traffic before.

The tennis courts on the upper deck are a half-acre of sleeping men now—men, feet, and equipment. MPs are everywhere, on stairs and passages, directing and watching. This embarkation must go on smoothly, for one little block might well lose hours in the loading, just as one willful driver, making a wrong turn in traffic, may jam an avenue for a long time. But in spite of the shuffling gait, the embarkation is very rapid. About midnight the last man is aboard.

In the staff room the commanding officer sits behind a long table, with telephones in front of him. His adjutant, a tired blond major, makes his report and places his papers on the table. The CO nods and gives him an order.

Throughout the ship the loudspeakers howl. Embarkation is complete. The gangways slide down from the ship. The iron doors close. No one can enter or leave the ship now, except the pilot. On the bridge the captain of the ship paces slowly. It is his burden now. These thousands are in his care, and if there is an accident it will be his blame.

The ship remains against the pier and a light breathing sound comes from deep in her. The troops are cut off now and gone from home, although they are not a hundred steps from home. On the upper decks a few men lean over the rails and look down on the pier and away at the city behind. The oily water ripples with the changing tide. It is almost time to go. In the staff room, which used to be the ship's theater, the commanding officer sits behind his table. His tired, blond adjutant sits beside him. The phone rings, the CO picks it up, listens for a moment and hangs up the receiver. He turns to the adjutant.

"All ready," he says.

Waiting

Bomber station in England, July 4, 1943 —

THE FIELD is deserted after the ships have left. The ground crew go into barracks to get some sleep, because they have been working most of the night. The flag hangs limply over the administration building. In the hangars repair crews are working over ships that have been injured. *Bomb Boogie* is brought in to be given another overhaul and *Bomb Boogie*'s crew goes disgustedly back to bed.

The crews own a number of small dogs. These dogs, most of which are of uncertain or, at least, of ambiguous breed, belong to no one man. The ship usually owns each one, and the crew is very proud of him. Now these dogs wander disconsolately about the field. The life has gone out of the bomber station. The morning passes slowly. The squadron was due over the target at 9:52. It was due home at 12:43. As 9:50 comes and passes you have the ships in your mind. Now the flak has come up at them. Perhaps now a swarm of fighters has hurled itself at them. The thing happens in your mind. Now, if everything has gone well and there have been no accidents, the bomb bays are open and the ships are running over the target. Now they have turned and are making the run for home, keeping the formation tight, climbing, climbing to avoid the flak. It is 10 o'clock, they should be started back — 10:20, they should be seeing the ocean by now.

The crew last night had told a story of the death of a Fortress, and it comes back to mind.

It was a beautiful day, they said, a picture day with big clouds and a very blue sky. The kind of day you see in advertisements for air travel back at home. The formation was flying toward St. Nazaire and the air was very clear. They could see the little towns on the ground, they said. Then the flak came up, they said, and some Messerschmitts parked off out of range and began to pot at them with their cannon. They didn't see where the Fortress up ahead was hit. Probably in the controls, because they did not see her break up at all.

They all agree that what happened seemed to happen very slowly. The Fortress slowly nosed up and up until she tried to climb vertically and, of course, she couldn't do that. Then she slipped in slow motion, backing like a falling leaf, and she balanced for a while and then her nose edged over and she started, nose down, for the ground.

The blue sky and the white clouds made a picture of it. The crew could see the gunner trying to get out and then he did, and his parachute fluffed open. And the ball-turret gunner—they could see him flopping about. The bombardier and navigator blossomed out of the nose and the waist gunners followed them. *Mary Ruth*'s crew was yelling, "Get out, you pilots." The ship was far down when the ball-turret gunner cleared. They thought the skipper and the copilot were lost. They stayed with the ship too long and then—the ship was so far down that they could hardly see it. It must have been almost to the ground when two little puffs of white, first one and then the second, shot out of her. And the crew yelled with relief. And then the ship hit the ground and exploded. Only the tail gunner and ball-turret man had seen the end. They explained it over the intercom.

Beside the No. 1 hangar there is a little mound of earth covered with short, heavy grass. At 12:15 the ground men begin to congregate on it and sweat out the homecoming. Rumor comes with the crew chief that they have reported, but it is rumor. A small dog, which might be a gray Scottie if his ears didn't hang down and his tail bend the wrong way, comes to sit on the little mound. He stretches out and puts his whiskery muzzle on his outstretched paws. He does not close his eyes and his ears twitch. All the ground crews are there now, waiting for their ships. It is the longest set of minutes imaginable.

Suddenly the little dog raises his head. His body begins to tremble all over. The crew chief has a pair of field glasses. He looks down at the dog and then aims his glasses to the south. "Can't see anything yet," he says. The little dog continues to shudder and a high whine comes from him.

And here they come. You can just see the dots far to the south. The formation is good, but one ship flies alone and ahead. "Can you see her number? Who is she?" The lead ship drops altitude and comes in straight for the field. From her side two little rockets break, a red one and a white one. The ambulance, they call it the meat wagon, starts down the runway. There is a hurt man on that ship.

The main formation comes over the field and each ship peels to circle for a landing, but the lone ship drops and the wheels strike the ground and the Fortress lands like a great bug on the runway. But the moment her wheels are on the ground there is a sharp, crying bark and a streak of gray. The little dog seems hardly to touch the ground. He streaks across the field toward the landed ship. He knows his own ship. One by one the Fortresses land and the ground crews check off the numbers as they land. *Mary Ruth* is there. Only one ship is missing and she landed farther south, with short fuel tanks. There is a great sigh of relief on the mound. The mission is over.

Stories of the Blitz

London, July 10, 1943 —

PEOPLE WHO try to tell you what the blitz was like in London start with fire and explosion and then almost invariably end up with some very tiny detail which crept in and set and became the symbol of the whole thing for them. Again and again this happens in conversations. It is as though the mind could not take in the terror and the noise of the bombs and the general horror and so fastened on something small and comprehensible and ordinary. Everyone who was in London during the blitz wants to describe it, wants to solidify, if only for himself, something of that terrible time.

"It's the glass," says one man, "the sound in the morning of the broken glass being swept up, the vicious, flat tinkle. That is the thing I remember more than anything else, that constant sound of broken glass being swept up on the pavements. My dog broke a window the other day and my wife swept up the glass and a cold shiver went over me. It was a moment before I could trace the reason for it."

You are going to dine at a small restaurant. There is a ruin across the street from the place, a jagged, destroyed stone house. Your companion says, "On one of the nights I had an engagement to have dinner with a lady at this very place. She was to meet me here. I got here early and then a bomb hit that one." He points to the ruin. "I went out in the street. You could see plainly, the fires lighted the whole city. That front wall was spilled into the street. You could see the front of a cab sticking out from the pile of fallen stone. Thrown clear, right at my feet as I came out of the door, was one pale blue evening slipper. The toe of it was pointing right at me."

Another points up at a wall; the building is gone, but there are five fireplaces, one above another, straight up the wall. He points to the topmost fireplace. "This was a high-explosive bomb," he says. "This is on my way to work. You know, for six months there was a pair of long stockings hanging in front of that fireplace. They must have been pinned up. They hung there for months, just as they had been put up to dry."

"I was passing Hyde Park," says a man, "when a big raid came over. I went down into the gutter. Always did that when you couldn't get a shelter. I saw a great tree, one like those, jump into the air and fall on its side not so far from me—right there where that scoop is in the ground. And then a sparrow fell in the gutter right beside me. It was dead all right. Concussion kills birds easily. For some reason I picked it up and held it for a long time. There was no blood on it or anything like that. I took it home with me. Funny thing, I had to throw it right away."

One night, when the bombs screamed and blatted, a refugee who had been driven from place to place and tortured in all of them until he finally reached London couldn't stand it anymore. He cut his throat and jumped out of a high window. A girl, who was driving an ambulance that night, says, "I remember how angry I was with him. I understand it a little now, but that night I was furious with him. There were so many who got it that night and they couldn't help it. I shouted at him I hoped he would die, and he did.

"People save such strange things. One elderly man lost his whole house by fire. He saved an old rocking chair. He took it everywhere with him; wouldn't leave it for a moment. His whole family was killed, but he hung on to that rocking chair. He wouldn't sit in it. He sat on the ground beside it, but you couldn't get it away from him."

Two reporters sat out the blitz in the Savoy Hotel, playing chess and fortifying themselves. When the bombs came near they went under the table. "One or the other of us always reached up and cheated a little," the reporter says.

Hundreds of stories, and all of them end with a little incident, a little simple thing that stays in your mind.

"I remember the eyes of people going to work in the morning," a man says. "There was a quality of tiredness in those eyes I haven't forgotten. It was beyond a tiredness you can imagine—a desperate kind of weariness that never expected to be rested. The eyes of the people seemed to be deep, deep in their heads, and their voices seemed to come from a long distance. And I remember during a raid seeing a blind man standing on the curb, tapping with his stick and waiting for someone to take him across through the traffic. There wasn't any traffic, and the air was full of fire, but he stood there and tapped until someone came along and took him to a shelter."

In all of the little stories it is the ordinary, the commonplace thing or incident against the background of the bombing, that leaves the indelible picture.

"An old woman was selling little miserable sprays of sweet lavender. The city was rocking under the bombs and the light of burning buildings made it like day. The air was just one big fat blasting roar. And in one little hole in the roar her voice got in—a squeaky voice. 'Lavender!' she said. 'Buy lavender for luck.' "

The bombing itself grows vague and dreamlike. The little pictures remain as sharp as they were when they were new.

Lilli Marlene

London, July 12, 1943—

THIS IS THE STORY of a song. Its name is "Lilli Marlene" and it was written in Germany in 1938 by Norbert Schultze and Hans Leit. In due course they tried to publish it and it was rejected by about two dozen publishers. Finally it was taken up by a singer, Lala Anderson, a Swedish girl, who used it for her signature song. Lala Anderson has a husky voice and is what you might call the Hildegarde type.

"Lilli Marlene" is a very simple song. The first verse of it goes: "Underneath the lanterns, by the barracks square, I used to meet Marlene and she was young and fair." The song was as simple as that. It went on to tell about Marlene, who first liked stripes and then shoulder bars. Marlene met more and more people until, finally, she met a brigadier, which was what she wanted all along. We have a song with much the same amused cynicism.

Eventually Lala made a record of the song and even it was not very popular. But one night the German station in Belgrade, which sent out programs to Rommel's Afrika Korps, found that, due to a little bombing, it did not have many records left, but among a few uninjured disks was the song "Lilli Marlene." It was put on the air to Africa and by the next morning it was being hummed by the Afrika Korps and letters were going in demanding that it be played again.

The story of its popularity in Africa got back to Berlin, and Madame Goering, who used to be an opera singer, sang the song of the inconstant "Lilli Marlene" to a very select group of Nazis, if there is such a thing. Instantly the song was popular and it was played constantly over the German radio until Goering himself grew a little sick of it, and it is said that, since inconstancy is a subject which is not pleasant to certain high Nazi ears, it was suggested that the song be quietly assassinated. But meanwhile "Lilli Marlene" had got out of hand. Lala Anderson was by now known as the "Soldiers' Sweetheart." She was a pin-up girl. Her husky voice ground out of portable phonographs in the desert.

So far, "Lilli" had been solely a German problem, but now the British Eighth Army began to take prisoners and among the spoils they got "Lilli Marlene." And the song swept through the Eighth Army. Australians hummed it and fastened new words to it. The powers hesitated, considering whether it was a good idea to let a German song about a girl who did not have all the sterling virtues become the favorite song of the British Army, for by now the thing had crept into the First Army and the Americans were beginning to experiment with close harmony and were putting an off-beat into it. It wouldn't have done the powers a bit of good if they had decided against the song.

It was out of hand. The Eighth Army was doing all right in the field and it was decided to consider "Lilli Marlene" a prisoner of war, which would have happened anyway, no matter what the powers thought about it. Now "Lilli" is getting deeply into the American Forces in Africa. The Office of War Information took up the problem and decided to keep the melody, but to turn new words against the Germans. Whether this will work or not remains to be seen. "Lilli Marlene" is international. It is to be suspected that she will emerge beside the barrack walls—young and fair and incorruptly inconsistent.

There is nothing you can do about a song like this except to let it go. War songs need not be about the war at all. Indeed, they rarely are. In the last war, "Madelon" and "Tipperary" had nothing to do with war. The great Australian song of this war, "Waltzing Matilda," concerns itself with sheep-stealing. It is to be expected that some groups in America will attack "Lilli," first, on the ground that she is an enemy alien, and, second, because she is no better than she should be. Such attacks will have little effect. "Lilli" is immortal. Her simple desire to meet a brigadier is hardly a German copyright. Politics may be dominated and nationalized, but songs have a way of leaping boundaries.

And it would be amusing if, after all the fuss and heiling, all the marching and indoctrination, the only contribution to the world by the Nazis was "Lilli Marlene."

Bob Hope

London, July 26, 1943 —

WHEN THE TIME for recognition of service to the nation in wartime comes to be considered, Bob Hope should be high on the list. This man drives himself and is driven. It is impossible to see how he can do so much, can cover so much ground, can work so hard, and can be so effective. He works month after month at a pace that would kill most people.

Moving about the country in camps, airfields, billets, supply depots, and hospitals, you hear one thing consistently. Bob Hope is coming, or Bob Hope has been here. The Secretary of War is on an inspection tour, but it is Bob Hope who is expected and remembered.

In some way he has caught the soldiers' imagination. He gets laughter wherever he goes from men who need laughter. He has created a character for himself—that of the man who tries too hard and fails, and who boasts and is caught at it. His wit is caustic, but it is never aimed at people, but at conditions and at ideas, and where he goes men roar with laughter and repeat his cracks for days afterward.

Hope does four, sometimes five, shows a day. In some camps the men must come in shifts because they cannot all hear him at the same time. Then he jumps into a car, rushes to the next post, and because he broadcasts and everyone listens to his broadcasts, he cannot use the same show more than a few times. He must, in the midst of his rushing and playing, build new shows constantly. If he did this for a while and then stopped and took a rest it would be remarkable, but he never rests. And he has been doing this ever since the war started. His energy is boundless.

Hope takes his shows all over. It isn't only to the big camps. In little groups on special duty you hear the same thing. Bob Hope is coming on Thursday. They know weeks in advance that he is coming. It would be rather a terrible thing if he did not show up. Perhaps that is some of his drive. He has made some kind of contract with himself and with the men that nobody, least of all Hope, could break. It is hard to overestimate the importance of this thing and the responsibility involved.

The battalion of men who are moving half-tracks from one place to another, doing a job that gets no headlines, no public notice, and yet which must be done if there is to be a victory, are forgotten, and they feel forgotten. But Bob Hope is in the country. Will he come to them, or won't he? And then one day they get a notice that he is coming. Then they feel remembered. This man in some way has become that kind of bridge. It goes beyond how funny he can be or how well Frances Langford sings. It has been interesting to see how he has become a symbol.

This writer, not knowing Hope, can only conjecture what goes on inside the man. He has seen horrible things and has survived them with good humor and made them more bearable, but that doesn't happen without putting a wound on a man. He is cut off from rest, and even from admitting weariness. Having become a symbol, he must lead a symbol life.

Probably the most difficult, the most tearing thing of all is to be funny in a hospital. The long, low buildings are dispersed in case they should be attacked. Working in the gardens or reading in the lounge rooms are the ambulatory cases in maroon bathrobes. But in the wards, in the long aisles of pain the men lie, with eyes turned inward on themselves, and on their people. Some are convalescing with all the pain and itch of convalescence. Some work their fingers slowly, and some cling to the little trapezes which help them to move in bed.

The immaculate nurses move silently in the aisles at the foot of the beds. The time hangs very long. Letters, even if they came every day, would seem weeks apart. Everything that can be done is done, but medicine cannot get at the lonesomeness and the weakness of men who have been strong. And nursing cannot shorten one single endless day in a hospital bed. And Bob Hope and his company must come into this quiet, inward, lonesome place, and gently pull the minds outward and catch the interest, and finally bring laughter up out of the black water. There is a job. It hurts many of the men to laugh, hurts knitting bones, strains at sutured incisions, and yet the laughter is a great medicine.

This story is told in one of those nameless hospitals which must be kept safe from bombs. Hope and company had worked and gradually they got the leaden eyes to sparkling, had planted and nurtured and coaxed laughter to life. A gunner, who had a stomach wound, was gasping softly with laughter. A railroad casualty slapped the cast on his left hand with his right hand by way of applause. And once the laughter was alive, the men laughed before the punch line and it had to be repeated so they could laugh again.

Finally it came time for Frances Langford to sing. The men asked for "As Time Goes By." She stood up beside the little GI piano and started to sing. Her voice is a little hoarse and strained. She has been working too hard and too long. She got through eight bars and was into the bridge, when a boy with a head wound began to cry. She stopped, and then went on, but her voice wouldn't work anymore, and she finished the song whispering and then she walked out, so no one could see her, and broke down. The ward was quiet and no one applauded. And then Hope walked into the aisle between the beds and he said seriously, "Fellows, the folks at home are having a terrible time about eggs. They can't get any powdered eggs at all. They've got to use the old-fashioned kind that you break open."

There's a man for you—there is really a man.

Vietnam War:
No Front, No Rear

Saturday, January 14, 1967
Saigon

Dear Alicia:

THIS WAR in Vietnam is very confusing not only to old war watchers but to people at home who read and try to understand. It is mainly difficult because of our preconceptions accumulated over several thousand years. This war is not like any we have ever been involved in. I'll try to tell you some of the points of difference as I have observed them.

It was easy to report wars of movement, places taken and held or lost, lines established and clear, troops confronting each other in force and fighting until one side or the other lost. Big battles are conceivable, can be reported like a bullfight. You could see if only on a map all previous wars—on one side of a line our friends, on the other our enemies. Vietnam is not like that at all and I wonder whether it can be described. Maybe the inability to communicate its quality is the reason for the discontent and frustration of the press corps here. Many of the fine reporters here understand this war, but their readers don't and often their editors demand the kind of war they are used to and comfortable with.

Maybe I can't tell you what it is like, Alicia, but I'm going to try so you can feel it. It's a feeling war with no fronts and no rear. It is everywhere like a thin ever-present gas. I am writing this in a comfortable hotel room in Saigon, which was once a beautiful city and now has a worn and sagging look like a worn-out suit that once was well tailored. And the war is here—in the street below, on the roofs, always present.

When I leave my wife here and go out to the hard-bitten sandbag re-doubts in the countryside, she is in as much danger as I am and perhaps in more because I am armed with alertness while she, walking in a civilized street to post a letter, may run into a murderous exchange of fire.

At night when we have drinks and dinner on the roof we can see the flares and hear the thunder of artillery all night long, and very often the quick-sharp rattle of automatic small arms fire. Both she and I know the sound of mortar fire and we are conditioned, if it comes close, to roll off the beds pulling the mattresses over us with one motion to veer off fragments and flying glass. This city is heavily fortified, but the bridge you cross to go to a small restaurant may be blown up before you return. The smiling man in the street selling colored etchings from a bulging briefcase may have a gummy lump of high explosive under the pictures—and he may not. There is the problem—he may be simply a smiling man selling pictures. That is the feeling all over the city. Any person, any place may suddenly erupt into violence and destruction. You have it with you every minute. You avoid clots of people in the streets and are prepared almost automatically to fall to the sidewalk or the street and to be perfectly still. Bob Capa's first instruction to me years ago was "Don't move. If they haven't hit you they haven't seen you." No better advice was ever given.

I realize that this account makes it seem that we are surrounded by thousands of enemies, and that is just not true. The armed forces radio and television station was riddled with about two hundred rounds from automatic rifles, by just two men. The airport, the largest in the world and surely the most guarded, was penetrated recently by fifteen heavily armed teenage boys, and they would have done great damage if the guard dogs had not smelled them out. You see, it isn't that the enemies are many but that you don't know which ones they are. And three with modern weapons can do the destruction of a hundred. One man, saun-tering slowly past with a basket of fruit on his head, can slaughter half the peasants in a village market with one grenade and he does not hesitate to do it. In many areas, we completely control the place by day, but no one moves about by night. Then the secured road is mined. Then a dreadful claymore mine is aimed to be exploded by the first man who opens the village gate.

On Christmas Day Gen. Westmoreland took me with him to visit the farthest outposts. The 101st Airborne has not been to its base camp for nearly a year. The special forces, Green Berets, are dug in in redoubts far in the hills. They range the countryside day and night like casting setters and very gradually they clear out the snakes. We called on the special forces at Plei Mrong and Polei Klong, elements of the 25th Division and the Eighth Infantry at Pleiku, the airborne and three battalions of infantry at Kontum and the First Cavalry at An Khe. The general must have rabbit blood. I had to run to keep up with him. The finest Army we have ever had, he said, the best-trained, most experienced soldiers in our history and with morale that clanged through the valleys like a struck gong.

Does it make you feel hopeless that these wonderful troops plus the equally fine allied troops cannot bring this thing to a quick victory? I find I am very hopeful but not of a quick victory. It is a large subject and I'll try to tell you more about it in my next. There is far too much to try to get in one letter.

Yours,
John

Action in the Delta

Saturday, January 21, 1967
Can Tho

Dear Alicia:

B Y CHOPPER to Delta region of Vietnam, a vast level plain much bigger than Kansas and just as flat. It is a watery plain through which the great Mekong River, split into many sinuous silver snakes, winds in looping curves to the sea.

In this respect it is like the Nile delta, but only in this. From three thousand feet up in this enormous rice bowl of Asia stretches from horizon to horizon a checkerboard of irregular-shaped rice paddies, some rich green, some harvested and some flooded for planting, for the growing season is the whole year and if the 5,500,000 people who live here wished they could grow three crops a year. That they do not is because for a thousand years they have had it taken away from them.

The potential of the Delta is staggering. It is crossed and recrossed by thousands of waterways, some natural and some man-made but all of them navigable by some kind of craft. The main channels of the river take seagoing traffic far up into Cambodia, but even the smallest water paths swarm with traffic. The VC are everywhere for the very good reason that here is the richest source of rice and money in all of Vietnam. The Viet Cong tax collectors roam through the countryside almost at will.

I came down to the Delta to go with the patrol boats which inspect the river traffic for contraband arms supplies and VC personnel. It is a long and a frustrating job and the best it can hope for now is to inhibit and to make difficult the movement of supplies.

Two boats make up a patrol. When the leader intercepts and inspects, the second stands by covering against surprise attack. I went on River Patrol Boat 37 (PBR) to cover a ten-mile stretch of the Bassac River. These are thirty-one-foot craft with water propulsion. The hull is not armored but the steersman is protected by a steel box, and two plates aft give some protection against shore fire. She is armed with twin .50-cal. machine guns forward and a single .50 aft. She also carries an M-70 .30 machine gun with two M-16 automatic rifles and two M-79 rocket launchers. On the 37, the boat captain was Harold Chase, engineman first class of New Bedford, Mass., a quiet red-haired man with restless eyes. In addition to the gunners and crew, we had aboard a Vietnamese river policeman to do the interrogation and inspection. We put out shortly after noon under a flaring sun. The river banks are surprising. From the air the flat country seems to be nothing but endless rice paddies but now I could see that the waterways are edged with high and dense fringes of palm, of bananas and of all manner of fruit trees with little thatched houses nestled among them. The banks are pierced with many small canals and half-concealed entrances. A boat attempting to escape inspection, if it has time, can literally disappear into what appears to be solid riverside.

As our two-boat patrol moved downriver there was little river traffic under the noonday sun. The junks and sampans were tied up near to the bank in the shade of overhanging trees. In the middle of the river a black tube about six inches in diameter bobbed up and down in the water. Mines are not practical in the main river course because of the current but booby traps are often encountered.

Our boat circled the canister warily keeping well clear. Then, making sure of a clear field of fire, one of our gunners opened on it with his M-16 and sank it with his first burst. Whatever it was, it did not explode.

Now the river traffic began to move up and down river but staying close to the bank, and I saw everywhere an engine new to me. It is a one-cylinder Briggs gas engine of the kind and power we use on lawn mowers. Extending from its driveshaft is a piece of pipe about eight feet long housing a propeller shaft and ending with a small two-blade screw. The whole affair is socketed in a hole bored in the stern of the boat and it can be turned 360 degrees or lifted out of the water. At right angles to the boat it can push the thing sideways. When clogged with eel grass, it is simply raised out of the water to spin in the air. It is the simplest contraption I have ever seen and it pushes even fairly large riverboats along at surprising speed. It would be ideal for trolling in the weedy inland waters of Long Island. The cheap little air-cooled engine uses very little fuel. I'm going to make one for myself when I get home.

Now we begin the job of stopping and inspecting boats. The procedure is always the same—a shrill whistle and a waving hat and if the called boat does not turn outward at once, a few shots ahead of it. When the boat comes alongside, two rifleman stand ready. The Vietnamese river policeman scrambles aboard, collects identity cards and manifest papers, which he inspects closely. The cards with photographs and fingerprints are passed to our boat captain, who checks them against lists of violators or known VC. The piles of loose rice are probed for weapons, baskets and packages opened and unwrapped. And in the poorest raggedest boats strange things come to light—transistor radios, painted vases, sets of hinges, a china doll, bits of tin and metal. Our policeman must have a decent approach. When the boats first came alongside the people, the women and children were worried and apprehensive, and why not? The VC tell them that we enslave them and steal their children. But in a few moments, even while probing through their effects, our policeman had them laughing and relieved. I watched the faces closely. These are very poor people, their clothing ragged, their possessions pitifully few. Most of the shallow-draft boats are roofed with thatch or corrugated iron against rain and sun. Some were so poor and old and leaky that the women could not pause in bailing and others were beautifully trim and well built and one in particular I admired because its deckhouse was completely shingled with flattened Hills Brothers Coffee cans, the printing and colors still bright. In the distance the thing seemed to be made of stained glass.

And I remember one poor boat that came alongside. A father with one eye, a wife tiny and shriveled and three little boys. I can't forget the pain of worry on the faces, the eyes haunted and the little boys' faces wounded with fear. They looked over the side into our boat, at the guns and the ammunition belts and all the gadgetry with which we surround ourselves. And nothing happened to the boys, no one pounced or shouted at them, and I saw the fear slide away and the eyes brighten with normal curiosity. And then one, the biggest, put out a timid hand and touched the fiberglass of our siding and then he looked up and laughed and his brothers laughed because he had touched a snake and had not been bitten. And his tiny mother laughed and the one-eyed father laughed. And maybe it's overhopeful but I like to think that a bit of carefully planted poison got flushed away in that laughter.

In all we stopped and inspected eighty boats of all sizes and with every kind of cargo, but mostly rice and fruits, stems of bananas, piles of mottled papayas and lots of produce I have not yet learned to identify. After inspections our policeman would report. "They say the VC are out collecting. They are moving the rice to save it." Charley is pushing them harder than ever, taking more and more. The afternoon waned into evening and the tree-clustered banks were black and threw even blacker shadows on the water and from the little hidden houses—glimmers of yellow light like fireflies. The slow-moving boats pulled near to the shore to anchor for the night for with the darkness comes the curfew when a sampan can legally move. This is the time when the VC move on the waters, creeping stealthily across with their sacks of stolen rice and their wads of crumpled small bills collected by threat and terror.

In the black night we moved quietly on the river, showing no lights, watching the soft glowing radar screen for anything moving. Sometimes we stopped our engines and listened for the sound of a putt-putt or the dip of oars. But there was nothing, or if there was, we didn't know it, just the quiet and the unshiny blackness of the hooded shores and faint stars reflected in the steel gray river. Now and then small islands of lily pads floated by detached from someplace far upriver. Any place on that dark tangle can belch fire and it often does from bunkers hidden in the undergrowth. But this night—quiet—quiet.

I've only been in country a few weeks but everywhere I've gone there has been the intimacy of the war. I went in with the lead ship of an assault team of the First Cav. In the north I've seen the volcano of a B-52 strike from a chopper five or six kilometers away. And I've been with the Marines in their forward positions, burning up in helmet and steel vest and glad to be so burning. The heavy drum of artillery and the lazy floating flares and the quick tearing of rockets have become almost commonplace. Perhaps that is why the dark quiet of the night river with faint stars and squinty yellow hut lights made such a deep impression on me.

When our time was up our two-boat river patrol went back to base to report no action, no activity—but it didn't last. I'll have to tell you about that when I can write again.

Yours,
John

Terrorism

Saturday, January 21, 1967
Can Tho

Dear Alicia:

I WROTE TO YOU about the quiet patrol on the river, the silent shores and the stars doubly twinkly because of the damp atmosphere. We came into dock a little before nine o'clock. Part of Operation Game Warden is based on Can Tho, the largest city in the Delta region. There are a few small restaurants in Can Tho where Viet people, always with their children, go to eat and talk in their language, which sounds like singing. The lights are not bright in such places. Because of power shortage most of them are lighted with flickering lamps.

At about ten o'clock in the evening two strolling young men paused in front of a crowded restaurant and suddenly threw two grenades in at the wide-open door. One was a dud. The other exploded and tore up the people and their children. There were no soldiers in the restaurant either American or Vietnamese. There was no possible military advantage to be gained. An American captain ran in and carried out a little girl of seven. He was weeping when he got her to the hospital and she was dead. Ambulances carried the broken bodies to the long building, once a French hospital and now ours. Then the amputations and the probing for pieces of jagged metal began and the smell of ether filled the building. Some of the tattered people were dead on arrival and some died soon after but those who survived were treated and splinted and bandaged. They lay on the wooden beds with a glazed questioning in their eyes. Plasma needles were taped to the backs of their hands, if they had hands, to their ankles if they had none. The children who had been playing about on the floor of the restaurant were the worst hit by the low-exploding grenade. The doctors and nurses of the brutal, aggressive, imperialist American force worked most of the night on the products of this noble defense of the homeland.

Meanwhile the grenade throwers had been caught and they proudly admitted the act, in fact boasted of it.

I find I have no access to the thinking of the wanton terrorist. Why do they destroy their own people, their own poor people whose freedom is their verbal concern? That hospital with all its useless pain is like a cloud of sorrow. Can anyone believe that the VC, who can do this kind of thing to their own people, would be concerned for their welfare if they had complete control? I find I can't. We and our allies too often kill and injure innocent people in carrying out a military operation. The VC invariably wash themselves with innocents. They set up a machine gun in the doorway of a peasant's house and herd the children close around it knowing our reluctance to return fire at the cost of people. They build their bunkers in thickly populated areas for the same reason. And people do get hurt. I've seen the care we take to avoid it, and instant care when it cannot be helped.

One wing of the old French hospital at Can Tho is for VC casualties. The doors and windows are barred, of course, but inside the treatment is the same we give our own. But in the eyes of the injured prisoners I saw another atrocity, the long conditioning of these minds to expect only torture and death from us and their uneasy suspicion when it did not come. These minds are crippled by the same plan which plants the satchel charge in a market or throws a grenade into a crowded theater.

I must believe that the plodding protest marchers who spend their days across from the UN and around the White House hate war. I think I have more reason than most of them to hate it. But would they enlist for medical service? They could be trained quickly and would not be required to kill anyone. If they love people so much, why are they not willing to help to save them? Their country is woefully short of medical help. Couldn't some of the energy that goes into carrying placards be diverted to emptying bedpans or cleaning infected wounds? This would be a real protest against war. They would have to be told of course that their VC heroes do not respect peaceful intentions. They bomb hospitals and set mines for ambulances. It might be dangerous to see this method of protest and besides, if they left the country, their relief checks might stop. But in return they might gain a little pride in themselves as being for something instead of only against.

The question comes from home so often—when will it be over? I can only guess, Alicia, but at least I am guessing on a base of observation from one end of this country to the other. I guess that a cease-fire is not too far in the future because we and our allies can meet and defeat any military foe that will face us. But a cease-fire is only the beginning. During the Christmas truce, which amounts to a cease-fire, there were over a hundred violations of the truce and not one by us. But that is not the finality of this war. The trained, professional hard-core VCs in their cells of three infest the country. They must be rooted out one by one until the villages and hamlets are able to defend themselves. And that may take a generation. But anyone who doubts that it can be done should look at South Korea. In one generation that is a changed people, proud, efficient and self-reliant. Their troops here in Vietnam are as fine as any in the world. And what happened to them can happen here—and must. If we are too quick to pull out or too stupid to understand the price, we may win the battle and lose the war.

Yours,
John

Puff, the Magic Dragon

Saturday, February 25, 1967
Saigon

Dear Alicia:

IT IS TIME for us to continue our journey on to Thailand. We made the reservations to Bangkok and said goodbye to many friends. I know that I have not written to you about everything I have seen. That would take a lifetime. But I have been six weeks here, about five of them in the field, and perhaps my years tell on me a little. I have often wished that if a war is necessary, it might be fought by men of my age rather than by boys with their whole lives ahead of them. The difficulty is that we wouldn't do it very well. Our bones would creak and our eyes might not have the clear sharpness required. Let's face it, Alicia, I get tireder quicker than the kids do and I don't recover as fast.

It was my last night and I had reserved it for a final mission. Do you remember or did I even mention Puff, the Magic Dragon? From the ground I had seen it in action in the night but I had never flown in it. It was not given its name by us but by the VC who have experienced it. Puff is a kind of a crazy conception. It is a C-47—that old Douglas two-motor ship that has been the workhorse of the world since early on in World War II.

The one I was to fly in was celebrating its twenty-fourth birthday and that's an old airplane. I don't know who designed Puff but whoever did had imagination. It is armed with three six-barreled Gatling guns. Their noses stick out of two side windows and the open door. And these three guns can spray out 2,800 rounds a minute—that's right, 2,800. In one quarter-turn, these guns fine-tooth an area bigger than a football field and so completely that not even a tuft of crabgrass would remain alive. The guns are fixed. The pilot fires them by rolling up on his side. There are cross hairs on his side glass. When the cross hairs are on the target, he presses a button and a waterfall of fire pours on the target, a Niagara of steel.

These ships, some of them, are in the air in every area at night and all night. If a call for help comes, they can be there in a very short time. They carry quantities of the parachute flares we see in the sky every night, flares so bright that they put an area of midday on a part of the night-bound earth. And these flares are not mechanically released. They are manhandled out the open door by the flare crew. I know the technique but I have never flown a night mission with Puff. I had reserved it for my last night in South Vietnam. We were to fly at dark and hoped to be back by midnight.

My lady-wife Elaine, who has taken everything in her proud stride to my admiration, did not want to sit alone in the Caravelle Hotel waiting for me, so Johnny Floyd, Regular Army, third hitch, recently wounded but recuperating, asked her to have dinner with him in a small restaurant near the hotel to wait out my return.

I went by chopper to the field where the Puffs live, met the pilot and his crew and had supper with them. Our mission was not general call. A crossroad area had been observed to be used after dark recently by Charley, who was rushing supplies from one place to another for reasons best known to Charley. We were to be directed by one of the little Forward Air Control planes I spoke of in an earlier letter.

Because it was hot and no wind in prospect, I wore only light slacks and a cotton shirt. We flew at dusk and very soon I found myself freezing. Puff is not a quiet ship, her door is open, her gun ports open, her engines loud and everything on her rattles. I did not wear a headset because I wanted to move about, so one of the flare crew, a big man, had to offer me an extra flight suit and he said it in pantomime. I accepted with chattering teeth and struggled into it and zipped it up. Then they fitted me with a parachute harness and showed me where my pack was in case of need. But even I knew that flying at low altitude, if the need should arise, there wouldn't be much time to get out even if I were young and clever.

Forward of the guns and aft by the open door were the racks where the flares stood, three feet high, four inches in diameter. I think they weigh about forty pounds. Wrestling two or three hundred of them out of the door would be a good night's work. The ship was dark, except for its recognition lights and a dim red light over the navigator's table.

They gave me ear plugs. I had heard that the sound of these guns is unique, so I put the rubber stoppers in my ears but they were irritating so I pulled them out again and only hoped to get my mouth open when we fired.

There was a line of afterglow in the western sky, only it was not west the way Puff flies. Sometimes it was overhead, sometimes straight down. Without an instrument you couldn't tell up from down but my feet were held to the steel floor by this centrifuge of the turning, twisting ship. Then the order came and a flare was thrown out and another and another. They whirled down and the brilliant lights came on. We upsided and looked down on the ghost-lighted earth. Far below, us almost skimming the earth, I could see the shape of the tiny skimming FAC plane inspecting the target and reporting to our pilot. We dropped three more flares, whirled and dropped three more. The road and the crossroads were very clearly defined on the ground and then there was a curious unearthly undulating mass like an amoeba under a microscope, a pseudopod changing its shape and size as it moved. Now Puff went up on its side. I did know enough to get my mouth open. The sound of those guns is like nothing I have heard. It is like a coffee grinder as big as Mt. Everest compounded with a dentist's drill. A growl but one that rocks your body and flaps your eardrums like wind-whipped flags. And out through the door I could see a stream, a wide river of fire that seemed to curve and wave toward the earth.

We flared and fired again and once again. Out on the edges of darkness there were the little winking lights that were ground fire aimed at us.

During the last five weeks, I guess I have been in areas and under conditions of danger. I've had a good normal fear that makes one keep his head down and take cover when it offers, the tenseness and crystal awareness danger brings. I guess it is fear all right but it brings compensations. But now, on the last night, with the mission completed and only the winking ground fire and that receding behind us, I was afraid. More

than that—I was scared. I could see the stray and accidental shot hit a
flare and the whole ship go up in a huge Roman candle of incandescent
searing light. I thought how silly it would be on my last night. I think it
was the first time I had thought of myself, me, as being in danger. And
then curious memories came to me like movie shorts. I had a drink with
Ernie Pyle in San Francisco. Ernie ordinarily dressed like a tossed salad
but now he was wearing a new Eisenhower jacket. I said, "Just because
you're going to the Pacific do you have to be a fashion plate?"

Ernie said, "It's new. I shouldn't have bought it. I'm not going to
need it." And his first time on the line he got a bullet between the eyes.

And Capa leaving Paris for the war in East Asia. We made a date for
dinner in Paris a week away. And Capa said, "I hate to go on this one. If I
didn't need the money, I wouldn't go. I've had it. I tell you this is the last
time." And it was.

And only last week lying in the bunker with a boy who said, "Five
more days—no, four days and thirteen hours, and I'll be going home. I
thought the time would never come." And it didn't. He was killed on the
next patrol.

I was cold all over and trembling maybe somewhat from the grinding
of the guns. And already we were landing and the mission was done and
we were back early.

I got to the hotel at a little before ten and of course Elaine was not
back from dinner. So I went around the corner to the restaurant. She and
Johnny Floyd were sitting quietly and when they saw me come in they
both jumped up. "How was it?" Elaine asked.

We have our privacies but not in big things.

I said, "I was scared."

"So was I. I had three martinis and they didn't help."

And Johnny Floyd said, "I kept telling her you were all right, but I
guess I oversold it. Because I was scared too."

Isn't that funny and strange the way the mind works? But that's the
way it works.

And soon we will be in Bangkok and it will be very different.

Yours,
John

An Open Letter
to Poet Yevtushenko

My dear friend Genya:

I HAVE JUST NOW read those parts of your poem printed in the *New York Times*. I have no way of knowing how good the translation is, but I am pleased and flattered by your devotion.

In your poem, you ask me to speak out against the war in Vietnam. You know well how I detest all war, but for this one I have a particular and personal hatred. I am against this Chinese-inspired war. I don't know a single American who is for it. But, my beloved friend, you asked me to denounce half a war, our half. I appeal to you to join me in denouncing the whole war.

Surely you don't believe that our "pilots fly to bomb children," that we send bombs and heavy equipment against innocent civilians? This is not East Berlin in 1953, Budapest in 1956, nor Tibet in 1959.

You know as well as I do, Genya, that we are bombing oil storage, transport and the heavy and sophisticated weapons they carry to kill our sons. And where that oil and those weapons come from, you probably know better than I. They are marked in pictograph and in Cyrilic characters.

I hope you also know that if those weapons were not being sent, we would not be in Vietnam at all. If this were a disagreement between Vietnamese people, we surely would not be there, but it is not, and since I have never found you to be naive you must be aware that it is not.

This war is the work of Chairman Mao, designed and generaled by him in absentia, advised by Peking and cynically supplied with brutal weapons by foreigners who set it up. Let us denounce this also, my friend, but even more, let us together undertake a program more effective than denunciation.

I beg you to use your very considerable influence on your people, your government, and on those who look to the Soviet Union for direction, to stop sending the murderous merchandise through North Vietnam to be used against the South.

For my part, I will devote every resource I have to persuade my government to withdraw troops and weapons from the South, leaving only money and help for rebuilding. And, do you know, Genya, if you could accomplish your part, my part would follow immediately and automatically.

But even this is not necessary to stop the war. If you could persuade North Vietnam to agree in good faith to negotiate, the bombing would stop instantly. The guns would fall silent and our dear sons could come home. It is as simple as that, my friend, as simple as that, I promise you. I hope to see you and your lovely wife Galya soon.

With all respect and affection,
John Steinbeck

VIII.

AMERICA AND AMERICANS

JOHN STEINBECK'S stature as a writer was solidified in the 1930s by three searing books about California migrants; his career closed with an equally stringent trilogy, books not about marginalized Americans but about mainstream America: *The Winter of Our Discontent* (1961), *Travels with Charley* (1962), and *America and Americans* (1966). In the decade since publication of *East of Eden* in 1952, Steinbeck had declared with some regularity that he wanted to leave the past behind, to write about something other than his California childhood or his apprenticeship on Monterey's Cannery Row. He had not been entirely successful, since *Sweet Thursday* carried him back, as did a projected short-story cycle, never completed, about his Salinas boyhood. But with increasing insistence, he declared that the past was the "disease of modern writers." "If this is a time of confusion, then that should be the subject of a good writer if he is to set down his time" (Benson 759). If confusion is the subject, however, a form to contain confusion is not easily found. He was drawn to the "hard discipline of play," the drama's "iron discipline of form," and throughout the 1950s he started a number of plays, all aborted. The more relaxed form of the letter served, as in "Letters to Alicia," for he could move from subject to subject. Brief journalistic pieces recorded impressions. But the longer works—a travel narrative, a novel capturing America's converging voices of past and present, and a collection of essays—most clearly indicate Steinbeck's struggle to contain the present.

It's not true that Steinbeck failed to understand America after World War II; it's not true that he swerved to the right politically; but it may be true that in trying to locate the source of American malaise, he could not find an adequate form or a convincing tone to contain his discontent.

"The better tone for a book such as [*America and Americans*]," observes Warren French, "is one that shares unique experiences rather than universalizing one's own" (110). Indeed, the essays in *America and Americans*, lacking Charley, lack a certain humor and charm; not fiction, they lack plot and character and setting. But they are impassioned pleas from a man who cared deeply about his country. They are jeremiads, exhorting America to take heed.

The writing of *America and Americans* came to him almost by accident. He was discouraged by his failure to make progress in his ten-year project of transforming Malory's *Le Morte d'Arthur* into modern English. He wrote to his agent that "the words sound pretentious and sour and unreal. It just makes me sick. Maybe the fire has gone out" (23 July 1964). He was rescued from despondency by an offer from his publisher. Viking's Thomas H. Guinzburg came to him with a collection of photographs that he had commissioned to be taken all over the country and suggested that the author write an introduction to the collection. Guinzburg's idea was to present the American spirit, to show Americans at work and play, in every corner of the country.

But what had started out as a thin volume of pictures was transformed into a collection of essays with the photos grouped together at various places in the text. The essays spring not from the photos, however, but from Steinbeck's recent tour of the country for *Travels with Charley*. He had a number of things he had wanted to say in that book which the form did not allow. The frustration of working on *Le Morte d'Arthur* pushed him forward to a more thoughtful and extensive job than he had originally agreed to, but also his thoughts about *Arthur* gave him a basis for developing his *America and Americans* essays.

A "cut version of the Caxton *Morte d'Arthur*" (Benson 21) had been his favorite book as a child, and he had used it as a framework for telling the story of the paisanos in *Tortilla Flat*. What attracted him as a child was its sense of mystery and adventure, but what attracted him as an adult was its sense of values—honor, duty, trustworthiness, and courage—as well as the sense of community as demonstrated by the knights of the roundtable. "The American," he writes in the last of these essays, "has never been a perfect instrument, but at one time he had a reputation for gallantry, which, to my mind, is a sweet and priceless quality. It must still exist, but it is blotted out by the dust cloud of self-pity." He would seem to have wanted to do the *Arthur* as a way of commenting indirectly on what he perceived was going wrong in American society, primarily its growing materialism and dishonesty. Frustrated with the translation, he took his concerns to express them in *America and Americans,* but he was led to go further, to discover just what the American was and how that person developed. He wrote to John Huston while the manuscript was in progress, "I may have to run for my life when it comes out. I am taking 'the American' apart like a watch to see what makes him tick and some very curious things are emerging" (*SLL* 807).

Few had tried to identify the American in such a way since St. John de Crèvecoeur had done it in *Letters from an American Farmer* at the time of the American Revolution. "What, then, is the American, this new man?" (63) Crèvecoeur asks and goes on to idealize him as the yeoman farmer, industrious, community-minded, family-centered, and optimistic. He is a new breed, having "arrived on a new continent; a modern society offers itself to his contemplation, different from what he had hitherto seen. It is not composed, as in Europe of great lords who possess everything, and a herd of people who have nothing" (63). Two centuries later, this was no longer a country that depended on the farmer and the opportunity to own land in order to ensure democracy, but John Steinbeck found it still inimitable and matchless: "I believe that out of the whole body of our past, out of our differences, our quarrels, our many interests and directions, something has emerged that is itself unique in the world: America—complicated, paradoxical, bullheaded, shy, cruel, boisterous, unspeakably dear, and very beautiful."

At the same time both writers found much to criticize. For Crèvecoeur one of the central problems in eighteenth-century America was the wild man, the frontiersman who has left behind all civilizing restraints. Without rules, examples, or a sense of morality, these "men appear to be no better than carnivorous animals of a superior rank, living on the flesh of wild animals when they can catch them, and when they are not able, they subsist on grain" (66). Two centuries later, Steinbeck saw a society that suffered from a similar lack of morality, but not because it was without resources out in the wilderness—just the opposite. Americans have food, shelter, transportation, and leisure, but have compromised values:

I strongly suspect that our moral and spiritual disintegration grows out of our lack of experience with plenty. . . . [We] are also poisoned with things. Having many things seems to create a desire for more things, more clothes, houses, automobiles. Think of the pure horror of our Christmases when our children tear open package after package and, when the floor is heaped with wrappings and presents, say, "Is that all?"

Crèvecoeur saw the wild man, his drunkenness and idleness, as being replaced by the settlers, who brought hard work, rules, and a sense of purpose to the frontier. Steinbeck envisioned a similar evolution in our nation, beginning with a biological necessity, the will to survive: "Every pursuit, no matter what its stated end, had as its foundation purpose, survival, growth, and renewal." But after our survival would seem to be assured, we will lose our will to go on if we do not have faith and a sense of a larger purpose:

It is probable that here is where morals—integrity, ethics, even charity—have gone. The rules allowed us to survive, to live together and to increase. But if our will to survive is weakened, if our love of life and our memories of a gallant past and faith in a shining future are removed—what need is there for morals or for rules? Even they become a danger. . . . We have succeeded in what our fathers prayed for and it is our success that is destroying us.

He wrote to Harry Guggenheim in January 1966: "Today I have spent the time correcting galley proofs on my new book. And it's a better book than I thought. It should raise some smoke. There's an argument in every sentence, or at least there will be if anyone reads it."

Foreword

I N TEXT and pictures,* this is a book of opinions, unashamed and individual. For centuries America and the Americans have been the
target for opinions—Asian, African, and European—only these opinions have been called criticism, observation, or, God help us, evaluation.
Unfortunately, Americans have allowed these foreign opinions the value
set on them by their authors. For our own part, we have denounced,
scolded, celebrated, and lied about facets and bits and pieces of our own
country and countrymen; but I know of no native work of inspection of
our whole nation and its citizens by a blowed-in-the-glass American, another opinion.

So long as our evaluators indulged in simple misconceptions and
discourtesies, the game was harmless and sometimes interesting. But
when, after 1918, systems arose which required a *bête noire* to balance
their homegrown *bête blanche*, America as a powerful nation and a successful system became the natural patsy for those governments which
were not doing so well. Since those same governments had closed their
frontiers to their own people, they were free to make any generalizations
they wished without the disadvantage of having to base them on observation.

This essay is not an attempt to answer or refute the sausage-like propaganda which is ground out in our disfavor. It cannot even pretend to be
objective truth. Of course it is opinion, conjecture, and speculation.
What else could it be? But at least it is informed by America, and inspired by curiosity, impatience, some anger, and a passionate love of

*The photographs from the original 1966 edition of *America and Americans* are not
included.

America and the Americans. For I believe that out of the whole body of our past, out of our differences, our quarrels, our many interests and directions, something has emerged that is itself unique in the world: America—complicated, paradoxical, bullheaded, shy, cruel, boisterous, unspeakably dear, and very beautiful.

If the text is opinionated, so are the pictures. The camera may record exactly, but it can set down only what its operator sees, and he sees what he wants to see—what he loves and hates and pities and is proud of. So that the pictures in this book, taken by photographers whose ancestral origins cover the whole world, whose backgrounds and experiences are as diversified as their styles and methods and camera techniques, are also opinions—American opinions. None of these pictures could have been taken anywhere but in America. A European, an African, or an Asian will not find in them an America that he has seen or would see here. But if he is open and sensitive he may learn of what our country is like to us, what we feel about it: our shame in its failures, our pride in its successes, our wonder at its size and diversity, and, above all, our passionate devotion to it—to all of it, the land, the idea, and the mystique.

I know of course that every country has its parallel. No foreigner can know and feel about England as an Englishman does, with his two thousand years in depth. I have seen a Pole kiss the earth of his homeland on returning, and a Dane shyly caress with his hand a ruddy iron stanchion on a Copenhagen dock. It is not that Americans are different in the quality of their feeling; but this feeling has rarely been set down about our whole country.

E Pluribus Unum

OUR LAND is of every kind geologically and climatically, and our people are of every kind also—of every race, of every ethnic category—and yet our land is one nation, and our people are Americans. Mottoes have a way of being compounded of wishes and dreams. The motto of the United States, "*E Pluribus Unum*," is a fact. This is the strange and almost unbelievable truth; and even stranger is the fact that the unit America has come into being in slightly over four hundred years—almost exactly the same amount of time as that during which England was occupied by the Roman legions.

It is customary (indeed, at high-school graduations it is a requirement) for speakers to refer to America as a "precious inheritance"—our heritage, a gift proffered like a sandwich wrapped in plastic on a plastic tray. Our ancestors, so it is implied, gathered to the invitation of a golden land and accepted the sacrament of milk and honey. This is not so.

In the beginning, we crept, scuttled, escaped, were driven out of the safe and settled corners of the earth to the fringes of a strange and hostile wilderness, a nameless and hostile continent. Some rulers granted large sections of unmapped territory, in places they did not own or even know, as cheap gifts to favorites or to potential enemies for the purpose of getting rid of them. Many others were sent here as a punishment for penal offenses. Far from welcoming us, this continent resisted us. The Indigenes fought to the best of their ability to hold on to a land they thought was theirs. The rocky soils fought back, and the bewildering forests, and the deserts. Diseases, unknown and therefore incurable, decimated the early comers, and in their energy of restlessness they fought one another. This land was no gift. The firstlings worked for it, fought for it, and died for it. They stole and cheated and double-crossed for it, and when they had taken a little piece, the way a fierce-hearted man ropes a wild mustang, they had then to gentle it and smooth it and make it habitable at all. Once they had a foothold, they had to defend their holdings against new waves of the restless and ferocious and hungry.

America did not exist. Four centuries of work, of bloodshed, of loneliness and fear created this land. We built America and the process made us Americans—a new breed, rooted in all races, stained and tinted with all colors, a seeming ethnic anarchy. Then in a little, little time, we became more alike than we were different—a new society; not great, but fitted by our very faults for greatness, *E Pluribus Unum*.

The whole thing is crazy. Every single man in our emerging country was out for himself against all others—for his safety, his profit, his future. He had little care for the land; he ripped it, raped it, and in some cases destroyed it. He cut and burned the forests, fired and plowed the plains, dredged the beautiful rivers for gold, leaving a pebbled devastation. When his family grew up about him he set it against all other families. When communities arose, each one defended itself against other communities. The provinces which became states were each one a suspicious unit, with jealously held borders and duties, tolls, and penalties against strangers. The surges of the new restless, needy, and strong— grudgingly brought in for purposes of hard labor and cheap wages—were resisted, resented, and accepted only when a new and different wave came in. Consider how the Germans clotted for self-defense until the Irish took the resented place; how the Irish became "Americans" against the Poles, the Slavs against the Italians. On the West Coast the Chinese ceased to be enemies only when the Japanese arrived, and they in the face of the invasions of Hindus, Filipinos, and Mexicans. Nor were the dislikes saved exclusively for foreigners. When dust and economics rooted up the poor dirt farmers of Oklahoma and pushed them westward, they were met with perhaps even more suspicion and resentment than the other waves.

All this has been true, and yet in one or two, certainly not more than three generations, each ethnic group has clicked into place in the union without losing the *pluribus*. When we read the lineup of a University of Notre Dame football team, called the "Fighting Irish," we do not find it ridiculous that the names are Polish, Slovak, Italian, or Fiji, for that matter. They *are* the Fighting Irish.

How all these fragments of the peoples of the world who settled America became one people is not only a mystery but quite contrary to their original wishes and intentions. The first European settlers on the eastern shores of America not only did not want to merge with other peoples but made sure by their regulations and their defenses that they did not. The Pilgrim Fathers who landed in Massachusetts turned their guns on anyone, English or otherwise, who was not exactly like themselves. The Virginia and Carolina planters, with royal grants of land, wanted slaves and indentured servants, not free and dangerous elements; but in many cases their only sources of supply were the prisons of England, so that they got their dangerous elements anyway. Every wavelet of early settlers either went to remote and distance-protected areas or set up defenses against future waves. The poor Irish, fleeing from the potato famine, in the face of North American hostility foregathered with the Irish, the Jews with the Jews. On the West Coast the Chinese formed their Chinese communities. Every large city had its national areas, usually known as "Irishtown," "Chinatown," "Germantown," "Little Italy," "Polacktown." The newcomers went to where the languages and customs were their own, and each community in its turn defended itself against the inroads of other nationalities.

Some groups abandoned or were forced away from the cities and took up their positions in the inexhaustible wilderness. In the Kentucky mountains to this day there are people all of a sort who still speak Elizabethan English. The Mormons, heckled, murdered, and driven from the East, made the terrible trek to Utah and formed their society around the Great Salt Lake. In California there were communities of Russians; in eastern Oregon the Basques took their language, their sheep, and their white sheep dogs to the inaccessible mountains. On the West Coast there were communities of Cornishmen, speaking only Cornish. These isolated groups went to places as nearly like their homeland as they could find, and tried to maintain the old customs and the old life. In the centers, synagogues sprang up, and onion-topped Russian Orthodox churches. Since California was Spanish and then Mexican, therefore

Catholic, the schools were parochial; Protestants arriving from the East had to send their sons to Hawaii for a Protestant education. Colonies of Germans settled in Texas and around the Great Lakes, and tried to keep their identities, their cooking, and their language.

From the first we have treated our minorities abominably, the way the old boys do the new kids in school. All that was required to release this mechanism of oppression and sadism was that the newcomers be meek, poor, weak in numbers, and unprotected—although it helped if their skin, hair, eyes were different and if they spoke some language other than English or worshiped in some church other than Protestant. The Pilgrim Fathers took out after the Catholics, and both clobbered the Jews. The Irish had their turn running the gantlet, and after them the Germans, the Poles, the Slovaks, the Italians, the Hindus, the Chinese, the Japanese, the Filipinos, the Mexicans. To all these people we gave disparaging names: Micks, Sheenies, Krauts, Dagos, Wops, Ragheads, Yellowbellies, and so forth. The turn against each group continued until it became sound, solvent, self-defensive, and economically anonymous—whereupon each group joined the older boys and charged down on the newest ones. It occurs to me that this very cruelty toward newcomers might go far to explain the speed with which the ethnic and national strangers merged with the "Americans." Having suffered, one would have thought they might have pity on the newer come, but they did not; they couldn't wait to join the majority and indulge in the accepted upper-caste practice of rumbling some newer group.

It is possible that the first colonist on these shores, as soon as he got the seaweed out of his shoes, turned and shouted toward the old country, "No more, now—that's enough!" The extraordinary ferocity with which each colony resisted newcomers lasted until finally the immigration laws slowed the river of strangers to a stream and then to a drip. Then we had come full turn, and had arrived at a curious and ridiculous position: the very men who were most influential in getting the restrictive immigration laws passed were forced to advocate the admission of new cheap labor, and in some cases to admit it illegally. In fact it can almost be said of us that if we didn't have patsies we'd have to invent them.

In earliest times, vulnerability consisted in strangeness, weakness, and poverty; but in the twentieth century a new thing came into being, probably because we had attracted every kind of stranger, except perhaps Eskimos and Australian bushmen. Once the saturation point was reached, minorities began to exert an influence simply as minorities. Perhaps communications, publicity, access to pictures, radio, and print had something to do with this; but there was a further factor involved. As each minority became solvent it ceased to be a target and became a market, and you do not run down someone to whom you hope to sell something. Minorities, sensing their power, began to use it, and to a large extent this was a good thing; but there were losses, of culture, and just pure amusement, which is plain unfortunate. Today, one cannot tell a Jewish joke in public, although the Jews have created some of the funniest stories we know.

With our history, every law of probability forecast a country made up of tight islands of ethnic groups held together by a common language and by the humility heaped on them by their neighbors. Even settlers from the same nation should have divided up according to language and custom, just as Welshmen keep separate from Lancashiremen, or Scots from men of Somerset or Kent. What happened is one of the strange quirks of human nature—but perhaps it is a perfectly natural direction that was taken, since no child can long endure his parents. It seemed to happen by instinct. In spite of all the pressure the old people could bring to bear, the children of each ethnic group denied their background and their ancestral language. Despite the anger, the contempt, the jealousy, the self-imposed ghettos and segregation, something was loose in this land called America. Its people were Americans. The new generations wanted to be Americans more than they wanted to be Poles or Germans or Hungarians or Italians or British. They wanted this and they did it. America was not planned; it became. Plans made for it fell apart, were forgotten. From being a polyglot nation, Americans became the worst linguists in the world.

There is no question in my mind that places in America mark their natives not only in their speech patterns but physically—in build, in stance, in conformation. Climate may have something to do with this, as well as food supply and techniques of living; in any case, it seems to be true that people living close together tend to look alike. Why not? If a man and his dog become the same in appearance, why not a man and his neighbor?

Each of us can detect a stranger, a strange accent. Once I prided myself on being able to tell where a man or woman came from after hearing him speak. But we do not think that we ourselves are so marked. Some years ago when I was living with the migrant people from the Southwest, it was my pride that I could tell an Oklahoman from a man from Arkansas, and either from one from another area. The Oklahoman spoke a regional dialect, it is true; but there were other signs, such as posture, facial structure, way of walking. Once, when I was smugly indulging my ability, a tall, rangy Okie boy said to me, "You're a Californian."

"How do you know that?" I asked with some surprise.

"You look like a Californian," he said; and I had not been aware that Californians had a look.

I have lived and traveled in foreign countries where my bloodlines of Scottish-Irish, English, and German are common. Let us say that my shoes and hats were made in England, my clothing in Italy cut from British cloth, my shirts and ties in France or Italy, my raincoat in Scotland. In addition, I have a parrot tongue, and quickly and unconsciously pick up the accent, speech mannerisms, and idioms of the people among whom I live. My face has the features, good or bad, of my ancestry. My eyes are northern blue, my hair before it whitened was that no-color which is described as brown. My cheeks are florid, with the tiny vesicles showing through, so characteristic of the Scottish and the North Irish. But in spite of all this, I have never been taken for a European. Any sensitive European knows instantly that I am an American. The Okie boy I mentioned did not remotely resemble me; his dark eyes, shining black hair, high cheekbones, and dark skin all spoke of his Cherokee blood. But if this boy should walk through any city in Europe, he too would instantly be picked out as an American. Somewhere there is an American look. I don't know what it is, and foreigners cannot describe it; but it is there.

The American look is not limited to people of Caucasian ancestry. In northern California, where I grew up, there was a large Japanese population, many of whom I knew well. The father and mother would be short, square, wide in the hip, and bowlegged, their heads round, the skin quite dark, the eyes almond with that fullness of the upper lid which is called Oriental. How does it happen, then, that their children and grandchildren are as much as a foot to eighteen inches taller than their parents, that their hips are narrow, their legs long and straight, the skin lighter, and the eyes, while still recognizable as Oriental, much less almond in shape and the fleshy upper lid much less pronounced? Furthermore, their heads are mostly long instead of round. This happens through no intermixture of other blood. It is easy to say that a change of diet has accomplished this change, but that cannot be the only factor; and it is interesting that when one of these Nisei go to Japan they are spotted immediately as Americans. These boys and girls are pure-blooded Japanese—and yet they are pure Americans.

Two racial groups did not follow the pattern of arrival, prejudice, acceptance, and absorption: the American Indian, who was already here, and the Negro, who did not come under his own volition. To begin with, the Indians were not a minority but a majority. In some cases they seem to have tried to get along with their guests, and when it became apparent that this was impossible—it is difficult to be friendly with someone who wants to take everything you have—the Indians not only defended themselves but inflicted telling losses on the settlers. Over the years the ratio changed as well as the weapons, but the Indians continued to defend themselves for a long, long time—a practice which not only cut them off from their white brothers but welded the Indians themselves much more tightly together. When the white settlers finally achieved supremacy, they found to their indignation that some of the best and most profitable places were inhabited by Indians. The process then was, by force of arms, to move the Indians little by little to areas so poor that nobody else wanted them. This process took an unconscionably long and bloody time, and mistakes were made, such as the prime one of moving the Cherokee tribes from the Appalachian Mountains to the West and settling them on unpromising-looking Oklahoma. When oil was discovered there, the mistake was apparent; but for some of the Indians it was too late—they kept the oil.

One of the American Indian tendencies which led to our distress was their abiding passion for survival. During the latter part of the last century, when some of the Southwestern tribes such as the Apaches were not only surviving but actually fighting back, a bounty was offered for scalps, and a good number were brought in and the bounty collected. It was after that that the Mexican government complained bitterly that the scalps were not Apache but Mexican. The hunters were crossing the border for the ugly little bits of skin and hair; it was much safer to kill a Mexican than an Apache, and they couldn't be told apart. Then, so it is said, a company of forward-looking businessmen began importing Chinese and Filipino scalps, smoked and dried, which could be got with no personal danger at all; but they overdid it and broke the bounty market.

For a time it looked as though the Indians might completely disappear, but then about fifty years ago something—or perhaps a series of things—happened. The Indians developed an immunity to extinction. Their birth rate began to pick up and their death rate dropped. Some of the young men emerged from their reservations to take dangerous jobs, such as top-falling in the forests and high steel work on the new skyscrapers of the growing cities, and at the same time it ceased to be a hidden disgrace to have Indian blood, and people began boasting of grandparents who were Cheyenne or Cherokee, even if it wasn't true. In recent years, no candidate would think of running for the Presidency without being made an honorary member of some tribe or other and being photographed wearing the feathered war bonnet that had once caused a chill of fear in the borderlands.

The Indians survived our open intention of wiping them out, and since the tide turned they have even weathered our good intentions toward them, which can be much more deadly. The myth of the Indian as a savage, untrustworthy, dangerous animal, wily, clever, and self-sufficient as an opponent, gave way to the myth of the Indian as a child, incapable of learning and of taking care of himself. Hence he was made a minor under the law, no matter what his age might be. The problem, of course, was, in the beginning, that he was the only person who *could* take care of himself. His crops served our first settlers, his skills in hunting were absorbed so that our people could live; and his method of warfare, being learned, was not only turned against him but was turned against our other enemies. Oh, yes, he could take care of himself—against everybody but us.

Many white people, after association with the tribesmen, have been struck with the dual life—the reality and super-reality—that the Indians seem to be able to penetrate at will. The stories of travelers in the early days are filled with these incidents of another life separated from this one by a penetrable veil; and such is the power of the Indians' belief in this other life that the traveler usually comes out believing in it too and only fearing that *he* won't be believed. An experience I once had illustrates, I think, the way the tribesmen can slip back and forth between their two realities and between one culture and another.

For several years I worked for the California Fish and Game Commission in a trout hatchery in the Lake Tahoe area. Our job was to trap big lake trout when they ran into a stream to spawn, to strip the eggs from the females and milt the males to fertilize the eggs, raise the little fish, and bring them up in tanks until they were ready to be transplanted into California streams. A young man named Lloyd Shebley and I were assigned to the Tallac hatchery and spent considerable time there. The hatchery had to be prepared in the winter for the run of the fish in the early spring before the snow melted. When the fish began to run, we were very busy; but later in the year our job was simply to feed and care for the fish, and so it was pleasant and highly interesting work, and also we got to know all the people in the area; and among those people were members of a tribe which I believe is a branch of the Piutes. In the summer they came up from Nevada, where their reservation is, to live in the mountains, to hunt, and to pick the piñons from which they made their bread. Among the friends we made was Jimmy, the chief of the tribe, and far from being a savage—noble or otherwise—Jimmy was like any American with a high-school education. He had been to high school in Reno, and looked and spoke like any other American, except that he was an Indian—rather a quiet, good-looking, well-mannered man of about forty. We liked him very much.

It has usually been a convention in Indian country that the game laws do not apply to Indians. They are permitted to hunt when their white brothers are forbidden to, and also to fish. This is just generally known and generally respected. One day in the spring when we were trapping, and the snow was still very high on the edge of the turbulent little stream, Jimmy appeared on foot—indeed, that was the only way he could get anywhere; he was walking on a pair of bear paws—and came to the trap and asked us for a fish. We were used to giving fish to the Indians when they asked for them. One of us reached into the trap with a net and pulled out a fine, big buck trout, drew the milt, and gave the fish to Jimmy. He put the flopping trout down in a snowbank, and in the freezing cold took off his clothes, got into the stream and washed himself carefully, got out, put his clothing back on, picked up his fish, and started right up the sides of Mount Tallac, a very steep mountain that rises in that back country; and that was the last we saw of him until the following summer.

It was in August, I think, that Jimmy came by the hatchery to pass the time of day and stay to dinner. We cooked him a good meal and when we were sitting afterward having coffee and whisky I said to him, "Jimmy, what was that thing about the fish last winter?"

He looked rather taken aback and answered naturally, "What fish?"

I said, "You remember, Jimmy—that trout we gave you when you jumped in the stream and then climbed up the mountain. What was that all about?"

He said, "Oh, yes—that fish," and he was silent again.

I said, "Of course, if you don't want to talk about it, it's all right with us. I was just interested."

He took quite a long time before he spoke again. "Yes, I guess I could tell you, maybe," he said. "You see, I was sick all last summer—bad stomach trouble—and I went to all the doctors in Reno and they looked me over and gave me medicine and it didn't do me a bit of good. They couldn't find out what was causing it and they couldn't cure it, and I was just miserable, and finally I just got sicker and sicker; and so I went to one of our own men."

I said, "You mean one of your medicine men?"

And Jimmy said, "Yes, I guess you could call them that—that's not what we call them. He told me what was wrong with me."

I asked, "Well, what *was* wrong with you?"

He said, "Well, you know, the last season my boys and I killed four deer and we didn't get to jerking the meat and some of it spoiled, and that was what was wrong with my stomach."

"You mean you ate spoiled meat?"

"No, we wasted meat."

"What did the man suggest?" I asked.

Jimmy said, "He told me to come and get one of the earliest trout I could, and to bathe in the stream it came from, and to take it up to Half Moon Lake, over in back of the peak of Tallac, and give it to a mermaid." He said, "Oh, no, now don't get this idea that this is a half-woman, half-fish sort of thing that you see in pictures. That's not what it was." And he was quiet.

I said, "But you did climb up the mountain to Half Moon Lake, and you did give the fish to something or somebody."

"Yes," he said, "I did."

"Could you describe what it was or who it was you gave the fish to?"

"No, it would be hard. I don't know how to describe it."

I said, "Was it a person?"

He said, "In a way; but it was an un-person too."

I said, "Male or female?"

He said, "It seemed to be a woman."

I said, "And she took the fish?"

And he said, "Yes."

"And she went into the lake?"

He said, "I don't know. I turned and walked away."

"Well," I said, "how is your stomach?"

He said, "I've had no more trouble with the stomach. It went away right then."

Well, that's what happened, and you can make anything you want of it; but of one thing I am certain: Jimmy was not a liar. But it is more than probable that if I had been alone at that time and did not have the corroboration of Lloyd Shebley I never would have repeated that story.

Paradox and Dream

ONE OF THE generalities most often noted about Americans is that we are a restless, a dissatisfied, a searching people. We bridle and buck under failure, and we go mad with dissatisfaction in the face of success. We spend our time searching for security, and hate it when we get it. For the most part we are an intemperate people: we eat too much when we can, drink too much, indulge our senses too much. Even in our so-called virtues we are intemperate: a teetotaler is not content not to drink—he must stop all the drinking in the world; a vegetarian among us would outlaw the eating of meat. We work too hard, and many die under the strain; and then to make up for that we play with a violence as suicidal.

The result is that we seem to be in a state of turmoil all the time, both physically and mentally. We are able to believe that our government is weak, stupid, overbearing, dishonest, and inefficient, and at the same time we are deeply convinced that it is the best government in the world, and we would like to impose it upon everyone else. We speak of the American Way of Life as though it involved the ground rules for the governance of heaven. A man hungry and unemployed through his own stupidity and that of others, a man beaten by a brutal policeman, a woman forced into prostitution by her own laziness, high prices, availability, and despair—all bow with reverence toward the American Way of Life, although each one would look puzzled and angry if he were asked to define it. We scramble and scrabble up the stony path toward the pot of gold we have taken to mean security. We trample friends, relatives, and strangers who get in the way of our achieving it; and once we get it we shower it on psychoanalysts to try to find out why we are unhappy, and finally—if we have enough of the gold—we contribute it back to the nation in the form of foundations and charities.

We fight our way in, and try to buy our way out. We are alert, curious, hopeful, and we take more drugs designed to make us unaware than any other people. We are self-reliant and at the same time completely dependent. We are aggressive, and defenseless. Americans overindulge their children and do not like them; the children in turn are overly dependent and full of hate for their parents. We are complacent in our possessions, in our houses, in our education; but it is hard to find a man or woman who does not want something better for the next generation. Americans are remarkably kind and hospitable and open with both guests and strangers; and yet they will make a wide circle around the man dying on the pavement. Fortunes are spent getting cats out of trees and dogs out of sewer pipes; but a girl screaming for help in the street draws only slammed doors, closed windows, and silence.

Now there is a set of generalities for you, each one of them canceled out by another generality. Americans seem to live and breathe and function by paradox; but in nothing are we so paradoxical as in our passionate belief in our own myths. We truly believe ourselves to be natural-born mechanics and do-it-yourself-ers. We spend our lives in motor cars, yet most of us—a great many of us at least—do not know enough about a car to look in the gas tank when the motor fails. Our lives as we live them would not function without electricity, but it is a rare man or woman who, when the power goes off, knows how to look for a burned-out fuse and replace it. We believe implicitly that we are the heirs of the pioneers; that we have inherited self-sufficiency and the ability to take care of ourselves, particularly in relation to nature. There isn't a man among us in ten thousand who knows how to butcher a cow or a pig and cut it up for eating, let alone a wild animal. By natural endowment, we are great rifle shots and great hunters—but when hunting season opens there is a slaughter of farm animals and humans by men and women who couldn't hit a real target if they could see it. Americans treasure the knowledge that they live close to nature, but fewer and fewer farmers feed more and more people; and as soon as we can afford to we eat out of cans, buy frozen TV dinners, and haunt the delicatessens. Affluence means moving to the suburbs, but the American suburbanite sees, if anything, less of the country than the city apartment dweller with his window boxes and his African violets carefully tended under lights. In no country are more seeds and plants and equipment purchased, and less vegetables and flowers raised.

The paradoxes are everywhere: We shout that we are a nation of laws, not men—and then proceed to break every law we can if we can get away with it. We proudly insist that we base our political positions on the issues—and we will vote against a man because of his religion, his name, or the shape of his nose.

Sometimes we seem to be a nation of public puritans and private profligates. There surely can be no excesses like those committed by good family men away from home at a convention. We believe in the manliness of our men and the womanliness of our women, but we go to extremes of expense and discomfort to cover any natural evidence that we are either. From puberty we are preoccupied with sex; but our courts, our counselors, and our psychiatrists are dealing constantly with cases of sexual failure or charges of frigidity or impotence. A small failure in business can quite normally make a man sexually impotent.

We fancy ourselves as hardheaded realists, but we will buy anything we see advertised, particularly on television; and we buy it not with reference to the quality or the value of the product, but directly as a result of the number of times we have heard it mentioned. The most arrant nonsense about a product is never questioned. We are afraid to be awake, afraid to be alone, afraid to be a moment without the noise and confusion we call entertainment. We boast of our dislike of highbrow art and music, and we have more and better-attended symphonies, art galleries, and theaters than any country in the world. We detest abstract art and produce more of it than all the rest of the world put together.

One of the characteristics most puzzling to a foreign observer is the strong and imperishable dream the American carries. On inspection, it is found that the dream has little to do with reality in American life. Consider the dream of and the hunger for home. The very word can reduce nearly all of my compatriots to tears. Builders and developers never build houses—they build homes. The dream home is either in a small town or in a suburban area where grass and trees simulate the country. This dream home is a permanent seat, not rented but owned. It is a center where a man and his wife grow graciously old, warmed by the radiance of well-washed children and grandchildren. Many thousands of these homes are built every year; built, planted, advertised, and sold—and yet, the American family rarely stays in one place for more than five years. The home and its equipment are purchased on time and are heavily mortgaged. The earning power of the father is almost always overextended, so that after a few years he is not able to keep up the payments on his loans. That is on the losing side. But suppose the earner is successful and his income increases. Right away the house is not big enough, or in the proper neighborhood. Or perhaps suburban life palls, and the family moves to the city, where excitement and convenience beckon.

Some of these movements back and forth seem to me a result of just pure restlessness, pure nervousness. We do hear, of course, of people who keep the same job for twenty years, or thirty years, or forty years, and get a gold watch for it; but the numbers of these old and faithful employees are decreasing all the time. Part of the movement has to do with the nature of business itself. Work in factories, in supermarkets, for contractors on the construction of houses, bridges, public buildings, or more factories is often temporary; the job gets done, or local taxes or wage increases or falling sales may cause a place of business to move to a new area. In addition, many of the great corporations have a policy of moving employees from one of their many branches to another. The employee with the home dream finds that with every removal he loses money. The sellers of homes make their profit on the down payment and on the interest on the loan; but the private owner who wants to turn over his dream home and move on to another finds that he always takes a loss. However, the dream does not die—it just takes another form.

Today, with the ancient American tendency to look for greener pastures still very much alive, the mobile home has become the new dream. It is not a trailer; it is a house, long and narrow in shape, and equipped with wheels so that it can, if necessary, be transported over the highway to a new area. In a mobile home, a man doesn't have to take a loss when he moves; his home goes with him. Until recently, when the local authorities have set about finding means of making Mr. Mobile pay his way, a mobile home owner living in a rented space in a trailer park could avoid local taxes and local duties while making use of the public schools and all the other facilities American towns set up for their people. The mobile way of life is not a new thing in the world, of course. It is more than probable that humans lived this way for hundreds of thousands of years before they ever conceived of settling down—the herdsmen followed the herds, the hunters followed the game, and everybody ran from the weather. The Tartars moved whole villages on wheels, and the diehard gypsies have never left their caravans. No, people go back to mobility with enthusiasm for something they recognize, and if they can double the dream—have a symbol home and mobility at the same time—they have it made. And now there are huge settlements of these metal houses clustered on the edges of our cities. Plots of grass and shrubs are planted, awnings stretched out, and garden chairs appear. A community life soon springs up—a life having all the signs of status, the standards of success or failure that exist elsewhere in America.

There is no question that American life is in the process of changing, but, as always in human history, it carries some of the past along with it; and the mobile home has one old trap built into it. Automobile manufacturers discovered and developed the American yearning for status. By changing the appliances and gadgetry on each new model, they could make the car owner feel that his perfectly good automobile was old-fashioned and therefore undesirable. His children were afraid to be seen in it; and, since a family's image of success in the world, or status, is to a certain extent dependent on the kind of a car the man drives, he was forced to buy a new one whether he needed it or not. Outdated mobile homes carry the same stigma. Every year new models appear, costing from five thousand to fifty thousand dollars, with new fixtures, colors—new, and therefore desirable. A family with an old model, no matter how comfortable and sound, soon feels *déclassé*. Thus the turnover in mobile houses is enormous, and thus the social strata reestablish themselves: the top people have the newest models, and lesser folk buy the used homes turned in as down payments on the newer ones. And the trailer cities have neighborhoods as fiendishly snobbish as have any other suburban developments—each one has its Sugar Hill, its upper-middle-class area, and its slums. The pattern has not changed; and none of this has in any way affected the American dream of home, which remains part

Grandma Moses and part split-level ranch house in an area where to keep a cow or a pen of chickens is to break the law.

Of course, the home dream can be acted out almost anywhere. A number of years ago, when I lived on East 51st Street in New York City, I saw an instance of it every day on my morning walk, near Third Avenue, where great numbers of old red brick buildings were the small, walk-up cold-water flats in which so many New Yorkers lived. Every summer morning about nine o'clock a stout and benign-looking lady came down the stairs from her flat to the pavement carrying the great outdoors in her arms. She set out a canvas deck chair, and over it mounted a beach umbrella—one of the kind which has a little cocktail table around it—and then, smiling happily, this benign and robust woman rolled out a little lawn made of green raffia in front of her chair, set out two pots of red geraniums and an artificial palm, brought a little cabinet with cold drinks—Coca-Cola, Pepsi-Cola—in a small icebox; she laid her folded copy of the *Daily News* on the table, arranged her equipment, and sank back into the chair—and she was in the country. She nodded and smiled to everyone who went by, and somehow she conveyed her dream to everyone who saw her, and everyone who saw her was delighted with her. For some reason I was overwhelmed with a desire to contribute to this sylvan retreat, and so one day when she had stepped inside for a moment, I deposited on her table a potted fern and a little bowl with two goldfish; and the next morning, I was pleased to see that these had been added to the permanent equipment. Every day through that summer the fern and the goldfish were part of the scene.

The home dream is only one of the deepset American illusions which, since they can't be changed, function as cohesive principles to bind the nation together and make it different from all other nations. It occurs to me that all dreams, waking and sleeping, are powerful and prominent memories of something real, of something that really happened. I believe these memories—some of them, at least—can be inherited; our generalized dreams of water and warmth, of falling, of monsters, of danger and premonitions may have been prerecorded on some kind of genetic tape in the species out of which we evolved or mutated, just as some of our organs which no longer function seem to be physical memories of other, earlier processes. The national dream of Americans is a whole pattern of thinking and feeling and may well be a historic memory surprisingly little distorted. Furthermore, the participators in the dream need not have descended physically from the people to whom the reality happened. This pattern of thought and conduct which is the national character is absorbed even by the children of immigrants born in America, but it never comes to the immigrants themselves, no matter how they may wish it; birth on American soil seems to be required.

I have spoken of the dream of home that persists in a time when home is neither required nor wanted. Until very recently home was a real word, and in the English tongue it is a magic word. The ancient root word *ham*, from which our word "home" came, meant the triangle where two rivers meet which, with a short wall, can be defended. At first the word "home" meant safety, then gradually comfort. In the immediate American past, the home meant just those two things; the log houses, even the sod houses, were havens of safety, of defense, warmth, food, and comfort. Outside were hostile Indians and dangerous animals, crippling cold and starvation. Many houses, including the one where President Johnson was born, built only a few generations back, have thick walls and gunslits for defense, a great hearth for cooking and for heat, a cellar under the floor and an attic for the storage of food, and sometimes even an interior well in case of siege. A home was a place where women and children could be reasonably safe, a place to which a man could return with joy and slough off his weariness and his fears. This symbol of safety and comfort is so recent in our history that it is no wonder that to all of us it remains dear and desirable.

It is an American dream that we are great hunters, trackers, woodsmen, deadshots with a rifle or a shotgun; and this dream is deeply held by Americans who have never fired a gun or hunted anything larger or more dangerous than a cockroach. But I wonder whether our deep connection with firearms is not indeed a national potential; not long ago we had to be good hunters or we starved, good shots or our lives were in danger. Can this have carried over? Early in World War II, I worked for the Training Command of the Air Force, and spent a good deal of time at the schools for aerial gunnery. The British, having been in the war for a long time, sent teams of instructors to teach our newly inducted men to handle the tail and ball-turret guns in our B-17 bombers, but the instruction began with small arms, since all shooting is pretty much the same. I remember an Englishman saying to me, "It is amazing how quickly these men learn. Some of them have never handled a weapon, and yet it seems to come to them as though they knew it; they pick it up much faster than the English lads do. Maybe they're just born with the knack."

I suggested, "Think of the time of Crécy and Agincourt, when the longbow dominated battlefields. Now, the yew of the longbows was not English, it was Spanish. The French had access to the longbow and surely they knew its effectiveness, and still they never used it."

"That's right," he said. "Our lads had the knack, didn't they? But also they had practice and habit; the bow was in their blood. Maybe they were bowmen before they ever handled a bow, because it was expected of them. You may have genes of firearms in your systems."

The inventiveness once necessary for survival may also be a part of the national dream. Who among us has not bought for a song an ancient junked car, and with parts from other junked cars put together something that would run? This is not lost; American kids are still doing it. The dreams of a people either create folk literature or find their way into it; and folk literature, again, is always based on something that happened. Our most persistent folk tales—constantly retold in books, movies, and television shows—concern cowboys, gunslinging sheriffs, and Indian fighters. These folk figures existed—perhaps not quite as they are recalled nor in the numbers indicated, but they did exist; and this dream also persists. Even businessmen in Texas wear the high-heeled boots and big hats, though they ride in air-conditioned Cadillacs and have forgotten the reason for the high heels. All our children play cowboy and Indian; the brave and honest sheriff who with courage and a six-gun brings law and order and civic virtue to a Western community is perhaps our most familiar hero, no doubt descended from the brave mailed knight of chivalry who battled and overcame evil with lance and sword. Even the recognition signals are the same: white hat, white armor—black hat, black shield. And in these moral tales, so deepset in us, virtue does not arise out of reason or orderly process of law—it is imposed and maintained by violence.

I wonder whether this folk wisdom is the story of our capability. Are these stories permanent because we know within ourselves that only the threat of violence makes it possible for us to live together in peace? I think that surviving folk tales are directly based on memory. There must have been a leader like King Arthur; although there is no historical record to prove it, the very strength of the story presumes his existence. We know there were gunslinging sheriffs—not many, but some; but if they had not existed, our need for them would have created them. It interests me that the youthful gangs in our cities, engaging in their "rumbles" which are really wars, and doing so in direct and overt disobedience of law and of all the pressures the police can apply—that these gangs take noble names, and within their organizations are said to maintain a code of behavior and responsibility toward one another and an obedience to their leaders very like that of the tight-knit chivalric code of feudal Europe; the very activities and attitudes which raise the hand of the law against these gangs would, if the nation needed them, be the diagnostics of heroes. And indeed, they must be heroes to themselves.

A national dream need not, indeed may not be clear-cut and exact. Consider the dream of France, based on a memory and fired in the furnace of defeat and occupation, followed by the frustration of a many-branched crossroads until Charles-le-plus-Magne polished up the old word "glory" and made it shine. La Gloire brightened French eyes; defensive arrogance hardened and even the philosophically hopeless were glorious and possessive in their hopelessness, and the dark deposits of centuries were washed from the glorious buildings in Paris. When this inspired people looked for examples of glory they remembered the Sun King, who left them bankrupt, and the Emperor Napoleon, whose legacy was defeat and semi-anarchy; but glory was in both men and both times—and France needed it, for glory is a little like dignity: only those who do not have it feel the need for it.

For Americans too the wide and general dream has a name. It is called "the American Way of Life." No one can define it or point to any one person or group who lives it, but it is very real nevertheless, perhaps more real than that equally remote dream the Russians call Communism. These dreams describe our vague yearnings toward what we wish we were and hope we may be: wise, just, compassionate, and noble. The fact that we have this dream at all is perhaps an indication of its possibility.

Government of the People

OUR MEANS of governing ourselves, while it doubtless derives from European and Asiatic sources, nevertheless is not only unique and a mystery to non-Americans but a matter of wonder to Americans themselves. That it works at all is astonishing, and that it works well is a matter for complete amazement. Americans' attitude toward their government is a mixture perhaps best expressed by the phrase "the American Way of Life" followed by "Go fight City Hall." In our thinking about conferring the blessings of our system on other people we forget that ours is the product of our own history, which has not been duplicated anywhere else in the world. We have amassed a set of prejudices and feelings which doubtless grew out of one time or fact in our background, but which are just as strongly held when we do not know that background.

For example, Americans almost without exception have a fear and a hatred of any perpetuation of power—political, religious, or bureaucratic. Whether this anxiety stems from what amounts to a folk memory of our own revolution against the England of George III, or whether in the family background of all Americans from all parts of the world there is an alert memory of the foreign tyrannies which were the cause of their coming here in the first place, it is hard to say. Perhaps it is a combination of both; but, whatever its source, it is a very real thing. An obvious concentration of power or an official with a power potential causes in Americans first a restiveness, then suspicion, and finally—if the official remains in office too long—a downright general animosity; and this happens whether or not the officer in question is ambitious. Many a public servant has been voted out of office for no other reason than that he has been in too long. In President Roosevelt's third and fourth terms, many people who had been his passionate partisans were turned against him by pure uneasiness over the perpetuation of power. On the crest of this feeling it was easy to put through a law limiting the Presidency to two terms—a law which soon after embarrassed its Republican proponents, who would have liked to keep President Eisenhower in office indefinitely for no other reason than that he could win.

It is our national conviction that politics is a dirty, tricky, and dishonest pursuit and that all politicians are crooks. The reason for this attitude is fairly obvious—we have had cynical and dishonest officials on all levels of our government. When their practices have been exposed, it has been with pyrotechnical publicity which has dazzled us to blindness toward the great number of faithful, honest, and efficient political men who make our system workable. When Adlai Stevenson was asked why he had gone into politics he replied that he wanted to raise the threshold and perhaps to give politics a better name, so that it could be a decent and honorable profession, thereby leading our best citizens to participate. But we have had over the years every reason to be suspicious of politicians. Such is the ruggedness of the path to election—the violence, the charges, the japes and hurtful tricks—that it takes a special kind of man to run for public office, a man with armored skin and a practical knowledge of gutter fighting. And this is true on every level, from village school board to the Presidency of the nation. It is little wonder that shy and sensitive men, no matter what their qualifications, are repelled. Such men will accept appointment when they shrink from election.

In the short history of our nation—190 years—we have managed to accumulate customs inviolable, deep-seated, and below the inspection level. One such fiesta is the nominating convention at which political parties decide on the candidates for President and Vice-President. The ritual of these conventions is binding, the prayers endless, the committees appointed to conduct so-and-so to the rostrum large and complacent. The nominating speeches are like litanies in their faithful orthodoxy. Then, after each contestant's name is put in nomination, the roof comes off; there are parades, marches, costumes, banners, posters, noisemakers. A pandemonium of enthusiasm rips the air and destroys eardrums and vocal cords. It is a veritable volcano of enthusiasm, and it is

in no way lessened or abated by the generally known fact that the sponta-
neous eruption is rehearsed, bought, and paid for, and that the same cel-
ebrants will in half an hour change their hats and posters and explode in
favor of another contestant; and the odd thing is that, although the technique is cut and dried, the enthusiasm is genuine.

The business of these conventions could be concluded in a very
short time, but it is not. For four or five days it continues, with parties,
celebrations at night, with great drinking affairs and every kind of excess
known to the American away from home. The reason for the duration is
obvious but no longer valid: when the first conventions met, most of the
delegates had to ride on horseback for days or even weeks to get to the
convention city, and those hard-riding delegates were not content to cast
their votes and mount their horses and go home; they wanted some fun
too; and they still do, even though they arrive by airplane.

Once the nominations are completed, the campaigns for election
begin—hurtful, libelous, nasty, murderous affairs, wherein motives are
muddied, names and reputations beshitten, families tarred and tawdried,
friends and associates mocked, charged, and clobbered. This, of course,
for the opposition. At the same time, one's own candidate becomes
saintly in character, solonic in statesmanship, heroic in war, humble toward the poor and weak, implacable toward wrongdoers, a sweet and
obedient son to his mother, grateful to his first-grade teacher who taught
him everything he knows. The ideal candidate leaps toward the bright
and beckoning future, while his feet are firmly planted in the golden
past. He worships children, venerates his parents, and creates an image of
his wife that is part mother, part friend, part goddess—but never bed-
mate. In fact, the rules of nonsense are suspended during a Presidential
election, as well as memories of honesty and codes of decency. I remember in Chicago, when Governor Stevenson had been nominated for the
Presidency, his first demand was for an open convention for the nomination of a Vice-Presidential candidate. This suggestion shocked Mr. Sam
Rayburn clear through, but he soon recovered and went to work on
Stevenson to prove to him that an open or uncontrolled convention was
disaster. Governor Stevenson held firm, and the argument went well into
the night, and when it got through to Mr. Sam that there would be no ca-
pitulation, he said with a sad, wise kindness, "Look, son—look, Gover-

nor—I'm an old man, and I've been through this for many years, and I
tell you I don't *mind* an open convention—as long as it's rigged!"

I have observed our politics as practiced in village and city wards, in
county, in state, and in nation; and it is just as crazy and just as venal as I
have suggested. How does it happen, then, that what emerges is a government more stable, more responsible, more permanent, trustworthy, and
respected than any other in the world? It is another of our paradoxes. In
this we are lucky—watched over by a kindly and humorous deity—or
there is something inherent in our system which protects us from ourselves. Our large, rich slice of the earth has survived even our efforts to
strip it bare. History treated us kindly in the days of our national infancy;
predatory countries, which might have wiped us out, had other business
while we were learning the lessons of nationhood. In fact, we find our
history strewn with good fortune. Our nation was designed by a group of
men ahead of their time and in some ways ahead of ours. They conceived a system capable of renewing itself to meet changing conditions,
an instrument at once flexible and firm. We constantly rediscover the excellence of the architecture of our government. It has been proof not
only against foreign attack but against our own stupidities, which are
sometimes more dangerous.

In reviewing our blessings we must pay heed to our leadership. It is
said of us that we demand second-rate candidates and first-rate Presidents. Not all our Presidents have been great, but when the need has
been great we have found men of greatness. We have not always appreciated them; usually we have denounced and belabored them living, and
only honored them dead. Strangely, it is our mediocre Presidents we
honor during their lives.

The relationship of Americans to their President is a matter of
amazement to foreigners. Of course we respect the office and admire the
man who can fill it, but at the same time we inherently fear and suspect
power. We are proud of the President, and we blame him for things he
did not do. We are related to the President in a close and almost family
sense; we inspect his every move and mood with suspicion. We insist that
the President be cautious in speech, guarded in action, immaculate in
his public and private life; and in spite of these imposed pressures we are
avidly curious about the man hidden behind the formal public image we

have created. We have made a tough but unwritten code of conduct for him, and the slightest deviation brings forth a torrent of accusation and abuse.

The President must be greater than anyone else, but not better than anyone else. We subject him and his family to close and constant scrutiny and denounce them for things that we ourselves do every day. A Presidential slip of the tongue, a slight error in judgment—social, political, or ethical—can raise a storm of protest. We give the President more work than a man can do, more responsibility than a man should take, more pressure than a man can bear. We abuse him often and rarely praise him. We wear him out, use him up, eat him up. And with all this, Americans have a love for the President that goes beyond loyalty or party nationality; he is ours, and we exercise the right to destroy him.

To all the other rewards of this greatest office in the gift of the people, we add that of assassination. Attempts have been made on the lives of many of our Presidents; four have been murdered. It would be comparatively easy to protect the lives of our Presidents against attacks by foreigners; it is next to impossible to shield them from the Americans. And then the sadness—the terrible sense of family loss. It is said that when Lincoln died African drums carried the news to the center of the Dark Continent that a savior had been murdered. In our lifetime two events on being mentioned will bring out the vivid memory of what everyone present was doing when he or she heard the news; those two events are Pearl Harbor and the death of John F. Kennedy. I do not know anyone who does not feel a little guilty that out of our soil the warped thing grew that could kill him.

It is said that the Presidency of the United States is the most powerful office in the world. What is not said or even generally understood is that the power of the chief executive is hard to achieve, balky to manage, and incredibly difficult to exercise. It is not raw, corrosive power, nor can it be used willfully. Many new Presidents, attempting to exert executive power, have felt it slip from their fingers and have faced a rebellious Congress and an adamant civil service, a respectfully half-obedient military, a suspicious Supreme Court, a derisive press, and a sullen electorate. It is apparent that the President must have exact and sensitive knowledge not only of his own office but of all the other branches of government if his program is to progress at all. The power of the President is great if he can use it; but it is a moral power, a power activated by persuasion and discussion, by the manipulation of the alignments of many small but aggressive groups, each one weak in itself but protected in combination against usurpation of its rights by the executive; and even if the national government should swing into line behind Presidential exercise of power, there remain the rights, prejudices, and customs of states, counties, and townships, management of private production, labor unions, churches, professional organizations of doctors, lawyers, the guilds and leagues and organizations. All these can give a President trouble; and if, reacting even to the suspicion of overuse or misuse of power, they stand together, a President finds himself hamstrung, straitjacketed, and helpless.

Americans are quite conscious that there are jagged holes in our system. Wishing to move, to meet new conditions and attitudes, we are nevertheless reluctant to change existing and traditional law. What has been written on paper long enough is written in our hearts, and it is very difficult to remove such lesions. Such a maze of connection and confusion is our curious trap of states' rights as opposed to federal rights.

When the Constitution was written, there were thirteen separate commonwealths which not only had their own economic, social, religious, and geographic identities, but—because of distances, lack of communication, roads, and so forth—necessarily maintained their separate polities. The original states could not have conceived of appealing for federal aid in education, health, harbor control, disaster, roads, rail and communications control and subsidy. It is true that some of the states formed loose alliances, such as those in New England and the South; but they remained thirteen individual, more or less self-sustaining small nations.

Survival has changed that condition, but the greatest change came when, during the deep Depression, the federal government assumed responsibility for the health and well-being of all citizens. This was a true second revolution. Today states' rights are, to a large extent, anachronisms. Though the Constitution says clearly that all powers not specifically reserved to the federal government are to remain with the states, in matters of interstate commerce, health, education, banking, communications, agriculture, and many other fields the government has had increasingly to assume control, because the states are incapable of doing so.

On the other hand, civil rights and universal suffrage are specifically mentioned in three constitutional amendments, backed by the Civil Rights Act of Congress, as being unquestionably the responsibility of the federal government, which is clearly charged with carrying out the law and with the punishment of anyone who disobeys it. And here we find one of America's most notable paradoxes. Those groups and individuals, official and private, whose purpose it is to reject the civil-rights laws and by appeal to states' rights to nullify federal law cry out like banshees against the injustice of federal regulation. Either crimes of violence, in such cases, are ignored or, if the criminals are brought to trial—this happens very rarely—they are acquitted. The federal government cannot enforce a law when the methods of subversion are beyond its reach. Court orders and contempt proceedings have little force in the face of unpunished violence. The government's only recourse, the employment of troops to control civil commotion, is a means that has never failed to do more harm than good. Now a government which is unable to enforce its own law soon ceases to be a government. The force of Negro pressure, backed by a majority of white Americans, will not allow us to retire civil rights to the limbo in which the constitutional amendments hid their heads for a hundred years. The only alternative is a federal law making any crime committed for the purpose of denying or inhibiting civil rights a federal offense, subject to federal judges and federal juries, with the option of change of venue if the local authorities flout the law. The very great threat of such a law might possibly be effective in causing the states to take over their own salvation. The changes of the last twenty years have been enormous, but we have come finally to the entrenched core of rebellion, which must be removed before we can travel on into a livable future. No good society can grow if its roots are in sterile soil.

Created Equal

TODAY WE BELIEVE that slavery is a crime and a sin, as well as being economically unsound under our system. Further, we can believe that it has always been a crime and always a sin, although ignored in some earlier periods. Nothing could be farther from the truth; our present attitude toward slavery came into our thinking less than two hundred years ago. We consider slavery a denial of the dignity of man; but human dignity has never been taller or more treasured than in Greece during the Golden Age, when the only Athenians who did not have slaves were those who were too poor to own them and consequently were due to become slaves themselves. From the beginning of known history the great empires grew, conquered, built their lasting monuments, and carved their immortality entirely through the use of slaves. And when the twin continents of North and South America were opened to the world, there was no question but that slave labor would be used to prepare and comb and gentle their intractable land with its hostile climates. The indigenous peoples were used as much as possible in Latin America, but there was always a difficulty in using Indians as slaves: it was their country and they knew it; with their neighbors and their tribe mates, they were susceptible to revolts and to self-defense. The opening of Africa to the slave trade solved the problem; the black men and women and children were rounded up, dragged to the coast, chained in their hundreds in kennels between the decks, and transported—those who survived—to the new land. In the process they lost not only their nativity but their identity, their names, their families, and any possible future.

As the concentration of slaves grew greater in those parts of America where the use of them was practical, one of the impractical manifestations became apparent. The Spartans, who were outnumbered by their Helots, were always in danger from revolt; in the American South the problems of control became apparent just as soon as the numbers of Negroes made them capable of any kind of resistance. There is no way to keep a man from resenting slavery; the best a slave-owning community can do is to make resistance seem hopeless. One way of doing this is to brainwash the slave from childhood with the conviction that he is inferior, stupid, weak, and irresponsible. A second method is to catch resistance in the bud and to punish it mercilessly; a third, to break up families and friends so that no possible tribal association can gather or establish itself; and fourth, and perhaps most important, to keep education, with its inevitable questioning and communication, from the slaves at all costs. All these methods were used, and still there were slave revolts, some of them of very serious proportions.

Students of brainwashing agree that it does not reach deeply into consciousness and that its effects disappear unless the pressure is maintained. The slave owner who by work, attitude, and action constantly maintained "I am not afraid of you Negroes because you are inferior, spiritually and mentally, to me" was like a man shouting that he is not afraid of the dark, unaware that he would not mention it if he were not afraid. In the South this fear of the Negro went deeper and deeper into the white population, and was kept deep by constant reiteration of their inferiority. But it is one of the paradoxes of slavery that, by its very nature, the slave becomes stronger than his master. He is there to do the hard, the strenuous, the dangerous, and the unpleasant work instead of the master. Furthermore, a slave soon loses his value as property if he is crippled, weak, or sick; not only is he useless to his master, he is valueless for resale. The Negroes captured in Africa and transported under appalling conditions to the coast caused considerable losses to the traders, for the weak died, the savage killed themselves or were killed in reprisals or in attempts to escape, the spiritually weak died of pure heartbreak and hopelessness. Then they were subjected to the many diseases of new climates and countries, and only those Negroes who developed immunities survived. Then, those who were not clever enough to conceal their feelings and to bide their time were destroyed; and finally, a diet of coarse, natural foods in small quantities and a diet low in sugars and fats did for them what any doctor counsels for his weak and flabby patients. Meanwhile a complete lack of medical care sent the slaves to herbs and soothing teas as well as to the powerful and psychiatric safety of religion. Lastly, being always in the presence of an active and overwhelmingly armed enemy gave the Negroes a community of spirit and a reliance on one another which whites have only vaguely felt in wartime when they have been under siege.

In the antebellum South, it was generally known that the Negroes were, by and large, physically strong and virile, and that, as with most physically strong people, they were sexually potent and active. This made for one more stage in the tower of fear; it was generally considered that Negroes were just that way—strong and sexy—and the fact that this strong, resistant breed had been developed by selection never occurred to the Southern whites.

It was not kindness or ethics or delicacy of feeling that kept slavery out of the Northern states in the nineteenth century; it was economics. There were some slaves in the cities and on the large farm holdings, and many of the ships that brought their dreadful cargoes of misery from the Gold Coast to the slave blocks of the South were owned, captained, and navigated by New Englanders. But the small farms of New England, poor and rocky and tiny, would not support slaves. It is easy to be uncompromisingly against an evil one does not need and cannot enjoy or profit by. But how did the Yankee abolitionists come by the idea that slavery was evil? Perhaps the Puritan strain so deeply set by the Pilgrim Fathers in the souls of their descendants could not tolerate the idea of warm climates and lush crops and the storied ease, the comfort and luxury of the great plantations of the South. The Pilgrims had hated such things in the Church and the crown in England, and they distrusted it in America; and if slavery was the foundation of such a way of life, slavery was evil, even sinful. It followed that slaves must be innocent and good. In the South many slave owners were beginning to doubt the value of the institution, and a number of the more intelligent landowners were beginning slowly to get rid of their slaves, either by sale or by emancipation. Then the power of Northern disapproval struck the South. All slave owners were evil, brutal men. Well, they weren't, and they knew they weren't. So it came about that the Southerners had to defend slavery in order to defend themselves.

By this time the question of slavery in the popular mind was no longer a matter for reason and analysis; it had become purely emotional. The American, Northern or Southern, before the war walked a jiggling tightrope. Consider, for example, my own great-grandfather. He was a Yankee from Leominster, Massachusetts, and his name was Dickson (when his family had come to Leominster in the middle of the seventeenth century it was spelled Dixon). He was a man of large family and even larger ideas. About 1840, he picked up his wife and children, put them in a sailing ship, and departed for the Holy Land. He was a farmer and a Christian; his purpose was to convert the Jews to Christianity, but he had devised a method Jesus had not thought of: he intended to teach the Jews agriculture. Once he had his toe in the door he would gradually move Christianity in on them. It was a fairly pragmatic piece of reasoning. If the first part worked, his clients, the Jews, would be open to the second step.

Israel was at that time a Turkish province; agriculture, even the most enlightened kind of 1840 agriculture, requires labor. There was only one kind of labor—slaves. And Mr. Dickson was a convinced and unchangeable antislavery man. You can almost feel his clever, practical, honest Yankee mind studying the problem, perhaps as he had studied the checkerboard in a Leominster general store. He worked it out, too. He did not buy slaves; he made life contracts for some men to work his farm, the laborers signing the contract themselves, proving their free will—though of course their owners got the money. It absolved my great-grandfather from the sin of slave owning. If his people ran away, he could have them apprehended by the Turkish police, not for escaping but for breach of contract.

Antebellum American Negroes, if they could have known their double image, would have been very confused. To the Yankee, informed by sermons, pictures, prejudice, travelers' tales, and novels, the Negro was a mistreated, brutalized, overworked, and starved creature, sometimes a hero, sometimes a saint, but never, by any chance, a man like other men. To the Southerner, informed by his fears, his prejudices, and the necessity for maintaining discipline, the Negro was a lazy, stupid animal, who was also dangerous, clever, tricky, thievish, and lecherous.

We know very little about what the Negroes thought of their masters.

They shared their thoughts and feelings only with one another and communicated with their masters with a studied, practical politeness. I do not mean to say there were no loyalties or loves or kindnesses between white and black. There were, but not of the texture of the feeling for their own kind, and this withdrawn separateness, driven deep into the generations, still exists. A friend of mine, a Southerner, said recently, "I can never talk to a Negro. I want to, but I just don't know what to talk about to him."

In the years leading up to 1861 the North and South growled and argued, compromised and were split again, muttered and grumbled toward war. New territories were layering and thrusting themselves, preparing to be states; and the border extended westward with quarreling over whether the new states should be slave or free. This was just a way of deciding on one kind of economy or another. Slavery had little to do with it except to give the differers an emotional platform. And the slaves, except as vehicles for that emotion, had nothing whatever to do with it.

In the dreadful war that ensued, the slaves were never taken into consideration; and after years of destruction and death, when the great Proclamation of Emancipation was issued it was timed and announced, not as an instrument of freedom, but as a military measure designed to confuse and dismay the already tottering South. We do not know what Lincoln would have done or could have done to smooth the way of transition had he lived on. What did happen was dreadful. Millions of slaves, blinking and helpless, emerged into the blinding light of freedom, and they were no more fitted or prepared for it than a man would be who after a lifetime spent in prison was forced into the complication, the uncertainty, and the responsibility of the outside world. If time could have been allowed for training, for transition; if the South had been able to understand that the change was necessary and inevitable and had put it into motion locally and slowly, the story might have been different. But emancipation was forced on the South and the white Southerner found himself surrounded by a vengeful, savage, and untrained enemy. He no longer had any responsibility for the Negro. He had only to consider self-defense and the protection of his family and his neighbors.

Southern Americans have throughout our history shown a gift for the military. They fought the Civil War with incredible bravery and ingenuity, and held out with pure spirit against the overwhelming Northern superiority in numbers, equipment, and supplies. When they were finally defeated and the slaves were freed against their will, they reacted as a military nation will when it is beaten, surrounded, occupied, and infiltrated. They invented a new kind of guerrilla warfare and went right on fighting. Their secret and close-knit orders were designed to keep a constant pressure of terror on the bewildered and angry Negroes. Preserving "law and order" meant keeping a tight and ferocious rein on the Negroes through the armed strength of law-enforcement officers of the whites' own choosing, and at the same time making the laws to be enforced—particularly those laws which denied the blacks access to the making or changing of the laws. And Southern representatives to the Northern government developed techniques of minority control through the infiltration of legislative committees, while their brilliant use of the filibuster closed off nearly every avenue of investigation and change.

The efforts of the Southerners were vastly successful; the amendments to the Constitution guaranteeing the Negroes their freedom and their right to participate in government were completely annulled by local custom, law, and law-enforcement officers, so that for nearly one hundred years Negroes, who often outnumbered the whites, were neither enfranchised nor free. Schools, neighborhoods, professions, and white facilities were closed against them. Infractions of the law drew one kind of punishment for Negroes and another for whites, while any organization designed for the self-protection of the Negro was mercilessly broken up and scattered by the law when possible, and by secret terror tactics when the law did not suffice. For slavery there were substituted the servitudes of debt, of need, of ignorance, and the constant reminders of inferiority. It is true that Negroes were free to go away if they wished to and could; and many did, only to find that the North, which had fought for their emancipation, would not accept them save on the same terms as those the South applied.

During Reconstruction, when many Negroes were elected to the state legislatures in the South, they voted for things they had never had; and among these was education. In the few short years of Negro participation in the Reconstruction of the South more school laws were written than at any time before or since; and when the black legislators were kicked out of office and disenfranchised by the growing power of the whites, these laws were removed from the books. Such was the rage of the whites that the very word "school" seems to have come under a ban, and many Southern schools, which had once been very fine, slipped into a shadow from which they have not yet emerged. It's a crazy thing; the whites denied themselves candy for fear someone else might get some!

When the war was over, my Great-Aunt Carrie, a tiny woman of whalebone and steel, daughter of that same Dickson who had gone to Palestine to convert the Jews to Christianity, this wee woman carrying a little satchel of contributions from her neighbors in Leominster, Massachusetts, went South and opened a school for Negro children. She was as tough as her father had been. No sooner had she opened her school and assembled a class of pickaninnies than the Ku Klux Klan burned it down; she opened another and kept the children in at night, and the white-robed horsemen fired through the walls while the children and Great-Aunt Carrie lay on the floor. With the little black kids helping her, she raised a sandbag defense inside the building, and cooked grits in the school fireplace to feed herself and her charges. Her spirit never gave out, but her money did; and the grits ran out, too—for, while Negroes crept near late at night bringing what food they could scrape together, the Klan soon closed that gap, and finally, weak from starvation and weighing less than her smallest charge, Aunt Carrie capitulated and retreated with her flag flying. It must be admitted that the Southern gentlemen did not disarm her; she marched away carrying her weapons—a Bible, *Pilgrim's Progress*, and *McGuffey's First Reader*.

Now, a hundred years later, American Negroes are surging toward the equality we promised them and did not give them in 1867, and that surge was started by four things, three of which Aunt Carrie was allowed to take away: religion, art, and learning. The fourth thing she did not have, but the Negroes have it now: economic importance and impact. Negro leaders are for the most part educated, literate, thoughtful, and experienced men. The thrust of the movement, based on religion, has almost the discipline and force of religion itself. And Negroes now have access to the wealth and to the ability to distribute it; businessmen all over the country have finally come to see that what is bad for Negroes is eventually bad for business, and so for America.

In the constant pressure of the Negro causes, some thoughtless people ask, "What are they after? What do they want?" It's very simple. They want exactly the same things other Americans want—peace, comfort, security, and love. The human wants everything he can conceive of and, as through education and understanding his concepts grow broader, he will want more and different things—perhaps even better things.

There is no question that Negroes will get their equality—at law; not as soon as they should, but sooner than pessimists believe. But legal equality is only the smallest part of being equal. It is one of the less attractive of human traits that everyone wants to look down on someone, to be better than someone else; and, since this is symptomatic of insecurity, humans in general do not seem to be very secure. The hurt in the Negro and the deep-seated suspicion of the white is matched only by the fear and suspicion of the white toward the Negro; and while there remains any vestige of such feeling, true equality cannot be achieved.

Some years ago, a very intelligent Negro man worked for me in New York. One afternoon through the window I saw this man coming home from the store. As he rounded the corner, a drunk, fat white woman came barreling out of a saloon, slipped on the icy pavement, and fell. Instantly, the man turned at right angles and crossed the street, keeping as far away from the woman as he could. When he came into the house I said, "I saw that. Why did you do it?"

"Oh, that. Well, I guess I thought if I went to help her she was so drunk and mad she might start yelling 'rape.' "

"That was a pretty quick reaction," I said.

"Maybe," he said; "but I've been practicing to be a Negro for a long time."

I have written at such length about this problem because any attempt to describe the America of today must take into account the issue of racial equality, around which much of our thinking and our present-day attitudes turn. We will not have overcome the trauma that slavery has left on our society, North and South, until we cannot remember whether the man we just spoke to in the street was Negro or white.

Genus Americanus

MEMBERS OF a classless society must work out changes in status levels without violating their belief that there are no such levels. In an aristocracy this problem is solved and the changes are in effect rather than in name. In America, and perhaps in Russia, the reverse is true. In name we are classless, while in practice the class structure is subtle, ever-changing.

The American Revolution was different from the French Revolution and the later Russian Revolution in that the revolting American colonists did not want a new kind of government; they wanted the same kind, only run by themselves. If they had been a united and cohesive polity, they might well have wanted a king—but their own king. Americans did not come by the theory of government by the common man all at once; that growth was gradual and is still going on. We want a common candidate but an uncommon office holder.

What Americans did discover earlier than most of the world was that ability had nothing to do with birth. Of course we have to some extent overdone this, as we often do; a national leader was required to be of log-cabin background, even if he had to invent the lowliness of his own ancestry and upbringing. But here again our paradoxical tendency took charge: we had learned to distrust inherited position, property, and money, but we quickly proceeded to admire the same things if self-acquired. When we revolted against the old country and set up our own stalls, we were careful to eliminate the hated symbols of aristocracy—titles, honors, inherited prerequisites. But since every man wants admiration and perhaps some envy, we had only money and possessions to admire and envy. The rich in America of the middle period may have been cursed and disparaged, but they had chosen the one way to be noticed.

The aristocrats our ancestors remembered and loathed invariably kept their positions and paid their expenses through landholding. The greater the aristocrat, the larger the landholding. It was natural that our early settlers tried to emulate the people they detested and perhaps envied. In open, untenanted America, apart from the royal colonial grants some men did accumulate enormous pieces of land through seizure, purchase, or chicanery. Because of the debilitating effect of some crops such as cotton, large areas were required to make the land show profit. Later, with the development of farm machinery it became possible for very few men to farm very large tracts. The only difficulty lay in increasing taxes, the cost of machinery and fertilizer, and that new thing in the world—overproduction: too much food, with the resulting drop in prices, came to haunt large farmers. The need to borrow and the advantages of corporate organizations made the huge farms into factories, owned mostly by banks or stock companies. Great holdings owned by one man or family became fewer and fewer, so that where once there were many estates as large as provinces, at the present there are very few; and the ones that do survive are almost museum pieces.

The world dearly loves the figure of the American capitalist: the hated robber baron, Mr. Moneybags, slopping up champagne fermented from the blood of the workers; feared and revered Uncle Sam in striped coat and a great dollar-sign belly, a crude, almost bestial figure. The curtain countries, Iron and Bamboo, particularly love this figure. Sometimes the "Capitalist" carries bombs or tanks and doubles as a warmonger, the soulless maker and seller of destruction. Any inspired protest against America is bound to have this figure in effigy. In the course of the pageant he is either burned or hanged. Unfortunately he doesn't exist anymore, and we miss him. The great robbers, fat, free-spending, vicious, top-hatted, and glittering with precious stones—the Diamond Jim Bradys, Lucky Baldwins, Leland Stanfords, with their pretty women, fast horses, and baronial mansions—were rich and proud of it, and they gloried in showing the world how rich they were. In the latter part of the last century these vital, boisterous figures were at once our curse and our ornament—and then something happened, and they disappeared. The railroad barons, the oil barons, the iron and copper barons became giants, were hated, were admired—and disappeared.

The giants of money were usually the sons of poor men who clawed and grappled their way to great fortune, driven by memory of poverty and hardship. Quite naturally, they protected their children from the experience which had been the driving force, and since there was no government approval or backing of individual families, the second generation of great wealth as a rule went to pieces in weakness, self-indulgence, and stupidity. A few families have continued in power through money, but they are rare. Most of the descendants who have remained rich are protected by trust funds and safeguards, which amount to about the same thing as entailment did in the old country and are designed to keep the grubby little hands of the sons out of the pot of the fathers. A goodly number of our earlier self-made millionaires even entertained dynastic notions. From the banks of the Hudson River to Nob Hill in San Francisco we can still see their efforts—castellated fortress-like seats, sometimes of shingle, with arrow slits, sally ports, barbicans—which, far from holding off enemies from without, could not even defend against creeping decay from within. When the flame of the founder was gone, only a wreathy smolder remained, and, without the stern defense of the trust fund, went out altogether.

Today there are probably more and much richer men than ever before; but far from boasting of their wealth they live almost like fugitives, secret and shy. No doubt the income tax and the ways of circumventing it have made them timid. We know about our tycoons only when they are giving something away, and their gifts and foundations are usually a means of keeping their money out of the hands of the tax collector.

Today, instead of the old, highly visible capitalist we have the corporation—one of the strangest organisms in the present world. It may manufacture goods for sale, operate mines, manipulate money, bore oil wells and crack the product into usable components, produce steel, copper, nickel, or tungsten, operate farms, or it may purchase the products of other corporations and distribute them; but its purpose is always to make money.

The corporation, to exist at all, must be efficient, must produce its product or perform its function for a minimum of cost and a maximum of profit. Since the most costly ingredient of any business operation is labor, the early corporations tried to keep labor costs at a minimum.

They settled in areas where labor, because of its competition with itself, was cheap. When workingmen began to organize, to pit group action against the employing agent, the corporations fought tooth and nail against the growing organization of labor. Every expedient was used to overcome or bypass organized labor—hiring of the hopeless and the ignorant, lockouts of labor unions, even armed defense and retaliation—a kind of civil war within the business structure.

We can all remember the warfare: company thugs against union goons; the riots, the murders, the wreckage; and particularly the loud and piercing charges, on the one hand that labor was treasonable to business, and on the other that fat, cold-hearted capitalism was exploiting the workingman and requiring enforced poverty for its purposes.

Shares in the early corporations were held by few investors, and those usually in upper financial brackets. The shareholders were against socialism certainly—but they were much more against no dividends. The warfare against organized labor was costly, as all wars are; and furthermore, the workers willing to accept the wages and conditions required were so ignorant, inept, and inefficient that production costs went up and profits went down. Also, as Americans generally acquired more money they bought shares in the more efficient corporations, so that the whole nature of the ownership changed and broadened. Gradually, the fat cartoon figure of Capitalism with a dollar sign on its distended vest ceased to be accurate. Shareholders became increasingly a cross-section of lively Americans. And it was early discovered that eleven men each with a hundred shares could outvote one man with a thousand. The shareholders ask one simple question: Is the corporation making money, or isn't it?

With all its power in the economy, its influence through the economy on states, governments, and nations, the great corporation has remained almost morbidly sensitive to criticism. A few letters critical of a product or a policy can and often do cause a nervous and fearful meeting of the board of directors and a sharp self-examination. Bad publicity, as every corporation head knows, can cause a fall-off in sales which automatically stirs up a hornets' nest among the stockholders. Therefore these giants spend great sums on public relations.

In America we have developed the Corporation Man. His life, his family, his future—as well as his loyalty—lie with his corporation. His training, his social life, the kind of car he drives, the clothes he and his wife wear, the neighborhood he lives in, and the kind and cost of his house and furniture are all dictated by his corporate status. His position in the pyramid of management is exactly defined by the size of his salary and bonuses. The pressures toward conformity are subtle but inexorable, for his position and his hopes for promotion to a higher status are keyed to performance of duties, activities, and even attitudes which make the corporation successful. In the areas of management, sales, and public relations, the position of the corporation man is secure only from one stockholders' meeting to the next; a successful revolt there may sweep out whole cadres of earnest men and replace them with others.

By reason of the simplicity of its end—making money—the corporation is much more efficient than any existing government. As my friend Ed Ricketts put it, "If General Motors or Du Pont or General Foods should form an army, no national army could last against it for a moment." To a fairly large extent a public army's purpose is just to stay in existence at all. We have found in the past, on entering into conflict, that the public professional army is not very well prepared. A great corporation, on the other hand, if its purpose were to win a war, would devote its total energy to that end with maximum speed and efficiency and a minimum of waste. "What public army," Ed Ricketts said, "could stand against such versatility and singleness of purpose?"

An oil company may extend into transportation, or a food-processing firm invest its profits in magazines, but there is one thing the corporation cannot do. When it enters fields of individual creativeness it not only fails but it shrivels the creator. It cannot order the writing of good books and plays, the painting of great pictures, the composing of exquisite music. Where it has entered such fields, it has succeeded only in adulterating the product and eventually destroying the producer. In the production of food, clothing, shelter, minor entertainment, and the gadgetry of comfort the corporation has not only fulfilled our needs but sometimes created them. Only in our yearning toward greatness is it helpless.

While our rich men were growing richer and we were all living high on the hog in the nineteenth century—all equal, all common, democratic, mostly Protestant, materialistic and down-to-earth—there must have been a profound yearning for the flamboyance, the trappings, the ritual, the fancy titles and postures and litanies we had denied and cast out. There was, and we did something about it. We created unofficial orders, kingdoms, robes, and regalia and complicated forms of procedure and secret recognitions among the elect. The meeting hall over the firehouse in the grubby little town would be transformed—one night into Solomon's temple, the next to a select and benign witches' coven, the next to the chapel of an order of knighthood complete with regalia, shining swords, and ostrich feathers. For one night a week we became noble. I remember well seeing Louis Schneider, the good butcher of Salinas—a round and red-faced man, in a bloody apron most of the time—wearing a golden crown, an imitation ermine robe, holding the symbols of power in his hands and speaking ritual phrases I am sure he didn't understand and would have laughed at if he had. His box-toed shoes peeped from under the gold and purple of his robe, but nothing could change his yellow waterfall mustache or his wrinkled and much-reddened neck. It was glorious. At every parade the noble knights marched, a little shy and very unmilitary, but with their plumes fluttering and silver-plated swords reflecting the light.

It is a strange thing how Americans love to march if they don't have to. Every holiday draws millions of marchers, sweating in the sun, some falling and being carted away to hospitals. In hardship and in some danger they will march, clad in any imaginable outlandish costume, carrying heavy banners with them too. Everything from Saint Patrick's Day to the Grandmothers of America, Inc., draws milling marchers; but let the Army take them and force them to march, and they wail like hopeless kelpies on a tidal reef, and it requires patience and enormous strictness to turn them into soldiers. Once they give in, they make very good soldiers; but they never cease their complaints and their mutinous talk. This, of course, does not describe our relatively small class of professional soldiers: they are like professionals in any army; but national need calls up the citizen soldier, and he is a sight. He kicks like a steer going in, bitches the whole time, fights very well when he is trained and properly armed. He lives for the day when he can get out of uniform, and once out spends a large part of his future life at reunions, conventions, marching his heart out while his uniform gets tighter and tighter, and his collar and waist-band torture him. Then the war he loathed becomes the great time of his life, and he can conscientiously bore his wife and children to death with it.

Along with the veterans' organizations, Americans have developed scores of orders, lodges and encampments, courts—some simple insur-ance organizations, some burial agreements, some charitable associa-tions, but all, all noble. Anyone who has lived long enough will remember some of these as an enrichment of his youth. Elks, Masons, Knight Templars, Woodmen of the World, Redmen, Eagles, Eastern Star, Foresters, Concatenated Order of Whowho, International—the *World Almanac* lists hundreds of such societies and associations, military and religious, philosophic, scholarly, charitable, mystic, political, and some just plain nuts. All were and perhaps still are aristocratic and mostly secret and therefore exclusive. They seemed to fulfill a need for grandeur against a background of commonness, for aristocracy in the midst of democracy. And the ritual perhaps satisfied the nostalgia of the Protes-tant for the fulsome litany and ritual of the denounced Catholic Church. A great many orders had rules against admitting any Catholic. And then the Catholics formed their own orders, their own knighthoods and clubs, and that kind of ruined the whole thing.

We are a very strange people; we love organizations, and hate them. I remember something that happened in Salinas at a time when the Hearst papers were whipping up anger against the Japanese, and when, in our schools—I guess I was about twelve or thirteen years old—at least thirty percent of the pupils were Japanese. Some of them were my good friends, but, stimulated by the ferocity of the Hearst campaign, we formed a little club for espionage against the Japanese. We had secret signs and secret message places and codes. We prowled about Japanese gardeners' farms, peered in their windows, and found that they went to bed very early—and got up very early, too. But we were content to snoop, and we were happy. Then a terrible thing happened. Takasi Yatkumi, who was one of our dearest friends, asked to join. We were horrified; it tore the whole structure of racial dislike down to the roots. We explained to Takasi that his action was not cricket; that he was the enemy; that he couldn't join an anti-Japanese organization. He thought about it awhile and said that if we would let him in he would help us to spy on his mother and father. And because he was our friend we had to take him in, but it ruined the fine, ferocious quality of our organization, just as the Catholic lodges in a way broke down the ferocity of the Protestant groups.

The desire and will to spy on, to denounce, to threaten, and to punish, while not an American tendency, nevertheless inflames a goodly number of Americans. The ones I have inspected at close range are people just past middle age, both men and women, who feel that life has cheated them or passed them by; the feeling may have something to do with the climacteric. They seem to believe that the blame for their own unhappiness lies in the nature of the society in which they live. The sexually dissatisfied are appalled at the immorality of youth. Those who have failed or not succeeded in business become convinced that a great wrongness directs our economy. Feelings of social inadequacy emerge in hatred of society.

All such sickness of the soul must find a target to shoot at—and the targets are available in the happy, the successful, the efficient, and the recognized. The attacker usually finds himself a high moral or religious purpose. He is not attacking something; he is defending something. Beautiful women, if publicized, must be whores, and attractive men lechers or deviates. The quality and direction of the attack diagnoses the failure or the sickness of the attacker. Politicians and statesmen are prime targets; and, above everyone else, our Presidents are sitting ducks. The letters of threat and denunciation sent to the White House are, in many cases, hysterical with hatred and jealousy. No President has escaped this deluge of rebuke, from Washington to Johnson. It is my firm belief that President Kennedy was murdered not for what he was but for what his murderer wasn't; a man with a beautiful and loving wife, a high position, and the respect and admiration of his countrymen could not be forgiven by a man who had failed in everything he had undertaken—his marriage, his politics, and his aching desire to be accepted and admired.

Writers do not draw quite as much fire as those whose personal lives are publicized, but in my time I have received some ferocious letters accusing me of sins both of commission and of omission. I think my favorite was one which, after several pages of furious and vengeful attack, ended with the beautiful threat: "You will never get out of this world alive!"

To guard us against taste, judgment, and self-reliance in our critical attitudes—particularly toward the arts—the American species has produced a sport which may be unique in the world today. We have identified her and named her "Mom." She seems to be related to the arachnids. She resembles *Latrodectus mactans,* and also the Salticidae and the Lycosidae, in their mating habits. The males of those species often dance for hours before the females will submit to mating, although sometimes, as with the Pisauridae, the female will accept from her mate a present such as a fly wrapped in silk. After mating, of course, she eats her spouse. Our counterpart *Moma Americana,* sometimes known as the "Haywire Mother," breathes fire and cries havoc while setting herself to defend her children from the withering effects of literature. She turns up to exorcise the pale and ghostly books from our haunted house of culture. Her victims, in effect, are not books but children.

The odd thing is that this March Hare mother need never have had children nor have read a book—indeed often has done neither. The object of her violence may be a little vague; sometimes morals are involved, sometimes politics, sometimes a confusion of both. It is her conviction that normal children, preoccupied as they are with normal and exciting thoughts and experiments with their own sexual potential, will learn to do what they are already doing by reading certain books. Again, a berserk mother gets into a belligerent panic in the belief that children, exposed to the turgid political litany of the last century, will become inflamed with uncontrollable revolutionary ecstasy approximating orgasm. It does not occur to this mother that the children are successfully resisting reading of any kind, and that she herself has never been able to read two paragraphs of Marx or Engels or Lenin even if she has heard of them. It is her conviction that the poison may even be fiendishly concealed in novels.

The field of action of this curious woman is the library of the public school, and her immediate victims are the teachers, the school board, and sometimes county or state officials, who are nervous of criticism of any kind. This noble creature infiltrates the school and demands that certain books be removed from the library shelves. Her action brings reaction. Defenders of the denounced books arise, newspapers are drawn in, stories are written, pictures taken. In many cases it develops that no one—supervisor, principal, teacher, student, or the Iron Mother herself—has ever read the books in question. The result is that school officials are forced to the dreary duty of reading the offending volumes and some of the children even dip into them briefly, just to be naughty. I don't suppose these Saint Georgias are very destructive. When, as happens pretty often, one or more of my books is purged from the shelves of a school or library, the immediate effect is an increased sale in that community, but perhaps for the wrong reasons. Once a number of years ago when a town wanted to make a burnt offering of an offending book of mine, they found to their horror that there was no copy to be had. It was necessary to order ten copies for the *auto-da-fé*, and that was more books than had been bought in that town for years.

America has its fair share of screwballs—we took the term from the kind of pitch in baseball which twists and turns in the air so that the batter can't figure how it will come over the plate, and it is a very apt description. While some of our screwballs are charming, original, and theatrical, others are malign and vicious, and a few are downright dangerous. Of our people, the most timid and subject to passion are those—some old, some idle through retirement—who live on fixed incomes from investments. There are many thousands of these, and they are usually to be found where a bad climate does not further their anxieties. Southern California and Florida attract them in great numbers. They gather in tightly knit groups and share their fears with one another. Any fluctuations in the cost of living, changes in the tax laws, or international situations which cause variations in stock prices or in the real-estate market affect their immediate income, with the result that they live in a state of constant apprehension. This makes them fair game for the man or group with dictatorial desires.

Such leaders are surely screwballs, but they are wise in the uses of timidity. They have only to bring charges, no matter how ridiculous or improbable, of plots to disturb the delicate balance of the fixed and unearned income in order to arouse fear, which is the mother of ferocity. The poor, idle people sitting in the sun are drawn together in positions of furious defense. The leaders who feed and abet their anxieties are able to hit them with dues and contributions while adding new fuel to their fears. The stalking horror is "Communism," with its thread of confiscation of private wealth, and "Socialism," which implies that they might be forced to share their wealth with less fortunate citizens. Once they have been frightened into organization for self-defense, the Messiah who has planted the fear is able to use it for his own ends. He has only to bring some cruel, stupid, and untrue charge against an official, and particularly against any reform movement, to set these cohorts in noisy motion and to draw from them large amounts of money which, devoted to publications and radio and television programs, keep these poor people further off balance; and, as Joseph McCarthy proved, the more ridiculous the charge, the less possibility there is of defense.

What is the purpose of such leaders or stimulators or catalysts? Probably a simple desire for power. But their stated purpose is invariably patriotic—they promise to preserve the nation by techniques which will inevitably destroy it. They may even have convinced themselves of the virtue of their mission; and yet, over all such activities there is the smell that caused Doctor Johnson to say that patriotism is the last refuge of a scoundrel.

Even more cynical are the screwball organizations which teach hatred and revenge to the ignorant and fearful people, using race or religion as the enemy. One of the oldest, most primitive and surviving of human groupings, after the family, is the totem; and the rules of the totem have never changed, from the beginning, when the animal totems branded and scarred their initiates, to the most recent activities of the Ku Klux Klan. The totem has certain rules, almost natural laws. It must be secret, exclusive, mysterious, cruel, afraid, dangerous, and monstrously ignorant. The mask, whether it be animal, skin, or sheet, is invariably present. The initiate must take a new name, thereby magically becoming a new, brave, shining person as opposed to the frightened, confused thing he knows himself to be. Spectacular, half-understood symbols must be used; and invariably torture and human sacrifice are appealed to as stimulants to release fear into ferocity. The steps never change; it is true there is less of it than there once was, but it still exists as a memory of our savage past and as an instrument on which the witch doctor, the wizard, or the Kleagle can play for his own profit.

Such are some of the ugly and evil aspects of American screwballery; but we have also pleasant, benign, and interesting screwballs who contribute to our gaiety. Of such was the gentle Emperor Norton, who lived in San Francisco and called himself "Emperor of the United States and Protector of Mexico." Of such is the man who runs for the Presidency on a vegetarian ticket, and of such was One Eye Connelly the gate crasher, and Leaping Lena Levinsky the lady prizefight promoter; of such was Canvasback Cohen, the prizefighter who was maintained by the Marx Brothers because he lost all contests.

We have poets in flowing robes, inventors of new religions, people who spend their lives warning us and painting on fences that the end of the world is at hand. Such screwballs are very valuable to us and we would be a duller nation without them, as our economy and our means of production gently shove us nearer and nearer to a dull and single norm.

One kind of eccentrics are the show-offs, who by outlandish costume or unusual gesture or speech spend their time drawing attention to themselves—some foolishly and some with a terrible mock dignity. But one must be sure, in observing such people, whether it is a true eccentricity or simply a matter of advertising. A number of years ago when I was working on a New York newspaper the police picked up a pretty young girl walking naked on Park Avenue, leading a fawn with a collar and leash. She was brought into the precinct station, booked, and then brought before a magistrate, who said that he found it eccentric but he wondered if she might not be opening in some show someplace; and it turned out that she was.

In addition to the show-offs there are the hiders—those who secrete themselves from society. I was twelve or thirteen years old when I became deeply involved with my first real eccentric. There are verities beyond question when one is thirteen—a haunted house is a haunted house, and there is no sense or purpose in questioning it. There is good luck and bad luck, and the penalty for inspection of these is bad luck. Then there are misers, and misers hoard gold. We had a miser; I shall call him Mr. Kirk. Kirk and his wife and daughter lived in a little, old, dark house in a five-acre orchard not far from the center of Salinas. Of course it had once been in the country, until the town crept out and surrounded it. The Kirk place was much too valuable as town lots to be left as a grove of apples and pears and plums, and even those trees so old that they were long past good bearing. The Kirks had been a decent, well-to-do farm family for generations, and it occurred to me only much later why Mr. Kirk was known as a miser. He couldn't be tempted, or bribed, or threatened into selling his valuable acres, to root out his trees, take his profit, and build a white house with a wrought-iron fence and a grave-plot-sized lawn. He hoarded his five acres; and he was peculiar.

Kirk dressed in a blue shirt and overalls like all farm people, but he left his orchard only once a week. On Saturday he came to a little feed store my father owned and bought ten cents' worth of middlings—about five pounds, I suppose. Middlings were simply ground wheat with the chaff left in; it would be called whole wheat now, but then it was sold for chicken and pig feed. His weekly purchase was remarkable because the Kirks had neither chickens nor pigs. Mrs. Kirk and the daughter were rarely seen. They never left the orchard, but we could peer through the black cypress hedge which surrounded the orchard and see two gaunt, gray women, so much alike that you couldn't tell which was mother and which was daughter. As far as anyone ever knew, the ten cents' worth of middlings was all Mr. Kirk ever bought. First the daughter faded and sickened and died, and soon after, Mrs. Kirk went the same way. The coroner said they had starved to death; we would call it malnutrition now—but there was no evidence of violence. People did mind their own business then. But I do know that after they died, Mr. Kirk bought five cents' worth of middlings a week.

Having a genuine miser of our own had a great impact on me and on the three other little boys I ran with. The dark and gloomy orchard and the little unpainted house, mossy with dampness, drew us. I remember being out at night a good deal and I can't for the life of me remember how I got out or back into my own house again. The four of us chicken-necked kids hid in the black shadow of the cypress hedge and looked at the lighted window glowing among the trees, and eventually, by boasting and daring one another, we overcame our cowardice and moved quietly into the orchard and crept with held breaths toward the uncurtained window. Mr. Kirk's face and his right hand and forearm seemed to hang in the air, yellow-lighted by the butterfly flame of a kerosene barn lantern.

He was writing feverishly in a big old ledger with red leather corners, his face twisted and contorted with concentration. Now and then his upper teeth clamped on his lower lip. Suddenly he looked up, I presume in thought, but in our timid state we thought he looked right into our peering faces. All of us jumped back, but one boy's foot slipped and fetched a heavy kick on the wall of the house.

Mr. Kirk leaped to his feet, and we froze in the darkness. He did not look at the window; he addressed a presence to his left so that his profile stood against the lantern. Through the closed window we could hear his voice; he cried out on Satan, on the Devil, on Beelzebub. He argued, pleaded, threatened, and after a few moments collapsed into his chair by the table and put his head down on his arms while we trembled in fear and ecstasy. Nothing there is in nature as thoughtlessly cruel as a small boy, unless it be a small girl. As we hid in the deep shadows, our terror abated and we felt that our entertainer had let us down. Then one of us, and I don't know which of us it was, crept back to the house and struck the wall three great, portentous raps. Instantly Mr. Kirk was on his feet again, fighting his brave and hopeless combat against Satan, while we glowed with excitement and a sense of power. Again he collapsed, and again we roused him, until finally he fell to the floor and did not get up. Now I am horrified at our wantonness, but I cannot remember that we felt any pity whatever.

In the ensuing weeks we ranged the darkness of the orchard every night, so that our parents wondered at our sluggishness in the daytime and put it down to what was called "growing pains." Since Mr. Kirk was a known miser, we began to dig about the roots of the fruit trees, searching for his golden hoard, while, to keep him busy, one of us would crouch under his window and with measured knockings employ him at his job against Satan.

We found no gold, but we were making a horrid mask of paper mounted on a stick to stimulate our victim to new heights of despair, when Mr. Kirk disappeared. No light glowed in his window, and a strange, sweet sickliness hung over the night orchard. Two weeks later we heard that Mr. Kirk had not gone away. He had died in his house, probably helped on by us, and he was in very bad shape when the sheriff and the coroner took him out and splashed the house with creosote.

We could hardly wait for the darkness to fall; we invaded through a window, our pockets full of candles. Every cranny we inspected for his gold; we dug up the earthen floor of his cellar, knocked on walls, searching for hidden hiding places, and we found nothing but his big ledgers. I took one away and read it: gibberish; words and word sounds repeated, "read, reed, wrote, rotten, Robert," or, "sea, sky, sin, sister, soon." I know now that these were symptoms of his sickness.

In the end we were fortunate, but it was long before we knew it to be good fortune. We found no gold, but when Kirk's distant cousins took over their inheritance and prepared to sell off the orchard for building lots, they found a canvas bag wedged in a U-pipe of the sink trap, and in the bag were gold pieces—over five thousand dollars' worth. If we had found them, we would have tried to spend them and—well, it's better we were unlucky.

This was our eccentric; every town must have one or more—strange, hidden, frightened, half-mad people are always with us. Only when they hurt someone or die do we discover them.

The Pursuit of Happiness

IN NOTHING are the Americans so strange and set apart from the rest of the world as in their attitudes toward the treatment of their children. In most Americans this is more than a symptom—it is a syndrome which often becomes trauma; and it is not surprising that even Americans are often frightened by their child-raising activities, and even more by the products. Indeed, in America paedotrophy has caused what amounts to a national sickness which might be called paedosis. Americans did not always fear, hate, and adore their children; in our early days a child spent its helpless and pre-procreative days as a child, and then moved naturally into adulthood. This was true across the world. I have studied the children in many countries—Mexico, France, England, Italy, and others—and I find nothing to approximate the American sickness. Where could it have started, and is it a disease of the children or of the parents? One thing we know: children seem to be able to get over it; parents rarely.

Maybe it might be this way—for the X millions of years of our existence as a species, the odds against a child's surviving to adulthood were very great. Germs, malnutrition, accidents, infections made the bringing up of a child to manhood or womanhood a kind of triumph in itself. My own grandparents thought themselves lucky to save half the children they bore. In parts of Mexico it was true that until recently the infant mortality was five to one. Miscarriages caused by overwork and too little food were far more numerous than they are now, while the plagues of smallpox, diphtheria, scarlet fever, cholera and finally colic were not unknown. It is possible but not provable that this screening for manhood and womanhood weeded out the weaklings, the whiners, the chronic failures, the neurotic, the violent, and the accident-prone; but we know from history that these factors did not eliminate all the stupid. Anyway, before American paedosis appeared, parents were delighted to have children at all and content that they might grow up to be exactly like themselves. The children also seem to have had no quarrel with this. Soldier begat soldier's son, farm boys grew to farmers, housewives trained their daughters to be housewives. Population explosion was taken care of by wars, plagues, and starvation.

The great change seems to have set in toward the end of the last century; perhaps it came with the large numbers of poor and bewildered immigrants suddenly faced with hope of plenty and liberty of development beyond their dreams. Our child sickness has developed very rapidly in the last sixty years and it runs parallel, it would seem, with increasing material plenty and the medical conquest of child-killing diseases. No longer was it even acceptable that the child should be like his parents and live as they did; he must be better, live better, know more, dress more richly, and if possible change from his father's trade to a profession. This dream became touchingly national. Since it was demanded of the child that he or she be better than his parents, he must be gaited, guided, pushed, admired, disciplined, flattered, and forced. But since the parents were and are no better than they are, the rules they propounded were based not on their experience but on their wishes and hopes.

If the hope was not fulfilled, and it rarely was, the parents went into a tailspin of guilt, blaming themselves for having done something wrong or at least something not right. They had played the wrong ground rules. This feeling of self-recrimination on the part of the parents was happily seized upon by the children, for it allowed them to be failures through no fault of their own. Laziness, sloppiness, indiscipline, selfishness, and general piggery, which are the natural talents of children and were once slapped out of them, if they lived, now became either crimes of the parents or sickness in the children, who would far rather be sick than disciplined.

In this confusion the experts entered, and troubled American parents put their difficulties and their children in the hands of the professionals—doctors, educators, psychologists, neurologists, even psychoanalysts. The only trouble was and is that few of the professionals agreed with one another except in one thing: it was the consensus that the child should be the center of attention—an attitude which had the full support of the children.

For the last half-century we have changed our approach about every ten years, from extreme permissiveness to extreme discipline, back and forth. We have thought of children as uncalculated risks, and they have responded. There has even been one school of thought which held that children are born good and are spoiled only by association with unworthy adults. Another school, observing that the first word a child learns is "no" and the second is "mine," believes that the process of growing up is one of reform.

While all this was on an emotional level, it was bad enough; but when it was discovered by advertising groups that children and adolescents could be used, first, as a market for clothes, foods, cosmetics, and second, as selling agents to the parents, then it became really dangerous. Since the parents are scared to death of youth, they become the victims of any kind of nonsense planted in the children by the agents of the sellers. One evening of television commercials shows the horrid results. Children dictate what foods are served, what clothes are worn. There is a child on the television screen selling noodles, soups, and soft drinks. A little child draws the father's attention to the fact that he has dandruff or any number of uglier, smellier, disgusting tendencies, thereby losing contracts and other valuable considerations. Once the delinquent parent takes the child's advice about shampoos or deodorants, everything goes well and happiness ensues.

Now since children and adolescents are bribed with allowances, they have money to spend and are therefore a market in themselves. Campaigns, even whole publications, are addressed to teen-agers; their ideas and suggestions are courted, even though it becomes quickly apparent that the ideas are far from original and the suggestions invariably take the form of complaints of a lack of understanding when not allowed to do anything they wish.

Meanwhile, the laws fumble along trying to keep up with the confusion of the times. Teenagers cannot be punished on the same basis as adults for the same crimes. Blame for the misdeeds of the young falls on the parents and the schools. Little or no effort has been made to teach children responsibility for their acts, for this is supposed to come automatically on the stroke of twenty-one. The fact that it doesn't is a matter of perpetual surprise to us. The reign of terror, which is actually a paedarchy, increases every day, and the open warfare between adults and teenagers becomes constantly more bitter. It doesn't occur to the adult that he has allowed the rules of warfare to be rigged against him; that he has permitted himself to be bound, defanged, and emasculated. I do not blame the youth; no one has ever told him that his tricks are obvious, his thoughts puerile, his goals uncooperative and selfish, his art ridiculous. Psychoanalysts constantly remind their little patients that they must find the real "me." The real "me" invariably turns out to be a savage, self-seeking little beast. Indeed, if the experts expected to be paid by the patient, rather than by the harassed parents, the couches would be empty.

The foregoing is not a diatribe; it is an exact description of what has been happening to Americans, and it doesn't work in that it does not create adults. Actually, the whole American approach to the young has extended adolescence far into the future, so that very many Americans have never and can never become adults. What has caused this?

If it is indeed the result of the parent's dissatisfaction with his own life, of his passionate desire to give his children something better or at least different, it is doubly apparent that he has failed at both. Very recently, studies of Little League baseball, for example, have shown that many parents so want or demand that their children become publicized athletes that they have caused definite mental and physical strain on their children, to the detriment of their health. We do not permit them to be children and insist that they become adults. Then, when they are approaching adulthood, we insist that they be children—with the result that there is a warping effect on the whole American personality.

There are exceptions. For the first time, numbers of American college students are beginning to take an active interest in politics; the movements toward improvement in racial understanding are engaging the effective interest of more and more young people; and the applicants for the Peace Corps far exceed the number who can be accepted. If the parents are harassed, so are the children, and all the harassment may be for the wrong reasons.

.   .   .   .

It may well turn out that modern medicine is saving handicapped children whom natural selection would have eliminated. But this is only one aspect of the inroads science is making on the laws of natural balance. Just as we are keeping more children alive who in other times would have died, we have prolonged life in many millions of people for whom we have no use or place—and this also is having a profound effect on America. We remember all too well how, in the past, the old were revered and admired. Certain ancients from other centuries are remembered for no other reason than that they were old; but with medical breakthroughs life expectancy has leaped. Once the main body of humans consisted of effective adults—say from twenty to fifty. At one end there were enough children for replacements and at the other a few old people as ornaments. But at present, children and old people outnumber the more effective middle group, and we have not yet found use for either. We keep the children young and retire the old to make room for replacements. It is true that we give such retired humans honorable titles such as "senior citizens" and "oldsters," but we have yet to find a place for them. Quite often we retire a man at sixty-five when his mental powers are at their peak, and replace him with an inferior who happens to be younger. As a result, we have a great burden of unhappy, unused, unfulfilled people; far from looking forward to age, the American dreads it— and his children dread it even more.

When America was being settled, the burdens of work, exposure, and infection were much greater on women than on men. Many of the old graveyards carry a record in one tombstone of a husband surrounded by several wives who predeceased him. Present-day American life has reversed this process. Once a man married a woman younger than himself because her term of life, due to work and childbearing, was shorter than his. Present-day pressures of American life, particularly on men in the business world, make it almost the rule that the husband dies first, usually of those difficulties which are the result of strain, pressure, and perhaps indulgence in fats, alcohol, and so forth. The result is a great oversupply of widows, mostly reluctant or too old to remarry. In many cases they are able to live minimal lives on the insurance or investments which were a part of the pressures which killed their husbands, for it is a bit of the American man's duty to live and act in the almost certain knowledge that his wife will survive him. And perhaps this very expectation has something to do with his demise. People do tend to act as they are expected to act. And again, we have found no use for this great supply of aging women.

Some, of course, try to find work; but age places a bar in that path. Of course I know that there are great numbers of useful and fulfilled women without men. Many apply themselves to social, political, or charitable duties, self-imposed; but by far the greater part find only a low-keyed social life without much pleasure or satisfaction—and that with other women exactly like themselves. Dorothy Parker wrote a wonderful play about these women—a heartbreaking play. I see them in New York, in the delicatessens buying a quarter of a pound of sausage, a small dab of cheese, a minuscule plate of potato salad for their suppers. But luncheon seems to be the widow's meal, and they congregate in restaurants—the rich ones in the fine restaurants, and the poor ones in the little places, sometimes vegetarian—where they talk together and look around brightly for acquaintances and for something to do.

Many a hopeless widow is better endowed socially as well as sexually than the illiterate child-women, all hair and false bosoms, who so excite the American man. Indeed, the cult of sexual excitement over undeveloped females seems one more evidence of the American preservation of adolescence beyond its normal span. And one of the curious and revealing symptoms of immaturity in many American men lies in their erotic preoccupation with the female breast. They catalogue women by the measurements of breast, waist, and hips—42-38-43, for example—completely overlooking the more obvious and healthier target. An overdeveloped bosom can arouse these men-children to heights of enthusiasm. I have often thought that when another species inherits the earth, if it should develop sufficient curiosity about extinct man to dig archaeologically among our records and artifacts, the scholarly ants or cockroaches would come to the justifiable conclusion that *Homo sapiens americanus* was born from the mammary gland.

How did this curious fixation arise? The female bosom is a lovely thing which should arouse warm and comforting memories of food and love and protection. It should, and it once did; but male titillation by the breast has caused our females to place great pride in these precious possessions. Employing them for their designed purpose of suckling babies has a tendency to cause bosoms to sag a little, a condition repulsive to men and women alike. This has been solved by bottle feeding, freeing the breasts from their ancient duties and conferring on them a purely ornamental and erotic function, while removing from human experience the association with the breast as a center of food and security.

Some years ago I ended a novel with an ancient symbolic act. I did not invent it; the symbol existed for thousands of years. In my book I had my heroine, who had lost her baby, give her breast to a starving man. I was astonished at the reaction. The scene was denounced as "dirty," "erotic," "filthy." As a baby I was nursed by my mother, and the breast had no such significance to me. As a matter of shocked curiosity, I began questioning those people who had found my scene erotic, and I discovered that the ones who were upset by my scene had invariably been bottle-fed. Such was the effect of a lack of mammary association, and I wonder what the effect on our women may be of retiring from its function a complicated part of their equipment.

What all these problems of youth and age—and of women—indicate is that we are living in two periods. Part of our existence has leaped ahead, and a part has lagged behind, because the problems have not been faced as problems, and the mores have not kept up with methods and techniques. The young dread to grow up, the grown dread growing old, and the old are in a panic about sickness and uselessness. As for the use of leisure, we are due to feel that pressure more and more as automation and increase of population force more and more leisure on us; and so far, in human history, leisure has caused us to get into destructive and unsatisfactory trouble. Unless some valuable direction can be devised and trained for in America, leisure may well be our new disease, dangerous and incurable.

From earliest times and perhaps because our earliest settlers brought little with them but their restless imagination, America has produced first craftsmen and then inventors. Sometimes a man trying to improvise a known tool with saw and pocket knife devised a new one. The small farmer of New England and later of the Middle West created not only the machines he needed to work with but also the furniture from which to enjoy his life. He made new things, new designs, new techniques—

almost as though a faulty memory caused him to start from the beginning. Invention and improvisation were, for a long time, almost national traits, destroyed only when mass production made cheaper but not necessarily better things people could afford to buy.

And yet, the yearning for hand craftsmanship survived, as the enormous sales of do-it-yourself tools testify. Nearly every garage in America has in it some kind of workshop, sometimes never used but kept on as a memory of self-sufficiency. The man who cannot saw a plank end square will furnish himself with complicated machine tools designed to do almost anything. And year after year, thousands of families, having accumulated a nest egg through hard, monotonous, boring work, go back to the country and try with puzzled failure to re-create a self-sufficient island against the creeping, groping assembly-line conformity which troubles and fascinates them at the same time.

Americans and the Land

I HAVE OFTEN wondered at the savagery and thoughtlessness with which our early settlers approached this rich continent. They came at it as though it were an enemy, which of course it was. They burned the forests and changed the rainfall; they swept the buffalo from the plains, blasted the streams, set fire to the grass, and ran a reckless scythe through the virgin and noble timber. Perhaps they felt that it was limit-less and could never be exhausted and that a man could move on to new wonders endlessly. Certainly there are many examples to the contrary, but to a large extent the early people pillaged the country as though they hated it, as though they held it temporarily and might be driven off at any time.

This tendency toward irresponsibility persists in very many of us today; our rivers are poisoned by reckless dumping of sewage and toxic industrial wastes, the air of our cities is filthy and dangerous to breathe from the belching of uncontrolled products from combustion of coal, coke, oil, and gasoline. Our towns are girdled with wreckage and the de-bris of our toys—our automobiles and our packaged pleasures. Through uninhibited spraying against one enemy we have destroyed the natural balances our survival requires. All these evils can and must be overcome if America and Americans are to survive; but many of us still conduct ourselves as our ancestors did, stealing from the future for our clear and present profit.

Since the river-polluters and the air-poisoners are not criminal or even bad people, we must presume that they are heirs to the early con-viction that sky and water are unowned and that they are limitless. In the light of our practices here at home it is very interesting to me to read of the care taken with the carriers of our probes into space, to make utterly sure that they are free of pollution of any kind. We would not think of doing to the moon what we do every day to our own dear country.

When the first settlers came to America and dug in on the coast, they huddled in defending villages hemmed in by the sea on one side and by endless forests on the other, by Red Indians and, most frightening, the mystery of an unknown land extending nobody knew how far. And for a time very few cared or dared to find out. Our first Americans organized themselves and lived in a state of military alertness; every community built its blockhouse for defense. By law the men went armed and were required to keep their weapons ready and available. Many of them wore armor, made here or imported; on the East Coast, they wore the cuirass and helmet, and the Spaniards on the West Coast wore both steel armor and heavy leather to turn arrows.

On the East Coast, and particularly in New England, the colonists farmed meager lands close to their communities and to safety. Every man was permanently on duty for the defense of his family and his village; even the hunting parties went into the forest in force, rather like raiders than hunters, and their subsequent quarrels with the Indians, resulting in forays and even massacres, remind us that the danger was very real. A man took his gun along when he worked the land, and the women stayed close to their thick-walled houses and listened day and night for the signal of alarm. The towns they settled were permanent, and most of them exist today with their records of Indian raids, of slaughter, of scalpings, and of punitive counterraids. The military leader of the community became the chief authority in time of trouble, and it was a long time before danger receded and the mystery could be explored.

After a time, however, brave and forest-wise men drifted westward to hunt, to trap, and eventually to bargain for the furs which were the first precious negotiable wealth America produced for trade and export. Then trading posts were set up as centers of collection and the exploring men moved up and down the rivers and crossed the mountains, made friends for mutual profit with the Indians, learned the wilderness techniques, so that these explorer-traders soon dressed, ate, and generally acted like the indigenous people around them. Suspicion lasted a long time, and was fed by clashes sometimes amounting to full-fledged warfare; but by now these Americans attacked and defended as the Indians did.

For a goodly time the Americans were travelers, moving about the country collecting its valuables, but with little idea of permanence; their roots and their hearts were in the towns and the growing cities along the eastern edge. The few who stayed, who lived among the Indians, adopted their customs and some took Indian wives and were regarded as strange and somehow treasonable creatures. As for their half-breed children, while the tribe sometimes adopted them they were unacceptable as equals in the eastern settlements.

Then the trickle of immigrants became a stream, and the population began to move westward—not to grab and leave but to settle and live, they thought. The newcomers were of peasant stock, and they had their roots in a Europe where they had been landless, for the possession of land was the requirement and the proof of a higher social class than they had known. In America they found beautiful and boundless land for the taking—and they took it.

It is little wonder that they went land-mad, because there was so much of it. They cut and burned the forests to make room for crops; they abandoned their knowledge of kindness to the land in order to maintain its usefulness. When they had cropped out a piece they moved on, raping the country like invaders. The topsoil, held by roots and freshened by leaf-fall, was left helpless to the spring freshets, stripped and eroded with the naked bones of clay and rock exposed. The destruction of the forests changed the rainfall, for the searching clouds could find no green and beckoning woods to draw them on and milk them. The merciless nineteenth century was like a hostile expedition for loot that seemed limitless. Uncountable buffalo were killed, stripped of their hides, and left to rot, a reservoir of permanent food supply eliminated. More than that, the land of the Great Plains was robbed of the manure of the herds. Then the plows went in and ripped off the protection of the buffalo grass and opened the helpless soil to quick water and slow drought and the mischievous winds that roamed through the Great Central Plains. There has always been more than enough desert in America; the new settlers, like overindulged children, created even more.

The railroads brought new hordes of land-crazy people, and the new Americans moved like locusts across the continent until the western sea put a boundary to their movements. Coal and copper and gold drew them on; they savaged the land, gold-dredged the rivers to skeletons of pebbles and debris. An aroused and fearful government made laws for the distribution of public lands—a quarter section, one hundred and sixty acres, per person—and a claim had to be proved and improved; but there were ways of getting around this, and legally. My own grandfather proved out a quarter section for himself, one for his wife, one for each of his children, and, I suspect, acreage for children he hoped and expected to have. Marginal lands, of course, suitable only for grazing, went in larger pieces. One of the largest landholding families in California took its richest holdings by a trick: By law a man could take up all the swamp or water-covered land he wanted. The founder of this great holding mounted a scow on wheels and drove his horses over thousands of acres of the best bottomland, then reported that he had explored it in a boat, which was true, and confirmed his title. I need not mention his name; his descendants will remember.

Another joker with a name still remembered in the West worked out a scheme copied many times in after years. Proving a quarter section required a year of residence and some kind of improvement—a fence, a shack—but once the land was proved the owner was free to sell it. This particular princely character went to the stews and skid rows of the towns and found a small army of hopeless alcoholics who lived for whisky and nothing else. He put these men on land he wanted to own, grubstaked them and kept them in cheap liquor until the acreage was proved, then went through the motions of buying it from his protégés and moved them and their one-room shacks on sled runners on to new quarter sections. Bums of strong constitution might prove out five or six homesteads for this acquisitive hero before they died of drunkenness.

It was full late when we began to realize that the continent did not stretch out to infinity; that there were limits to the indignities to which we could subject it. Engines and heavy mechanical equipment were allowing us to ravage it even more effectively than we had with fire, dynamite, and gang plows. Conservation came to us slowly, and much of it hasn't arrived yet. Having killed the whales and wiped out the sea otters and most of the beavers, the market hunters went to work on game birds; ducks and quail were decimated, and the passenger pigeon eliminated. In my youth I remember seeing a market hunter's gun, a three-gauge shotgun bolted to a frame and loaded to the muzzle with shingle nails. Aimed at a lake and the trigger pulled with a string, it slaughtered every living thing on the lake. The Pacific Coast pilchards were once the raw material for a great and continuing industry. We hunted them with aircraft far at sea until they were gone and the canneries had to be closed. In some of the valleys of the West, where the climate makes several crops a year available, which the water supply will not justify, wells were driven deeper and deeper for irrigation, so that in one great valley a million acre-feet more of water was taken out than rain and melting snow could replace, and the water table went down and a few more years may give us a new desert.

The great redwood forests of the western mountains early attracted attention. These ancient trees, which once grew everywhere, now exist only where the last Ice Age did not wipe them out. And they were found to have value. The Sempervirens and the Gigantea, the two remaining species, make soft, straight-grained timber. They are easy to split into planks, shakes, fenceposts, and railroad ties, and they have a unique virtue: they resist decay, both wet and dry rot, and an inherent acid in them repels termites. The loggers went through the great groves like a barrage, toppling the trees—some of which were two thousand years old—and leaving no maidens, no seedlings or saplings on the denuded hills.

Quite a few years ago when I was living in my little town on the coast of California a stranger came in and bought a small valley where the Sempervirens redwoods grew, some of them three hundred feet high. We used to walk among these trees, and the light colored as though the great glass of the Cathedral at Chartres had strained and sanctified the sunlight. The emotion we felt in this grove was one of awe and humility and joy; and then one day it was gone, slaughtered, and the sad wreckage of boughs and broken saplings left like nonsensical spoilage of the battle-ruined countryside. And I remember that after our rage there was sadness, and when we passed the man who had done this we looked away, because we were ashamed for him.

From early times we were impressed and awed by the fantastic accidents of nature, like the Grand Canyon and Yosemite and Yellowstone Park. The Indians had revered them as holy places, visited by the gods, and all of us came to have somewhat the same feeling about them. Thus we set aside many areas of astonishment as publicly owned parks; and though this may to a certain extent have been because there was no other way to use them, as the feeling of preciousness of the things we had been destroying grew in Americans, more and more areas were set aside as national and state parks, to be looked at but not injured. Many people loved and were in awe of the redwoods; societies and individuals bought groves of these wonderful trees and presented them to the state for preservation.

No longer do we Americans want to destroy wantonly, but our new-found sources of power—to take the burden of work from our shoulders, to warm us, and cool us, and give us light, to transport us quickly, and to make the things we use and wear and eat—these power sources spew pollution on our country, so that the rivers and streams are becoming poisonous and lifeless. The birds die for the lack of food; a noxious cloud hangs over our cities that burns our lungs and reddens our eyes. Our ability to conserve has not grown with our power to create, but this slow and sullen poisoning is no longer ignored or justified. Almost daily, the pressure of outrage among Americans grows. We are no longer content to destroy our beloved country. We are slow to learn; but we learn. When a superhighway was proposed in California which would trample the redwood trees in its path, an outcry arose all over the land, so strident and fierce that the plan was put aside. And we no longer believe that a man, by owning a piece of America, is free to outrage it.

But we are an exuberant people, careless and destructive as active children. We make strong and potent tools and then have to use them to prove that they exist. Under the pressure of war we finally made the atom bomb, and for reasons which seemed justifiable at the time we dropped it on two Japanese cities—and I think we finally frightened ourselves. In such things, one must consult himself because there is no other point of reference. I did not know about the bomb, and certainly I had nothing to do with its use, but I am horrified and ashamed; and nearly everyone I know feels the same thing. And those who loudly and angrily justify Hiroshima and Nagasaki—why, they must be the most ashamed of all.

Americans and the World

THE AMERICAN ATTITUDE toward foreign nations, foreign people, and foreign things is closely tied historically to our geographical position and our early history on this continent. Our land was many months' journey by sea from the civilized sectors of Europe and Asia from which all of us originally came. Until recently, the chance that the average native-born American would ever see a foreign country was remote. Since we had little actual communication we had no need to learn other languages than our own. The immigrants brought every tongue in the world to our shores and tried their best to keep them; but their children were Americans and somehow ashamed that their parents once were not. The second generation did its best to forget the past, including the past languages. In our earlier, colonial days, every foreign ship sighted was a potential enemy, bent on conquest and settlement—English, Dutch, French, Spanish, Portuguese—all were on the prowl looking for new territory and new conquest. New York changed hands twice, New Orleans three times, Texas five. The power politics and changing alliances of Europe in our colonial days involved us in wars which were not our concern. As a newborn nation we did not understand world politics, and consequently were afraid of being involved. When Washington advised us against entangling alliances, he was voicing what everyone felt. Only our rich and sophisticated visited Europe and they, by their education and background, were more European than their stay-at-home brothers.

Our years of isolation were based on a very real fear of the unknown, and this attitude was not helped by the kind of visitors who came to our country, or by their attitudes and what they said about us. These callers were usually of the upper class and provincial in the sense that they disapproved of everything that was not their own. They found only contempt for our manners and speech, the hardship of our lives, our ignorance of them—which was equaled only by their ignorance of us—and because they usually emerged from the upper levels of a sharply classed society they disdained our clumsy attempts at equality and democracy. In their written reports they made fun of us and presented a picture of the Americans as dirty, drunken, ignorant savages. It was beyond the comprehension of these visitors that a man without accepted schooling, sometimes without formal schooling at all, should come from what they considered squalor to lead the American nation; and they were stridently puzzled that sometimes these products of our poverty were able, intelligent, informed, and efficient leaders. It was beyond even contemplation that a Lincoln could have become Prime Minister of England.

I remember a story told me by a friend, a well-turned-out, educated lady of enormous imagination, a good writer and a good observer who had moved about over the face of the world for many years. Once in London, over tea, an English lady whose only move in the world was a yearly journey from London to a watering place in, perhaps, Dorset said to my friend, "Where are you from, my dear?" To which my friend said, "I am from California." To which the English lady said, "Dear, dear, how you provincials do get about!"

The self-assured criticism by visitors may have angered some Americans, but mostly it made us feel shy and clumsy. We had no pattern of comparison which would have shown us that the recipients of our hospitality were insensitive, ill-mannered louts, so full of their parochial self-satisfaction that they did not bother, or were unable, to observe us. I have used the word hospitality advisedly; in a developing country where people in villages, or families in far-flung farmhouses, have little excitement outside of their daily working lives and their churches and their occasional trips to town for supplies, a visitor was welcomed as a bringer of news, an interpreter of the world over the horizon. The best we had was brought out for guests and the tables were loaded with food. Besides, in a country where hunger was always keyed to wind and weather, where danger of violence or even of being lost or injured was ever-present, hospitality was a built-in duty every man owed to every wayfarer—since he might need it himself. A man or a family always offered the best and most valued of his possessions to a passing stranger, and took in trade the interest and information the stranger brought.

My uncle Charlie told me a story about hospitality in the desolate northern plains. He was a surveyor, running a prospecting line for the Canadian Pacific Railway, and he was out far ahead of the main party. The houses in that part of the country were made of sod, half cave and half hut with grass growing on the roofs, but they were warm and they were secure and dry. One afternoon Uncle Charlie knocked on the door of a sod house, so low and overgrown that it looked like a barrow. A little old woman opened the door; the men were away hunting, she said, but yes, he could stay the night and she would cook his dinner. She rushed out, killed a chicken, and prepared it while Uncle Charlie looked about the poor little place. The floor was of earth, the furniture knocked together out of packing crates; and then he saw, to his astonishment, an upright piano. Uncle Charlie moved up on it and thumped out a few chords, whereupon the old lady whirled from her cooking with great excitement. "Professor," she said, "can you play 'The Maiden's Prayer'?" Charlie could and he did; and of course any stranger who could play piano was automatically a professor.

It was the same when we entertained visitors from abroad. The fact that they accepted our gift of hospitality and then turned on us made us feel inadequate. We were asking for approval, and we got kicked in the face. It did not occur to us that our guests were not representatives of their people or nations but a selected group of hypercritical snobs. Later, in two world wars when masses of our men who had not and probably never would have traveled were transported overseas and set down in English, French, or Italian countrysides, their most common reaction was "Why these aren't the English—or the French, or the Italians—we know; these are people just like us!"

And of course we had our share of slobs, but usually the Americans when they traveled have wanted desperately to be liked; they have overtipped, overpaid, and overpraised, in the hope that they might, as strangers, be liked. And they—or let us say we—have not discovered that a person who so wants to be liked usually draws dislike or even contempt.

I believe the time of our insularity is over. Americans travel more than any other people today, and we are learning the rules of the road.

I think the common feeling now is "I don't give a damn whether the British, the French, or the Russians like me or not." Once, if a so-called superior Frenchman was appalled at my failure to speak good French, I would have been shy and apologetic; now my feeling and my reply are that I am sad that my French leaves something to be desired, but how much sadder must a Frenchman be who has not troubled to learn English, which is a noble and a rapidly spreading language. It is not strange, and it is true, that this perceptible change in the American attitude makes us much better liked abroad. We no longer believe that all art, all culture, and all knowledge originate in Europe.

American literature, as it does in most countries, grew up twofold; the early, scholarly, traditional, and correct writers imitated English writing of the time and their thinking followed European trends and held in contempt the starveling, semiliterate organism that was growing up under their eyes. This attitude still obtains in many American writers, particularly in those critics who are descended from recent immigrants. On the other hand, the exotic nature of the new continent, with its unexplored and mysterious areas and its noble but savage Red Men, engaged the interest of some European writers who reported us with the childlike inaccuracy we now address to Africa and the upper ranges of the Amazon. However, we were fortunate quite early in developing some mature writers of eye, ear, and enthusiasm: Washington Irving, for instance, looked with joy on our people, our speech, stories, and patterns of thought; Cooper made up a fund of misinformation about the American Indians; while Longfellow searched for Hellenic meter and meaning in the life and history of Americans. Meanwhile, the true seedlings of our literature were sprouting in the tall tales, the jests, the boasting, and the humor of the storytellers in the forests and on the plains. Their product was printed in local newspapers and in publications fiercely ignored by the princely intellectual Brahmins of the East Coast, who felt that the indigenous must somehow be tainted. Even Edgar Allan Poe, who surely wrote more like a European than an American, had to be acclaimed in France before he was acceptable to upper-brow Americans. But the writers of America for Americans survived and expanded and, perhaps because their only outlet was in obscure and local journals, created a situation which even today exists only in America.

In Europe, a journalist is looked upon as a second- or third-rate writer. "Journalist," to a European aspirer to belles-lettres, is a dirty word. In America, on the contrary, journalism not only is a respected profession, but is considered the training ground of any good American author. The disciplines of clarity and simplicity imposed on writers by newspapers, far from being considered limiting and low, are held with considerable justification to be valuable in cleaning out the gaudy trash most new writers bring to their early work. The list of American writers of stature and performance who took their basic training and found their first outlet in newspapers is ample proof that for us, at least, the proposition is tenable. Alphabetically, beginning with George Ade, Maxwell Anderson, Benchley, Bierce, Crane, Dreiser, Faulkner, Hammett, Hearn, Lardner, London, Norris, Mark Twain, Artemus Ward, Thomas Wolfe, are only a few. And apart from the disciplines, newspaper work has other advantages. It sends the writer to the people to hear, see, and understand and report to peoples of all kinds, on all levels. Recently, in the Soviet Union, I was asked how a capitalist country like America produced so many of what the Russians call "proletarian writers." I replied that in the USSR when a writer is accepted by the Union—in other words, is underwritten by the state—he associates only with other writers and lives on a plane far above other people. In America, on the other hand, an aspiring writer is forced by the threat of starvation to learn his trade in the mass media and to keep his contacts with his people. Some, of course, escape into the esoteric towers of advertising or the semipaternal cloisters of teaching; but these are considered, and consider themselves, to have failed in the pattern of American literature.

At the time when the Golden Age of classic writing was flourishing in the East Coast centers of learning, when the accepted were members of an establishment endowed with the keys to the heaven of literary acceptance, at this very time Herman Melville was writing *Moby-Dick*, the first edition of which did not sell out for forty years; Stephen Crane was writing *The Red Badge of Courage*; Walt Whitman was printing his own *Leaves of Grass* and being fired from his job because it was a dirty book.

The incredible ear and eye and sense of form of Mark Twain were in communication not with classic Greeks but with Americans. He got by because people thought he was only funny and therefore not dangerous; and nobody of any importance considered that America had or ever would have a literature. The successful members of the Establishment lived and had their being on and sometimes physically emigrated to the Continent.

Perhaps someone knows how the great change came which elevated American writing from either weak imitation or amusing unimportance to a position of authority in the whole world, to be studied and in turn imitated. It happened quickly. A Theodore Dreiser wrote the sound and smell of his people; a Sherwood Anderson perceived and set down secret agonies long before the headshrinkers discovered them. Suddenly the great ones stirred to life: Willa Cather, then Sinclair Lewis, O'Neill, Wolfe, Hemingway, Faulkner. There were many others, of course— poets, short-story writers, essayists like Benchley and E. B. White. Their source was identical; they learned from our people and wrote like themselves, and they created a new thing and a grand thing in the world—an American literature about Americans. It was and is no more flattering than Isaiah was about the Jews, Thucydides about the Greeks, or Tacitus, Suetonius, and Juvenal about the Romans; but, like them, it has the sweet, strong smell of truth. And as had been so in other ages with other peoples, the Americans denounced their glory as vicious, libelous, and scandalous falsehood—and only when our literature was accepted abroad was it welcomed home again and its authors claimed as Americans.

Generations of social historians have assessed and assayed the past with the purpose of finding out what happened and why. The what is difficult enough to pin down, since records and reports tend to favor the recorder; but the why is almost impossible to come by. Individuals have a hard enough time finding a reason for their actions and thought; how much more difficult it is to determine what gives rise to group actions and attitudes. Reasons are usually arrived at after the fact, when the need arises for explanation.

When I was a child growing up in Salinas, I found in the attic of our house boxes of the *Atlantic Monthly*—almost a complete file—for the 1870s and 1880s. Apart from the charm that old advertising has, these magazines fascinated me. At the time of their publication the Civil War was near enough to be remembered and far enough in the past to be wondered about. In issue after issue, general officers of both the North and the South wrote descriptions of the actions in which they had commanded, and set down the reasons for their decisions and orders, many of which had turned out disastrously but all of which had been arrived at for the best possible reasons. In no case had a commander made a mistake or an error in judgment. Even as a child, I can remember wondering what really happened and realizing that I could never know; for if the men who had been there were confused, what chance had I, a child, or a historian, of finding out? And in the thousands of books written about that war right up to the present time, the guessing has grown more assertive and quarrelsome as the subject matter has become more remote.

For the most part, history is what we wish it to have been. A friend of mine, sent to England as a correspondent for a Midwestern paper in World War II, to vary his dispatches conceived the idea of visiting the seat in Ireland of the Cornwallis family, and of finding what recollections or records remained of the service of Lord Cornwallis in the American Revolution and of his surrender at Yorktown—certainly one of the most important events in our history. My friend found a monument to Lord Cornwallis, recounting his activities in the European wars of his time; but there was no mention on the monument, nor any memory among his descendants, of his ever having served in America—let alone having surrendered to the Americans. In that area, our slice of glory did not exist.

Not long ago, after my last trip to Russia, I had a conversation with an American very eminent in the field of politics. I asked him what he read, and he replied that he studied history, sociology, economics, and law.

"How about fiction—novels, plays, poetry?" I asked.

"No," he said, "I have never had time for them. There is so much else I have to read."

I said, "Sir, I have recently visited Russia for the third time. I don't know how well I understand Russians; but I do know that if I had only read Russian history I could not have had the access to Russian thinking I have had from reading Dostoevsky, Tolstoy, Chekhov, Pushkin, Turgenev, Sholokhov, and Ehrenburg. History only recounts, with some inaccuracy, *what* they did. The fiction tells, or tries to tell, *why* they did it and what they felt and were like when they did it."

My friend nodded gravely. "I hadn't thought of that," he said. "Yes, that might be so; I had always thought of fiction as opposed to fact."

But in considering the American past, how poor we would be in information without *Huckleberry Finn*, *An American Tragedy*, *Winesburg, Ohio*, *Main Street*, *The Great Gatsby*, and *As I Lay Dying*. And if you want to know about Pennsylvania of the last hundred years, you'll read O'Hara or you'll know less than you might.

This is no plea for fiction over history, but it does suggest that both are required for any kind of understanding. It is safe to say, I think, that the picture of America and the Americans which is branded on the minds of foreigners is derived in very large part from our novels, our short stories, and particularly from our moving pictures. To a certain extent this has been unfortunate; America is so enormous that our writers, of their own experience, could know only a small part of it. Because of this, the so-called sectional novel developed. The American novelist wrote almost exclusively of his own home countryside, and if he wrote interestingly enough or powerfully enough his picture became, in the European mind, the picture of America. Because the West of the Indians and cowboys was exotic and exciting, this became America—so that until recently travelers from abroad expected to find painted savages in war bonnets on the outskirts of New York and Boston. Also, because American novelists in the nineteen-twenties and thirties and forties attacked social injustices and inequalities with a savagery aimed at reform, conditions which have since changed and improved still linger as truths in the foreign mind. This is a compliment to the force of American writing, but it does not contribute to present truth. Finally, the American films in the golden early days of Hollywood, having no purpose but to excite, to amuse, to astonish, and thereby to sell tickets, created a life that never existed, based perhaps on the dreams and the yearnings of the inexperienced and ill-informed.

The films of the early days, like the great European cathedrals of medieval Europe, opened a glory to people who had none in their lives. For the price of a ticket, a person whose life was dull, sad, unexciting, ugly, and without hope could enter and become part of a dream life in which all people were rich and beautiful — or violent and brave — and in which, after the storied solution of a foretellably solvable problem, permanent happiness came like a purple and gold sunset. These films helped to create in the minds of foreign people a dismally untrue picture of an America of gangsters, penthouses, and swimming pools and an endless supply of elegant and available houris very like those promised by the Prophet to the faithful in heaven. The least informed American knew that he would emerge from the glory, the vice, and the violence, and return to the shrieking street, the eventless town, or the humdrum job; but poor immigrants were drawn to our golden dreams and the promise of happiness.

This naïve time is over, but it has left its mark — perhaps a deeper mark than we realize — both at home and abroad; for advertising has taken over where the dream film stopped. And any night of television commercials can convince a plain and lonely girl that a hair rinse, along with false eyelashes and protuberances, can magically transform her into an exciting, magnetic sex kitten and guarantee her entrance into the garden of happiness.

But these frills and trappings are believed and not believed at the same time. What all these exploding dreams have contributed, it seems to me, is a kind of sullen despair and growing anger and cynicism, which is another kind of escape. Perhaps the urge toward happiness has taken the place of the urge toward food and warmth and shelter.

Americans and the Future

I FIND I have been avoiding or at least putting off one of the most serious problems, if not the most serious one, that Americans are faced with, both as a people and as individuals. In very many people this problem is a gray and leaden weight heavy to all and unbearable to some. We discuss it constantly and yet there is not even a name for it. Many, not able to face the universal spread and danger of the cancerous growth, split off a fragment of the whole to worry about or to try to cure. But it seems to me that we must inspect the disease as a whole because if we cannot root it out we have little chance of survival.

First, let us try to find something to call this subtle and deadly illness. Immorality does not describe it, nor does lack of integrity, nor does dishonesty. We might coin the word "anethics," but that would be too scholarly an approach to a subject that is far more dangerous than anything that has happened to us. It is a creeping, evil thing that is invading every cranny of our political, our economic, our spiritual, and our psychic life. I begin to think that the evil is one thing, not many, that racial unrest, the emotional crazy quilt that drives our people in panic to the couches of the psychoanalysts, the fallout, dropout, copout insurgency of our children and young people, the rush to stimulant as well as hypnotic drugs, the rise of narrow, ugly, and vengeful cults of all kinds, the distrust and revolt against all authority, political, religious, or military, the awful and universal sense of apprehension and even terror, and this in a time of plenty such as has never been known—I think all these are manifestations of one single cause.

Perhaps we will have to inspect mankind as a species, not with our usual awe at how wonderful we are but with the cool and neutral attitude we reserve for all things save ourselves. Man is indeed wonderful, and perhaps his gaudiest achievement has been to survive his paradoxes. He is not a herd animal, nor has he any of the built-in rules which permit the ruminants to graze and mate and survive together, reserving their fear and their ferocity for protection against foreign species. Mankind seems more nearly related to the predators, possessive, acquisitive, fearful, and aggressive. He is omnivorous, can and will eat anything living or dead, two endowments shared by the cockroach and the common rat. He is aggressively individual and yet he swarms and goes to hive in the noise and discomfort of his tenements and close-packed cities. Once, when enemies roamed the open, there was a reason for thronging in caves and castle courtyards, but with these dangers removed he is drawn to packed subways, crowded streets, howling traffic, and penal quarters in apartment houses. And in America this human tendency seems to be increasing. The small towns grow smaller so that men and women can breathe poisoned air and walk fearfully through streets where violence does not even wait for darkness. We are afraid to be alone and afraid to be together. What has happened to us? Something deep and controlling and necessary.

I'm not going to preach about any good old days. By our standards of comfort they were pretty awful. What did they have then that we are losing or have lost? Well, for one thing they had rules—rules concerning life, limb, and property, rules governing deportment, manners, conduct, and rules defining dishonesty, dishonor, misconduct, and crime. The rules were not always obeyed but they were believed in, and breaking them was savagely punished.

Because of our predatory nature, the hive or the herd were always beyond us but the pack and the crowd were open to us. When two humans get together rules are required to keep them from stripping or killing each other. These rules are simply pragmatic brakes on our less than fraternal instincts. Early on to make the rules effective they were put out as the commands of a God and therefore not open to question. By this means, it was simple for obedience to the rules to be equated with virtue or good, and disobedience with bad or evil. Since so many of our instincts lead to rape, rapine, mayhem, and plunder, it was necessary not only to punish the bad, or natural, but to reward the good people who lived by the rules in peace and safety. Since it was impractical to make these rewards in physical form, more and more of the payments were put over into a future life.

In many of our activities, opposites in the world of rules are placed in juxtaposition one to another. It is said that the convict and the keeper are more alike than they are different; that cop and robber are skin brothers. All armies, regardless of their missions, carry death and destruction in their hands, and this is so frightening to us that the rules we make for armies are rigid beyond all others, while punishment for infringement is immediate and savage. In this way we show our awareness of the dark danger lurking in us always. Over the millennia most of us have learned to obey the rules or suffer punishment for breaking them. But, most important, even the rule-breaker knew he was wrong and the other right; the rules were understood and accepted by everyone. At intervals in our history, through unperceived changes usually economic, the rules and the enforcing agents have come a cropper. Inevitably the result has been a wild and terrible self-destructive binge, a drunken horror of the spirit giving rise to the unspeakable antics of crazy children. And this dark maze-mania has continued until rules were reapplied, rewritten, or re-enforced.

Once Adlai Stevenson, speaking of a politician of particularly rancid practices, said, "If he were a bad man, I wouldn't be so afraid of him. But this man has no principles. He doesn't know the difference." Could this be our difficulty, that gradually we are losing our ability to tell the difference? The rules fall away in chunks and in the vacant place we have a generality: "It's all right because everybody does it." This is balanced with another cry of cowardice. In the face of inequity, dishonesty in government, or downright plundering the word is "Go fight City Hall!" The implication is, of course, that you can't win. And yet in other times we did fight City Hall and often we won.

The American has never been a perfect instrument, but at one time he had a reputation for gallantry, which, to my mind, is a sweet and priceless quality. It must still exist, but it is blotted out by the dust cloud of self-pity. The last clear statement of gallantry in my experience I heard in a recidivist state prison, a place of two-time losers, all lifers. In the yard an old and hopeless convict spoke as follows: "The kids come up and they bawl how they wasn't guilty or how they was framed or how it was their mothers' fault or their father was a drunk. Us old boys try to tell 'em, 'Kid, for Chrise sake do your *own* time and let us do ours.' " In the present climate of whining self-pity, of practiced sickness, of professional goldbricking, of screaming charges about whose fault it is, one hears of very few who do their own time, who take their rap and don't spread it around. It is as though the quality of responsibility had atrophied.

It is hard to criticize the people one loves. I knew this would be a painful thing to write. But I am far from alone in my worry. My mail is full of it—letters of anxiety. The newspapers splash so much of it that perhaps we have stopped seeing. How is one to communicate this sadness? A simile occurs to me again and again. Our national nervousness reminds me of something—something elusive.

Americans, very many of them, are obsessed with tensions. Nerves are drawn tense and twanging. Emotions boil up and spill over into violence largely in meaningless or unnatural directions. In the cities people scream with rage at one another, taking out their unease on the first observable target. The huge reservoir of the anger of frustration is full to bursting. The cab driver, the bus or truck driver, pressed with traffic and confusion, denounces Negroes and Puerto Ricans unless he is a Negro or a Puerto Rican. Negroes burn up with a hateful flame. A line has formed for the couches of the psychoanalysts of people wound so tight that the mainspring has snapped and they deliver their poisons in symbolic capsules to the doctor. The legal and criminal distribution of sleeping pills and pep pills is astronomical, the first opening escape into sleep and the second access to a false personality, a biochemical costume in which to strut. Kicks increasingly take the place of satisfaction. Of love, only the word, bent and bastardized, remains.

It does remind me of something. Have you ever seen a kennel of beautiful, highly bred and trained and specialized bird dogs? And have you seen those same dogs when they are no longer used? In a short time their skills and certainties and usefulness are gone. They become quarrelsome, fat, lazy, cowardly, dirty, and utterly disreputable and worthless, and all because their purpose is gone and with it the rules and disciplines that made them beautiful and good.

Is that what we are becoming, a national kennel of animals with no purpose and no direction? For a million years we had a purpose—simple survival—the finding, planting, gathering, or killing of food to keep us alive, of shelter to prevent our freezing. This was a strong incentive. Add to it defense against all kinds of enemies and you have our species' history. But now we have food and shelter and transportation and the more terrible hazard of leisure. I strongly suspect that our moral and spiritual disintegration grows out of our lack of experience with plenty. Once, in a novel, I wrote about a woman who said she didn't want a lot of money. She wanted just enough. To which her husband replied that just enough doesn't exist. There is no money or not enough money. A billionaire still hasn't enough money.

But we are also poisoned with things. Having many things seems to create a desire for more things, more clothes, houses, automobiles. Think of the pure horror of our Christmases when our children tear open package after package and, when the floor is heaped with wrappings and presents, say, "Is that all?" And two days after, the smashed and abandoned "things" are added to our national trash pile, and perhaps the child, having got in trouble, explains, "I didn't have anything to do." And he means exactly that—nothing to do, nowhere to go, no direction, no purpose, and worst of all no needs. Wants he has, yes, but for more bright and breakable "things." We are trapped and entangled in things.

In my great-grandmother's time things were important. I know, because I have read her will, and the things she found important enough to bequeath by legal instrument we would have thrown away—such things as four pewter spoons, one broken in the handle, a square of black cotton lace. I had from Grandmama the little box of leaves from the Mount of Olives, a small bowl carved from one piece of onyx and beautiful to see, twelve books, and eight sheets of music. These were valuable things.

It is probable that the want of things and the need of things have been the two greatest stimulants toward the change and complication we call progress. And surely we Americans, most of us starting with nothing, have contributed our share of wanting. Wanting is probably a valuable human trait. It is the means of getting that can be dangerous.

It's a rare morning when our newspapers do not report bribery, malfeasance, and many other forms of cheating on the part of the public officials who have used the authority vested in their positions for personal gain. Of course we don't hear of the honest men, but the danger lies no in the miscreants but in our attitude toward them. Increasingly we lose our feeling of wrong. Huge corporations are convicted of price fixing and apparently the only shame is in being caught. It is a kind of a game. On the other hand, these same corporations, if Senate testimony is correct, offer bribes to members of other corporations, install listening devices and use all manner of spying methods against each other. I am dwelling on these clandestine practices not as wrong but as impractical. Businesses must not only watch rivals but must constantly spy on their own people to forestall treachery. And this is regarded as normal. Actually the use of both espionage and security in business is unworkable, expensive, and indicative of the collapse of the whole system, for any system which cannot trust its own people is in deep trouble.

When students cheat in examinations, it may be bad for them as individuals but for the community it means that the graduate is traveling with false papers and very shortly the papers—in this case the college degree—lose their value. When military cadets cheat it is in effect a kind of treason, for it means they have not learned to do the things they will be assigned to do. John Kennedy said his famous lines "Ask not what your country can do for you—ask what you can do for your country," and the listening nation nodded and smiled in agreement. But he said it not because this selfishness might become evident but because it is evident, and increasingly so. And it is historically true that a nation whose people take out more than they put in will collapse and disappear.

Why are we on this verge of moral and hence nervous collapse? One can only have an opinion based on observation plus a reading of history. I believe it is because we have reached the end of a road and have no new path to take, no duty to carry out, and no purpose to fulfill. The primary purpose of mankind has always been to survive in a natural world which has not invariably been friendly to us. In our written, remembered, and sensed history, there has always been more work to do than we could do. Our needs were greater than their possible fulfillment. Our dreams were so improbable that we moved their reality into heaven. Our ailments, our agonies, and our sorrows were so many and so grievous that we accepted them either as inevitable or as punishments for our manufactured sins.

What happened to us came quickly and quietly, came from many directions and was the more dangerous because it wore the face of good. Almost unlimited new power took the place of straining muscles and bent backs. Machinery took the heavy burden from our shoulders. Medicine and hygiene cut down infant mortality almost to the vanishing point, and at the same time extended our life span. Automation began to replace our workers. Where once the majority of our people worked the land, machines, chemistry, and a precious few produced more food than we needed or could possibly use. Leisure, which again had been the property of heaven, came to us before we knew what to do with it, and all these good things falling on us unprepared constitute calamity.

We have the things and we have not had time to develop a way of thinking about them. We struggle with our lives in the present and our practices in the long and well-learned past. We have had a million years to get used to the idea of fire and only twenty to prepare ourselves for the productive-destructive tidal wave of atomic fission. We have more food than we can use and no way to distribute it. Our babies live and we have no work for their hands. We retire men and women at the age of their best service for no other reason than that we need their jobs for younger people. To allow ourselves the illusion of usefulness we have standby crews for functions which no longer exist. We manufacture things we do not need and try by false and vicious advertising to create a feeling of need for them. We have found no generally fulfilling method for employing our leisure. To repeat—we have not had time to learn inside ourselves the things that have happened to us.

And finally we can come back to morals.

Ethics, morals, codes of conduct, are the stern rules which in the past we needed to survive—as individuals, as groups, as nations. Now, although we give lip service to survival, we are embarrassed and beginning to be smothered by our own numbers. Americans, who are makers and lovers of statistics, are usually puzzled and irritated when it is suggested that we are a statistic. But neither the sleeping pill, the Church, nor the psychiatrist can long hide from us that economic laws apply to ourselves, that increased supply causes a drop in value, that we already have too many people and are in process of producing far too many. Remember when we gave our Occidental sniff and observed that in China life was cheap? It never occurred to us that it could become cheap to us. Those codes of conduct we call morals were evolved for this thinly inhabited continent when a man's life was important because he was rare and he was needed. Women were protected to the point of worship because only they could bear children to continue the race. A cry for help brought out Americans buzzing like bees. Homosexuality brought down community rage on the practices because it was unconcerned and wasteful. Every pursuit, no matter what its stated end, had as its foundation purpose, survival, growth, and renewal.

Perhaps one can judge the health of a society by the nature as well as the incidence of crimes committed against it. Consider us today not only in the cities but in small towns and the country as well. There are of course the many crimes against property, but increasingly these are destructive rather than for gain. But the greatest increase is in crimes against people, against the physical bodies of people. The rapes have little to do with sexuality and much to do with destructive murder. The mugging in the streets and the violence which has turned our parks into jungles have little to do with robbery, although, as in the modern rape the ritual of sex is added, so in mugging there is robbery but its purpose and its drive seem to be destructive, the desire to hurt, to maim, to kill. Where need for money is the motive of the violence, the reason is again sad and sick and destructive, this time self-destructive, the need for drugs to abolish consciousness or stimulants to give shape and substance to a schizoid twin, hallucinatory aids in the creation of another world to take the place of this hated one. This too is a kind of murder, and finally what is known as kicks, the whipping of reluctant nerves, the raising of savage specters that even the maudlin witchcraft of the Middle Ages could not evoke—and this is another kind of murder of the self that might be called upon for responsibility.

These things are true for the practicers of our present-day necromancy, but how about the bystanders? Remember the windows slammed against a girl's cry for help in the night? People seeing or hearing a violence look away, walk away, refuse to talk to the police. Life is indeed cheap, and moreover it is becoming hateful. We act as though we truly hated one another, and silently approved the killing and removal of one among us.

Could it be that below the level of thought our people sense the danger of the swarming, crowding invasion of America by Americans? Starvation, pestilence, plague, which once cut us down, are no longer possible. And war? Well, during the *last* war, with all its slaughter, the world's population increased. Are people genuinely afraid of the bomb or do they look to it to do the job we have eliminated from nature? There seems to be little sense of horror when authority states that with the first exchange of bombs a hundred million Americans will die.

It is probable that here is where morals—integrity, ethics, even charity—have gone. The rules allowed us to survive, to live together and to increase. But if our will to survive is weakened, if our love of life and our memories of a gallant past and faith in a shining future are removed—what need is there for morals or for rules? Even they become a danger.

We have not lost our way at all. The roads of the past have come to an end and we have not yet discovered a path to the future. I think we will find one, but its direction may be unthinkable to us now. When it does appear, however, and we move on, the path must have direction, it must have purpose and the journey must be filled with a joy of anticipation, for the boy today, hating the world, creates a hateful world and then tries to destroy it and sometimes himself. We have succeeded in what our fathers prayed for and it is our success that is destroying us.

If I inspect my people and study them and criticize them, I must love them if I have any self-love, since I can never be separate from them and can be no more objective about them than I am about myself. I am not young, and yet I wonder about my tomorrow. How much more, then, must my wonder be about the tomorrow of my people, a young people. Perhaps my questioning is compounded of some fear, more hope, and great confidence.

I have named the destroyers of nations: comfort, plenty, and security—out of which grow a bored and slothful cynicism, in which rebellion against the world as it is and myself as I am are submerged in listless self-satisfaction. A dying people tolerates the present, rejects the future, and finds its satisfactions in past greatness and half-remembered glory. A dying people arms itself with defensive weapons and with mercenaries against change. When greatness recedes, so does belief in greatness. A dying people invariably concedes that poetry has gone, that beauty has withered away. Then mountains do not rise up as they once did against the sky, and girls are not as pretty. Then ecstasy fades to toleration, and agony subsides to a dull aching; then vision dims like the house lights in a theater—and the world is finished. As it is with a poet, so it is with a people.

It is in the American negation of these symptoms of extinction that my hope and confidence lie. We are not satisfied. Our restlessness, perhaps inherited from the hungry immigrants of our ancestry, is still with us. Young Americans are rebellious, angry, searching like terriers near a rat's nest. The energy pours out in rumbles, in strikes and causes, even in crime; but it is energy. Wasted energy is only a little problem, compared to its lack.

If the world were walled and boundaried as it once was in feudal towns, we could destroy the irritant of creative restlessness, punish the lively guilty—and subside. But the world is open as it has never been before, and the skies are open, and for the first time in human experience we have the tools to work with. Three-fifths of the world and perhaps four-fifths of the world's wealth lie under the sea, and we can get to it. The sky is open at last, and we have the means to rise into it. Revolt against what is is in the air—in the violence of the long, hot summer; in the resentment against injustice and inequality, and against imperceptible or cynical cruelty. There is blind anger against delay, against the long preparation for the long journey—perhaps the longest, darkest journey of all, with the greatest light at the end of it.

In our prehistory—only now beginning to open its cloak a little—we have set a guard of secrecy and holiness on the unknown. The forest, the sky—the unconceivable large, the unseeable small—we once placed beyond our reach in mystery; taboo to approach, forbidden to inspect. Our dreams we gave to ancestors, cantankerous and selfish and dead, while our closest and most precious possession we gave into the hands of God or gods, not kindly or wise, but vain and jealous and greedy—in the image not of ourselves but of the ugly things, precarious and usurped, that power makes of us. Here is a world or a universe unknown, even unconceived of, and perhaps at last open for exploration: the great and mysterious mind and soul of man, a land full of marvels.

Americans do not lack places to go and new things to find. We have cut ourselves off from the self-abuse of war by raising it from a sin to an extinction. Far larger experiences are open to our restlessness—the fascinating unknown is everywhere. How will the Americans act and react to a new set of circumstances for which new rules must be made? We know from our past some of the things we will do. We will make many mistakes; we always have. We are in the perplexing period of change. We seem to be running in all directions at once—but we are running. And I believe that our history, our experience in America, has endowed us for the change that is coming. We have never sat still for long; we have never been content with a place, a building—or with ourselves.

Afterword

THE PICTURES in this book are of our land, wide open, fruitful, and incredibly dear and beautiful. It is ours and we will make of it what we are—no more, no less.

Something happened in America to create the Americans. Perhaps it was the grandeur of the land—the lordly mountains, the mystery of deserts, the ache of storms, cyclones—the enormous sweetness and violence of the country which, acting on restless, driven peoples from the outside world, made them taller than their ancestors, stronger than their fathers—and made them all Americans.

Maybe the challenge was in the land; or it might be that the people made the challenge. There have been other strange and sudden emergences in well-remembered and documented history. A village on the Tiber spread its fluid force and techniques through the known world. A blaze from Mongolia spread like a grass fire over most of Asia and Europe. These explosions of will and direction have occurred again and again, and they have petered out, have burned up their material, smoked awhile, and been extinguished. Now we face the danger which in the past has been most destructive to the human: success—plenty, comfort, and ever-increasing leisure. No dynamic people has ever survived these dangers. If the anaesthetic of satisfaction were added to our hazards, we would not have a chance of survival—as Americans.

From our beginning, in hindsight at least, our social direction is clear. We have moved to become one people out of many. At intervals, men or groups, through fear of people or the desire to use them, have tried to change our direction, to arrest our growth, or to stampede the Americans. This will happen again and again. The impulses which for a time enforced the Alien and Sedition Laws, which have used fear and illicit emotion to interfere with and put a stop to our continuing revolution, will rise again, and they will serve us in the future as they have in the past to clarify and to strengthen our process. We have failed sometimes, taken wrong paths, paused for renewal, filled our bellies and licked our wounds; but we have never slipped back—never.

WORKS CITED

Abbreviations used for Steinbeck works are in parentheses.

Benchley, Nathaniel. "The Art of Fiction, XLV." *Paris Review*, Fall 1969: 161–88.

Benson, Jackson. *The True Adventures of John Steinbeck, Writer*. New York: Penguin, 1984.

Brinkley, Douglas. "The Other Vietnam Generation." *New York Times Book Review*, 28 Feb. 1999: 27.

Cousins, Norman. *Present Tense: An American Editor's Odyssey*. New York: McGraw-Hill, 1967.

Crèvecoeur, J. Hector St. John de. *Letters from an American Farmer*. New York: Signet Classics, 1963.

DeMott, Robert. *Working Days: The Journals of "The Grapes of Wrath."* New York: Penguin, 1989. (Cited as WD.)

Fench, Thomas, ed. *Conversations with John Steinbeck*. Jackson: University Press of Mississippi, 1988.

French, Warren. *John Steinbeck's Nonfiction Revisited*. New York: Twayne, 1996.

Guggenheim, Harry, correspondence. Library of Congress. (Cited by date of letter.)

Kaplan, Justin. *Lincoln Steffens: A Biography*. New York: Simon & Schuster, 1974.

Kluger, Richard. *The Paper: The Life and Death of the New York Herald Tribune*. New York: Alfred A. Knopf, 1986.

Lopez, Barry. *Crossing Open Ground*. New York: Random House, 1989.

McElrath, Joseph, Jesse Crisler, Susan Shillinglaw, eds. *John Steinbeck: The Contemporary Reviews*. Cambridge: Cambridge University Press, 1996.

Parini, Jay. *John Steinbeck: A Biography*. New York: Henry Holt, 1995.

Shillinglaw, Susan. Introduction to *Of Mice and Men*. New York: Penguin, 1994.

Simmonds, Roy. *John Steinbeck: The War Years, 1939–1945*. Lewisburg: Bucknell University Press, 1996.

Steinbeck, Elaine, and Robert Wallsten. *Steinbeck: A Life in Letters*. New York: Viking, 1978. *(SLL)*

Steinbeck, John. *The Acts of King Arthur and His Noble Knights*. New York: Farrar, Straus & Giroux, 1976. *(Acts)*

——. Foreword to *Between Pacific Tides*, by Edward Ricketts and Jack Calvin. Stanford: Stanford University Press, 1939.

——. In memoriam. *Pascal Covici, 1888–1964*. Meriden Gravure Company, 1964: 19–20.

——. *Journal of a Novel: The "East of Eden" Letters*. New York: Penguin, 1969. *(JN)*

——. *Once There Was a War*. New York: Penguin, 1994. *(OWW)*

——. Preface to *Story Writing*, by Edith Ronald Mirrielees. New York: Viking, 1962.

——. *Sea of Cortez*. New York: Viking, 1941. *(SOC)*

——. "Some Thoughts on Juvenile Delinquency." *The Saturday Review*, 28 May 1955: 22.

Street, Toby. Interview with Jackson Benson. Benson papers, Special Collections at Stanford University.

SELECTED BIBLIOGRAPHY OF STEINBECK'S NONFICTION

Only the first appearance of magazine and newspaper articles is noted, with a few exceptions where reprints are cited: *Their Blood Is Strong* (articles that originally ran in the *San Francisco News* in October 1936 with "Starvation Under the Orange Trees"), *Once There Was a War* (a selection of Steinbeck's World War II journalism that ran in the *New York Herald Tribune* in 1943), and known English-language versions of pieces first published in French in *Le Figaro* in 1954. Newspaper series are cited as series, not by individual pieces.

BOOKS

Their Blood Is Strong. San Francisco: Simon J. Lubin Society, 1938. Reprinted as *The Harvest Gypsies*. Berkeley, CA: Heyday Press, 1989.

A Letter Written in Reply to a Request for a Statement About His Ancestry. Stamford, CT: Overbrook Press, 1940. 350 copies.

Sea of Cortez: A Leisurely Journal of Travel and Research, with Edward F. Ricketts. New York: Viking, 1941.

Bombs Away: The Story of a Bomber Team. Photographs by John Swope. New York: Viking, 1942.

Vanderbilt Clinic. Photographs by Victor Kepler. New York: Presbyterian Hospital, 1947.

The First Watch. Los Angeles: Ward Ritchie Press, 1947. 60 numbered copies.

A Russian Journal. Photographs by Robert Capa. New York: Viking, 1948.

The Log from the "Sea of Cortez." New York: Viking, 1951.

Un Américain à New-York et à Paris. French translation by Jean-François Rozan. Paris: René Julliard, 14 May 1956.

Once There Was a War. New York: Viking, 1958.

Travels with Charley in Search of America. New York: Viking, 1962.

Speech Accepting the Nobel Prize for Literature. New York: Viking, 1962.

A Letter from John Steinbeck. San Francisco and Los Angeles: Roxburghe and Zamorano Clubs, 1964. 150 copies.

America and Americans. New York: Viking, 1966.

Journal of a Novel: The "East of Eden" Letters. New York: Viking, 1969.

John Steinbeck, His Language. Introduction by James B. Hart. Aptos, CA: Roxburge and Zamorano Clubs, 1970.

Steinbeck: A Life in Letters. Edited by Elaine Steinbeck and Robert Wallsten. New York: Viking, 1975.

Letters to Elizabeth. Edited by Florian J. Shasky and Susan F. Riggs. San Francisco: Book Club of California, 1978. 500 copies.

Your Only Weapon Is Your Work: A Letter by John Steinbeck to Dennis Murphy. Introduction by Robert DeMott. San Jose, CA: Steinbeck Research Center, 1985. 500 copies.

Working Days: The Journals of "The Grapes of Wrath," 1938–1941. Edited by Robert DeMott. New York: Viking, 1989.

FILMSCRIPTS

The Forgotten Village. New York: Viking, 1941.

Viva Zapata! Edited by Robert Morsberger. New York: Viking, 1975.

Zapata: A Narrative in Dramatic Form on the Life of Emiliano Zapata. Woodcuts by Karin Wickstrom. Covelo, CA: Yolla Bolly Press, 1991. 257 numbered copies. Reprint edited by Robert Morsberger. New York: Penguin, 1993.

INTRODUCTIONS, FOREWORDS, AND MISCELLANY

"The How, When and Where of the High School." *El Gabilan* (Salinas High School yearbook), 1919: 19.

"Class Will." *El Gabilan*, 1919: 36.

"Student Body." *El Gabilan*, 1919: 43.

"Woodwork." *El Gabilan*, 1919: 50.

"Tortilla Flat." *Famous Recipes by Famous People, Hotel Del Monte.* Compiled and commented upon by Herbert Cerwin. Del Monte, CA: Hotel Del Monte, 1936: 18. Reprinted as "Of Beef and Men" in *Famous Recipes by Famous People.* San Francisco: Lane Publishing Co., 1940: 11.

"Steinbeck's Letter." *Writers Take Sides: Letters About the War in Spain from 418 American Authors.* New York: League of American Writers, 1938: 56–57.

Foreword to *Between Pacific Tides,* by Edward Ricketts and Jack Calvin. Revised edition. Stanford, CA: Stanford University Press, 1948: v–vi. Reprinted as *Foreword to "Between Pacific Tides."* Stanford, CA: Stanford University Press for Nathan Van Patten, 1948. 10 copies.

Foreword to *Burning Bright*. New York: Viking, 1950: 9–13.

"The 'Inside' on the Inside." *The Iron Gate of Jack & Charlie's "21."* Edited by Francis T. Hunter. New York: Jack Kriendler Memorial Foundation, 1950: 27.

"About Ed Ricketts." Preface to *The Log from the "Sea of Cortez."* New York: Viking, 1951: vii–xvii.

"Un Grand Romancier de Notre Temps." *Hommage à André Gide, 1869–1951*. Paris: La Nouvelle Revue Française, 1951: 30. Tribute to Gide.

Foreword to *Speeches of Adlai Stevenson*. New York: Random House, 1952: 5–8.

Introduction to *The World of Li'l Abner*, by Al Capp. New York: Farrar, Straus & Young, 1953: np.

"An Appreciation." *Elia Kazan's Production of John Steinbeck's "East of Eden."* Warner Brothers, 1955. Souvenir booklet for the world premiere presentation of the film at the Astor Theater in New York City.

Foreword to *Much Ado About Me*, by Fred Allen. Boston: Little, Brown, 1956: np.

"A Postscript from Steinbeck." *Steinbeck and His Critics: A Record of Twenty-five Years*. Edited by Ernest W. Tedlock and C. V. Wicker. Albuquerque: University of New Mexico Press, 1957: 307–8.

"Rationale." *Steinbeck and His Critics*: 308–9.

Preface to *Story Writing*, by Edith Ronald Mirrielees. New York: Viking, 1962: vii–viii.

Letter of tribute to Oscar Hammerstein II. Program for the Oscar Hammerstein II Memorial Festival, 46th Street Theatre, New York City, 8 April 1962.

Letter of appreciation for publication of a Greek translation of *East of Eden*. *John Steinbeck: An Exhibition of American and Foreign Editions*. Austin: Humanities Research Center, University of Texas, 1963: 23. Reprint from *Antolica Tis Edhem*. Thessaloníki: Syropoulos, 1955.

"On Learning Writing." *Writer's Yearbook*. Cincinnati: F & W Publications, 1963.

"Robert Capa: An Appreciation by John Steinbeck." *Images of War by Robert Capa*. Assembled by Cornell Capa. New York: Grossman, 1964: 7.

"A Letter from Steinbeck." *The Thinking Man's Dog*. Edited by Ted Patrick. New York: Random House, 1964: 3–10.

"A President—Not a Candidate." *1964 Democratic National Convention*. 1964: 94–97.

"In memoriam. *Pascal Covici, 1888–1964*. [New York:] Meriden Gravure Company, 1964: 19–20.

"John Emery." *John Emery*. Zachary Scott. Privately printed, 1964. 200 copies. A tribute.

Foreword to *Hard Hitting Songs for Hard-Hit People*. Compiled by Alan Lomax. New York: Oak Publications, 1967: 8–9.

Foreword to *The Eddie Condon Scrapbook of Jazz*, by Eddie Condon and Hank O'Neal. New York: Galahad Books, 1973: np.

Foreword to *Bringing in the Sheaves*, by Windsor Drake (Thomas A. Collins). *Journal of Modern Literature*, April 1976: 211–13.

CONTRIBUTIONS TO MAGAZINES AND NEWSPAPERS

1936

"A Depiction of Mexico by an Author with No Pattern to Vindicate." *San Francisco Chronicle*, 31 May 1936: D4.

"Dubious Battle in California." *Nation*, 12 Sept. 1936: 302–4.

"The Harvest Gypsies." *San Francisco News*, 5–12 Oct. 1936.

"The Way It Seems to John Steinbeck." *The Occident* 29 (1936): 5.

1938

"The novel might benefit by the discipline, the terseness of the drama . . ." *Stage* 15 (Jan. 1938): 50–51.

"Starvation Under the Orange Trees." *Monterey Trader*, 15 Apr. 1938.

"A Letter to the Inmates of the Connecticut State Prison." *Monthly Record* (Connecticut State Prison), June 1938: 3.

"The Stars Point to Shafter." *Progressive Weekly*, 24 Dec. 1938: 2.

1941

"Steinbeck Lashes Out at Bungled Goodwill Drive in Latin States: A Reply to American Censorship." *Carmel Cymbal* 15, no. 10 (4 Sept. 1941): 3.

1942

" 'Our Best'—Our Fliers." *New York Times Magazine*, 22 Nov. 1942: 16–17, 29. Excerpt from *Bombs Away*.

1943

86 war dispatches. *New York Herald Tribune*, 21 June–15 Dec. 1943. Available through interlibrary loan from Center for Steinbeck Studies at San Jose State University, in Robert B. Harmon, *John Steinbeck, World War II Correspondent: An Annotated Reference Guide*. San Jose, CA: Dibco Press, 1997.

"John Steinbeck Writes Appeal for Third War Loan Drive." *Monterey Peninsula Herald*, 17 Sept. 1943.

1946

"This Is the Monterey We Love."*Monterey Peninsula Herald*, 3 July 1946: Sec. 3: 1.

1947

"The GI's War in a Book Far from Brass." *New York Herald Tribune Weekly Book Review*, 18 May 1947: 1.

1948

"A Russian Journal." *New York Herald Tribune*, 14–31 Jan. 1948.

"Women and Children in the USSR." *Ladies Home Journal*, Feb. 1948: 44–59.

"Journey into Russia: People of the Soviet." *Illustrated*, 1 May 1948: 5–22.

1950

"My Ideal Woman." *Flair*, July 1950:30–33.

"Critics, Critics Burning Bright." *Saturday Review*, 11 Nov. 1950: 20–21.

1951

"Do You Like Yourself?" *New York Herald Tribune*, 21 Jan. 1951: Sec. 7: 2.

"The Naked Book." *Vogue*, 15 Nov. 1951: 119, 161.

"The Farmer's Hotel." Letter to the editor. *New York Times Book Review*, 2 Dec. 1951: 40.

1952

"Who Said the Old Lady Was Dying?" *Evening Standard* (London), 1 Aug. 1952.

"Your Audiences Are Wonderful." *Sunday Times* (London), 10 Aug. 1952.

"Duel Without Pistols." *Collier's*, 23 Aug. 1952: 13–15.

"The Soul and Guts of France." *Collier's*, 30 Aug. 1952: 26–30.

"For Stevenson: Rivals Contrasted." Letter to the editor. *New York Times*, 26 Oct. 1952: Sec. 4: 9.

1953

"The Stevenson Letter." *New Republic*, 5 Jan. 1953: 13–14.

"The Secret Weapon We Were Afraid to Use." *Collier's*, 10 Jan. 1953: 9–13.

"Ballantine Ale." *Life*, 26 Jan. 1953: 92–93.

"I Go Back to Ireland." *Collier's*, 31 Jan. 1953: 48–50.

"Autobiography: Making of a New Yorker." *New York Times Magazine*, 1 Feb. 1953: 26–27, 66–67.

"Positano." *Harper's Bazaar*, May 1953: 158, 185, 187–90, 194. Reprinted as *Positano*. Salerno, Italy: Ente Provinciale Per Il Turismo, 1954.

"A Model T Named 'It.' " *Ford Times*, July 1953: 34–39.

"My Short Novels." *Wings*, Oct. 1953: 4–8.

1954

"Circus." Ringling Bros. and Barnum & Bailey Circus program, 1954: 6–7.

"Trade Winds: When, Two Summers Ago . . ." *Saturday Review*, 27 Feb. 1954: 8.

"In Awe of Words." *The Exonian*, 3 Mar. 1954: 4.

"One American in Paris." *Le Figaro Littéraire*, 12 June–18 Sept. 1954. A series of seventeen articles, as well as an eighteenth published in a French collection, *Un Américain à New-York et à Paris*, 1956. Manuscripts and typescripts of the seventeen articles written for *Le Figaro* are located in the Marlene Brody Collection at the Center for Steinbeck Studies, San Jose State University; transcriptions in this book are taken from the typescripts.

"Death with a Camera." *Picture Post* (London), 12 June 1954.

"Jalopies I Cursed and Loved." *Holiday*, July 1954: 44–45, 89–90.

"Fishing in Paris." *Punch*, 25 Aug. 1954: 248–49. Also published as "Of Fish and Fishermen." *Sports Illustrated*, 4 Oct. 1954: 45. From *Le Figaro*.

"Robert Capa: An Appreciation." *Photography*, Sept. 1954: 48.

"The Miracle of Joan." *John O'London's Weekly*, 19 Sept. 1954: 907. From *Le Figaro*.

"Good Guy—Bad Guy." *Punch*, 22 Sept. 1954: 375–78.

"Steinbeck's Voices of America." *Scholastic*, 3 Nov. 1954: 15.

"Reality and Illusion." *Punch*, 17 Nov. 1954: 616–17. From *Le Figaro*.

1955

"A Plea for Tourists." *Punch*, 26 Jan. 1955: 148–49. From *Le Figaro*.

"The Affair at 7, Rue de M——" *Harper's Bazaar*, Apr. 1955: 112, 202, 213. From *Le Figaro*.

"The Death of a Racket." *Saturday Review*, 2 Apr. 1955: 26.

"Cooks of Wrath." *Everybody's*, 9 Apr. 1955. From *Le Figaro*.

"Capital Roundup: Paris." *Saturday Review*, 16 Apr. 1955: 41. From *Le Figaro*.

"A Plea to Teachers." *Saturday Review*, 30 Apr. 1955: 24.

"The Summer Before." *Punch*, 25 May 1955: 647–51.

"Some Thoughts on Juvenile Delinquency." *Saturday Review*, 28 May 1955: 22.

"Always Something to Do in Salinas." *Holiday*, June 1955: 58–59, 152–53, 156. Reprinted as *Always Something to Do in Salinas*. Bradenton, FL: Opuscula Press, 1986. 300 copies.

"Report on America." *Punch*, 22 June 1955: 754–55.

"Bricklaying Piece." *Punch*, 27 July 1955: 92.

"How to Recognize a Candidate." *Punch*, 10 Aug. 1955: 146–48.

"Critics—from a Writer's Viewpoint." *Saturday Review*, 27 Aug. 1955: 20, 28.

"A Letter on Criticism." *Colorado Quarterly* 4 (Autumn 1955): 218–19.

"Random Thoughts on Random Dogs." *Saturday Review*, 8 Oct. 1955: 11.

". . . like captured fireflies." *CTA Journal*, Nov. 1955: 7.

"We're Holding Our Own." *Lilliput*, Nov. 1955: 18–19. Also published as "The Short-Short Story of Mankind." *Playboy*, Apr. 1958.

"Writer's Mail." *Punch*, 2 Nov. 1955: 512–13.

"Trade Winds: In a radio broadcast beamed to listeners in foreign countries, John Steinbeck had this to say about New York City." *Saturday Review*, 26 Nov. 1955: 8–9.

"Dreams Piped from Cannery Row." *New York Times*, 27 Nov. 1955: Sec. 2: 1, 3.

"What Is the Real Paris?" *Holiday*, Dec. 1955: 94. From *Le Figaro*.

"More About Aristocracy: Why Not a World Peerage?" *Saturday Review*, 10 Dec. 1955: 11.

1956

"The Yank in Europe." *Holiday*, Jan. 1956: 25. From *Le Figaro*.

"The Joan in All of Us." *Saturday Review*, 14 Jan. 1956: 17. From *Le Figaro*.

"Miracle Island of Paris." *Holiday*, Feb. 1956: 43. From *Le Figaro*.

"Madison Avenue and the Election." *Saturday Review*, 31 Mar. 1956: 11.

"Needles—Derby Day Choice for President?" Louisville *Courier-Journal*, 6 May 1956: 8.

"The Vegetable War." *Saturday Review*, 21 July 1956: 34–35.

"Discovering the People of Paris." *Holiday*, Aug. 1956: 36. From *Le Figaro*.

"The Mail I've Seen." *Saturday Review*, 4 Aug. 1956: 16, 34.

Reporting on 1956 Democratic and Republican Conventions. Louisville *Courier-Journal*, 12–25 Aug. 1956.

1957

"Trust Your Luck." *Saturday Review*, 12 Jan. 1957: 42–44. From *Le Figaro*.

"My War with the Ospreys." *Holiday*, Mar. 1957: 72–73, 163–65.

"John Steinbeck States His Views on Cannery Row." *Monterey Peninsula Herald*, 8 Mar. 1957: 1.

"Letters to the *Courier-Journal*." Louisville *Courier-Journal*, 17 Apr.–17 July 1957. Series of twenty-three travel articles.

"A Game of Hospitality." *Saturday Review*, 20 Apr. 1957: 24.

"The Trial of Arthur Miller." *Esquire*, June 1957: 86.

"Red Novelist's [Sholokoff's] Visit Produces Uneasy Talk." Louisville *Courier-Journal*, 17 July 1957.

"Television and Radio." *New York Herald Tribune*, 23 Aug. 1957: Sec. 2:1.

"Open Season on Guests." *Playboy*, Sept. 1957: 21.

"Steinbeck and the Flu." *Newsday*, 9 Sept. 1957: 37.

" 'D' for Dangerous." *McCall's*, Oct. 1957: 57, 82.

"Dichos: The Way of Wisdom." *Saturday Review*, 9 Nov. 1957: 13.

1958

"Dedication." *Journal of the American Medical Association*, 12 July 1958: 1388–89.

"The Easiest Way to Die." *Saturday Review*, 23 Aug. 1958: 12, 37.

"Healthy Anger." *Books and Bookman*, Oct. 1958: 24.

"The Golden Handcuff." *San Francisco Examiner*, 23 Nov. 1958.

1959

"Writer Catches Lions by Tale." *Monterey Peninsula Herald*, 3 Oct. 1959: 1, 3.

"Adlai Stevenson and John Steinbeck Discuss the Past and the Present." *Newsday*, 22 Dec. 1959: 34–35.

1960

"Have We Gone Soft?" *New Republic*, 15 Feb. 1960: 11–15.

"Steinbeck Replies." *Newsday*, 1 Mar. 1960: 27.

"A Primer on the Thirties." *Esquire*, June 1960: 85–93.

"Atque Vale." *Saturday Review*, 23 July 1960: 13.

1961

"Conversation at Sag Harbor." *Holiday*, Mar. 1961: 60–61, 129–31, 133.

"High Drama of Bold Thrust Through Ocean Floor." *Life*, 14 Apr. 1961: 110–18, 120, 122.

"In Quest of America," part one. *Holiday* 30, no. 1 (July 1961): [26], 27–33, 79–85.

"The Critic Defined." Letter to the editor. *Newsweek*, 10 July 1961: 2.

"Sorry—If I had any advice to give I'd take it myself." *Writer's Digest*, Sept. 1961

"In Quest of America," part two. *Holiday* 30, no. 6 (Dec. 1961): 60–65 116–18, 120–21, 124, 126–28, 130–31, 134–36.

1962

"In Quest of America," part three. *Holiday* 31, no. 2 (Feb. 1962): 58–63, 122.
"California: The Exploding State." *Sunday Times Colour Section* (London), 16 Dec. 1962: 2.

1963

"To the Swedish Academy." *Story*, Mar.–Apr. 1963: 6–8. Acceptance speech for Nobel Prize.
"Reflections on a Lunar Eclipse." *New York Sunday Herald Tribune*, 6 Oct. 1963: *Book Week* 3.
Quote about Berlin Wall. *Time*, 20 Dec. 1963: 28.

1964

"The Pure West." *Montana, the Big Sky Country: Official Publication of the Montana Territorial Centennial Commission* 1 (1964): 6–9, 30, 35. Text is from *Travels with Charley*.
Letter to Samuel Tankel, publisher. *Short Story International* 1 (Apr. 1964).
"The Language of Courtesy." *New World Review*, Dec. 1964: 26.

1965

"Letters to Alicia." *Newsday*, 20 Nov. 1965–28 May 1966.
"Then My Arm Glassed Up." *Sports Illustrated*, 20 Dec. 1965: 94–96, 99–102.

1966

"How Steinbeck's Religious Career Ended." Salinas *Californian*, 26 Feb. 1966: 16, 10.
"The Waiter Is Liable to Lose Face." *Newsday*, 28 Feb. 1966: 35.
"America and the Americans." *Saturday Evening Post*, 2 July 1966: 33–38, 40–41, 44, 46–47.
"An Open Letter to Poet Yevtushenko." *Newsday*, 11 July 1966: 3.
"Let's Go After the Neglected Treasures Beneath the Seas." *Popular Science*, Sept. 1966: 84–87.
"Henry Fonda." *Harper's Bazaar*, Nov. 1966: 215.
"John Steinbeck's America." *Newsday*, 12–19 Nov. 1966. Seven essays from *America and Americans*.
"Letters to Alicia." *Newsday*, 3 Dec. 1966–20 May 1967.

1967

"A Warning to the Viet Cong—Keep New Year's Truce or Else." *Los Angeles Times*, 1 Jan. 1967: C2.

"Challenge to Soviets." *Newsday*, 5 Jan. 1967: 5, 75.

"Steinbeck in Vietnam: 'Pravda Called Me an Accomplice in a Murder, but Do They Know the Facts?'" *Daily Sketch* (London), 6 Jan. 1967: 6.

"John Steinbeck vs. Erle Stanley Gardner" ("Camping Is for the Birds"). *Popular Science*, May 1967: 160, 204–5.

Quotation. *Weekly Messenger* (Presbyterian Hospital, New York City), 29 May 1967.

1969

"The Art of Fiction, XLV." *Paris Review*, Fall 1969: 161–88. Compilation of quotes from various sources.

1971

"On the Craft of Writing." *Intellectual Digest*, June 1971: 126–27. From *Journal of a Novel*.

1975

"Graduates: These Are Your Lives!" *Esquire*, Sept. 1975: 69, 142–43.

"The Art of Fiction, XLV (Continued)." *Paris Review*, Fall 1975: 180–94.

1992

"Steinbeck on Politics." *The Steinbeck Newsletter*, Spring 1992: 12.

1994

"Steinbeck on Politics, Part 2." *The Steinbeck Newsletter*, Winter 1994: 5.

1997

"Sag Harbor: Manifesto." *The Steinbeck Newsletter*, Fall 1997: 9.

INDEX